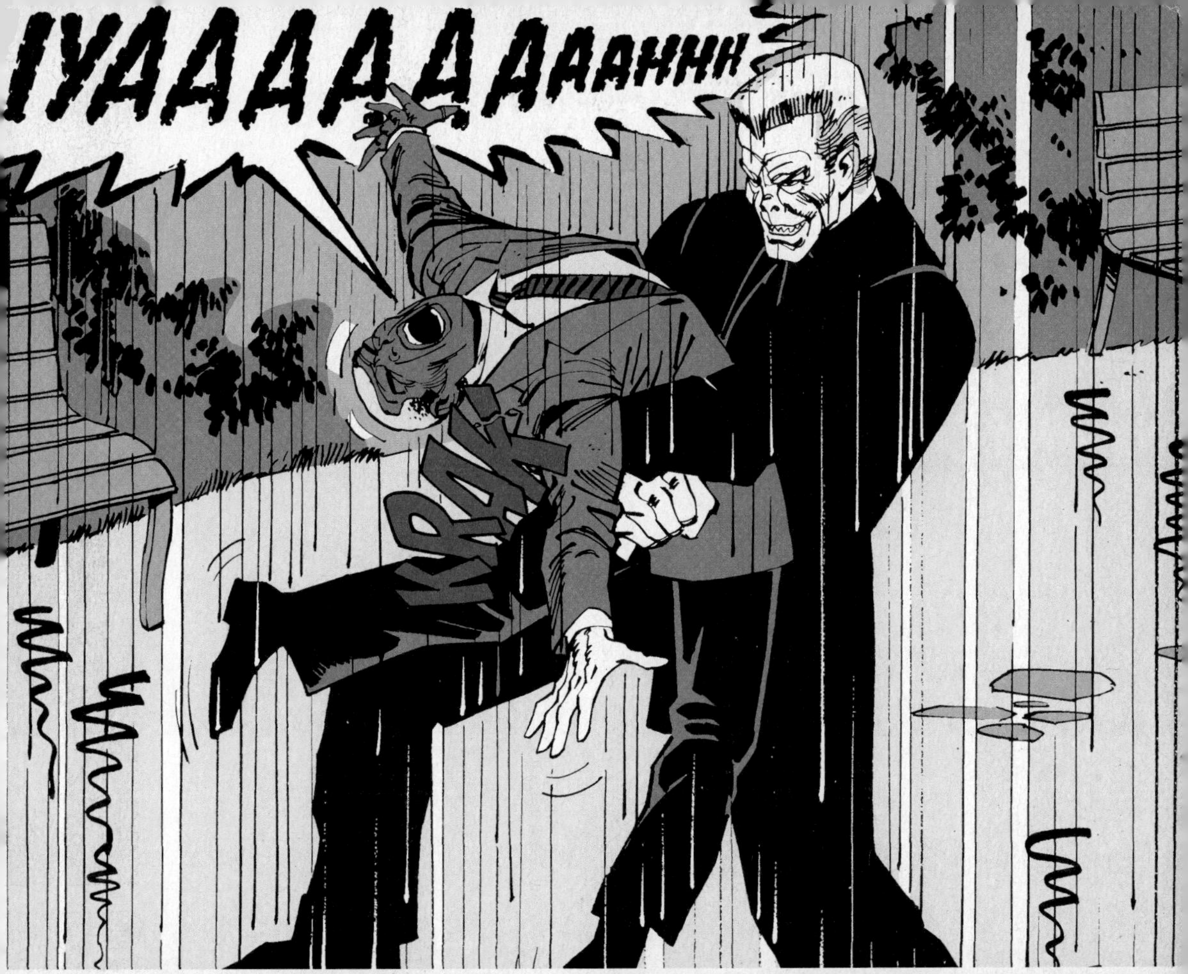
IYAAAAAAAAHHH
KRAK

SPIDER-MAN
TOMBSTONE!

SPIDER-MAN: TOMBSTONE VOL. 1. Contains material originally published in magazine form as SPECTACULAR SPIDER-MAN #137-150 and SPECTACULAR SPIDER-MAN ANNUAL #8. First printing 2016. ISBN# 978-1-302-90064-9. Published by MARVEL WORLDWIDE, INC., a subsidiary of MARVEL ENTERTAINMENT, LLC. OFFICE OF PUBLICATION: 135 West 50th Street, New York, NY 10020. Copyright © 2016 MARVEL. No similarity between any of the names, characters, persons, and/or institutions in this magazine with those of any living or dead person or institution is intended, and any such similarity which may exist is purely coincidental. **Printed in the U.S.A.** ALAN FINE, President, Marvel Entertainment; DAN BUCKLEY, President, TV, Publishing & Brand Management; JOE QUESADA, Chief Creative Officer; TOM BREVOORT, SVP of Publishing; DAVID BOGART, SVP of Business Affairs & Operations, Publishing & Partnership; C.B. CEBULSKI, VP of Brand Management & Development, Asia; DAVID GABRIEL, SVP of Sales & Marketing, Publishing; JEFF YOUNGQUIST, VP of Production & Special Projects; DAN CARR, Executive Director of Publishing Technology; ALEX MORALES, Director of Publishing Operations; SUSAN CRESPI, Production Manager; STAN LEE, Chairman Emeritus. For information regarding advertising in Marvel Comics or on Marvel.com, please contact Vit DeBellis, Integrated Sales Manager, at vdebellis@marvel.com. For Marvel subscription inquiries, please call 888-511-5480. **Manufactured between 4/1/2016 and 5/9/2016 by R.R. DONNELLEY, INC., SALEM, VA, USA.**

10 9 8 7 6 5 4 3 2 1

SPIDER-MAN
TOMBSTONE!

WRITER
GERRY CONWAY

PENCILERS
**SAL BUSCEMA &
MARK BAGLEY**

INKERS
**SAL BUSCEMA &
KEITH WILLIAMS**

COLORISTS
BOB SHAREN WITH
JOHN WILCOX

LETTERER
RICK PARKER

COLLECTION EDITOR
MARK D. BEAZLEY

ASSOCIATE EDITOR
SARAH BRUNSTAD

ASSOCIATE MANAGER, DIGITAL ASSETS
JOE HOCHSTEIN

ASSOCIATE MANAGING EDITOR
ALEX STARBUCK

EDITOR, SPECIAL PROJECTS
JENNIFER GRÜNWALD

VP, PRODUCTION & SPECIAL PROJECTS
JEFF YOUNGQUIST

RESEARCH
JOHN RHETT THOMAS

LAYOUT
JEPH YORK

PRODUCTION
COLORTEK & JOE FRONTIRRE

BOOK DESIGNER
ADAM DEL RE

SVP PRINT, SALES & MARKETING
DAVID GABRIEL

ASSISTANT EDITOR
GLENN HERDLING

EDITOR
JIM SALICRUP

EDITOR IN CHIEF
AXEL ALONSO

CHIEF CREATIVE OFFICER
JOE QUESADA

PUBLISHER
DAN BUCKLEY

EXECUTIVE PRODUCER
ALAN FINE

FRONT COVER ARTISTS
**SAL BUSCEMA &
VERONICA GANDINI**

SPECIAL THANKS TO
MIKE HANSEN

BACK COVER ARTIST
SAL BUSCEMA

SPIDER-MAN CREATED BY
STAN LEE & STEVE DITKO

The albino crimelord Tombstone made his menacing debut
in this short scene from *Web of Spider-Man #36*.

Writer: **Gerry Conway** • Penciler: **Alex Saviuk**
Inker: **Keith Williams** • Colorist: **Janet Jackson** • Letterer: **Rick Parker**
Assistant Editor: **Glenn Herdling** • Editor: **Jim Salicrup**

THERE HE GOES, MR. TOMBSTONE... THAT *RAYBURN* GUY.

YOU WANT I SHOULD *FOLLOW* HIM?

THAT'S WHAT YOU ARE PAID FOR, ISN'T IT?

UH, YEAH, SURE-- BUT I DON'T GET IT, MR. TOMBSTONE, HOW LONG WE GONNA TAG THIS GUY? WE'VE BEEN WATCHING HIM A WEEK NOW.

WE WATCH UNTIL OUR EMPLOYER TELLS US TO ACT.

BY THE WAY, DON'T CALL ME MR. TOMBSTONE.

OH?

MY NAME IS TOMBSTONE.

JUST *TOMBSTONE*.

AM I CLEAR?

AT THAT MOMENT, OUTSIDE...

AH, GOOD FOOD, GOOD CONVERSATION-- AND NO NEWSPAPER TALK. JUST WHAT I NEEDED FOR A BREAK FROM THE *DAILY BUGLE*.

MY WIFE ALWAYS TOLD ME--

Fluties

"ROBBIE ROBERTSON, KEEP WORKING SO HARD YOU'LL MAKE YOURSELF AN OLD MAN. THE *BUGLE* WON'T COLLAPSE IF ITS EDITOR IN CHIEF TAKES TIME OFF FOR A GOOD DINNER NOW AND THEN."

I SHOULD HAVE *LISTENED* TO HER WHEN I--

GOOD LORD! IN THAT CAR... IT'S *HIM!*

HE'S *BACK!*

AFTER ALL THESE YEARS, HE'S *BACK!*

END OF INTERLUDE 1.

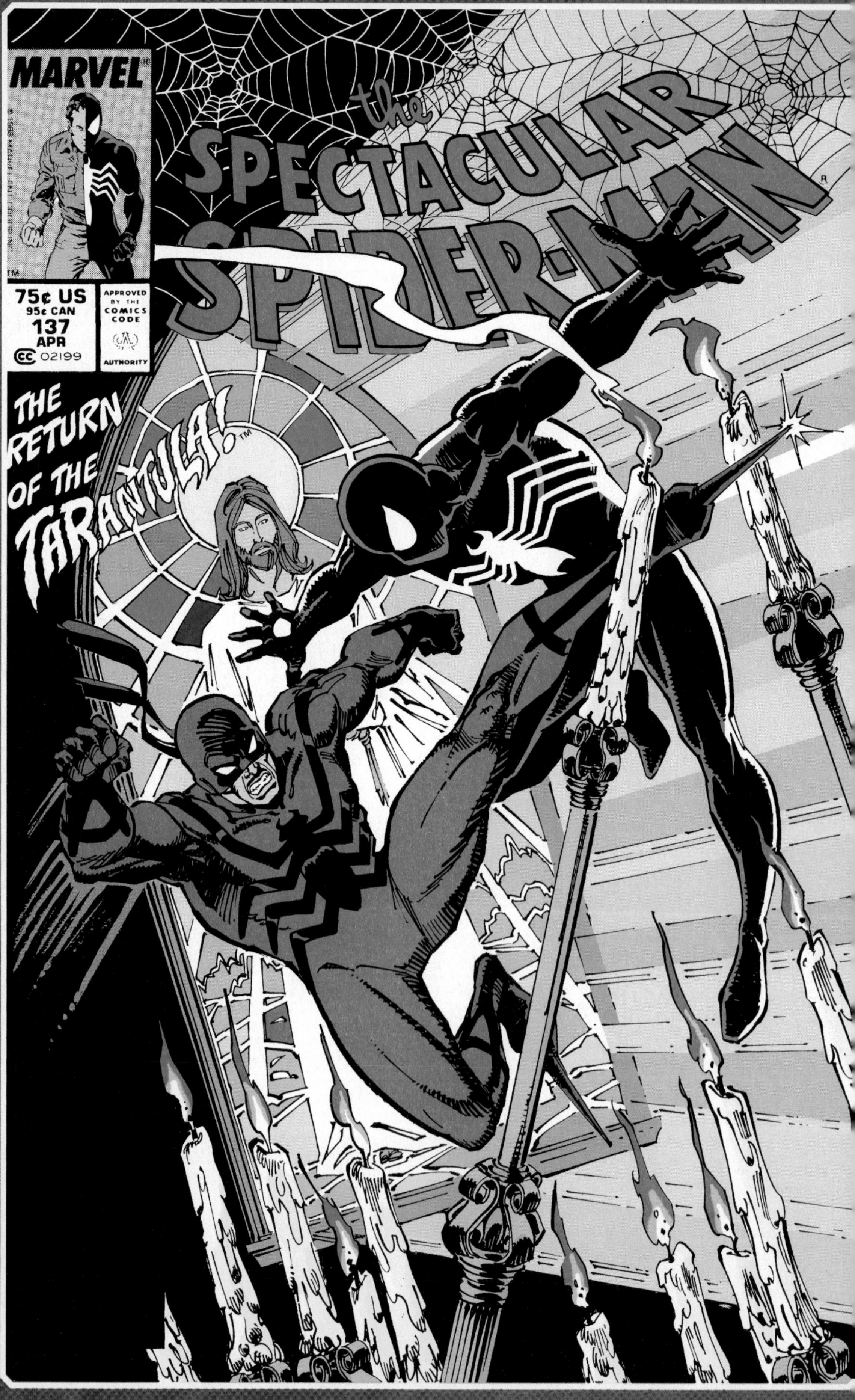
MARVEL
the SPECTACULAR SPIDER-MAN
75¢ US
95¢ CAN
137
APR
02199
APPROVED BY THE COMICS CODE AUTHORITY
THE RETURN OF THE TARANTULA!™

STan Lee PRESENTS: THE SPECTACULAR SPIDER-MAN!™

NOWHERE TO RUN, NOWHERE TO HIDE!

IN THE HOUR AFTER MIDNIGHT, THIS CITY IS AS TRANQUIL AS IT EVER GETS: A DROWSING MONSTER, RESTLESS AND UN-QUIET IN ITS SLEEP...

I'LL *NEVER* LEARN.

THIS WEEK IN NOW

NOW AMNISTIA FRAUD OR BOONDOGGLE?

NOW

EVERY TIME I TAKE AN ASSIGNMENT FOR THE *DAILY BUGLE* SOONER OR LATER, I REGRET IT.

IT'S JONAH JAMESON-- THE GUY JUST DRIVES ME *NUTS!*

GERRY CONWAY
SCRIPT

SAL BUSCEMA
ART

RICK PARKER
LETTERING

BOB SHAREN
COLOR

JIM SALICRUP
EDITOR

TOM DeFALCO
EDITOR IN CHIEF

YESTERDAY HE CALLS AND ASKS IF I CAN GET EXCLUSIVE PHOTOS OF A GANGLAND SUMMIT OVER IN *JERSEY* TONIGHT.

SO I TAKE THE RISK, I GET THE PICTURES, I BRING THEM TO THE *BUGLE* IN TIME FOR THE LATE MORNING EDITION--

--AND JONAH *SPIKES* THE STORY!

"WHO CARES ABOUT A BUNCH OF FAT OLD MOBSTERS MEETING IN JERSEY CITY?" HE SAYS. NEVER MIND THAT IT WAS *HIS* IDEA.

NOW

AMNISTIA
FRAUD OR BOONDOGGLE

TYPICAL. JUST *TYPICAL*.

"ANYBODY WHO WORKS FOR J. JONAH JAMESON *DESERVES* IT."

ARMANDO RUIZ WOULD *DISAGREE*.

HE'S GRATEFUL TO JONAH JAMESON FOR HIS JOB AS A JANITOR AT THE DAILY BUGLE.

SIX YEARS AGO, ARMANDO RUIZ ESCAPED THE DEATH SQUADS OF HIS HOMELAND, FLEEING TO A NEW LIFE IN *EL NORTE*.

BUT NOT ONCE IN THOSE SIX YEARS HAS HE FELT *SAFE*.

AND CERTAINLY NOT TONIGHT.

KLIK KLIK

KLIK KLIK

BUENAS NOCHES, ARMANDO.

YOUR FRIENDS AT HOME PRAY FOR YOUR SWIFT RETURN.

LA TARANTULA!

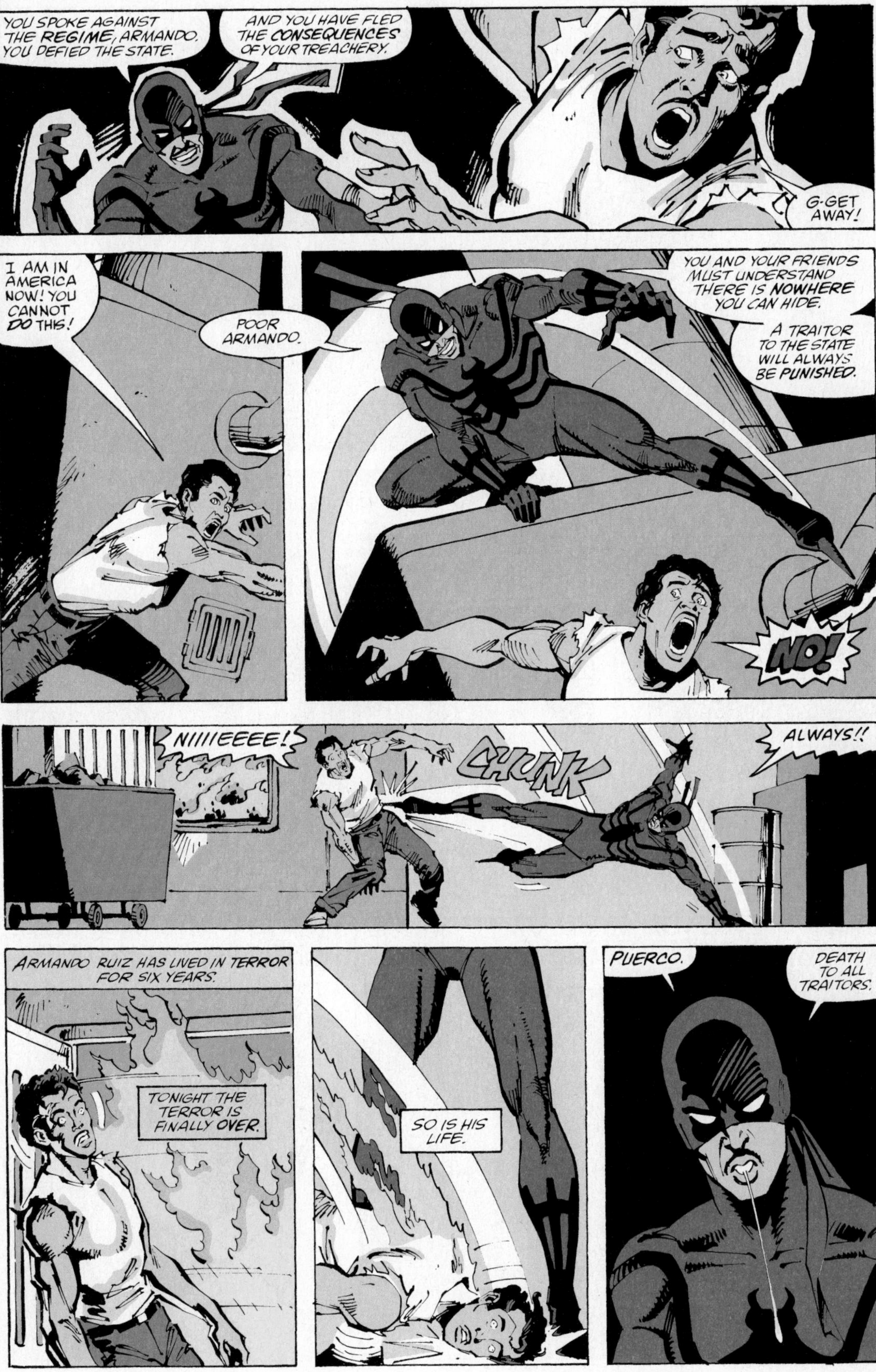
YOU SPOKE AGAINST THE REGIME, ARMANDO. YOU DEFIED THE STATE.
AND YOU HAVE FLED THE CONSEQUENCES OF YOUR TREACHERY.
G-GET AWAY!
I AM IN AMERICA NOW! YOU CANNOT DO THIS!
POOR ARMANDO.
YOU AND YOUR FRIENDS MUST UNDERSTAND THERE IS NOWHERE YOU CAN HIDE.
A TRAITOR TO THE STATE WILL ALWAYS BE PUNISHED.
NO!
NIIIIEEEE!
CHUNK
ALWAYS!!
ARMANDO RUIZ HAS LIVED IN TERROR FOR SIX YEARS.
TONIGHT THE TERROR IS FINALLY OVER.
SO IS HIS LIFE.
PUERCO.
DEATH TO ALL TRAITORS.

EIGHT SECONDS EARLIER AND THREE BLOCKS AWAY...

HUH?

THAT WAS A SCREAM--

--AND IT CAME FROM THE DAILY BUGLE BUILDING!

MUCH AS I'D LIKE TO HOPE IT'S J. JONAH GETTING A PARKING TICKET, I'VE GOT A BAD FEELING IT'S SOMETHING A WHOLE LOT WORSE.

BINGO! SOMEONE RUNNING FROM THE BASEMENT.

I CAN SMELL GUILTY A MILE OFF--

--AND THIS GUY PRACTICALLY REEKS OF IT, LIKE A CHEAP COLOGNE!

WHOA, PAL.

LET'S YOU AND ME TAKE A STROLL INSIDE AND SEE WHAT--

I DON'T BELIEVE IT.

TARANTULA!

BUT YOU'RE--

DEAD?

I AM LA TARANTULA. THE OTHER WAS MY PREDECESSOR, SEÑOR. AND YOU ARE THE ONE WHO KILLED HIM, SÍ?

I AM THE ONE WHO KILLED HIM, NO.

HE DIED A MONSTER, FRIEND.‡ BUT IT WASN'T MY FAULT.

*SEE AMAZING SPIDER-MAN # 236.-- J.S.

I'M MORE INTERESTED IN YOU, THOUGH, AND WHAT YOU'RE DOING H--

SPIDER-SENSE-- --WARNING ME--

TAKATAKA TAKA

--AMBUSH!

TAKATAK

YOU BOYS PLAY FOR *KEEPS*, DON'T YOU?

GOOD! SO DO--

--I?

WHERE DID THEY GO?

I COULDN'T HAVE BEEN DODGING BULLETS FOR MORE THAN A FEW *SECONDS*. HOW COULD TARANTULA AND HIS GOONS HAVE CLEARED OUT SO *QUICKLY?*

THE ONLY PLACE YOU SEE A MANEUVER THAT FAST AND PROFESSIONAL IS IN A *MILITARY* OPERATION.

AARROOAAA

SIRENS. TIME TO CHECK OUT.

THE *FIRST* TARANTULA USED TO WORK FOR HIS COUNTRY'S MILITARY DICTATORSHIP.

JUDGING BY THE *COMPANY* HE KEEPS, I'LL BET THIS GUY DOES THE SAME.

"*GREAT.*"

"JUST WHAT NEW YORK *NEEDS:* ANOTHER NUT IN A COSTUME, WITH HIS VERY OWN PARAMILITARY BACK-UP SQUAD."

MORNING...

IDIOTS!

WHAT DO I PAY *TAXES* FOR? SO THE POLICE DEPARTMENT CAN KEEP A GANG OF *MOUTH-BREATHERS* ON SALARY IN THE HOMICIDE DEPARTMENT?

ROBERTSON! GET IN HERE! TELL KATE CUSHING TO DROP EVERY-THING AND PUT OUR BEST PEOPLE ON THE *RUIZ* STORY.

...*RUIZ,* JONAH?

WAKE *UP,* MAN!

RUIZ! THE JANITOR WHO WAS KILLED LAST NIGHT-- ONE OF *MY* PEOPLE, IN *MY* BUILDING!

THOSE CLOWNS DOWNTOWN DON'T HAVE A *CLUE* WHO'S RESPONSIBLE.

I WANT ANSWERS, ROBBIE. IF THE *BUGLE'S* PEOPLE ARE IN *DANGER,* I WANT TO *KNOW.* PUT BEN URICH AND PARKER ON IT.

EXACTLY. AFTER ALL, I DON'T WANT TO LEAVE TOWN FOR NO GOOD *REASON,* DO I?

ANSWERS...

I CAN'T GET MY MIND OFF WHAT I SAW THE OTHER DAY *... WAS IT HIM? WAS IT REALLY *TOMBSTONE?*

AFTER ALL THE YEARS I'VE TRIED TO *FORGET* HIM...IS HE BACK IN MY LIFE?

ROBBIE, WHAT DID JONAH WANT?

WHO?

* IN WEB OF SPIDER-MAN #36.-- J.S.

JONAH JAMESON? CHEWS A CIGAR, SIGNS OUR *CHECKS?* YOU TALKED TO HIM--?

ROBBIE, ARE YOU OKAY? THE LAST COUPLE OF DAYS YOU HAVEN'T *LOOKED* SO GOOD...

JUST A FLU BUG, KATE.

CALL PETER PARKER IF HE WANTS IT, HE'S GOT ANOTHER *ASSIGNMENT...*

MORNING (PART 2)...

HOW ABOUT A **BREAK**, LEON?

ANOTHER MINUTE UNDER THESE LIGHTS, AND MR. PARKER'S BRAND NEW BRIDE WILL JUST **WILT.**

SURE, **MJ**, I'VE GOTTA CHANGE SCENERY FOR THE NEXT SERIES OF SHOTS, ANYWAY. TAKE FIVE.

IT'S FUNNY, ELVIRA. WHEN I WAS A GIRL, I **DREAMED** ABOUT BEING A MODEL SOMEDAY.

YES, MISSUS.

SOMETIMES THE **REALITY** ISN'T AS MUCH FUN AS THE DREAM, Y'KNOW?

SAY... WHY THE SAD FACE? WHAT'S WRONG? ARE YOU OKAY?

I JUS' WORRY SO MUCH, MISSUS. EVERY DAY I WORRY THEY'RE GOING TO COME...

WHO'S GOING TO COME, ELVIRA?

LA INMIGRACIÓN.

THE IMMIGRATION SERVICE? THE **I.N.S.?**

ELVIRA, ARE YOU AN **ILLEGAL?**

SÍ, MISSUS. FIVE YEARS I HAVE LIVED HERE, NOW THE **AMNISTIA** COMES...

... BUT THE **ABOGADO,** THE LAWYER SAYS I AM NOT HERE LONG ENOUGH. IF THEY FIND ME, **LA INMIGRACIÓN** WILL SEND ME HOME.

I WILL LOSE MY FAMILY... MY CHILDREN... **EVERYTHING.**

ELVIRA, MY HUSBAND WORKS FOR A **NEWS-PAPER** SOMETIMES. MAYBE HE CAN HELP.

NO ONE CAN HELP.

YOU'D BE SURPRISED. HERE'S MY PHONE NUMBER.

IF YOU'RE EVER IN TROUBLE, **CALL ME.** OKAY?

MJ! TELEPHONE-- SOMEBODY AT THE **DAILY BUGLE.**

OH, HI, KATE. WHAT'S UP?

PETER? SURE, WE'RE MEETING FOR LUNCH. I'LL TELL HIM YOU'RE TRYING TO REACH HIM.

THAT'S NOT ALL I'LL TELL HIM.

IF PETER PARKER CAN'T HELP ELVIRA, MAYBE THERE'S SOMETHING **SPIDER-MAN** CAN DO...

MORNING...
(PART 3)

PARK BY THE WHARF EDGE AND WAIT.

I WON'T BE LONG.

WAR

BEEP CLICK

HMMM

INTERESTING LOCATION FOR AN *OPERATIONS BASE*, SEÑOR TARANTULA-- INSIDE A GARBAGE SCOW. NO ONE WOULD EVER LOOK FOR YOU HERE.

THE SMELL ALONE IS QUITE A *DETERRENT*.

WE HAVE FOUND IT SO, SEÑOR--?

SOUTH. *GULLIVAR SOUTH*.

YOU ARE WITH THE *WHITE HOUSE*, MR. SOUTH?

NOT EXACTLY.

BUT MY COUNTRY WAS GIVEN TO UNDERSTAND WE HAVE YOUR GOVERNMENT'S COOPERATION...

NOT OFFICIALLY.

HOWEVER, CERTAIN POLICYMAKERS IN THE CAPITAL SUPPORT YOUR GOVERNMENT'S EFFORTS TO BRING *STABILITY* AND *DEMOCRACY* TO SOUTH AMERICA--

--AND WE'LL DO WHAT WE CAN TO *ASSIST* YOUR MISSION IN THE STATES.

14

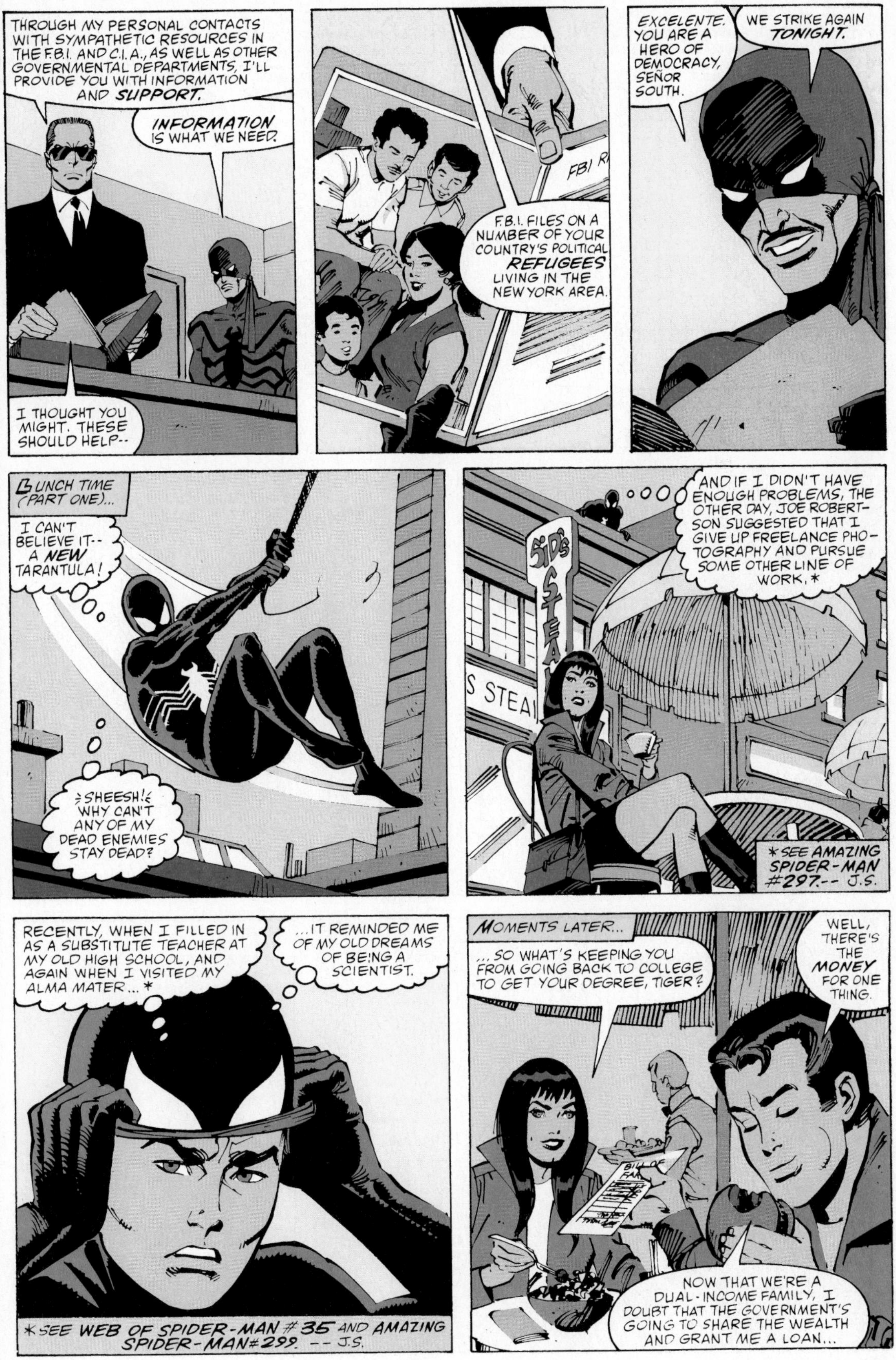

THROUGH MY PERSONAL CONTACTS WITH SYMPATHETIC RESOURCES IN THE F.B.I. AND C.I.A., AS WELL AS OTHER GOVERNMENTAL DEPARTMENTS, I'LL PROVIDE YOU WITH INFORMATION AND SUPPORT.
INFORMATION IS WHAT WE NEED.
I THOUGHT YOU MIGHT. THESE SHOULD HELP--
FBI R
F.B.I. FILES ON A NUMBER OF YOUR COUNTRY'S POLITICAL REFUGEES LIVING IN THE NEW YORK AREA.
EXCELENTE. YOU ARE A HERO OF DEMOCRACY, SEÑOR SOUTH.
WE STRIKE AGAIN TONIGHT.
LUNCH TIME (PART ONE)...
I CAN'T BELIEVE IT-- A NEW TARANTULA!
SHEESH! WHY CAN'T ANY OF MY DEAD ENEMIES STAY DEAD?
AND IF I DIDN'T HAVE ENOUGH PROBLEMS, THE OTHER DAY, JOE ROBERTSON SUGGESTED THAT I GIVE UP FREELANCE PHOTOGRAPHY AND PURSUE SOME OTHER LINE OF WORK.*
SID'S STEA
S STEA
*SEE AMAZING SPIDER-MAN #297.-- J.S.
RECENTLY, WHEN I FILLED IN AS A SUBSTITUTE TEACHER AT MY OLD HIGH SCHOOL, AND AGAIN WHEN I VISITED MY ALMA MATER...*
...IT REMINDED ME OF MY OLD DREAMS OF BEING A SCIENTIST.
*SEE WEB OF SPIDER-MAN #35 AND AMAZING SPIDER-MAN #299. -- J.S.
MOMENTS LATER...
...SO WHAT'S KEEPING YOU FROM GOING BACK TO COLLEGE TO GET YOUR DEGREE, TIGER?
WELL, THERE'S THE MONEY FOR ONE THING.
BILL OF FARE
NOW THAT WE'RE A DUAL-INCOME FAMILY, I DOUBT THAT THE GOVERNMENT'S GOING TO SHARE THE WEALTH AND GRANT ME A LOAN...

OH, *POO*, PETEY! HOW MANY TIMES DO WE HAVE TO GO THROUGH THIS?

I'LL BE MORE THAN HAPPY TO FOOT THE BILL FOR SOMETHING THAT MEANS SO MUCH TO YOU.

IT'S NOT THAT SIMPLE, MARY JANE.

WHEN I FIRST WENT TO COLLEGE I PAID MY OWN WAY. IT GAVE ME A GREATER SENSE OF ACCOMPLISHMENT. *I STILL* FEEL THAT WAY.

IN THAT CASE, MAN O'MINE, YOU'D BETTER RE-LOAD YOUR CAMERA. KATE CUSHING CALLED. SHE WANTS YOU TO MEET *BEN URICH* UPTOWN.

GREAT.

I GUESS I'D BETTER GO.

TILL I MAKE UP MY MIND, I'M *STILL* A PHOTOGRAPHER-- AND AN ASSIGNMENT IS STILL AN *ASSIGNMENT!*

MM-HMM.

PETER, WAIT--!

HE DIDN'T HEAR ME. I FORGOT TO TELL HIM ABOUT *ELVIRA* AND HER PROBLEM.

OH, WELL. WE CAN ALWAYS TALK *TONIGHT*--

BILL OF FARE

--IN BETWEEN *OTHER* THINGS.

LUNCHTIME (PART TWO)...

TWO BUCKS EVEN.

HOT DOGS · SODA · FI

THANKS.

THE *KINGPIN'S* NEW YORK HEADQUARTERS.

HOW MANY PEOPLE PASS IT EVERY DAY WITHOUT EVER *GUESSING* WHAT GOES ON INSIDE?

IS *HE* THERE...?

HE IS.

TOMBSTONE.

I WAS RIGHT.

WHEN I SAW HIM THE OTHER DAY, I HAD A SUSPICION HE WAS IN NEW YORK WORKING FOR THE *KINGPIN.*

WHO ELSE COULD *AFFORD* A MAN LIKE TOMBSTONE?

HE'S THE HIGHEST-PRICED *KILLER* IN THE BUSINESS.

I CAN'T LET IT PASS. NOT *THIS* TIME. I'VE GOT TO *DO* SOMETHING BEFORE--

HI, ROBBIE.

LONG TIME NO SEE.

UURK!

STILL THE SAME OLD ROBBIE ROBERTSON, SNOOPING AROUND, PLAYING REPORTER.

I TOLD YOU YEARS AGO, STAY OUT OF MY WAY AND YOU'LL LIVE A LONG, LONG TIME.

THAT WAS GOOD ADVICE THEN, AND IT'S GOOD ADVICE NOW.

NICE TALKING TO YOU, ROBBIE.

LET'S NOT DO IT AGAIN ANYTIME SOON.

LUNCH TIME (PART THREE)...

I CALLED KATE CUSHING AND SHE TOLD ME WHERE TO MEET BEN URICH UP IN SPANISH HARLEM.

APPARENTLY, A MAN NAMED RUIZ WAS *KILLED* AT *THE BUGLE* LAST NIGHT--AND I BET *TARANTULA* WAS INVOLVED.

"BEN AND I ARE SUPPOSED TO GET RUIZ'S *STORY* FROM A LEGAL AID LAWYER NAMED *MAGGIE MICHAELSON*..."

ARMANDO RUIZ WAS A *POLITICAL* REFUGEE, MR. URICH--BUT *NOT* ACCORDING TO THE *INS.*

RUIZ'S COUNTRY IS AN *ALLY* OF OUR COUNTRY--

--SO OUR GOVERNMENT WON'T RECOGNIZE THE POLITICAL STATUS OF ITS REFUGEES. RUIZ WAS AN *ILLEGAL*.

WHAT ABOUT THE *AMNESTY* PROGRAM?

MANY ILLEGALS WON'T APPLY FOR AMNESTY OUT OF *FEAR*.

FEAR OF *WHAT?*

FEAR OF BEING *DEPORTED*, MR. URICH. FOR SOME OF THEM, LIKE RUIZ, THERE'S THE REAL FEAR OF BEING SENT BACK TO A *DEATH SQUAD*.

HI, BEN. CAN I GET A *PICTURE?*

GO FOR IT, KID.

DID I HEAR YOU MENTION DEATH SQUADS, MS. MICHAELSON?

DO YOU THINK RUIZ WAS KILLED BY SOME KIND OF DEATH SQUAD *HERE?*

THERE ARE ALWAYS *RUMORS*. MILITARY DICTATORSHIPS CONTROL THEIR PEOPLE BY FORCE AND FEAR.

WHAT BETTER WAY TO EVOKE *TERROR* THAN BY SHOWING DISSENTERS THEY HAVE NOWHERE TO RUN, NOWHERE TO HIDE?

LOOK AROUND YOU.

THESE ARE FRIGHTENED PEOPLE. THEY'RE FRIGHTENED BY THE NIGHTMARE THEY BARELY ESCAPED--AND THE SADDEST PART IS, THEY'RE FRIGHTENED BY *US*.

THEY'RE AFRAID WE'LL SEND THEM *BACK*.

MAKES YOU THINK. HERE I AM WORRIED ABOUT MY CAREER, WHILE THESE PEOPLE ARE WORRIED ABOUT THEIR *LIVES*. I ALMOST--HUH?

SPIDER-SENSE TINGLING...!

SOMETHING ABOUT THAT *GUY* ACROSS THE STREET!

USUALLY MY SPIDER-SENSE WARNS ME OF *DANGER*... SO THAT GUY I SAW ENTER THIS ALLEY MUST BE A THREAT TO ME SOMEHOW!

THE WAY HE WALKED LOOKED SO *FAMILIAR.* WHERE DID I...?

LA TARANTULA! THAT'S WHO IT WAS!

BUT WHY IS HE HERE, OUT OF COSTUME, AND-- *GONE!*

HE MUST HAVE SLIPPED INTO ONE OF THE *BUILDINGS* OFF THIS ALLEY. I SHOULD HAVE--

HEY, INMIGRACIÓN.

YOU DON'T BELONG HERE, INMIGRACIÓN.

WE DON'T WANT YOU TAKING PICTURES.

HUH? LISTEN, YOU'RE MAKING A MISTAKE.

NO, INMIGRACIÓN-- YOU ARE MAKING THE MISTAKE.

MAYBE WE DEPORT *YOU,* EY?

--VÁYASE!

I DON'T KNOW HOW I GET INTO THESE THINGS--

--BUT I KNOW HOW TO GET *OUT!*

WHERE DID HE *GO?*

WHO CARES? HE'S *GONE.*

--PUERCA DE LA INMIGRACIÓN!

I'VE SEEN ANGRY BEFORE, BUT THOSE KIDS WERE *FURIOUS.*

MORE THAN FURIOUS... THEY WERE *TERRIFIED.*

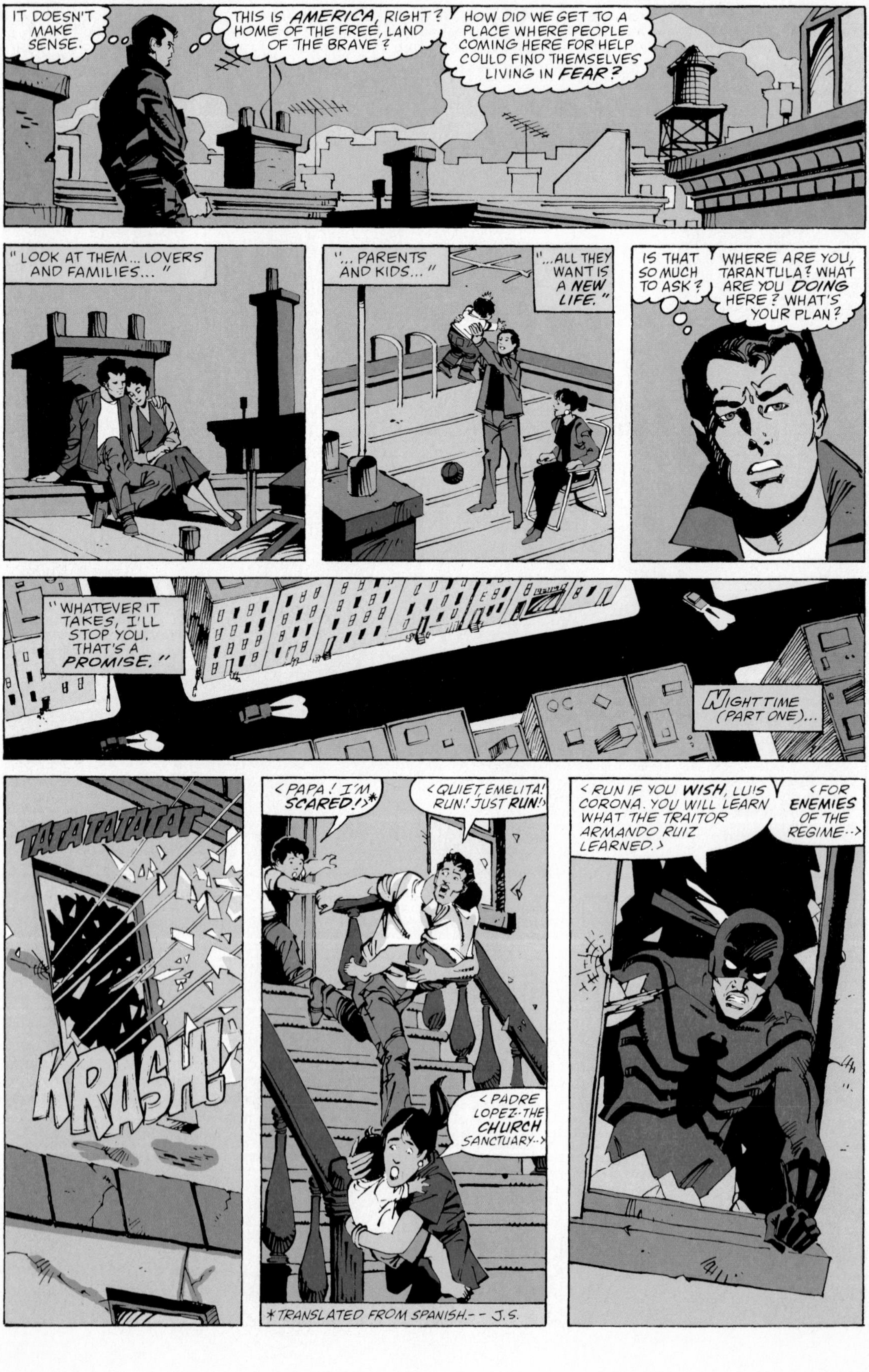
IT DOESN'T MAKE SENSE.
THIS IS AMERICA, RIGHT? HOME OF THE FREE, LAND OF THE BRAVE?
HOW DID WE GET TO A PLACE WHERE PEOPLE COMING HERE FOR HELP COULD FIND THEMSELVES LIVING IN FEAR?
"LOOK AT THEM... LOVERS AND FAMILIES..."
"...PARENTS AND KIDS..."
"...ALL THEY WANT IS A NEW LIFE."
IS THAT SO MUCH TO ASK?
WHERE ARE YOU, TARANTULA? WHAT ARE YOU DOING HERE? WHAT'S YOUR PLAN?
"WHATEVER IT TAKES, I'LL STOP YOU. THAT'S A PROMISE."
NIGHTTIME (PART ONE)...
TATATATATATAT
KRASH!
<PAPA! I'M SCARED!>*
<QUIET, EMELITA! RUN! JUST RUN!>
<PADRE LOPEZ--THE CHURCH SANCTUARY-->
*TRANSLATED FROM SPANISH.-- J.S.
<RUN IF YOU WISH, LUIS CORONA. YOU WILL LEARN WHAT THE TRAITOR ARMANDO RUIZ LEARNED.>
<FOR ENEMIES OF THE REGIME-->

‹--THERE IS *NO SANCTUARY!*›

‹JUAN, HIDALGO-- CALL THE OTHERS--›

--FOLLOW ME!

EARLIER TODAY I EXPLORED THIS PART OF THE CITY IN CIVILIAN CLOTHES. I FOUND CONFUSED, *FRIGHTENED* PEOPLE.

ON ALL SIDES THEY SEE ONLY *ENEMIES.*

AS WE LEARNED IN MY COUNTRY, THOSE WHO LIVE IN SUCH TERROR ARE *EASILY* CONTROLLED-- AND THOSE WHO RESIST THE TERROR ARE AS EASILY *DESTROYED.*

NIGHTTIME (PART TWO)...

HELLO?

SLOW DOWN, I CAN'T-- *ELVIRA?*

WHERE ARE YOU? WHAT'S *WRONG?*

ELVIRA--THAT'S THE WOMAN MARY JANE TOLD ME ABOUT OVER DINNER. IS SHE IN *TROUBLE--?*

I AM IN ST. JUDE'S CHURCH, MISSUS--ON SECOND AVENUE-- PADRE LOPEZ GIVES US SANCTUARY--BUT THAT WILL NOT STOP *HIM,* MISSUS--HE'S COME TO KILL US--MY HUSBAND--MY FAMILY--

WHO, ELVIRA? WHO'S TRYING TO KILL YOU?

LA TARANTULA?

GET THE DETAILS, M.J. I'M ON MY WAY.

MOMENTS LATER...

NOW I'M *CERTAIN* LA TARANTULA KILLED RUIZ AT *THE BUGLE--* AND FOR SOME REASON HE WANTS MJ'S FRIEND *ELVIRA* DEAD, TOO.

I DON'T KNOW WHY HE'S DOING THIS, BUT IT STOPS HERE. IT STOPS *NOW!*

NIGHTTIME (PART THREE)...

<YOU ARE SAFE HERE, MY CHILDREN.>

<THE CHURCH GIVES YOU SANCTUARY. EVEN THIS MADMAN OF WHOM YOU SPEAK MUST RESPECT THE CHURCH.>

<AND IF THE HOLINESS OF THIS PLACE DOES NOT DISSUADE HIM--->

RATTLE RATTLE

SURELY OUR STRONG LOCKS WILL!>

<I FEAR NOTHING WILL STOP HIM, FATHER!>

<HE HAS NO FEAR OF GOD OR MAN!>

<HE IS THE DEVIL HIMSELF! HE IS--->

PADRE!

KRASH

<DID I NOT WARN YOU?>

<THERE IS NO ESCAPE.>

BADDA TAK TAK BADAM

22

‹YOU AND THE OTHERS WHO HAVE FLED OUR COUNTRY MUST ALL *DIE* TO PROTECT THE STATE.›

‹THOSE WHO REMAIN IN OUR HOMELAND MUST UNDERSTAND THAT *DEFIANCE* OF THE STATE IS FUTILE--›

‹-- AND *SUICIDAL.*›

‹THAT IS WHY I WAS CHOSEN TO TAKE THE DRUGS THAT HAVE GIVEN ME THE STRENGTH OF *LA TARANTULA.*›

‹THAT IS WHY I HAVE *COME* TO EL NORTE!›

‹TO TEACH THE LESSON OF *TERROR.*›

GUESS WHAT, TEACH?

SCHOOL'S IN *RECESS.*

TAKA TAKA BDAM

BDAM

‹KILL HIM!›

SPTOW
SPTOW
SPTOW

SPTOW

UH-UH, BOYS. YOU CAN'T CATCH ME BY SURPRISE *TWICE.*

NO MATTER HOW FAST YOU ARE WITH THOSE GUNS..

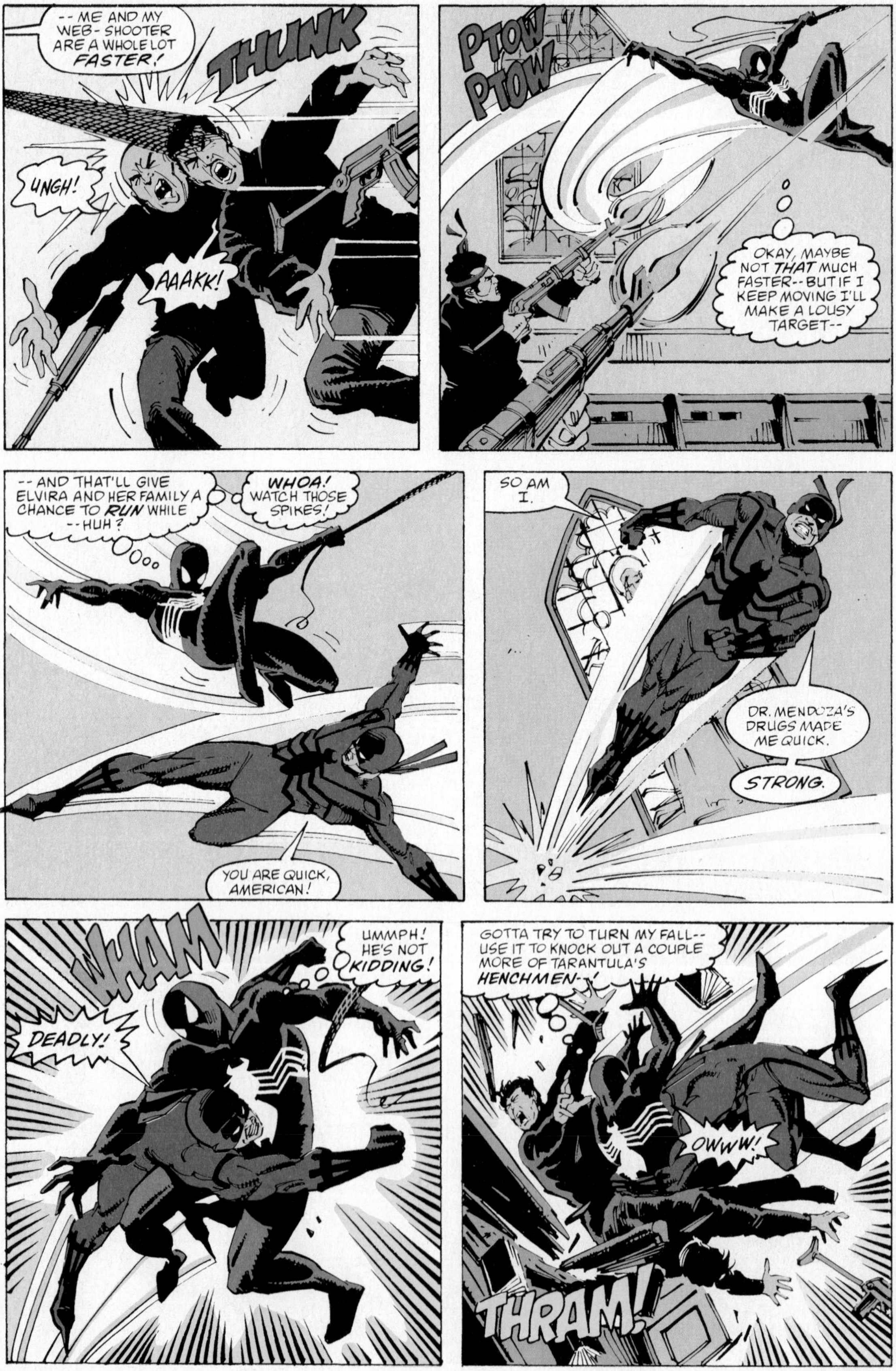

-- ME AND MY WEB-SHOOTER ARE A WHOLE LOT FASTER!
THUNK
UNGH!
AAAKK!
PTOW PTOW
OKAY, MAYBE NOT THAT MUCH FASTER--BUT IF I KEEP MOVING I'LL MAKE A LOUSY TARGET--
-- AND THAT'LL GIVE ELVIRA AND HER FAMILY A CHANCE TO RUN WHILE --HUH?
WHOA! WATCH THOSE SPIKES!
YOU ARE QUICK, AMERICAN!
SO AM I.
DR. MENDOZA'S DRUGS MADE ME QUICK.
STRONG.
WHAM
DEADLY!
UMMPH! HE'S NOT KIDDING!
GOTTA TRY TO TURN MY FALL-- USE IT TO KNOCK OUT A COUPLE MORE OF TARANTULA'S HENCHMEN--!
OWWW!
THRAM!

NIGHTTIME (PART FOUR)...

FIFTEEN MINUTES AGO, FIVE MINUTES AFTER THE FIRST SHOTS WERE FIRED, A BRAVE AND ANONYMOUS CITIZEN PHONED 911 TO REPORT THE SHOOTING.

FIVE MINUTES LATER, A PATROL CAR INVESTIGATING A FAMILY DISTURBANCE IN THE AREA CONFIRMED THE REPORT.

SIX MINUTES AGO, S.W.A.T. TEAMS WERE DISPATCHED.

THIRTY SECONDS AGO THEY ARRIVED.

HEAR ALL THAT NOISE OUTSIDE, AMIGO?

ARE YOU SO SURE?

THAT'S THE POLICE. THEY'RE GOING TO NAIL YOUR HIDE.

IN MY COUNTRY THE POLICE ARE THE SERVANTS OF THE STATE.

THE POLICE ARE HERE-- THEY WILL PUT AN END TO THIS MADNESS!

OH, NO, PADRE NOT LA POLICIA.

PADRE LOPEZ, ELVIRA IS AN ILLEGAL. THEY WILL SEND HER TO PRISON.

OH, MY LORD... BEHIND HIM--

SPIDER-MAN! THE OTHER GUNMEN--!

THRAM

THANKS FOR THE WARNING, PADRE--

--BUT MY *SPIDER-SENSE* WENT OFF A WHOLE TWO SECONDS BEFORE YOU YELLED!

I'VE GOT TO FORGET *LA TARANTULA.* THAT GUNFIRE'S GETTING TOO CLOSE TO ELVIRA AND HER *FAMILY!*

TRAKA TRAKA TRAK TRAK

HOW COULD A MAN MOVE SO *QUICKLY?*

<WE *MUST* HAVE WOUNDED HIM-- HE *MUST* HAVE FALLEN HERE-- BUT WHERE IS HIS *BODY?*>

LET'S SEE IF YOU CAN *GUESS.*

TIME'S UP.

THUNK!

SO MUCH FOR THE *COMEDY RELIEF.*

NOW I'LL GRAB THEIR *BOSS* BEFORE HE CAN--

<POR FAVOR! NO!>

HUH?

I DON'T BELIEVE IT!

26

BUT THIS WOMAN HAS *SANCTUARY*...

SORRY, FATHER. THE U.S. GOVERNMENT DOESN'T RECOGNIZE THE PROTECTION OF CLERICAL SANCTUARY.

THE LADY'S ON OUR LIST. I WAS COMING BY TO PICK HER UP TONIGHT WHEN ALL OF THIS--

HOLD IT!

WHAT LIST? WHO *ARE* YOU?

DUNPHY. *IMMIGRATION AND NATURALIZATION SERVICE.*

YOU MEAN AFTER ALL SHE'S BEEN THROUGH-- --THIS WOMAN IS BEING *ARRESTED?*

NOT ARRESTED-- *DETAINED* FOR A DEPORTATION HEARING.

DUNPHY, THAT *STINKS!* SHE'S A VICTIM, AND YOU'RE TREATING HER LIKE A CRIMINAL.

YOU THINK I LIKE THIS? THE LAW'S THE LAW. I JUST *ENFORCE* IT.

NO QUESTIONS ASKED? JUST FOLLOWING *ORDERS?*

IT'S THE LAW. YOU DON'T LIKE IT? WRITE YOUR *CONGRESSMAN.*

GREAT.

JUST... *GREAT.*

27

EPILOGUE 1: AN APARTMENT IN CHELSEA...

I CAN'T STAND IT, MJ.

LA TARANTULA GETS AWAY... YOUR FRIEND ELVIRA GETS "DETAINED"...

... AND I FEEL AS USEFUL AS A CLAM IN ROLLER SKATES.

WE'LL HELP HER, TIGER. YOU'LL THINK OF SOMETHING.

IT'S NOT OVER YET.

EPILOGUE 2: A SCOW ON THE HUDSON...

< I CANNOT STAND IT. >

< THE TRAITOR ESCAPED... MY AIDES WERE CAPTURED... AND THE AMERICAN MADE ME LOOK LIKE A FOOL! >

I AGREE.

< NEXT TIME I WILL-- EH? >

SMASH

AMMUNIT

I SAID, I AGREE-- AND SO DOES MY DEPARTMENT. WE DECIDED YOU NEED SPECIAL HELP IF YOU'RE GOING TO GO UP AGAINST SPIDER-MAN AGAIN.

YOUR GOVERNMENT CONCURS.

WE CONTACTED THE COMMITTEE FOR SUPER-POWERS. THEY SENT US A FREEDOM FIGHTER LIKE YOURSELF. LIKE YOU, A CHAMPION OF DEMOCRACY.

"CAPTAIN AMERICA!"

TO BE CONTINUED...

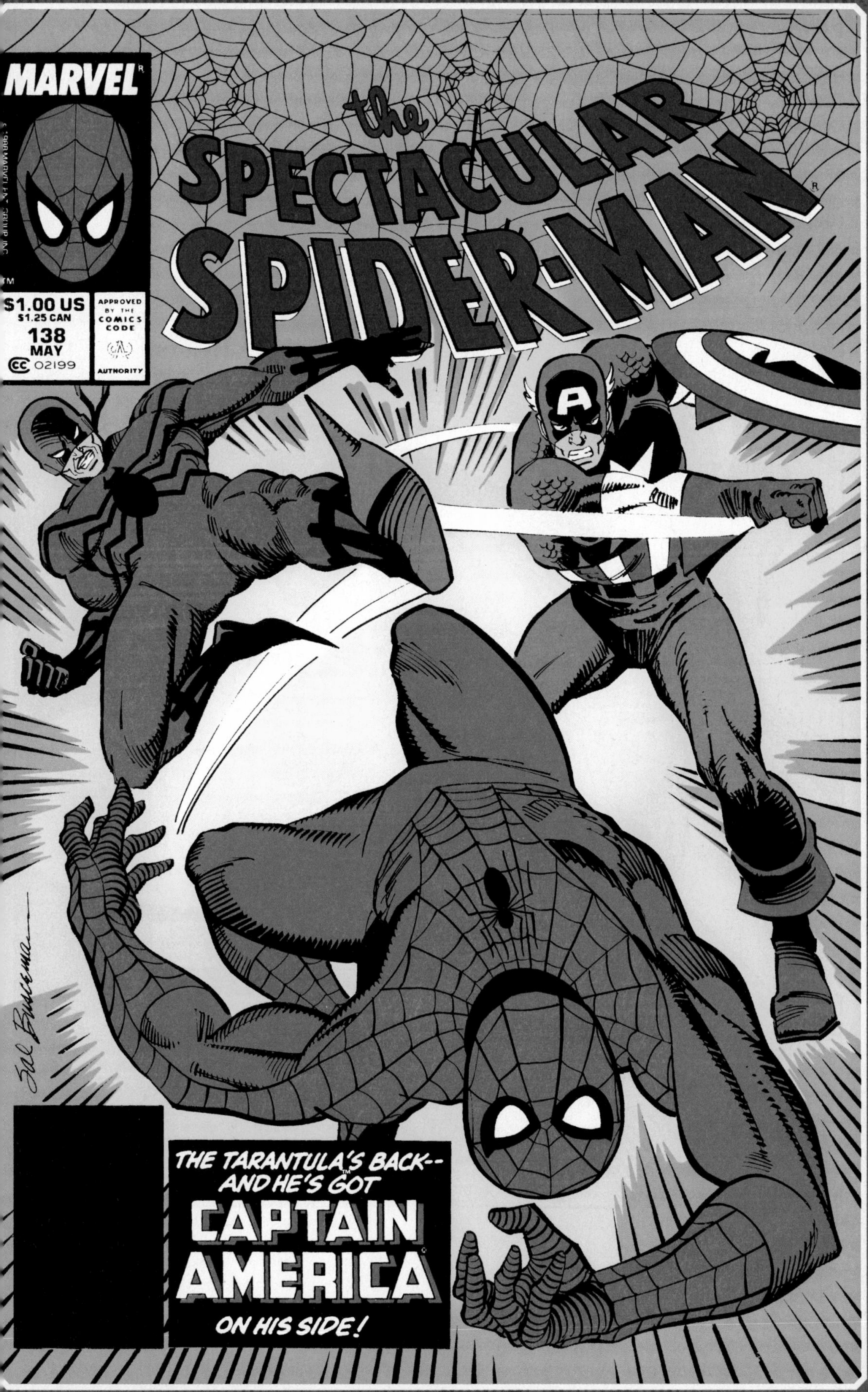

MARVEL
the SPECTACULAR SPIDER-MAN
$1.00 US
$1.25 CAN
138
MAY
02199
APPROVED BY THE COMICS CODE AUTHORITY
THE TARANTULA'S BACK--
AND HE'S GOT
CAPTAIN AMERICA
ON HIS SIDE!

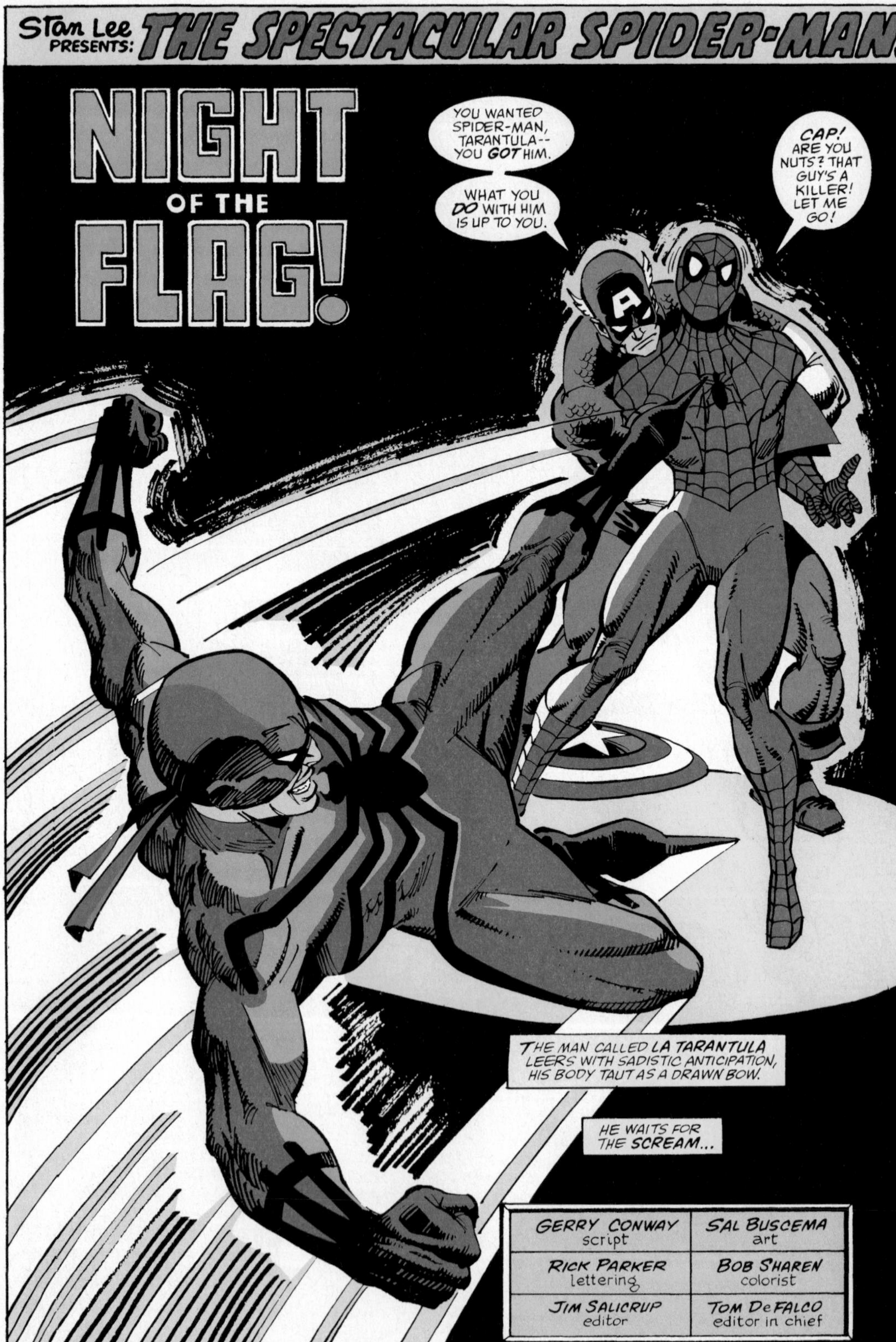

Stan Lee PRESENTS: THE SPECTACULAR SPIDER-MAN! TM
NIGHT OF THE FLAG!
YOU WANTED SPIDER-MAN, TARANTULA-- YOU GOT HIM.
WHAT YOU DO WITH HIM IS UP TO YOU.
CAP! ARE YOU NUTS? THAT GUY'S A KILLER! LET ME GO!
THE MAN CALLED LA TARANTULA LEERS WITH SADISTIC ANTICIPATION, HIS BODY TAUT AS A DRAWN BOW.
HE WAITS FOR THE SCREAM...
GERRY CONWAY script
SAL BUSCEMA art
RICK PARKER lettering
BOB SHAREN colorist
JIM SALICRUP editor
TOM DeFALCO editor in chief

...AND WHEN IT COMES, 'LA TARANTULA SHUD-DERS WITH A SENSATION OF EXQUISITE *RELEASE.*

AAYYHHHHHH

YOUR *PLEADING* WAS WITHOUT HOPE, SPIDER-MAN.

CAPTAIN AMERICA *KNOWS* YOU FOR WHAT YOU ARE:

≩ *FTUU* ≩

A TRAITOR TO YOUR COUNTRY AND TO THE CAUSE OF FREEDOM EVERYWHERE.

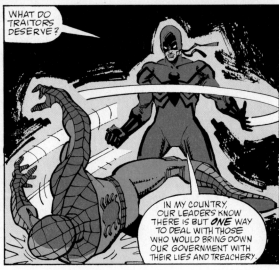

WHAT DO TRAITORS DESERVE?

IN MY COUNTRY, OUR LEADERS KNOW THERE IS BUT *ONE* WAY TO DEAL WITH THOSE WHO WOULD BRING DOWN OUR GOVERNMENT WITH THEIR LIES AND TREACHERY.

DEATH.

BUT BEFORE DEATH... *SUFFERING.*

BY YOUR SUFFERING YOU BECOME AN EXAMPLE TO THE PEOPLE. THE PEOPLE *UNDERSTAND* SUFFERING.

SUFFERING BREEDS FEAR, AND FEAR BREEDS *LOYALTY.*

ALL WE *WANT* FROM THEM IS LOYALTY.

REALLY, IS THAT SO MUCH TO *ASK?*

"*TIME TO MOVE OUT,* TARANTULA..."

DID YOU HEAR ME? IF WE'RE GOING TO FIND **SPIDER-MAN** BEFORE SUNRISE, WE BETTER START TRACKING HIM NOW.

I STILL DON'T UNDERSTAND THE RUSH, BUT YOUR FRIEND HERE FROM THE **STATE DEPARTMENT** CLAIMS IT'S IMPORTANT WE NAIL THE WALL-CRAWLER **TONIGHT.**

TO **ME.** I WILL ENJOY REPAYING SPIDER-MAN FOR THE **HUMILIATION** HE CAUSED ME. *

BUT I MUST FOCUS ON WHAT IS **AHEAD.** NO MORE DAYDREAMS.

LAST ISSUE. MORE LATER.--JIM

GOOD LUCK, AMIGO. REMEMBER, WHEN IT COMES TO THE BATTLE AGAINST INTERNATIONAL COM-- MUNISM, YOUR FIGHT IS **OUR** FIGHT.

ISN'T THAT **RIGHT,** CAPTAIN AMERICA?

THAT'S WHY I'M **HERE,** MR. SOUTH.

THAT, AND ORDERS FROM THE **COMMISSION ON SUPER-HUMAN ACTIVITIES.**

UH... THAT'S **COLONEL SOUTH,** CAPTAIN.

QUITE A GRIP YOU'VE GOT THERE.

I KNOW.

TELL ME SOMETHING, **TARANTULA.** WHY DID YOUR PEOPLE CHOOSE A **GARBAGE SCOW** FOR YOUR MISSION HEADQUARTERS?

THE TRAITORS I CAME HERE TO PUNISH ARE THEMSELVES **BASURA--** "GARBAGE," AS YOU SAY IN ENGLISH.

IN THIS WAY I AM REMINDED CONSTANTLY OF MY NOBLE **CAUSE.**

I SEE.

MAY I SAY WHAT AN *HONOR* IT IS FOR ME TO BE WORKING WITH THE GREAT *CAPITÁN AMERICA*?

YOU WERE THE MODEL FOR MY COUNTRY'S ORIGINAL *TARANTULA*.

WHAT HAPPENED TO *HIM*?

HE WAS *KILLED* BY SPIDER-MAN.

MAYBE YOU'D BETTER *BRIEF* ME.

THE *COMMISSION* ORDERED ME TO HELP YOU TRACK SPIDER-MAN. THEY SAID HE AIDED A KNOWN *TERRORIST*.

THAT IS SO.

HER NAME IS *ELVIRA CORONA*, A VICIOUS CRIMINAL.

"MY MEN AND I WERE SENT TO ARREST HER FOR TRANSGRESSIONS AGAINST THE STATE -- BUT SHE CAUGHT US BY SURPRISE, THREATENED TO *KILL* US.

"I WAS *PERSUADING* HER TO *SURRENDER*--

"--WHEN *SPIDER-MAN* BURST ONTO THE SCENE.

"THANKS TO HIM, SHE ALMOST *ESCAPED*. THAT WOULD HAVE BEEN A TRAGEDY.

"FORTUNATELY, AGENTS OF YOUR *IMMIGRATION SERVICE* WERE WAITING OUTSIDE.

" SHE PUT UP A TERRIBLE STRUGGLE. THANK GOD, NO ONE WAS *HURT*. * "

* A SOMEWHAT *TWISTED* VIEW OF EVENTS LAST ISSUE. -- J.S.

AND *SPIDER-MAN...?*

WHEN HE REALIZED THE ODDS WERE AGAINST HIM, HE FLED.

WHY ALL THESE *QUESTIONS?*

I'M ONLY WONDERING WHY SPIDER-MAN GOT INVOLVED WITH ALL THIS. IT DOESN'T FIT MY *PICTURE* OF THE MAN.

PERHAPS THE TRAITORS *HIRED* HIM. WE'LL ASK THE WOMAN ELVIRA CORONA.

SHE IS BEING HELD IN THE *FEDERAL BUILDING--* DOWN THERE.

LET'S GO.

I WISH I KNEW MORE. THE *ORIGINAL* CAPTAIN AMERICA KNEW SPIDER-MAN.

ALL I HAVE IS THE COMMISSION'S *BRIEFING.*

NONE OF THIS *FEELS* RIGHT.

BUT LIKE IT OR NOT, I'VE GOT MY *ORDERS...*

FIRST INTERLUDE: A FEW MILES NORTH IN SPANISH HARLEM...

AMNISTIA

LOOK, MS. MICHAELSON, ELVIRA CORONA IS MY WIFE'S FRIEND-- WE WANT TO *HELP* HER--

-- BUT THE GOVERNMENT IS GOING TO DEPORT HER--

-- AND YOU SAY YOUR LEGAL AID OFFICE CAN'T DO A THING TO STOP IT.

WHAT ABOUT THE ILLEGAL ALIEN *AMNESTY* PROGRAM?

I'M AFRAID ELVIRA CORONA ISN'T *ELIGIBLE,* MRS. PARKER.

HER HUSBAND AND CHILDREN QUALIFY, BUT SHE DOESN'T. SHE CAN'T PROVE SHE'S BEEN IN THIS COUNTRY *CONTINUOUSLY* SINCE *1981.*

CAN *YOU?* CAN *ANYONE?*

THIS IS *CRAZY!* IF SHE'S SENT BACK TO HER *HOMELAND,* SHE'LL BE *KILLED.* BUT ALL THE *GOVERNMENT* CARES ABOUT ARE ITS STUPID RULES AND REGULATIONS!

BELIEVE ME, MARY JANE, I'M AS *FRUSTRATED* AS YOU ARE. WE'LL TRY TO HELP, BUT RIGHT NOW--

"-- THE SITUATION LOOKS PRETTY *HOPELESS.* "

I SHOULDN'T HAVE YELLED AT HER, PETER. SHE WAS JUST BEING *HONEST.*

BUT I FEEL SO *USELESS...*

ME TOO, MJ.

MAGGIE MICHAELSON TOLD BEN URICH AND ME HOW SOME ILLEGALS ARE TOO *FRIGHT-ENED* TO APPLY FOR AMNESTY-- AFRAID THEY'LL BE SEPARATED FROM THEIR FAMILIES -- AND I DIDN'T UNDERSTAND IT.

SHE SAID THERE WERE SHYSTER LAWYERS WHO *PREYED* ON THAT FEAR, MAKING PROMISES THEY COULDN'T KEEP-- FOR A HEFTY *FEE.*

BUT THE REALITY DIDN'T *HIT HOME* UNTIL YOUR FRIEND ELVIRA PHONED FOR HELP LAST NIGHT. AS SPIDER-MAN, I COULD SAVE HER FROM *LA TARANTULA* AND HIS GOON SQUAD--

-- BUT ALL MY POWER COULDN'T RESCUE HER FROM "THE WHEELS OF JUSTICE."

ALL THESE PEOPLE, PETER, LIVING WITH SUCH FEAR... IT ISN'T *FAIR.*

" GIVE ME YOUR TIRED, YOUR POOR, YOUR HUDDLED MASSES YEARNING TO BREATHE FREE..."

...BUT *ONLY* IF THEY'VE BEEN HERE SINCE 1981.

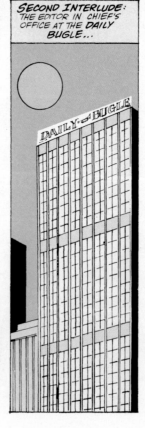

SECOND INTERLUDE: THE EDITOR IN CHIEF'S OFFICE AT THE *DAILY BUGLE...*

DAILY BUGLE

...WHERE A TIRED *JOE ROBERTSON* STARES BLANKLY INTO SPACE, UNAWARE OF THE ROOM AROUND HIM UNTIL A SOFT VOICE CALLS HIM BACK TO THE PRESENT...

YOU SHOULD GO HOME, ROBBIE. THE MORNING EDITION WENT TO BED AN *HOUR* AGO.

HMMM?

BESIDES, I CAN'T LEAVE TILL YOU LEAVE, AND I'M *TIRED.*

EVEN CITY EDITORS NEED TO SLEEP SOMETIME.

THANKS, KATE.

GUESS I GOT CARRIED AWAY WITH THIS *RESEARCH.*

ANYTHING I CAN HELP WITH? THE LAST FEW DAYS YOU SEEMED SO *PREOCCUPIED...*

PERSONAL BUSINESS, KATE. *PRIVATE* AND PERSONAL.

ROBERTSON IN CHIEF

UH-HUH. BEFORE I BECAME AN EDITOR, I WAS A *REPORTER--* AND I DIDN'T WIN MY PULITZER BY IGNORING MY INSTINCTS.

THOSE INSTINCTS TELL ME ROBBIE IS IN *TROUBLE.*

EVEN IF WE WEREN'T FRIENDS, I'D BE A POOR JOURNALIST IF I DIDN'T TRY TO FIND OUT WHAT KIND OF TROUBLE.

CHARGES DROPPED AGAINST ALLEGED "TOMBSTONE" KILLER

TOMBSTONE... THEY SAY HE'S THE MOST *FEARED* MOB HITMAN IN THE MIDWEST.

WHY WOULD ROBBIE BE INTERESTED IN *HIM?*

END OF SECOND INTERLUDE.

AT THE FEDERAL BUILDING IN DOWNTOWN MANHATTAN, ALL IS *QUIET,* THE BUREAUCRATS LEFT HOURS AGO, THE CLEANING STAFF HAS CLEANED AND DEPARTED...

...AND IN THE BASEMENT DEPORTATION DETENTION CENTER, ONE LONELY GUARD WAITS FOR HIS SHIFT TO END.

MAN, THIS CLAREMONT GUY SURE CAN *WRITE.* HE'S NO STEPHEN KING, BUT--

CLIK CLIK

HUH?

HEY! HOW'D YOU GET IN-- !AAAAHH!

PUBLIC BUILDINGS ARE *EASY* TO ENTER, MI AMIGO. EVEN AFTER HOURS.

SNAK

DETENTION CELLS, HOWEVER, ARE MORE *DIFFICULT* TO BREACH.

FOR THOSE, ONE REQUIRES A *KEY*-- IN THIS CASE AN ELECTRONIC KEY CARD, SUCH AS THE ONE IN YOUR DESK.

THE DRUG ON MY *TOE* SPIKE SHOULD HAVE RENDERED YOU *UNCONSCIOUS* INSTANTLY.

STOP.

YOU NEED A *SECOND* DOSE.

NO.

≈UUHHHH!≈

HE'S JUST DOING HIS JOB. ONE DOSE IS ENOUGH.

UHH-- I WAS ONLY TRYING TO PROTECT *YOU*, IF HE SAW YOU, IDENTIFIED YOU...

HE DIDN'T... AND HE'S OUT NOW.

CAN YOU FIND THE *CORONA* WOMAN'S *CELL?*

OF COURSE.

THEN FIND IT. I DON'T LIKE YOUR *METHODS*, TARANTULA.

THE SOONER WE'RE FINISHED WITH THIS MISSION, THE HAPPIER I'LL BE.

THE WAY THESE ILLEGALS *STARE* AT ME--AT THE *FLAG* I WEAR--WITH SUCH FEAR AND HATRED...

IT MAKES MY *SKIN* CRAWL.

I BELIEVE IN THE FIGHT AGAINST COMMUNISM. I BELIEVE IN HELPING OUR DEMOCRATIC ALLIES IN LATIN AMERICA.

BUT SOMETHING ABOUT ALL THIS FEELS SO *WRONG*.

DO YOU SPEAK ESPAÑOL, CAPTAIN?

SPANISH? NO.

THEN I WILL QUESTION HER.

ELVIRA CORONA. <DO YOU KNOW ME?>*

* TRANSLATED FROM THE SPANISH. -- J.S.

< YOU ARE THE DEMON. YOU ARE TARANTULA.>

< WHERE ARE MY CHILDREN? WHERE IS MY HUSBAND? WHAT WILL YOU DO TO THEM?>

<THEY WILL DIE IF YOU DO NOT TELL ME HOW TO FIND THE ONE THE AMERICANS CALL SPIDER-MAN.>

<BUT FIRST THEY WILL SUFFER EXQUISITE AGONY.>

<I DON'T KNOW. I SWEAR IT. HE JUST CAME.>

<PLEASE, MY BABIES...>

<YOUR BABIES WILL DIE. WHO DID YOU CALL? HOW DID YOU REACH HIM?>

< MRS. PARKER... MARY JANE PARKER...>

<...DON'T HURT HER...>

<...DON'T HURT MY BABIES...>

SPIDER-MAN IS IN CONTACT WITH SOMEONE NAMED MARY JANE PARKER.

WE ARE CLOSE. I FEEL IT.

VERY VERY CLOSE.

39

THIRD INTERLUDE:

TRUST ME ON THIS, TAKASURA.

BY THE TIME THE TOKYO MARKETS OPEN TOMORROW, THE STOCK INDEX WILL BE OFF BY FIVE PERCENT. AT *LEAST.*

MAKE YOUR MARGIN CALL NOW AND YOU'LL CLEAR SIXTY CENTS AMERICAN PER SHARE PROFIT MINIMUM.

HOW DO I KNOW?

I HAVE FRIENDS IN *HIGH PLACES,* TAKASURA. THEY TELL ME THINGS, I TELL YOU THINGS, THEN YOU--

PUT DOWN THE PHONE.

HUH?

THERE'S A MAN UPTOWN WANTS TO TALK WITH YOU, RAYBURN.

HEY! WHO ARE YOU? HOW DID YOU GET IN HERE? THIS IS A PRIVATE OFFICE--I'LL CALL *SECURITY.*

YOU'RE A TALKER. A RUNNER, TOO.

≤*GAAKK!*≥

GUYS LIKE YOU GIVE ME A RASH.

PLEASE--DON'T HURT ME-- MAKE IT WORTH YOUR WHILE--

UH-HUH. THE ARRANGER SAID YOU'D TRY THAT.

YOU DON'T... *WANT* TO HURT ME...

YOU *WANT* TO...LET GO... LET GO...

UH-HUH. THE ARRANGER SAID YOU'D TRY *THAT,* TOO. WON'T WORK, 'CAUSE I'M *READY* FOR YOU.

≤*AAG!*≥

HE SAID YOU HAVE SOME KIND OF *CHARISMA* THAT MAKES PEOPLE DO WHAT YOU TELL THEM TO DO.

HE SAID YOU PROBABLY DON'T EVEN KNOW IT.

ALL YOUR LIFE, MEN AND WOMEN JUST DID WHAT YOU *WANTED* THEM TO. YOU APPARENTLY NEVER EVEN WONDERED WHY.

BUT *THE ARRANGER* LEARNED ABOUT YOU FROM ONE OF YOUR WALL STREET BUDDIES.

HE SAYS YOU HAVE A *RAW* TALENT. HE WANTS WHAT YOU'VE GOT.

AND IF YOU THINK *YOU'RE* PERSUASIVE, ROLAND...

...JUST WAIT TILL YOU MEET *HIM.*

END OF THIRD INTERLUDE.

ONE HOUR LATER, IN A *DARKENED* WEST SIDE APARTMENT STILL CLUTTERED WITH THE DEBRIS OF A RECENT MOVE...

NO!

PETER?

PETER! YOU'RE HAVING A NIGHTMARE! WAKE UP!

ALONE... I WAS *ALONE,* MJ...

IT'S OK, PETEY, IT'S OK. I'M WITH YOU.

...ALL ALONE, IN A STRANGE PLACE... AND THEY STARTED COMING AT ME...

...DOC OCTOPUS...VENOM... MONGOOSE... HOBGOBLIN... ALL MY *ENEMIES*...

WE'RE IN A NEW *APARTMENT,* PETER.

NATURALLY, YOU FEEL DIFFERENT, *STRANGE...* BUT YOU DON'T HAVE TO FEEL *ALONE.*

IT ISN'T THE NEW PLACE, MJ.

41

SEEING THOSE ILLEGALS TONIGHT REALLY AFFECTED ME.

I GUESS I'VE ALWAYS FELT LIKE AN OUTSIDER HIDING ON THE INSIDE...

...BUT THEY REALLY ARE OUTSIDERS HIDING ON THE INSIDE.

I UNDERSTOOD HOW ALONE THEY MUST FEEL. ALONE AND DESPERATE.

WITHOUT FRIENDS, AND HUNTED BY ENEMIES.

I WISH--

BRING

UH-OH.

WHERE DID WE PUT THE PHONE...?

BRRING

MAYBE LEAVING A FORWARDING NUMBER WASN'T SUCH A GREAT IDEA, HUH?

WHO'D CALL US AFTER MIDNIGHT?

WHAT WE NEED IS A NICE NEW ANSWERING MACHINE, BUT TILL THEN-- HELLO?

WHO? ELVIRA?

HOW DID YOU-- WHERE?

ELVIRA, PLEASE TELL ME WHAT--

LET ME TALK TO HER!

HELLO? ELVIRA? HELLO?

THE LINE'S DEAD. WHAT DID SHE SAY, MJ?

SOMETHING ABOUT THE WESTSIDE FREIGHT YARD...

OKAY.

I CAN'T HELP THOSE PEOPLE WE SAW TONIGHT... AND THAT MAKES ME MAD.

BUT YOUR FRIEND ELVIRA IS ANOTHER STORY.

SOMEHOW SHE GOT AWAY FROM THE I.N.S.

NOW SHE'S HIDING, SCARED OUT OF HER MIND...

...AND *THAT'S* SOMETHING I CAN HELP HER DEAL WITH.

I'LL FIND ELVIRA AND BRING HER TO MAGGIE MICHAELSON. MAGGIE WILL KNOW WHAT TO DO.

AS SPIDER-MAN?

HEY, I'M NOT *COMPLETELY* STUPID.

LA TARANTULA TRIED TO KILL ELVIRA ONCE, TO MAKE HER AN *EXAMPLE* TO OTHER POLITICAL REFUGEES.

HE'S STILL OUT THERE, SOMEWHERE.

TAKE CARE, PETEY.

RELAX, MJ...

"...THESE DAYS, *CAREFUL* IS MY MIDDLE NAME."

TEN MINUTES LATER, THE WEST THIRTIES RAILROAD YARD.

I DIDN'T WANT TO WORRY MJ, BUT THE TRUTH IS, I'M PRETTY SURE THIS IS A *TRAP*.

THE *I.N.S.* DOESN'T LOSE ILLEGALS ONCE THEY'RE IN DETENTION.

SOMEONE COULD HAVE LEARNED THE CONNECTION BETWEEN ELVIRA AND MJ--

--AND THEN FAKED ELVIRA'S VOICE TO *LURE* ME HERE.

LA TARANTULA IS THE LOGICAL SUSPECT, WHICH MAKES ME-- EH?

SPIDER-SENSE... WARNING ME-- *DANGER*--!

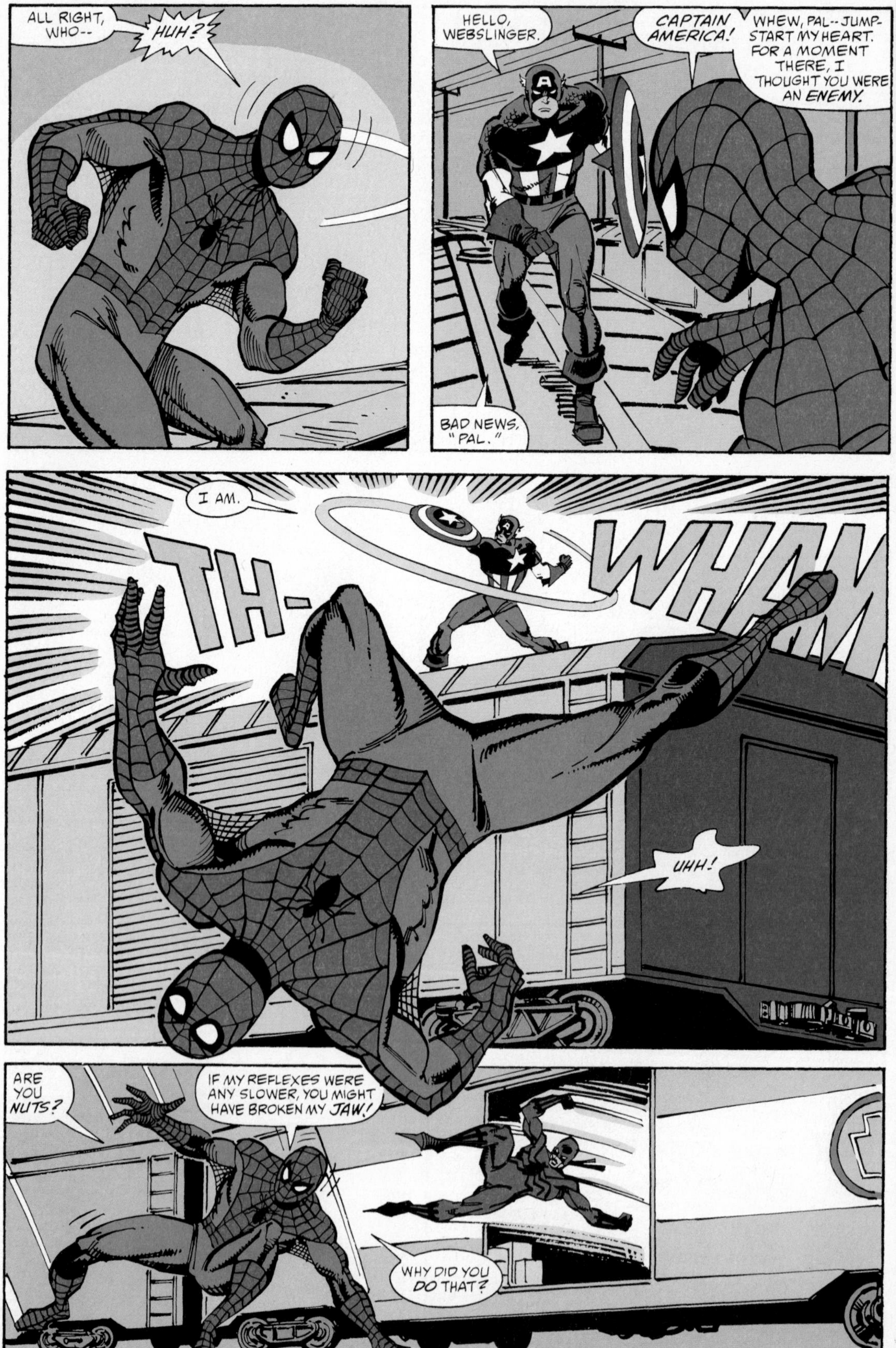

ALL RIGHT, WHO--
HUH?
HELLO, WEBSLINGER.
CAPTAIN AMERICA!
WHEW, PAL-- JUMP-START MY HEART. FOR A MOMENT THERE, I THOUGHT YOU WERE AN ENEMY.
BAD NEWS, "PAL."
I AM.
TH-
WHAM
UHH!
ARE YOU NUTS?
IF MY REFLEXES WERE ANY SLOWER, YOU MIGHT HAVE BROKEN MY JAW!
WHY DID YOU DO THAT?

TO DISTRACT YOU FROM *ME*, OF COURSE.

THAK

OWWW!

CAP AND *LA TARANTULA*-- WORKING TOGETHER?

I EXPECTED THAT SOUTH AMERICAN HITMAN AND MAYBE A FEW THUGS-- BUT THIS IS LOONEY TUNES TIME!

UHHH! MY SHOULDER FEELS LIKE SOMEONE'S *FRYING* IT WITH A *BLOWTORCH!*

CAN'T LET HIM GET A *SECOND* SHOT AT ME.

RUN, LITTLE SPIDER. BY NOW YOU BEGIN TO FEEL THE EFFECTS OF THE *DRUG* COATING MY *TOE-SPIKE*.

CAPTAIN AMERICA BELIEVES IT TO BE A *DILUTED* FORM OF *CURARE*, PRODUCING MUSCLE RELAXATION.

"IN FACT, LITTLE SPIDER THE DRUG IS AT *FULL STRENGTH*... AN 'ACCIDENT' THAT WILL LEAD TO DEATH FROM *HEART FAILURE* IN A MATTER OF MINUTES..."

ACHES SO BAD, TOE-SPIKE MUST'VE BEEN *POISONED.*

MY ENHANCED METABOLISM IS *FIGHTING* THE EFFECTS-- BUT I NEED TIME TO-- OH, NO--

SPLASH

THIS IS WRONG. ATTACKING A WOUNDED MAN ISN'T HEROISM. I HAVE TO ASK MYSELF-- IS THIS HOW THE ORIGINAL CAP WOULD ACT?

NO. WHAT SPIDER-MAN SAID WHEN I ATTACKED HIM: " I THOUGHT YOU WERE AN ENEMY."--THOSE PEOPLE IN THE I.N.S. DETENTION CENTER TONIGHT SEEMED TO BE THINKING THE SAME THING.

" THEY LOOKED AT THE FLAG I WEAR, AND THEIR FACES SHOWED FEAR.

"TO THEM, I AM THE ENEMY."

CAPTAIN AMERICA... AMERICA ITSELF... THE ENEMY.

I DON'T LIKE THE WAY THAT FEELS. NOT ONE BIT.

WHAT AM I DOING HERE?

WHO AM I TRYING TO HELP?

WHAT'S WRONG, LITTLE SPIDER? HAVE YOU CAUGHT YOUR FOOT?

-- QUÉ LASTIMA! THAT'S TOO BAD!

MUSCLES FEEL SO WEAK... LIKE I'M IN THE WORLD'S HOTTEST JACUZZI...

...CAN'T PULL FREE... HAVE TO REACH THE TRACK SWITCH...

THAT'S NOT FOR YOU, LITTLE SPIDER.

THAK

NO, I HAVE OTHER PLANS FOR YOU.

WHEN YOU KILLED THE FIRST TARANTULA YOU DISHONORED MY COUNTRY.

LIAR... DIDN'T KILL HIM... DIED BY ACCIDENT *...

PERHAPS. I DO NOT CARE.

*IN AMAZING SPIDER-MAN # 236.--JIM

WHAT DID HE SAY?

ONLY THE DISHONOR MATTERS.

FOR THE DISHONOR, AND FOR INTERFERING WITH MY MISSION OF TERROR AGAINST LA REFUGIDA YOU MUST BE PUNISHED.

NOT KILLED.

KILLING WOULD BE TOO QUICK.

THE DRUG WAS A MISTAKE. YES, I SEE THAT. IT IS GOOD YOU SURVIVE.

FOR YOU THERE MUST BE SUFFERING.

A SHATTERED LEG, THE LOSS OF A FOOT-- YOU WILL BE CRIPPLED, LITTLE SPIDER.

AND YOU WILL WISH YOU WERE DEAD!

BOY, TALK ABOUT A NEGATIVE ATTITUDE.

WANT SOME ADVICE?

SEE A SHRINK.

QUÉ ES ESTO?

YOU SHOULD BE PARALYZED-- TOO WEAK TO MOVE!

48

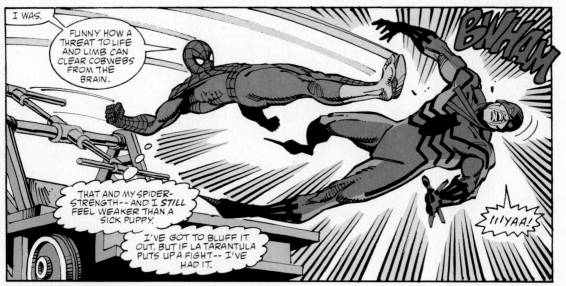

I WAS.

FUNNY HOW A THREAT TO LIFE AND LIMB CAN CLEAR COBWEBS FROM THE BRAIN.

BNHAM

THAT AND MY SPIDER-STRENGTH-- AND I *STILL* FEEL WEAKER THAN A SICK PUPPY.

I'VE GOT TO BLUFF IT OUT, BUT IF LA TARANTULA PUTS UP A FIGHT-- I'VE HAD IT.

IIIYAA!

SNAP

MADRE! MY LEG-- I BROKE MY KNEE--!

CONSIDERING WHAT YOU HAD PLANNED FOR ME, PAL, THAT MAKES ME FEEL JUST *AWFUL*.

CAPTAIN AMERICA! MI AMIGO! HELP ME!

OH, NO! FIGHTING LA TARANTULA, I FORGOT ABOUT CAP!

THE WAY HE'S *LOOKING* AT US-- WHAT IS HE GOING TO *DO*?

WAIT! WHERE ARE YOU GOING?

I'M YOUR *ALLY!* YOU CAN'T *ABANDON* ME--!

GUESS WHAT, TWINKLE TOES?

HE JUST DID.

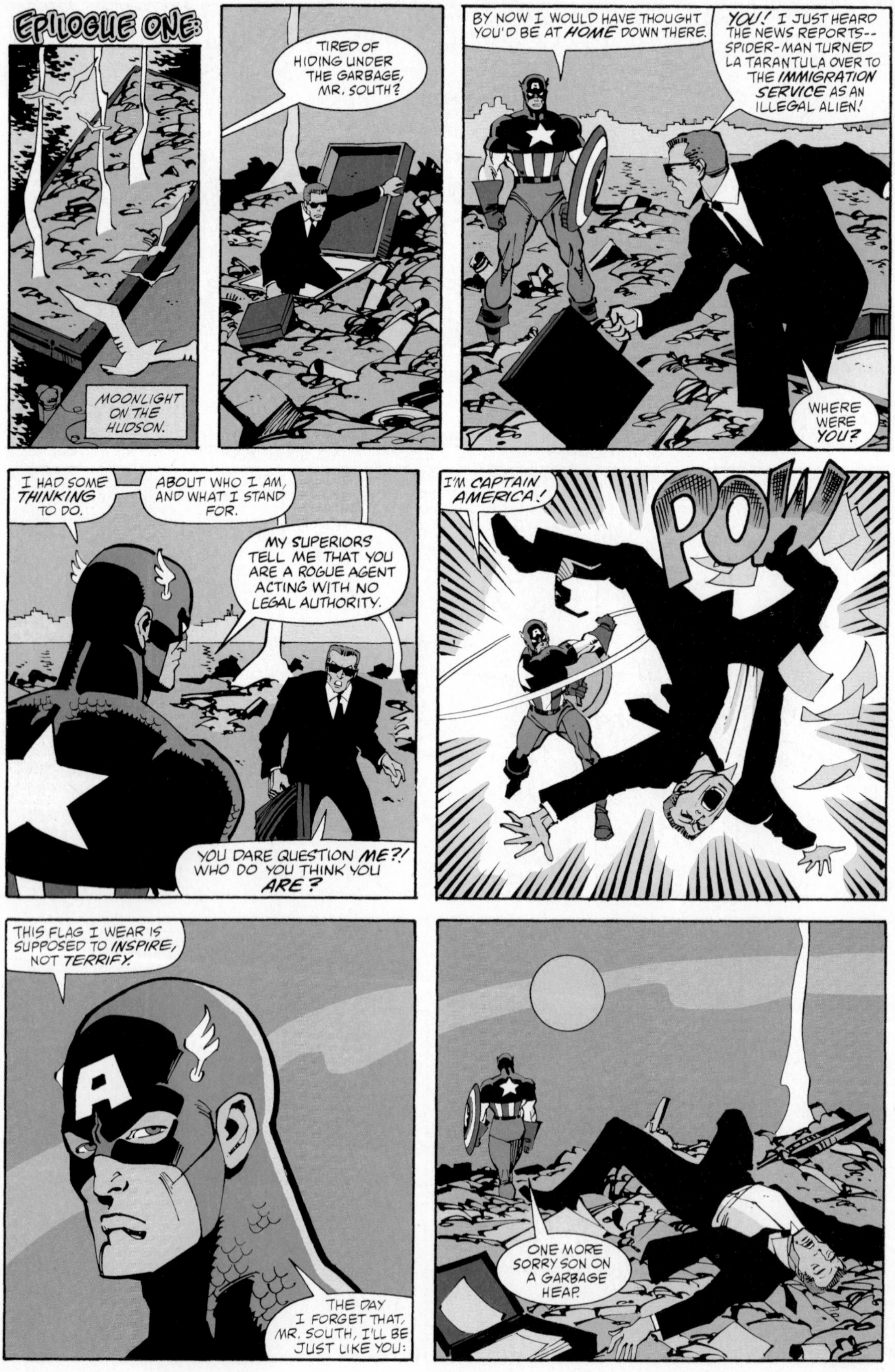
EPILOGUE ONE:
MOONLIGHT ON THE HUDSON.
TIRED OF HIDING UNDER THE GARBAGE, MR. SOUTH?
BY NOW I WOULD HAVE THOUGHT YOU'D BE AT HOME DOWN THERE.
YOU! I JUST HEARD THE NEWS REPORTS-- SPIDER-MAN TURNED LA TARANTULA OVER TO THE IMMIGRATION SERVICE AS AN ILLEGAL ALIEN!
WHERE WERE YOU?
I HAD SOME THINKING TO DO.
ABOUT WHO I AM, AND WHAT I STAND FOR.
MY SUPERIORS TELL ME THAT YOU ARE A ROGUE AGENT ACTING WITH NO LEGAL AUTHORITY.
YOU DARE QUESTION ME?! WHO DO YOU THINK YOU ARE?
I'M CAPTAIN AMERICA!
POW
THIS FLAG I WEAR IS SUPPOSED TO INSPIRE, NOT TERRIFY.
THE DAY I FORGET THAT, MR. SOUTH, I'LL BE JUST LIKE YOU.
ONE MORE SORRY SON ON A GARBAGE HEAP.

EPILOGUE TWO: ONE WEEK LATER, JFK INTERNATIONAL AIRPORT.

DON'T WORRY, MJ. THANKS TO ALL THE *PUBLICITY*--

--MAGGIE SAYS ELVIRA AND HER FAMILY SHOULD BE *SAFE* FROM REPRISALS IN THEIR HOMELAND.

FOR A WHILE, ANYWAY.

"YEAH. IN THE MEANTIME, MAGGIE WILL TRY TO ARRANGE POLITICAL REFUGEE STATUS FOR ELVIRA.

"IT'S A LONG-SHOT, BUT THERE'S A *CHANCE*.

I HOPE SO, PETER. I FEEL SO *HELPLESS*.

ME, TOO. HELPLESS AND ANGRY AND SAD.

AT LEAST *LA TARANTULA* AND HIS THUGS ARE GOING HOME, TOO--

--AND WITH LUCK, THEY'LL GET THE KIND OF *WELCOME* THEY DESERVE.

IT'S NOT MUCH, BUT SOMETIMES YOU HAVE TO SETTLE FOR SMALL *VICTORIES*.

I KNOW.

BUT IT'S THE SMALL *DEFEATS* THAT BREAK MY HEART...

"GIVE ME YOUR TIRED, YOUR POOR, YOUR HUDDLED MASSES YEARNING TO BREATHE FREE, THE WRETCHED REFUSE OF YOUR TEEMING SHORE. SEND THESE, THE HOMELESS, TEMPEST-TOST TO ME. I LIFT MY LAMP BESIDE THE GOLDEN DOOR."

-- THE NEW COLOSSUS: INSCRIPTION FOR THE STATUE OF LIBERTY, NEW YORK HARBOR.

FINI.

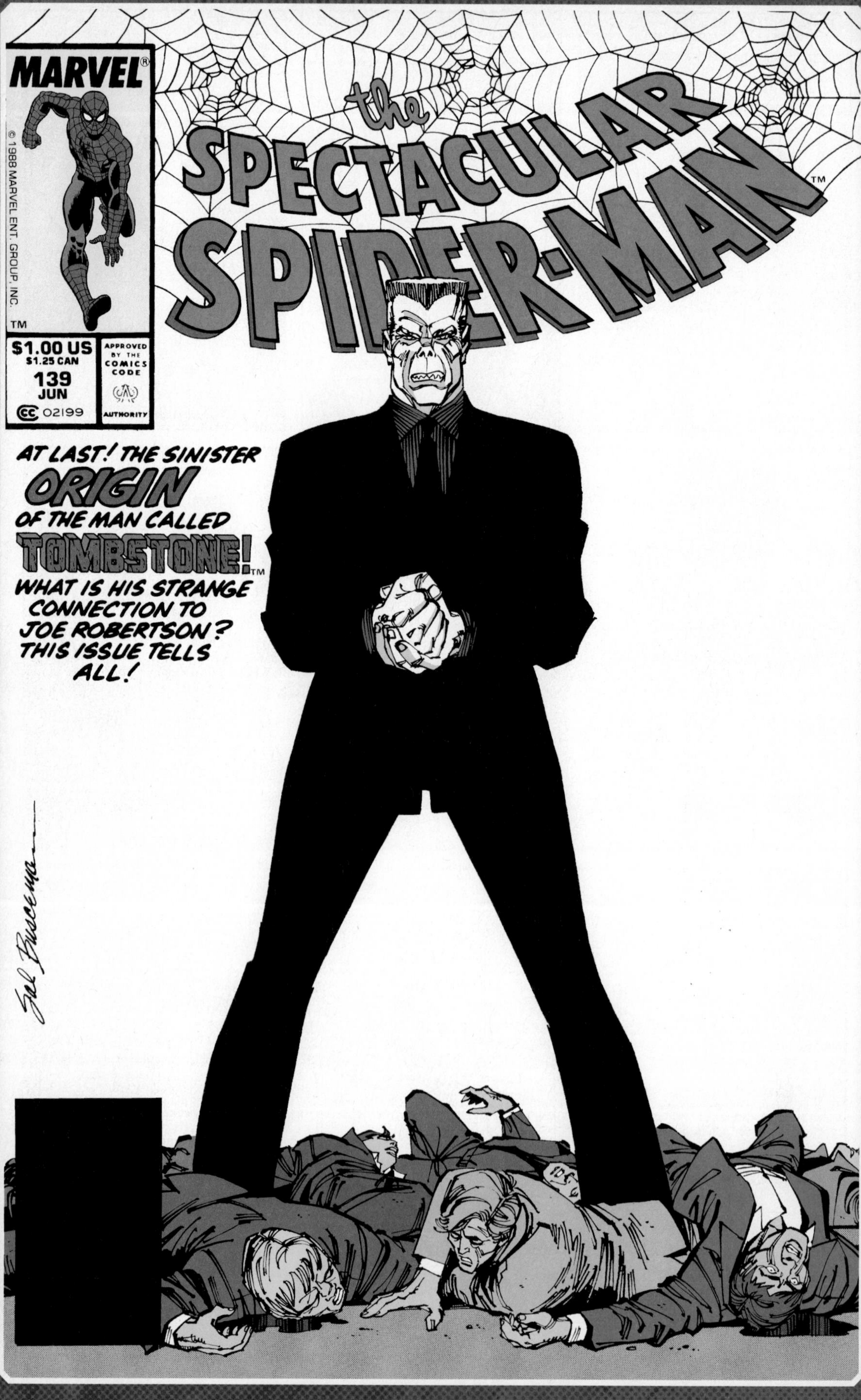
MARVEL®
© 1988 MARVEL ENT. GROUP, INC.
TM
$1.00 US
$1.25 CAN
139
JUN
CC 02199
APPROVED BY THE COMICS CODE AUTHORITY
the SPECTACULAR SPIDER-MAN™
AT LAST! THE SINISTER ORIGIN OF THE MAN CALLED TOMBSTONE!™
WHAT IS HIS STRANGE CONNECTION TO JOE ROBERTSON? THIS ISSUE TELLS ALL!
Sal Buscema

FIFTEEN MINUTES AGO, PETER PARKER WAS SITTING DOWN TO *DINNER* WITH HIS NEW BRIDE.

FOURTEEN MINUTES AGO, PETER PARKER RECEIVED AN URGENT PHONE SUMMONS FROM *JOE ROBERTSON,* EDITOR IN CHIEF OF THE *DAILY BUGLE.*

TWELVE MINUTES AGO, PETER PARKER PULLED ON THE FAMILIAR RED AND BLUE COSTUME OF *SPIDER-MAN.*

TEN SECONDS AGO, SPIDER-MAN SWUNG TOWARD ROBBIE ROBERTSON'S OFFICE WINDOW.

PZING!

HEY!

ONE SECOND AGO, SOMEONE TRIED TO USE HIS HEAD FOR *TARGET PRACTICE.*

"GRAVE MEMORY"

GERRY **CONWAY** ✶ SAL **BUSCEMA** ✶ RICK **PARKER** ✶ BOB **SHAREN** ✶ JIM **SALICRUP** ✶ TOM **DeFALCO**
SCRIPTER · ARTIST · LETTERING · COLORS · EDITOR · EDITOR IN CHIEF

GOOD THING MY *SPIDER-SENSE* WARNED ME TO FLINCH, OR I'D BE A SPLAT ON THE SIDEWALK RIGHT NOW!

THERE'S THE GUNMAN--

--AND HE DOESN'T LOOK *HAPPY* THAT HE MISSED.

YOU THINK YOU'RE UPSET NOW, PAL-- JUST *WAIT.*

HUFF HUFF HUFF--

YULP!

UHHH UHHH *UHHH*

THAT WEB'S GOT A TENSILE STRENGTH OF *120* POUNDS PER SQUARE MILLIMETER. DO YOURSELF A FAVOR.

TALK TO ME.

N-NO-- WON'T--

DUMB.

WOK

YOU WANT DRAMA, WE'LL DO *DRAMA.*

FADE OUT.

FADE IN:

.....

UH, HEY... WHERE... HOW...

YAAAA!

WELL, *HI,* THERE. REMEMBER ME? I'M THE GUY YOU POPPED A SHOT AT A FEW MINUTES AGO.

WAS IT YOUR IDEA OR DID SOMEONE HIRE YOU?

BETTER TALK FAST. THAT WEB MIGHT *MELT* IN ALL THIS RAIN.

GNNAAAH

"GNAH"?

COULD YOU BE MORE *SPECIFIC?*

B-BLIND HIRE... AGGIE'S PUB...10TH AVENUE... SUPPOSED TO HIT *ROBERTSON*... YOU JUST GOT IN THE WAY...

P-PLEASE... LEMME DOWN...

DON'T WORRY. I CALLED THE COPS WHILE YOU WERE OUT. THEY SHOULD BE BY TO PICK YOU UP ANY MINUTE.

BUT THE WEB... IT'LL *MELT...*

OH, ABOUT THAT? I LIED.

"BLIND HIRE"--THAT'S AN UNDERWORLD TERM FOR A CONTRACT HIT WHERE THE GUNMAN DOESN'T *KNOW* HIS EMPLOYER.

WHO WANTS YOU *DEAD*, ROBBIE?

AND *WHERE* ARE YOU?

FOR: PETER PARKER

ROBBIE PHONED LESS THAN HALF AN HOUR AGO-- ASKED ME, OR RATHER *PETER PARKER*, TO MEET HIM HERE IN HIS OFFICE.

HE MADE IT SOUND *URGENT*-- SO WHY ISN'T HE *HERE*?

HMM...

THE CASSETTE IN THIS TAPE RECORDER HAS *MY* NAME ON IT.

LET'S TAKE A LISTEN...

♪CLICK!♪ THANKS FOR COMING, PETER.

I'M SORRY I'M NOT THERE TO MEET YOU--

--BUT AS I HOPE YOU'LL UNDERSTAND ONCE YOU'VE HEARD THIS TAPE, I HAVE ANOTHER COMMITMENT TO FULFILL TONIGHT.

I CHOSE YOU TO RECEIVE THIS TAPE BECAUSE YOU'RE *FREELANCE*. YOU HAVE NO VESTED INTEREST IN PROTECTING EITHER MY REPUTATION OR THAT OF THE *DAILY BUGLE*.

AND WHAT I'M ABOUT TO TELL YOU WILL *DESTROY* MY REPUTATION,

PETER, I'M AN *ACCESSORY* TO MURDER,

THERE'S A FOLDER ON MY DESK. OPEN IT.

I'M AS *RESPONSIBLE* FOR THE KILLINGS IN THOSE CLIPPINGS AS IF I'D PULLED THE TRIGGER *MYSELF*...

TOMBSTONE AT LARGE

TRACE KILLING TO TOMBSTONE

TOMBSTONE ESCAPES CONVICTION FOR "LACK OF EVIDENCE"!!

ROBBIE? ROBBIE, IT'S KATE AND JONAH--WE NEED TO TALK. MAY WE COME IN?

UH-OH.

KATE CUSHING AND JONAH JAMESON ARE THE LAST PEOPLE ROBBIE WOULD WANT TO HEAR THIS.

≥CLICK!≤

UNTIL I LISTEN TO THE REST, I BETTER KEEP THIS TAPE SECRET.

IT'S THE LEAST I CAN DO FOR A FRIEND.

"ESPECIALLY A FRIEND WHO SOUNDS AS IF HE'S IN BIG TROUBLE..."

ROBBIE?

HMPH. I COULD'VE SWORN I HEARD HIS VOICE.

WHAT'S GOING ON HERE, KATE?

I DON'T KNOW, JONAH.

THE LAST FEW DAYS ROBBIE SEEMED PRE-OCCUPIED... DISTRACTED... I'M WORRIED ABOUT HIM...

IF YOU ARE, I AM.

BLAST IT, IF SOMETHING'S WRONG, I WANT TO HELP.

ROBERTSON'S THE BEST EDITOR IN CHIEF A PUBLISHER COULD ASK FOR.

HE'S ALSO MY FRIEND...

ELSEWHERE...

TO BE PRECISE, THE MIDTOWN TOWER BELONGING TO BUSINESS-MAN WILSON FISK, a.k.a., THE KINGPIN.

YOU'RE NOT BEING VERY COOPERATIVE, MR. RAYBURN.

SWAK!

THANK YOU, TOMBSTONE.

WE'LL GET ALONG MUCH BETTER, MR. RAYBURN, IF YOU CULTIVATE A MORE ACCOMMODATING ATTITUDE.

YOU SEE, ON MR. FISK'S BEHALF, I'VE FOLLOWED YOUR WALL STREET CAREER THESE LAST FEW MONTHS I KNOW WHAT YOU CAN DO.

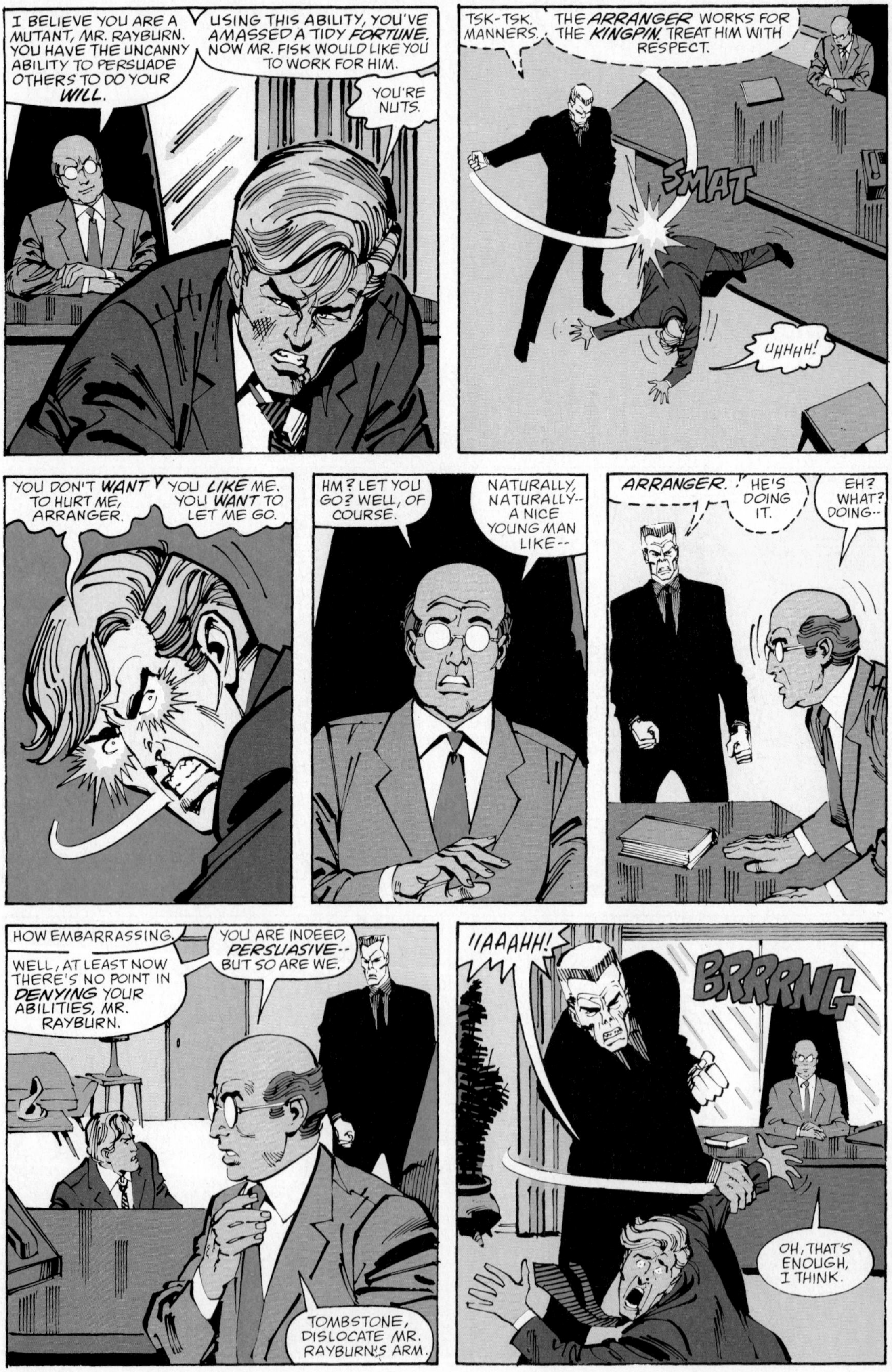
I BELIEVE YOU ARE A MUTANT, MR. RAYBURN. YOU HAVE THE UNCANNY ABILITY TO PERSUADE OTHERS TO DO YOUR WILL.
USING THIS ABILITY, YOU'VE AMASSED A TIDY FORTUNE. NOW MR. FISK WOULD LIKE YOU TO WORK FOR HIM.
YOU'RE NUTS.
TSK-TSK. MANNERS.
THE ARRANGER WORKS FOR THE KINGPIN. TREAT HIM WITH RESPECT.
SMAT
UHHHH!
YOU DON'T WANT TO HURT ME, ARRANGER.
YOU LIKE ME. YOU WANT TO LET ME GO.
HM? LET YOU GO? WELL, OF COURSE.
NATURALLY, NATURALLY-- A NICE YOUNG MAN LIKE--
ARRANGER.
HE'S DOING IT.
EH? WHAT? DOING--
HOW EMBARRASSING.
WELL, AT LEAST NOW THERE'S NO POINT IN DENYING YOUR ABILITIES, MR. RAYBURN.
YOU ARE INDEED, PERSUASIVE-- BUT SO ARE WE.
TOMBSTONE, DISLOCATE MR. RAYBURN'S ARM.
!AAAHH!
BRRRNG
OH, THAT'S ENOUGH, I THINK.

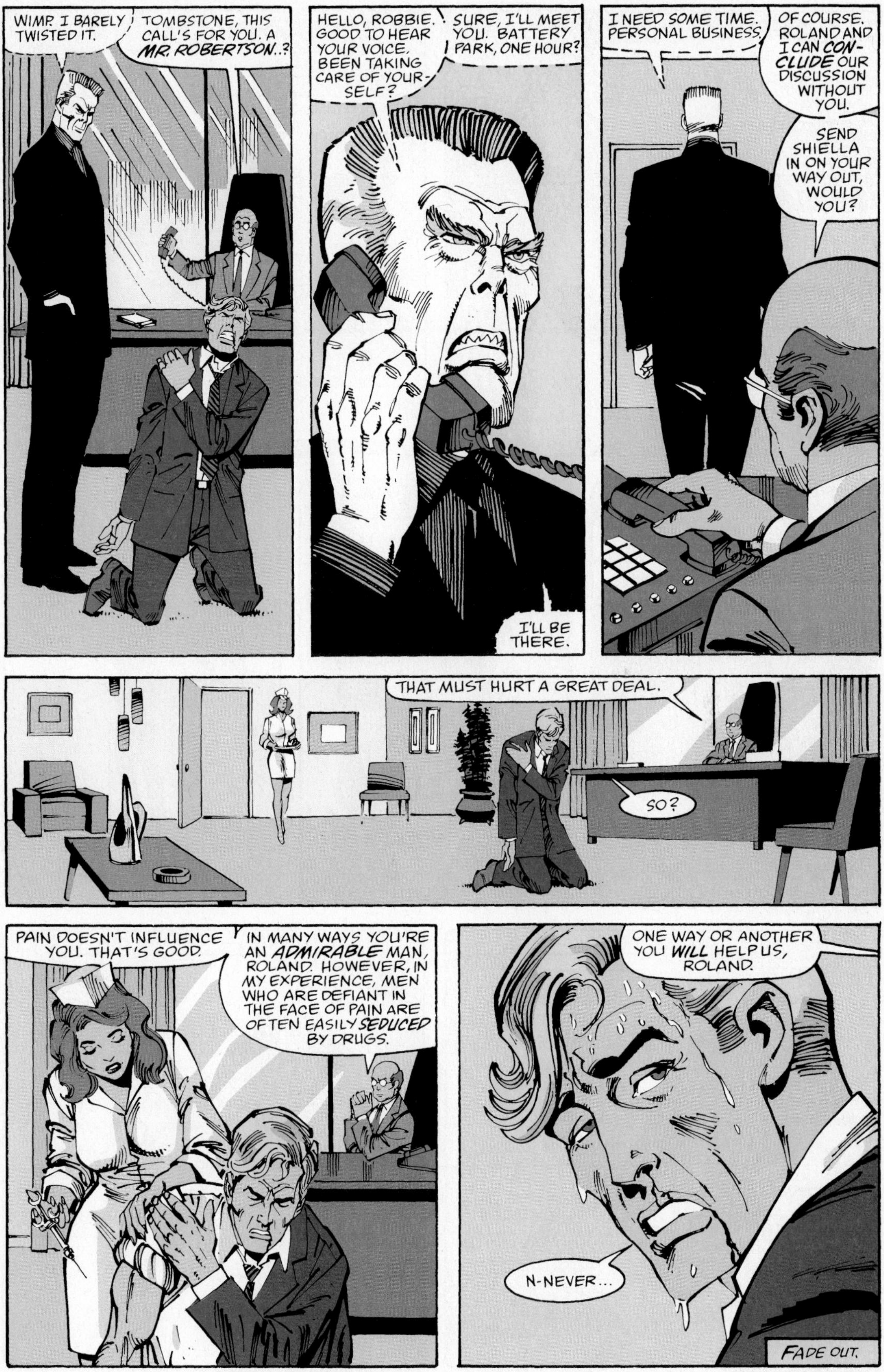
WIMP. I BARELY TWISTED IT.
TOMBSTONE, THIS CALL'S FOR YOU. A MR. ROBERTSON..?
HELLO, ROBBIE. GOOD TO HEAR YOUR VOICE. BEEN TAKING CARE OF YOURSELF?
SURE, I'LL MEET YOU. BATTERY PARK, ONE HOUR?
I'LL BE THERE.
I NEED SOME TIME. PERSONAL BUSINESS.
OF COURSE. ROLAND AND I CAN CONCLUDE OUR DISCUSSION WITHOUT YOU.
SEND SHIELLA IN ON YOUR WAY OUT, WOULD YOU?
THAT MUST HURT A GREAT DEAL.
SO?
PAIN DOESN'T INFLUENCE YOU. THAT'S GOOD.
IN MANY WAYS YOU'RE AN ADMIRABLE MAN, ROLAND. HOWEVER, IN MY EXPERIENCE, MEN WHO ARE DEFIANT IN THE FACE OF PAIN ARE OFTEN EASILY SEDUCED BY DRUGS.
ONE WAY OR ANOTHER YOU WILL HELP US, ROLAND.
N-NEVER...
FADE OUT.

FADE IN:

I'VE LIVED WITH THIS SECRET FOR MORE THAN THIRTY YEARS... IF YOU CAN CALL IT LIVING WHEN YOU WAKE SWEATING WITH *GUILT* AT NIGHT.

LET ME START AT THE BEGINNING.

"IF IT BEGAN ANYWHERE, IT BEGAN MY SENIOR YEAR AT *HARLEM HIGH SCHOOL*, BEFORE BLACK WAS BEAUTIFUL AND MARTIN LUTHER KING, JR. WAS STILL ALIVE TO DREAM OF BETTER THINGS...

"THAT SPRING, I WAS *EDITOR* OF THE SCHOOL NEWSPAPER.

"TWO WEEKS BEFORE, I'D GOTTEN NOTICE OF MY *SCHOLARSHIP* TO THE COLUMBIA SCHOOL OF JOURNALISM.

"THERE WAS ONLY ONE *CLOUD* ON MY PERSONAL HORIZON.

"A KID NAMED *LONNIE LINCOLN*.

"EVERYONE CALLED HIM *TOMBSTONE*.

"IT WAS A *FRIDAY*.

"I'D *WORKED LATE* TO CLOSE THAT WEEK'S PAPER.

"EVEN THEN, I PUT THE PAPER OVER MY PERSONAL LIFE.

"BY THE TIME I CLOSED UP, THE SCHOOL WAS *DESERTED*.

"*ALMOST* DESERTED.

HI, ROBBIE.

HEY-- AAAK!

"LONNIE WAS THERE, AND HE WAS *MAD*.

WE HAVE TO TALK.

60

WORD AROUND SCHOOL SAYS YOU'RE WRITING A STORY ABOUT ME FOR YOUR PAPER.

WHAT'S IT GONNA *SAY*, ROBBIE?

R-READ IT AND FIND OUT, LONNIE.

NOW, IS THAT NICE?

I HEAR YOU SAY SOME *BAD THINGS* ABOUT ME IN YOUR STORY, ROBBIE. YOU SAY I BEAT KIDS IF THEY DON'T PAY FOR INSURANCE.

YOU'RE NOT GONNA SAY THAT, ROBBIE.

W-WHY NOT?

GUESS.

=UNGH!=

THD!

I LIKE YOU, ROBBIE. YOU'RE A SMART KID. YOU'LL GO FAR.

WE SHOULD BE *FRIENDS*.

KRAK!

FRIENDS THAT TREAT EACH OTHER *NICE*.

THM!

YOU'RE GONNA TREAT ME NICE--

--AREN'T YOU, ROBBIE?

YES...

WHAT A GUY.

"I'LL TELL YOU, PETER, BAD AS I FELT AFTER TOMBSTONE'S BEATING, I FELT MUCH WORSE THE NEXT MORNING, WHEN--

I WAS WRONG.

YOU'RE *WITH-DRAWING* YOUR ARTICLE?

BUT, JOSEPH, YOU WORKED SO HARD TO *RESEARCH* THAT STORY.

WHY DON'T YOU LET ME *READ* IT? THEN WE CAN TALK--

THERE'S NOTHING TO *TALK* ABOUT, ALL RIGHT?

THE ARTICLE'S DEAD. I SPIKED IT.

IT'S OVER.

"BUT, OF COURSE, IT *WASN'T* OVER.

"PART OF ME KNEW IT WASN'T *EVER* GOING TO BE OVER.

KEEP UP THE GOOD WORK, ROBBIE-PAL.

"IN THAT MOMENT, I SAW MY FUTURE COMPROMISED. I ALMOST THREW UP. I SWORE TO MYSELF THEN I WOULD NEVER, EVER RETREAT ON ANOTHER STORY-- NO MATTER *WHAT* THE COST."

I *MEANT* IT, TOO.

KIDS ARE SO NAIVE.

"EIGHT YEARS LATER, I WAS A MARRIED MAN AND THE NIGHT DESK CATCHER FOR A PAPER IN *PHILADELPHIA.*"

"MOST NIGHTS, *MOST* OF THE CALLS I CAUGHT WERE FROM CRANKS OR INSOMNIACS."

"ONE NIGHT, ONE CALL WAS *DIFFERENT*..."

SAY AGAIN? YOU SAW *WHAT?*

I SAW THE GUY WHO POPPED OZZY MONTANA. YOU *DEAF?*

KEEP TALKING.

OVER THE PHONE? *FORGET* IT.

YOU WANT THIS, YOU COME SEE ME.

LISTEN, I'LL TELL YOU WHERE...

"I LISTENED. SOMETHING IN THE GUY'S VOICE TOLD ME HE WAS REAL. THIS WAS THE KIND OF TIP EVERY REPORTER *DREAMS* ABOUT."

COVER FOR ME, DAVE. I'VE GOT A HOT ONE.

YEAH, SO? DON'T GET BURNED, KID.

"THREE DAYS BEFORE, LOCAL CRIME-BOSS OZZY MONTANA HAD SHOWN UP *DEAD* IN THE TRUNK OF HIS LIMOUSINE."

"IF I EXPOSED MONTANA'S KILLER, I COULD WRITE MY OWN TICKET TO *ANY* PAPER IN THE COUNTRY."

"MY SOURCE HAD SAID HE'D MEET ME AT THE WATER-FRONT."

"HE'D WARNED ME NOT TO BE *LATE.*"

"I WASN'T, BUT HE *WAS.*"

HI, ROBBIE.

LONG TIME NO SEE, ROBBIE-PAL.

THUMP

"I KNEW.

"EVEN BEFORE THE BEAM OF MY FLASHLIGHT FOUND HIM...

"I KNEW.

TOMBSTONE!

"HAVE YOU EVER KNOWN *TERROR*, PETER?

"*REAL* TERROR, WHEN YOU THOUGHT YOUR HEART MIGHT COLLAPSE AND YOUR BRAIN TURN TO ICE IN YOUR SKULL?

"I SAW THAT DEAD MAN'S FACE, I HEARD TOMBSTONE'S WHISPER, AND I WAS SO AFRAID I THOUGHT I WAS GOING TO *DIE*.

"THE FEARS OF *CHILDHOOD* ARE THE FEARS THAT STAY WITH US FOREVER.

"TOMBSTONE WAS MY CHILDHOOD *HORROR*.

"THAT NIGHT MY CHILDHOOD HORROR CAME BACK TO *LIFE*.

"MARTHA WAS ASLEEP WHEN I GOT HOME, AN HOUR OR SO BEFORE *DAWN.*

"THANK HEAVEN FOR THAT SMALL MERCY.

"I SAT IN THE QUIET OF THE LIVING ROOM, TRYING TO THINK, TRYING TO DECIDE WHAT TO *DO.*

"I WASN'T SURPRISED WHEN THE *PHONE* RANG.

BRIIING

JOE?

WHO IS IT, HONEY?

" I DIDN'T ANSWER.

"FOR A LONG TIME I JUST LISTENED TO *SILENCE* ON THE OTHER END OF THE LINE.

"THEN ...

YOU DO GOOD WORK, ROBBIE-PAL.

⇒CLICK!⇐

JOE? ARE YOU ALL RIGHT? WHO WAS THAT ON THE PHONE?

NOBODY, HONEY.

NOBODY AT ALL...

HOW COULD I TELL HER? HOW COULD I TELL ANY-ONE?

HEAVEN FORGIVE ME, I WAS AFRAID.

THAT FIRST COMPROMISE IN SCHOOL HAD CRACKED MY SPIRIT SOMEHOW.

TOMBSTONE KILLED MY SOURCE. HE PROBABLY KILLED OZZY MONTANA.

AND IF I SAID ANYTHING, IF I SAID JUST ONE WORD, IN MY HEART I KNEW HE'D KILL ME.

"A MONTH LATER, MARTHA AND I LEFT PHILADELPHIA AND CAME BACK TO NEW YORK, WHERE I TOOK A JOB AT THE BUGLE.

"OVER THE NEXT TWENTY YEARS I FOLLOWED TOMB-STONE'S CAREER AS A PHILLY MOB ENFORCER WITH A KIND OF SICK FASCINATION.

"HE WAS ARRESTED A DOZEN TIMES FOR A DOZEN MURDERS, BUT NEVER TRIED.

"SOME WITNESSES RECANTED THEIR TESTIMONY. SOME WITNESSES DISAPPEARED.

CITY SUN
TOMBSTONE INDICTED!!

DAILY BUGLE
TOMBSTONE FOUND NOT GUILTY!!!

"TOMBSTONE ALWAYS WENT FREE.

"THEN ONE DAY A COUPLE OF WEEKS AGO, AS I WAS LEAVING A PUB NEAR SOUTH STREET, I *SAW* HIM. *

*YOU DID TOO, IN *WEB OF SPIDER-MAN* #36. -- JIM

"AND IT WAS AS IF SOMEONE HAD OPENED A *TRAPDOOR* IN MY HEART."

FOR TWENTY YEARS I MANAGED TO CONVINCE MYSELF IT DIDN'T *MATTER;* IT WAS ANOTHER CITY, ANOTHER TIME.

BUT NOW HE WAS HERE IN *MY CITY.*

I CAN'T EXPLAIN IT.

ALL THE FEELINGS I'D BURIED FOR TWO DECADES CAME *RISING* TO THE SURFACE LIKE OIL FROM AN UNDERSEA PIPELINE.

I FELT FRIGHTENED AND ANGRY-- AND BITTERLY *ASHAMED.*

MOVING AND STORAGE C WAREHOUSE

" AT FIRST, I COULDN'T CONCENTRATE ON ANYTHING AT ALL.

"THEN I FOUND MYSELF POURING THROUGH A COLLECTION OF *CLIPPINGS* I DIDN'T REALIZE I'D BEEN KEEPING OVER THE YEARS.

" PERHAPS I WAS LOOKING FOR A *JUSTIFICATION* FOR WHAT I'D DONE -- OR HADN'T DONE.

" IF SO, I DIDN'T *FIND* IT.

TOMBSTONE

TOMBSTONE

"THESE LAST FEW DAYS I'VE FELT AS IF MY LIFE WERE A BOAT THAT'S LOST ITS *ANCHOR.* I EVEN SAW TOMBSTONE, AND TALKED WITH HIM, OUTSIDE THE KINGPIN'S OFFICE TOWER.*

"AFTER THAT, NOTHING MADE *SENSE* ANYMORE. PEOPLE AROUND ME SEEMED TO BE TALKING IN A FOREIGN LANGUAGE. EVERYTHING FELT UNREAL.

TITANIC HIT BY ICEBERG

"THEN, TONIGHT...

* IN *SPECTACULAR SPIDER-MAN #137.* -- JIM

"...TONIGHT I WAS AT A BAR DOWN THE BLOCK FROM THE *BUGLE,* WHERE REPORTERS GATHER AFTER THE PAPER'S GONE TO PRESS. AND FROM THE BABBLE OF CONVERSATION A *NAME* JUMPED OUT AT ME...

...TOMBSTONE...

"BEN URICH WAS TALKING. EVERY WORD WAS LIKE A KNIFE WOUND TO MY HEART.

MY SOURCE AT POLICE PLAZA SAYS HE'S THE NUMBER ONE *HITMAN* IN PHILLY.

THE GUY'S A ONE-MAN *MURDER EPIDEMIC.*

SO WHAT BRINGS HIM *HERE?*

MAYBE HE'S A *KNICKS* FAN.

RUMOR HAS IT HE'S HIRED OUT TO THE *KINGPIN.* COULD BE HE'S--

RUMOR?

SINCE WHEN DOES A *JOURNALIST* DEAL IN RUMOR, URICH? GROW UP! YOU'RE NOT WRITING FOR SOME KIDDIE HIGH SCHOOL NEWSPAPER, *UNDERSTAND?*

HUH?

SURE, ROBBIE.

WE WERE JUST SCHMOOZING.

ROBBIE?

ARE YOU OKAY?

"WAS I OKAY?"

"OH, I WAS FINE."

DAILY BUGLE

MOB HITS MULTIPLY!!

25¢

SMASH

"HOW MANY PEOPLE HAD TOMBSTONE KILLED? THIRTY? FIFTY?"

"A HUNDRED?"

"THOSE DEATHS WERE ON MY HEAD, TOO."

"IF I'D HAD THE COURAGE TO FACE TOMBSTONE DOWN TWENTY YEARS AGO, HIS VICTIMS WOULD BE ALIVE TODAY."

"I CAN'T CHANGE THE PAST, PETER, BUT I CAN CHANGE THE FUTURE. I'M GOING TO MEET HIM TONIGHT."

"TONIGHT IT ENDS."

FADE OUT.

FADE IN:

ARRANGER!

I HEAR YOU'VE HIRED A MOB PUNK FROM PHILADELPHIA NAMED TOMBSTONE.

WHERE IS HE?

AND GOOD EVENING TO YOU, SPIDER-MAN.

YOU'RE MISINFORMED. THE MAN YOU CALL TOMBSTONE IS NOT CURRENTLY IN MR. FISK'S EMPLOY.

IS THERE SOME OTHER WAY I CAN ASSIST YOU--?

I DIDN'T COME HERE TO PLAY GAMES.

A FRIEND OF MINE MAY BE IN SERIOUS TROUBLE. IF YOU DON'T WANT SOME SERIOUS TROUBLE OF YOUR OWN, TALK TO ME.

ASSUME TOMBSTONE ISN'T WORKING FOR YOU. FINE, YOU'RE OFF THE HOOK.

NOW WHERE IS HE?

UNDER THAT ASSUMPTION, ANYTHING I SAY WOULD BE PURE SPECULATION.

SO SPECULATE.

IF YOU WISH...

"...YOU MIGHT TRY LOOKING IN BATTERY PARK,"

LONG TIME NO SEE, ROBBIE-PAL.

HELLO, LONNIE. IT'S FUNNY, IN THE CAB DOWN HERE I THOUGHT OF THINGS I WANTED TO *SAY*... BUT NOW THAT WE'RE HERE, NONE OF IT MATTERS.

NOBODY CALLS ME LONNIE ANYMORE, KIDDO.

YOU'VE GOT SOMETHING YOU WANT TO DO, *DO IT.*

YEAH.

I THOUGHT THAT'S WHAT YOU'D TRY. I SAW IT IN YOUR EYES DURING OUR LITTLE *TALK* THE OTHER DAY.

YOU GONNA *ARREST* ME OR *SHOOT* ME, ROBBIE-PAL?

ARREST YOU--

ROBBIE, ROBBIE...

HOW COULD A KID SO SMART GROW UP TO BE SO *DUMB*?

W-WHAT? G-GET BACK-- *DON'T*--

BAMM

DUMB, ROBBIE-PAL. YOU SHOULD'VE AIMED FOR THE HEAD.

UHHH

A PRO *ALWAYS* WEARS A KEVLAR VEST WHEN HE'S ON A JOB.

YOU KNOW, ROBBIE, I'VE ALWAYS *LIKED* YOU. I THOUGHT WE HAD AN UNDERSTANDING.

NOT ANYMORE... ...WE DON'T...

TOO BAD.

STILL, FOR OLD TIME'S SAKE, I'LL GIVE YOU ONE MORE *BREAK*, ROBBIE-PAL.

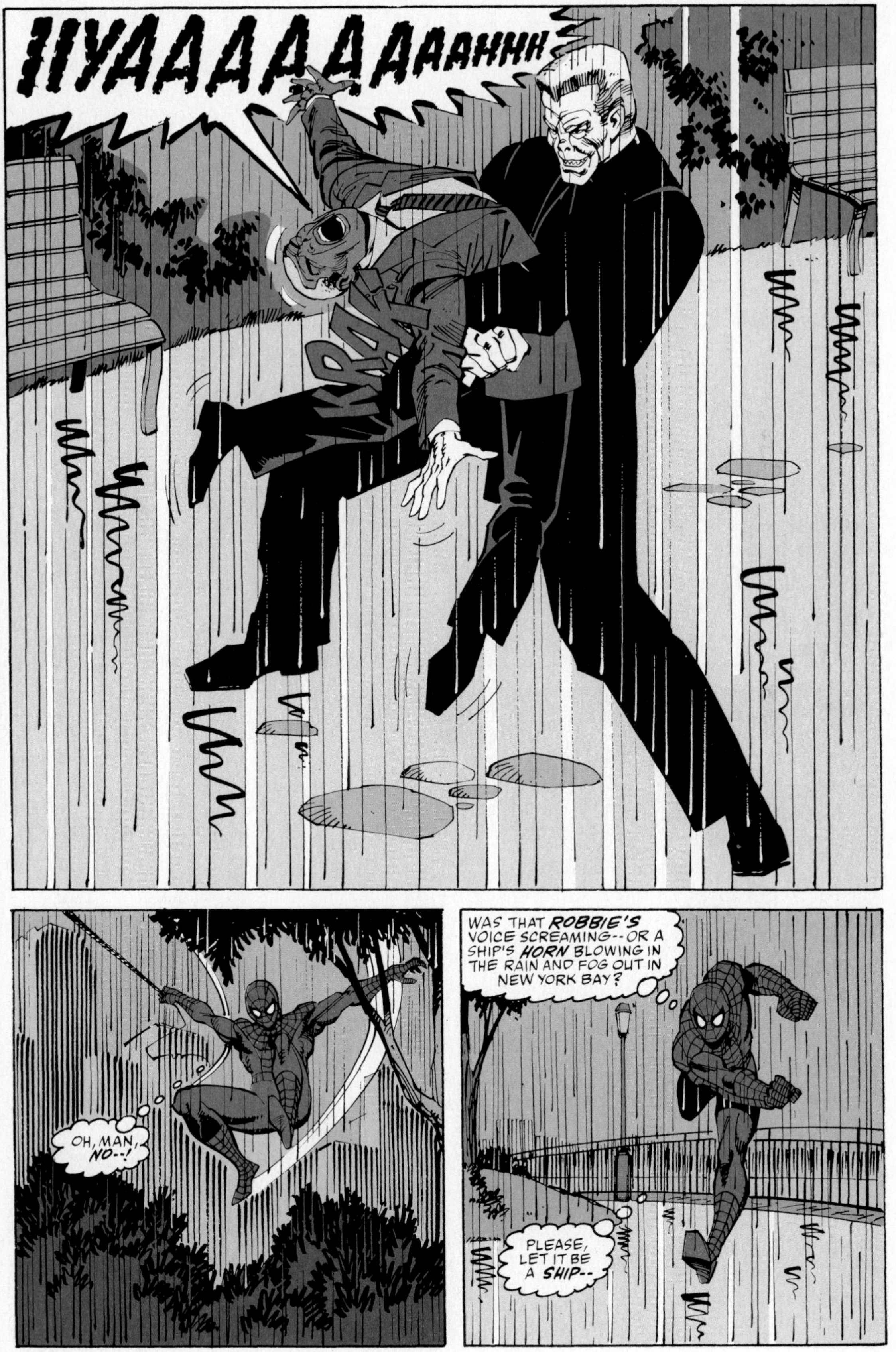
IIYAAAAAAAAHHH
KRAK
OH, MAN, NO--!
WAS THAT ROBBIE'S VOICE SCREAMING--OR A SHIP'S HORN BLOWING IN THE RAIN AND FOG OUT IN NEW YORK BAY?
PLEASE, LET IT BE A SHIP--

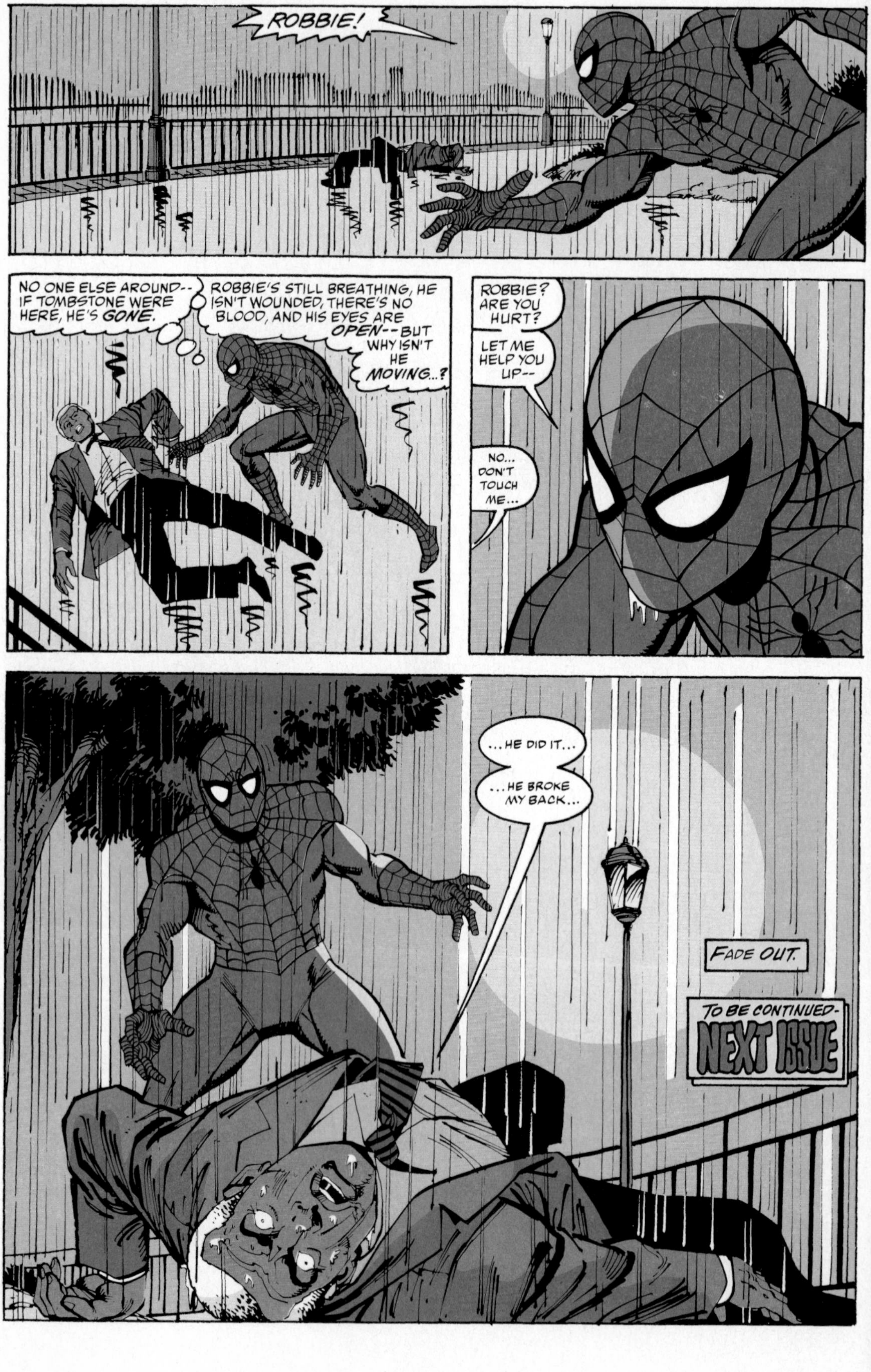
ROBBIE!
NO ONE ELSE AROUND-- IF TOMBSTONE WERE HERE, HE'S GONE.
ROBBIE'S STILL BREATHING, HE ISN'T WOUNDED, THERE'S NO BLOOD, AND HIS EYES ARE OPEN--BUT WHY ISN'T HE MOVING...?
ROBBIE? ARE YOU HURT?
LET ME HELP YOU UP--
NO... DON'T TOUCH ME...
...HE DID IT...
...HE BROKE MY BACK...
FADE OUT.
TO BE CONTINUED-
NEXT ISSUE

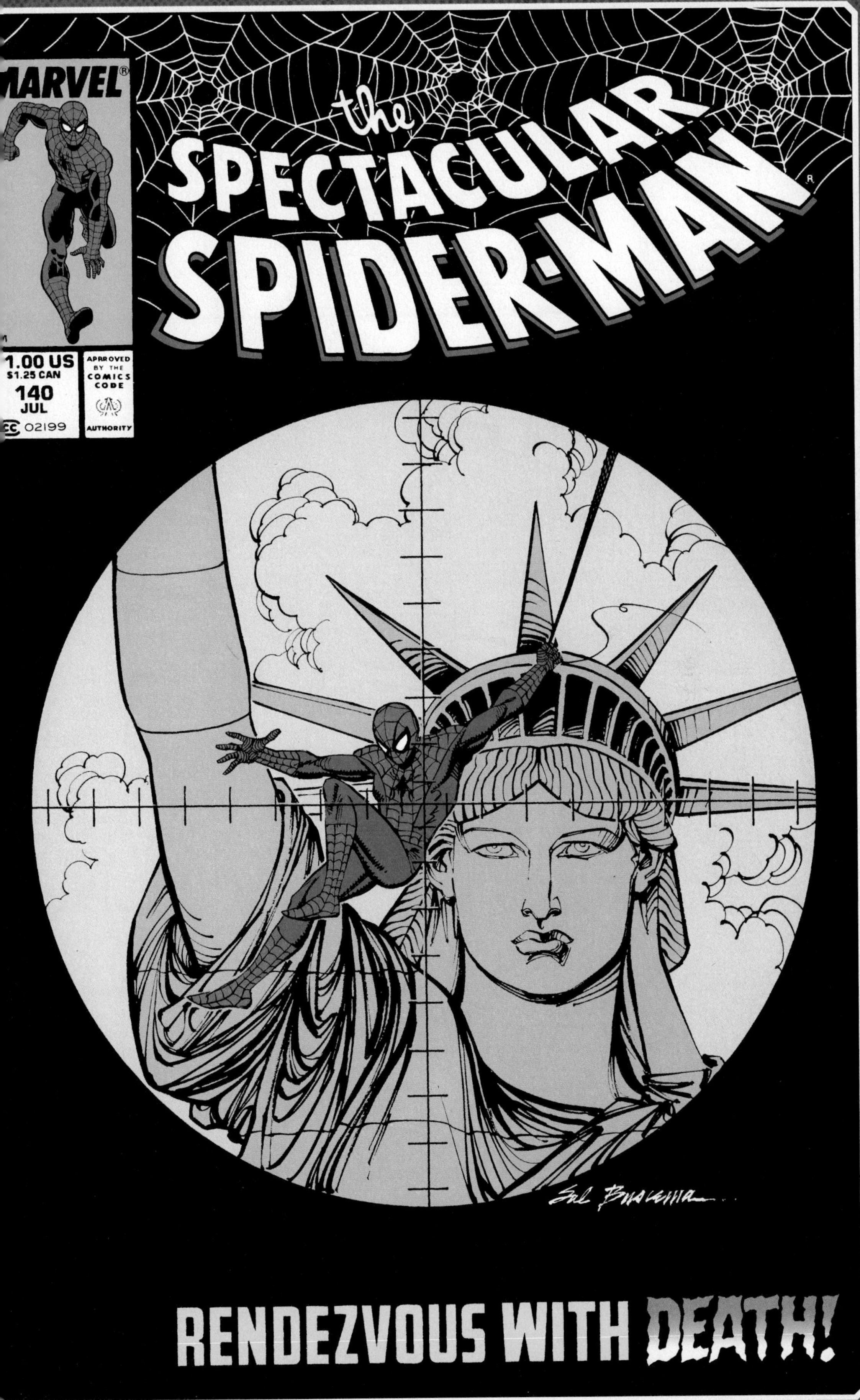
MARVEL
the SPECTACULAR SPIDER-MAN
1.00 US
$1.25 CAN
140
JUL
APPROVED BY THE COMICS CODE AUTHORITY
RENDEZVOUS WITH DEATH!

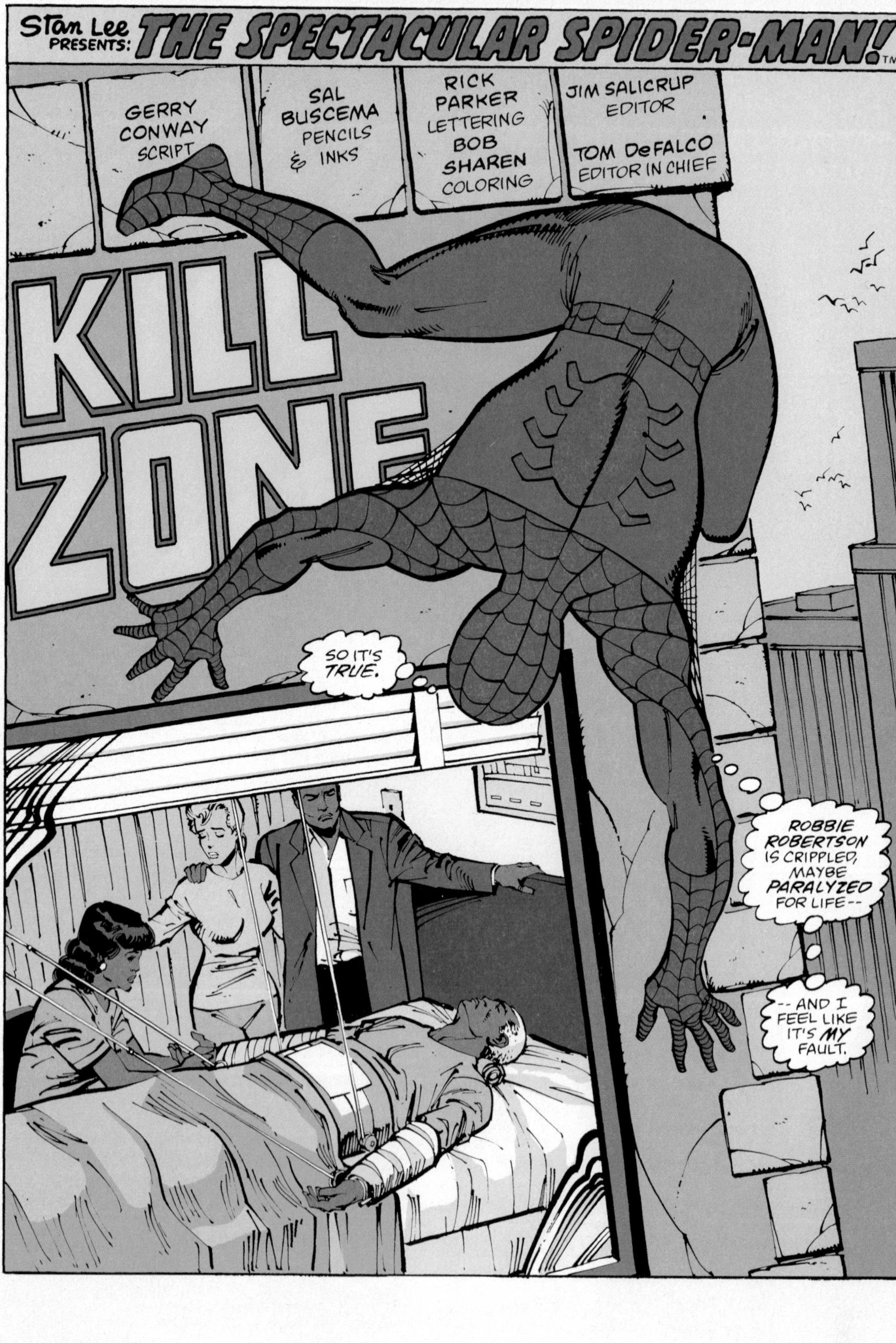
Stan Lee PRESENTS: THE SPECTACULAR SPIDER-MAN!™
GERRY CONWAY SCRIPT
SAL BUSCEMA PENCILS & INKS
RICK PARKER LETTERING
BOB SHAREN COLORING
JIM SALICRUP EDITOR
TOM DeFALCO EDITOR IN CHIEF
KILL ZONE
SO IT'S TRUE.
ROBBIE ROBERTSON IS CRIPPLED, MAYBE PARALYZED FOR LIFE--
--AND I FEEL LIKE IT'S MY FAULT.

BUT WHAT'S NEW ABOUT *THAT?*

I ALWAYS FEEL *EVERYTHING* IS MY FAULT.

"IF ONLY I GOT TO BATTERY PARK *SOONER,* I MIGHT HAVE STOPPED *TOMBSTONE* FROM CRUSHING ROBBIE'S SPINE.*"

*IT HAPPENED LAST ISSUE. -- JIM.

THAT'S WHAT I TELL MYSELF, AND IT'S *BUNK.*

WHAT HAPPENED, *HAPPENED.*.. AND THERE WASN'T A THING SPIDER-MAN *OR* PETER PARKER COULD HAVE DONE TO PREVENT IT.

AT LEAST I WAS THERE TO CALL AN *AMBULANCE.*

I WAITED WITH ROBBIE TILL THE PARAMEDICS ARRIVED--

-- THEN TOOK OFF TO FIND *TOMBSTONE.*

NO LUCK, BUT I'LL KEEP TRYING UNTIL I-- OBOY.

I NEVER SAW JONAH JAMESON LOOK *SAD* BEFORE.

THERE'S *MARTHA,* ROBBIE'S WIFE-- HIS WHOLE FAMILY--

-- AND FROM THE WAY THEY LOOK, THINGS MUST BE *WORSE* THAN I THOUGHT!

BEN-- WHAT'S THE STORY HERE?

ANY WORD FROM THE DOCTORS ABOUT ROBBIE'S CONDITION?

NOT MUCH, PARKER, AND NONE TOO *GOOD.*

THEY SAY HE'LL LIVE, BUT COULD BE HE'LL NEVER WALK AGAIN.

KNOWN HIM A LONG TIME, HUH?

YEAH. SINCE I STARTED SELLING PHOTOS TO THE *DAILY BUGLE* BACK IN HIGH SCHOOL.

HOSPITAL

ROBBIE WAS *CITY EDITOR* THEN, HE ALWAYS ENCOURAGED ME....

UH-HUH,

77

ROBERTSON WAS PRETTY **PREOCCU- PIED** THE LAST FEW WEEKS.

GOING THROUGH THE MORGUE FILES...LOCKED IN HIS OFFICE AFTER DEADLINE...WORKING ON SOME **SECRET** PROJECT.

WHAT WAS IT ABOUT, PETER?

HOW SHOULD **I** KNOW?

KID, I'M A **REPORTER**. FINDING OUT THINGS IS MY JOB.

ROBBIE PHONED YOU LAST NIGHT AND ASKED YOU TO **MEET** HIM AT THE BUGLE.

I HAPPENED TO BE PASSING HIS OFFICE WHEN HE MADE THE CALL.

WHAT DID HE **TELL** YOU, PETER?

I - I DON'T KNOW, BEN, BY THE TIME I ARRIVED, HE WAS **GONE**.

UH-HUH.

WELL, IF YOU WANT TO TALK, YOU KNOW WHERE TO FIND ME.

G'NIGHT, PARKER.

RIGHT. GOOD NIGHT.

NO NO NO

HOSPITAL

HIYA, ROBBIE.

LONG TIME NO SEE.

IF WE WEREN'T OLD FRIENDS, I COULD BE REAL *ANGRY* WITH YOU RIGHT NOW.

LURING ME TO BATTERY PARK, THEN TRYING TO *SHOOT* ME--ROBBIE, THAT WAS DUMB.

YOU'RE LUCKY I LIKE YOU.

WE'VE KNOWN EACH OTHER, WHAT-- TWENTY-FIVE YEARS?

ALL THAT TIME I THOUGHT WE HAD AN *UNDERSTANDING.*

I DO MY JOB FOR THE MOB, AND YOU KEEP YOUR MOUTH SHUT.

NO MORE.

STOP YOU... TOMBSTONE.

NOT AFRAID... YOU KILL ME.

NOT AFRAID, HUH?

LISTEN WHY YOUR OUT OF NO--

...THERE. NOW WE UNDERSTAND EACH OTHER.

PLEASANT DREAMS, ROBBIE-BOY.

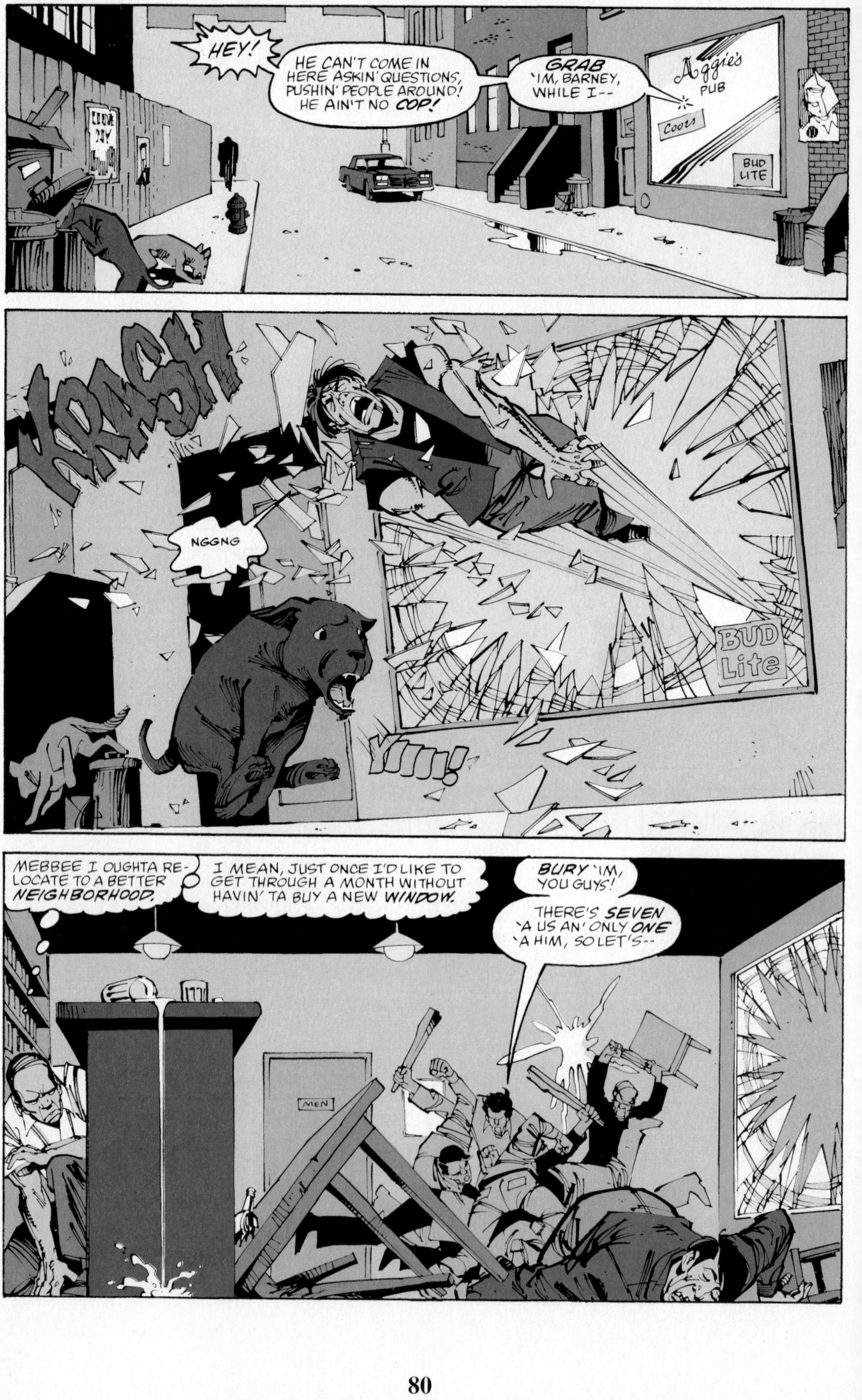

HEY!
HE CAN'T COME IN HERE ASKIN' QUESTIONS, PUSHIN' PEOPLE AROUND! HE AIN'T NO COP!
GRAB 'IM, BARNEY, WHILE I--
Aggie's PUB
Coors
BUD LITE
KRASH
NGGNG
BUD Lite
MEBBEE I OUGHTA RE-LOCATE TO A BETTER NEIGHBORHOOD.
I MEAN, JUST ONCE I'D LIKE TO GET THROUGH A MONTH WITHOUT HAVIN' TA BUY A NEW WINDOW.
BURY 'IM, YOU GUYS!
THERE'S SEVEN 'A US AN' ONLY ONE 'A HIM, SO LET'S--
MEN

WHAMMM

BOY, HAVE YOU BOZOS GOT A LOUSY SENSE OF *ODDS!*

WIND IT BACK AND TAKE IT FROM THE TOP, OKAY?

I CAME IN ASKING IF YOU GENTLEMEN HAD ANY IDEA WHO PUT A *CONTRACT* ON ROBBIE ROBERTSON'S LIFE.

NAIL THIS CREEP!

NAUGHTY.

KTHUNK

ONE OF YOUR ASSOCIATES TRIED TO *SHOOT* MR. ROBERTSON LAST NIGHT. *

HE *MISSED.*

*SEE LAST ISH.--- JIM.

81

AFTER I *CAUGHT* HIM, WE HAD A CHAT.

HE SAID HE WAS *BLIND-HIRED* TO DO THE HIT FROM THIS BAR.

S-S-SO?

SOOOO... I FIGURE THAT HIT WAS CONTRACTED BY A FELLOW NAMED *TOMBSTONE.*

DO I MAKE YOU NERVOUS, BUNKIE?

T-TA-TOMB-STONE?

Y-Y-YES.

GOOD. TELL ME WHERE I CAN FIND TOMB-STONE, OR SOME-BODY WHO *KNOWS* HIM.

A-AH-*ARRANGER*... WORKS FOR THE *KINGPIN*...

W-W-WORD ON THE S-STREET...

SPIDER-SENSE *TINGLING*--

...A-ARRANGER HIRED TOMBSTONE FOR SOME B-B-BIG SCHEME...!

C-COULD I GO NOW?

--WARNING ME--*DANGER*--

KTOW!

G-G-G

KLUD

SAY HUH? THAT *THUG* WAS GOING TO SHOOT ME-- BUT SOMEBODY SHOT HIM *FIRST!*

EXIT

AND THERE HE *GOES*--!

ONLY CAUGHT A *GLIMPSE*--

-- BUT THERE'S SOMETHING *FAMILIAR* ABOUT--

UH-OH.

KTOW-

SPAK!

83

GUESS YOUR LUCK BOTTOMED OUT AGAIN, PARKER.

--IF I GET HIM TO A HOSPITAL FAST ENOUGH, MAYBE THERE'S A CHANCE I CAN STILL *SAVE* HIM!

CAN'T LEAVE THAT GOON WHO WAS *SHOT* IN THE BAR--

AT LEAST THIS VISIT TO THE LIGHTER SIDE OF MANHATTAN WASN'T A *TOTAL* WASTE.

I HAD A SUSPICION WHO HIRED *TOMBSTONE*, AND NOW I KNOW FOR SURE.

A SLIMEY BALD-HEADED *WORM* KNOWN AS--

--*THE ARRANGER* HERE, MR. FISK.

THE *ROLAND RAYBURN PROJECT* IS PROCEEDING *NICELY,* YOU'LL BE PLEASED TO KNOW.

MR. RAYBURN AND I HAVE AN *APPOINTMENT* IN FIFTEEN MINUTES.

AT THAT TIME I HAVE EVERY *REASON* TO EXPECT HE'LL SIGN ON TO OUR LITTLE TEAM.

WHY, *THANK* YOU, MR. FISK, YOUR APPRECIATION IS-- EH?

MR. FISK?

ODD, WE'VE BEEN CUT--

--OFF.

HI, GUY. YOU AND I ARE GOING TO HAVE A *CHAT.*

SPIDER-MAN. I WON'T ASK HOW YOU GOT IN HERE.

I SUGGEST YOU USE THE SAME ROUTE *OUT.*

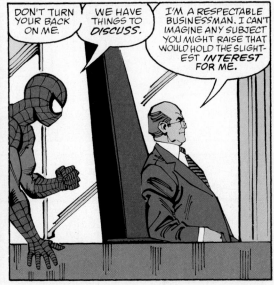

DON'T TURN YOUR BACK ON ME.

WE HAVE THINGS TO *DISCUSS.*

I'M A RESPECTABLE BUSINESSMAN. I CAN'T IMAGINE ANY SUBJECT YOU MIGHT RAISE THAT WOULD HOLD THE SLIGHTEST *INTEREST* FOR ME.

YOU, RESPECTABLE? WITH A PRIVATE OFFICE HERE IN *KINGPIN'S* MANHATTAN HEADQUARTERS?

WATCH ME *LAUGH.*

REMEMBER OUR TALK ABOUT *TOMBSTONE* EARLIER TONIGHT?*

DIMLY.

*SEE LAST ISSUE.-- JIM.

YOU TIPPED ME I'D FIND HIM IN *BATTERY PARK--* BUT WHEN I GOT THERE, TOMBSTONE WAS GONE, AND A FRIEND OF MINE WAS *HALF DEAD.*

I WANT HIM, ARRANGER. YOU'RE MY *ONLY* LEAD.

TELL ME WHERE HE IS, OR I'LL RE--

OH, I DON'T THINK SO.

YOU WON'T TAKE *ANY* ACTION AGAINST ME.

KLIK

WHIRR

NOT WHILE I HAVE THIS ENTIRE CONVERSATION-- AND YOUR RATHER APALLING *THREATS*--ON VIDEO TAPE.

NRRGGHH!

SKRAKK

SUCH A TEMPER.

UNPLEASANT AS THIS HAS BEEN--

--I THINK IT'S TIME YOU WERE *LEAVING.*

GENTLEMEN, SHOW OUR FRIEND THE DOOR, OPEN IT IF YOU MUST.

BREAKING AND ENTERING IS A SERIOUS OFFENSE, FRIEND.

I SUGGEST YOU COME ALONG NICE AND--

WELL, *GOOD, RUN* FOR IT.

WE'LL TELL THE POLICE YOU BROKE IN, RESISTED A CITIZEN'S ARREST--

--AND TOOK A NASTY *FALL.*

AND SINCE YOU WON'T BE *ALIVE* TO TELL THEM OTHERWISE, WE'LL BE OFF WITHOUT A--

WOW.

WHO WOULD'A FIGURED SPIDER-MAN FOR A *SUICIDE,* CHIEF?

YOU'RE *NEW* IN TOWN, SCOTTIE, SO I WON'T SAY WHAT I'M THINKING.

ON SECOND THOUGHT, MAYBE I *WILL,* YOU DUMB--

AN UNFORTUNATE INTERRUPTION, THAT. MR. FISK WAS MOST *ANNOYED* WHEN I CALLED HIM BACK.

WE REALLY WILL HAVE TO *DO* SOMETHING ABOUT SPIDER-MAN ONE OF THESE DAYS.

IF MR. FISK WERE NOT SO OBSESSED BY HIS VENDETTA AGAINST *DAREDEVIL*...

AH, WELL. IT'S NOT FOR *ME* TO SECOND-GUESS THE KINGPIN'S BUSINESS PRIORITIES.

I ONLY MAKE *ARRANGEMENTS*.

MR. RAYBURN, I TRUST SHIELLA HAS DONE HER BEST TO MAKE YOU-- *COMFORTABLE?*

...DRUGGED ME...

OF COURSE.

YOUR STUBBORN REFUSAL TO COOPERATE LEFT US LITTLE ALTERNATIVE.

WE NEED YOUR POWERS OF *MENTAL PERSUASION*, ROLAND.

ARE YOU WITH US NOW?

...YES...

FINE.

SHIELLA WILL REDUCE YOUR *MEDICATION.* YOU'LL BE YOURSELF AGAIN IN A MATTER OF HOURS.

...MYSELF...

QUITE, BUT YOU'LL *REMEMBER* THIS EXPERIENCE, AND NEVER AGAIN WILL YOU REFUSE WHAT WE REQUEST.

ARRANGER.

YES, TOMBSTONE?

HE'S HERE. IN TOWN.

ONE OF OUR PEOPLE *SPOTTED* HIM AT AGGIE'S PUB WHEN SPIDER-MAN WAS THERE ASKING QUESTIONS.

HE'S LOOKING FOR ME.

MY COMING TO NEW YORK LURED HIM INTO THE LIGHT.

JUST THE WAY YOU FIGURED.

OF COURSE, OF COURSE.

ALL MY PLANS ARE PROCEEDING EXACTLY AS *ARRANGED...*

TA-DA!

PRESENTING FOR YOUR AMUSEMENT AND ENTERTAINMENT *THIS AFTERNOON,* THE WATSON-PARKER TRAVELING TENT SHOW AND BOTTLE WASHER COMPANY ON ITS FIRST *OFFICIAL* ENGAGEMENT AT *MIDTOWN HOSPITAL--*

--DON'T ALL *APPLAUD* AT ONCE, AND *PLEASE* THROW MONEY!

UH, I DON'T THINK ROBBIE AND MARTHA ARE IN THE MOOD FOR *HUMOR*, MJ!

AH, DON'T BE A *SPOILSPORT*, PETEY!

EVERYBODY LOVES A YUCK WHEN THEY'RE SICK.

PETER, MARY JANE--

IT WAS GOOD OF YOU TO COME.

WHEN *ELSE* WOULD I GET A CHANCE TO PLANT A SMACKER ON THIS GUY WITHOUT HIM RUNNING AWAY?

HOW YA DOIN', ROBBIE?

DOCTOR SAYS... NO DANCING RIGHT AWAY.

MARTHA, MJ... LIKE TO TALK TO PETER... ALONE.

I'LL BE OUTSIDE.

HE'S LOOKING GOOD, MRS. R.

A COUPL'A WEEKS--

MARY JANE, I'M AFRAID I'M GOING TO *LOSE* HIM.

HIS DOCTORS CAN'T BE SURE UNTIL THE *SWELLING* GOES DOWN, BUT THEY THINK HIS SPINE IS *BROKEN*.

JOE MAY NEVER *WALK* AGAIN.

C'MON, HE'S STRONG. HE'LL *FIGHT* IT.

WILL HE?

WHOEVER DID THIS DID *MORE* THAN BREAK JOE'S BACK, MARY JANE.

THEY BROKE HIS *SPIRIT*...

BETTER GET WELL *FAST*, ROBBIE.

WITHOUT YOU AT THE *BUGLE* TO KEEP HIS BLOOD PRESSURE DOWN, JONAH WILL POP A STROKE ONE OF THESE--

PETER...

THE CASSETTE TAPE I LEFT FOR YOU...DO YOU HAVE IT?

SAFE AND SOUND.

THE INFORMATION ON THAT TAPE WILL PUT *TOMBSTONE* BEHIND BARS PERMANENTLY ONCE I--

...BURN IT.

WHAT?

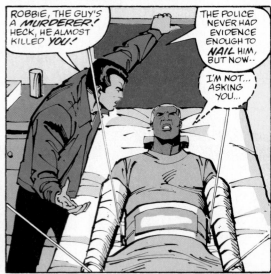

ROBBIE, THE GUY'S A *MURDERER!* HECK, HE ALMOST KILLED *YOU!*

THE POLICE NEVER HAD EVIDENCE ENOUGH TO *NAIL* HIM, BUT NOW--

I'M NOT... ASKING YOU...

...I'M TELLING YOU... DESTROY THE TAPE.

I KNOW WHAT TOMBSTONE IS... I KNOW WHAT HE'S DONE... I KEPT HIS SECRET FOR TWENTY-FIVE YEARS...

...AND I GUESS I'LL KEEP IT...TILL I DIE.

IT'S ON MY CONSCIENCE... NOT YOURS.

JUST...DO IT.

NO. I WON'T.

WHAT'S *WRONG* WITH YOU, ROBBIE? HOW CAN YOU *QUIT*?

SO HE *HURT* YOU-- SO *WHAT*?

ARE YOU GOING TO LET HIM WIN BECAUSE YOU'RE AFRAID TO *FIGHT BACK*?

NOT AFRAID... FOR *ME*.

TOMBSTONE WAS HERE.

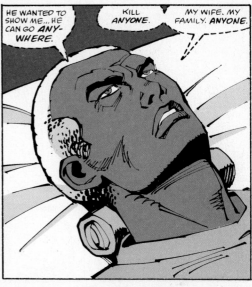

HE WANTED TO SHOW ME... HE CAN GO *ANY-WHERE*.

KILL *ANYONE*.

MY WIFE. MY FAMILY. *ANYONE*.

I DON'T CARE ABOUT MYSELF... BUT MARTHA, RANDY... THEY'RE MORE *IMPORTANT* TO ME THAN LIFE.

I *CAN'T* FIGHT HIM, PETER.

BURN THE TAPE.

TIGER, ARE YOU OKAY?

I'M MAD AND I FEEL SICK BUT OTHER THAN THAT--

--I'M *GREAT*.

TELL ME ABOUT IT?

ROBBIE ROBERTSON MADE A TAPE RECORD-ING WITH ENOUGH *DETAILS* TO NAIL TOMBSTONE'S COFFIN SHUT FOR GOOD.

ROBBIE LEFT *ME* THE TAPE AT HIS OFFICE LAST NIGHT.

BUT NOW, BECAUSE TOMB-STONE THREATENED ROBBIE'S FAMILY, ROBBIE WANTS THE TAPE *DESTROYED*.

WOW. WHAT WILL YOU DO?

I'VE GOT TO DROP BY THE BUGLE TO SEE BEN URICH, MAYBE GET HIS ADVICE, BUT OTHER THAN THAT, M J...

...I JUST *DON'T KNOW*.

HEY, BEN-- GOT A MINUTE?

YOU'RE A PRO FROM THE OLD SCHOOL...

DAILY BUGLE

...WHAT WOULD YOU DO IF YOU HAD EVIDENCE OF A CRIME, BUT YOUR INFORMANT FELT HIS FAMILY'S LIVES WOULD BE ENDANGERED IF YOU USED IT?

WHAT IS THIS, ETHICS IN JOURNALISM 101?

FAR AS I KNOW, THERE'S NO HARD RULE, PARKER. YOU'VE GOT TO DO WHAT YOU THINK IS RIGHT.

THIS IS FOR YOU.

IT'S A PHONE NUMBER.

AMAZING. I ALWAYS SAID YOU HAD A REPORTER'S INSTINCTS.

SOME GUY CALLED FOR YOU COUPLE'A MINUTES AGO.

HE LEFT THAT NUMBER. SOUNDED LIKE A REAL HARD CASE.

JUST WHAT I NEED, A MYSTERIOUS NUT.

...HELLO? THIS IS PETER PA--

PARKER.

I KNOW ABOUT THE ROBERTSON TAPE.

MEET ME ON LIBERTY ISLAND. ONE HOUR. ALONE.

GEE, YOU LOOK HAPPY.

STILL WANT TO TALK ABOUT THAT ETHICS PROBLEM--?

LATER.

...LIBERTY ISLAND, SPIDER-MAN. THIS IS AS FAR AS WE *GO*. GOTTA GET BACK TO *TRAFFIC REPORTS*.

THANKS, GUYS. I OWE YOU ONE.

THE LAST TOURIST FERRY LEFT HALF AN HOUR AGO.

WHOEVER PETER PARKER WAS SUPPOSED TO MEET HERE IS PROBABLY GETTING PRETTY *IMPATIENT*. GOOD. KEEP HIM GUESSING UNTIL--

UH-OH!

P*OOM!*

WELL NOW!

I WANTED TO PUT MY MYSTERY MAN ON *EDGE*--

AND IT LOOKS LIKE I *SUCCEEDED*--

--THAT *SHOT* CAME FROM LIBERTY'S CROWN!

TOO FAR TO *JUMP*--

93

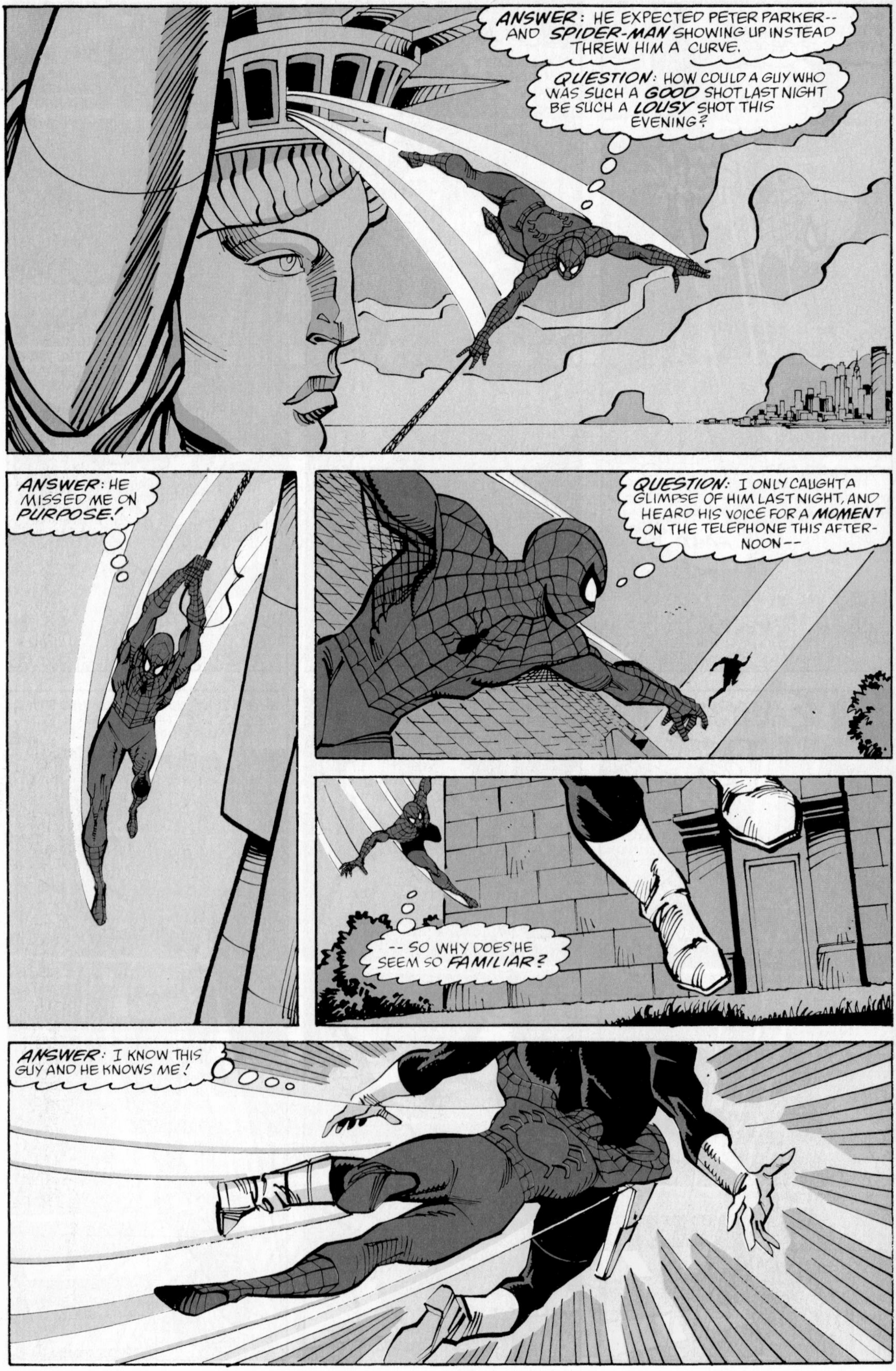
ANSWER: HE EXPECTED PETER PARKER-- AND SPIDER-MAN SHOWING UP INSTEAD THREW HIM A CURVE.
QUESTION: HOW COULD A GUY WHO WAS SUCH A GOOD SHOT LAST NIGHT BE SUCH A LOUSY SHOT THIS EVENING?
ANSWER: HE MISSED ME ON PURPOSE!
QUESTION: I ONLY CAUGHT A GLIMPSE OF HIM LAST NIGHT, AND HEARD HIS VOICE FOR A MOMENT ON THE TELEPHONE THIS AFTER-NOON--
-- SO WHY DOES HE SEEM SO FAMILIAR?
ANSWER: I KNOW THIS GUY AND HE KNOWS ME!

OK, WE'VE PLAYED GAMES *LONG ENOUGH,* FRIEND.

WHY DON'T YOU TELL ME WHAT YOU WANT WITH THE *ROBERTSON* TAPE, AND MAYBE WE CAN--

I'VE GOT A MUCH *BETTER* IDEA, SPIDER-MAN.

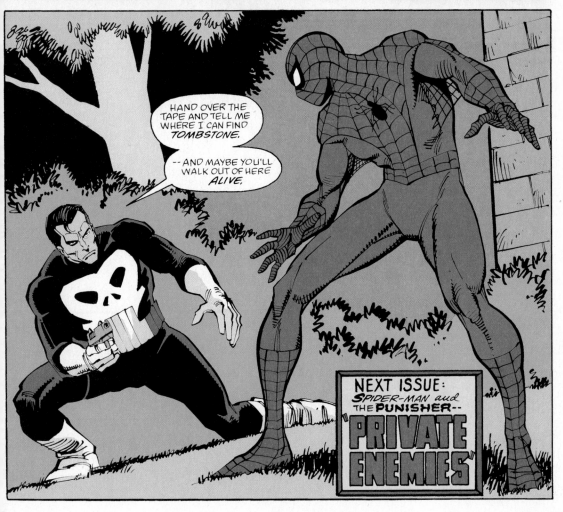

HAND OVER THE TAPE AND TELL ME WHERE I CAN FIND *TOMBSTONE.*

--AND MAYBE YOU'LL WALK OUT OF HERE *ALIVE.*

NEXT ISSUE: *SPIDER-MAN and* THE *PUNISHER*-- "PRIVATE ENEMIES"

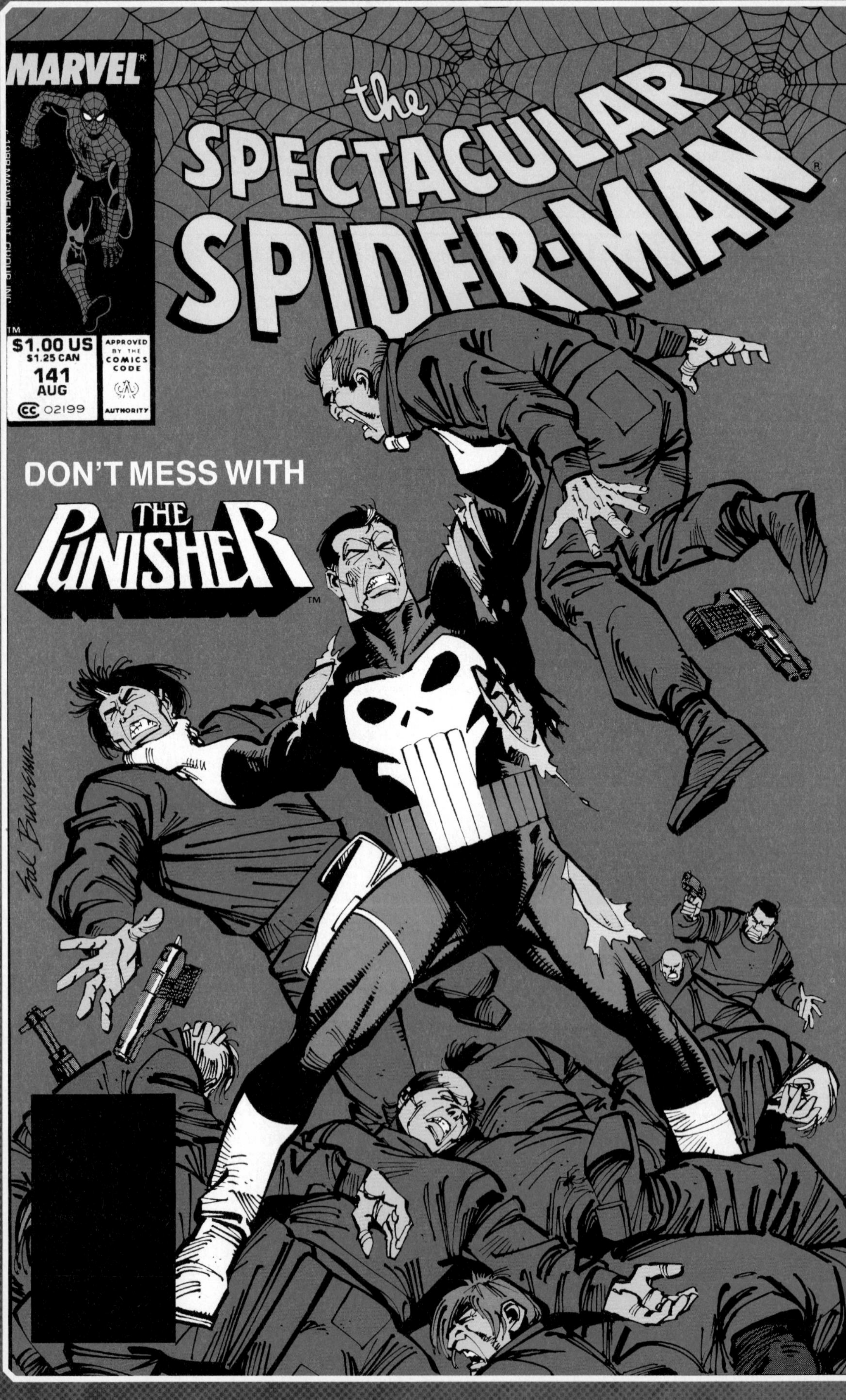
MARVEL
the SPECTACULAR SPIDER-MAN
$1.00 US
$1.25 CAN
141
AUG
02199
APPROVED BY THE COMICS CODE AUTHORITY
DON'T MESS WITH
THE PUNISHER

STAN LEE PRESENTS: **THE SPECTACULAR SPIDER-MAN!** ™

THE **TOMBSTONE TESTAMENT!**

THE HOUR BEFORE DAWN.

MANHATTAN'S WEST SIDE MARINA.

SIX-TO-ONE, PARKER, YOU'RE WALTZING INTO A *TRAP.*

FORTY-FIVE MINUTES AGO, THE GUY IN THAT VAN ALMOST TRIED TO *KILL* YOU.

NOW YOU'RE FOLLOWING HIM TO A PRIVATE MEETING, JUST THE *TWO* OF YOU ABOARD HIS BOAT.

SOMETIMES I'VE GOT TO WONDER-- ARE YOU CRAZY, OR JUST OUT OF YOUR MIND?

GERRY CONWAY
SCRIPT
SAL BUSCEMA
ART
RICK PARKER
LETTERS
BOB SHAREN
COLORIST
JIM SALICRUP
EDITOR
TOM DeFALCO
EDITOR IN CHIEF

SURE, HE *SAYS* HE WAS JUST TRYING TO SPOOK ME BY THAT AMBUSH ON *LIBERTY ISLAND.*＊

HE *SAYS* HE WAS EXPECTING PETER PARKER, AND GOT SUSPICIOUS WHEN *I* SHOWED UP INSTEAD.

GOLDEN GIRL

＊ *LAST ISSUE.*
-- JIM

AND MAYBE I BELIEVE HIM.

GOLDEN GIRL

" AFTER ALL, IF HE REALLY WANTED TO KILL ME, I'D BE WOUNDED NOW -- OR *DEAD.*

" *THE PUNISHER* DOESN'T MISS.

WELCOME ABOARD, SPIDER-MAN.

LET'S TALK.

YEAH, LET'S *DO* THAT, PUN.

FOR STARTERS, WHAT *IS* THIS PLACE? YOUR HOME AWAY FROM HOME?

IT LOOKS LIKE A *FLOATING ARSENAL.*

"GOLDEN GIRL" ONCE BELONGED TO A COLOMBIAN DRUG DEALER. HE'S DEAD.

I USE IT SOMETIMES AS A MOBILE TACTICAL STAGING AREA.

MY MAIN OPERATIONS BASE IS ELSEWHERE.

AND YOU'D JUST AS SOON I DON'T LEARN *WHERE*, RIGHT?

FAIR ENOUGH. I WON'T BE TAKING YOU HOME TO MEET THE FOLKS EITHER -- HUH?

QUITE A PHOTO GALLERY YOU'VE GOT, PUNISHER.

INTERESTING SCENERY -- SAN FRANCISCO, ST. LOUIS, PITTSBURGH -- BUT I DON'T THINK MUCH OF YOUR *MODEL...*

TOMBSTONE. THE MOST VICIOUS MOB HIT MAN WEST OF UNION CITY.

MY STREET INFORMANTS TELL ME HE'S IN NEW YORK.

I WANT TO KNOW WHY.

I BELIEVE YOUR FRIEND JOE ROBERTSON, THE DAILY BUGLE'S EDITOR IN CHIEF, HAS THE ANSWER.

ROBERTSON MADE AN AUDIO CASSETTE CONTAINING INFORMATION ABOUT TOMBSTONE'S CRIMES, AND GAVE IT TO A BUGLE PHOTOGRAPHER NAMED PETER PARKER.

YOU KNOW PARKER, DON'T YOU?

UH-HUH.

I WANT THAT TAPE, SPIDER-MAN.

AND ONE WAY OR THE OTHER, WITH OR WITHOUT YOUR FRIEND PARKER'S COOPERATION--

"-- I'M GOING TO GET IT."

GUESS KINGPIN'S INFORMERS WERE RIGHT, MR. TOMBSTONE.

THAT'S HIS VAN.

I SAW IT ONCE DURING A SHOOTOUT ON STATEN ISLAND WHEN I WAS WORKIN' FOR THE CARELLA FAMILY.

JUST DUMB LUCK I GOT OUTTA THERE IN ONE PIECE.

I FIGURE I OWE THE GUY.

WE'RE NOT HERE FOR REVENGE, WILLIS.

THE ARRANGER WANTS US TO ATTRACT THE PUNISHER'S ATTENTION, THAT'S ALL.

PERSUADER WILL DO THE REST.

WAIT TILL DAWN. THEN ATTACK.

YOU GOT IT, MR. TOMBSTONE.

ONE THING MORE, ALL OF YOU.

MY NAME ISN'T "MR."

IT'S *TOMBSTONE.*

GET IT RIGHT OR I'LL BREAK YOUR LEGS.

WE'RE AT WAR, SPIDER-MAN. OUR WHOLE SOCIETY IS AT WAR, AND I'M ON THE FRONT LINE.

OUR ENEMIES ARE VERMIN LIKE TOMB-STONE. YOU SEE IT IN THE NEWSPAPER AND ON TELEVISION EVERY DAY.

MAKE NO MISTAKE, CRIME *IS* WAR.

AND OUR SIDE IS LOSING.

TAKE THIS KIND OF *PERSONALLY,* DON'T YOU?

WHAT DID TOMBSTONE DO, KICK YOUR PUPPY WHEN YOU WERE KIDS?

UM.

HIS SORT OF SCUM MURDERED MY WIFE AND CHILDREN.

"AND THERE WAS A MAN, A DEPUTY *DISTRICT ATTORNEY* IN ST. LOUIS NAMED HAROLD ULLMAN.

"HAROLD ULLMAN WAS A FRIEND OF MINE FROM THE *CORPS.*

"HE HAD A WIFE, A DAUGHTER, AND A HOUSE IN THE SUBURBS.

"SIX WEEKS AGO, HAROLD CON-VENED A GRAND JURY TO INVESTI-GATE *MOB INFLUENCE* BACKING THE STREET CORNER 'MINI-MALL' BOOM.

"MY INFORMANTS SAY TOMBSTONE TOOK THE HIT.

"BUT THERE'S NO PROOF, NO WITNESSES, NO *EVIDENCE.*

"WITH TOMBSTONE, THERE NEVER IS."

THAT'S WHY I WANT THE *ROBERTSON* TAPE.

HOW'D YOU FIND OUT TOMBSTONE WAS IN NEW YORK?

CONTACTS.

" I HAVE FRIENDS IN LOW PLACES."

"AFTER HAROLD'S FUNERAL, I DID SOME *NETWORKING* IN ST. LOUIS."

" MY FRIENDS WERE VERY HELPFUL."

WHERE IS HE?

LOUDER.

YOUR MOTHER WEARS COMBAT BOOTS IF HER HAIR AND EYES

...NEW YORK... ...AGGIE'S PUB...

EVERY CITY HAS ITS MOB BAR. HANGOUT FOR LOWLIFE MERCENARIES AND WOULD-BE HIT MEN.

I WENT THERE LOOKING FOR *TOMBSTONE* OR SOMEONE WHO KNEW WHERE HE WAS.

"INSTEAD I FOUND YOU, DOING A JOB BREAKING HEADS.

"YOU WANTED TO KNOW WHO'D PUT A *CONTRACT* ON JOE ROBERTSON.

" YOU WERE TOLD IT WAS *TOMBSTONE*,

" WE'RE NOT EXACTLY ALLIES, YOU AND I, BUT AT TIMES WE SHARE A *COMMON* INTEREST.

" I DECIDED THIS WAS ONE OF THOSE TIMES."

"WHEN I SAW A THUG ABOUT TO *SHOOT* YOU, I SHOT FIRST.

" GETTING OUT BEFORE YOU COULD CATCH ME WASN'T EASY, BUT I LEARNED HOW TO HIDE IN THE NAM.

" OF COURSE, NEW YORK ISN'T THE NAM.

" HERE, THERE ARE A LOT FEWER TREES."

FUNNY. MY SPIDER-SENSE ALREADY WARNED ME ABOUT THAT *GUNMAN,* PUN.

YOU DIDN'T HAVE TO SHOOT HIM.

THEN WE HAVE A DIFFERENCE OF OPINION.

AT ANY RATE, I CALLED THE *BUGLE,* AND FOUND OUT ROBERTSON HAD BEEN HOSPITALIZED.

"AT THE HOSPITAL I OVERHEARD *PETER PARKER* TALKING ABOUT AN AUDIO TAPE ROBERTSON GAVE HIM."

"PARKER SAID HE WAS GOING TO THE *DAILY BUGLE.*"

"I CALLED HIM THERE, AND TOLD HIM TO MEET ME WITH THE TAPE."

INSTEAD OF PARKER, *YOU* SHOWED UP.

SO YOU *AMBUSHED* ME.

RULE ONE: NEVER LOSE THE INITIATIVE.

I WANTED YOU ON THE DEFENSIVE. PEOPLE WHO FEEL VULNER-ABLE TEND TO BE MORE FORTHCOMING.

UH-HUH. YOU HAD ME *GOING* THERE BEFORE WE BOTH CALMED DOWN.

I WANT THAT TAPE.

SORRY, IT'S NOT MINE TO GIVE.

JOE ROBERTSON GAVE IT TO PETER PARKER—

THEN I'LL ASK PETER *PERSONALLY.*

I'LL TELL HIM YOU SAID HELLO.

UH... HOLD IT, PUN.

NO NEED TO BOTHER OUR BOY PARKER.

HE WON'T MAKE A MOVE WITH THAT TAPE WITHOUT ROBBIE ROBERTSON'S SAY-SO.

YOU'RE SUGGESTING I TALK TO ROBERTSON?

I'M SUGGESTING YOU COOL DOWN.

ROBBIE ROBERTSON HAS BEEN THROUGH A LOT, TOMBSTONE MAY HAVE BROKEN HIS BACK. RIGHT NOW HE'S IN A ROUGH PLACE.

WE ALL HAVE OUR PROBLEMS, SPIDER-MAN. WHAT MATTERS IS HOW YOU DEAL WITH THEM.

THEN LET ME DEAL WITH THIS.

I'LL CHAT WITH PETER PARKER, HE'LL CHAT WITH ROBERTSON, AND WE'LL GET THE TAPE.

YOU HAVE TILL SUNDOWN TONIGHT. AFTER THAT...

I GET THE PICTURE.

HAVE A NICE DAY, PUN.

DON'T LET YOUR SHORTS RIDE UP.

BOATS

SPIDER-MAN-- VISITING THE PUNISHER. INTERESTING.

ALL MY YEARS WORKING IN THE MIDWEST AND ON THE COAST, I WONDERED HOW I'D HANDLE A COSTUMED CLOWN LIKE HIM.

MAYBE I'LL FIND OUT BEFORE THIS BUSINESS IS FINISHED.

"SO PETER PARKER HAS A TAPE MADE BY ROBBIE ROBERTSON. WELL, NOW.

"IF THAT TAPE CONTAINS WHAT I THINK IT DOES, PARKER AND ROBERTSON WILL FIND THEMSELVES IN SERIOUS TROUBLE."

I'LL HANDLE PARKER AND THE ROBERTSON TAPE.

OUR FRIEND IN BLACK HAS HAD A BUSY NIGHT. HE'LL BE TIRED. HE'LL NEED SOME SLEEP.

GIVE HIM AN HOUR TO SETTLE DOWN.

THEN RING HIS ALARM...

BEN URICH ISN'T QUITE SURE *WHICH* HE HATES MORE:

QUIET HOSPITAL ZONE

MORNINGS BEFORE 9:00 a.m., OR HOSPITALS WITH ANTI-SMOKING RULES.

HEY, BEN-- GOOD TO SEE YOU!

DID YOU HEAR THE *NEWS?*

DAD'S DOCTOR SAYS THERE WAS NO *PERMANENT* DAMAGE TO DAD'S SPINE.

A WEEK OR TWO OF PHYSICAL THERAPY, HE'LL BE DANCING WHATEVER IT IS YOU OLD FOLKS DANCE.

WE "OLD FOLKS" DON'T DANCE, KID.

MOSTLY WE JUST MOVE AROUND REAL *SLOW.*

HOW'S IT GOIN', ROBBIE?

NOT AS WELL AS RANDY WANTS TO THINK, BEN.

DAD'S STILL A LITTLE *DEPRESSED,* BEN-- THAT'S ALL.

WE ALL KNOW HE'LL BE *FINE.*

YOU BET, KID.

GIVE ME A FEW MINUTES *ALONE* WITH THE OLD MAN, OKAY?

DAD?

GO AHEAD, RANDY... WAIT OUTSIDE.

YOU NEVER HIT *THE BUGLE OFFICES* BEFORE *NOON,* BEN. WHAT BRINGS YOU HERE SO EARLY...?

I FIGURE WE NEED TO TALK.

HURTS *BAD,* HUH?

LIKE SOMEBODY RAMMED A STEEL BAR DOWN MY SPINE.

YEAH... GUESS YOU'RE LUCKY YOU'RE ALIVE.

WANT TO TELL ME ABOUT THE *TAPE* YOU GAVE PETER PARKER?

WHAT TAPE?

I DON'T KNOW WHAT YOU'RE--

SAVE IT, ROBBIE. I'M A REPORTER, REMEMBER?

DIGGING UP NASTY LITTLE SECRETS IS MY *JOB*-- EVEN WHEN THOSE SECRETS BELONG TO MY BOSS AND FRIEND.

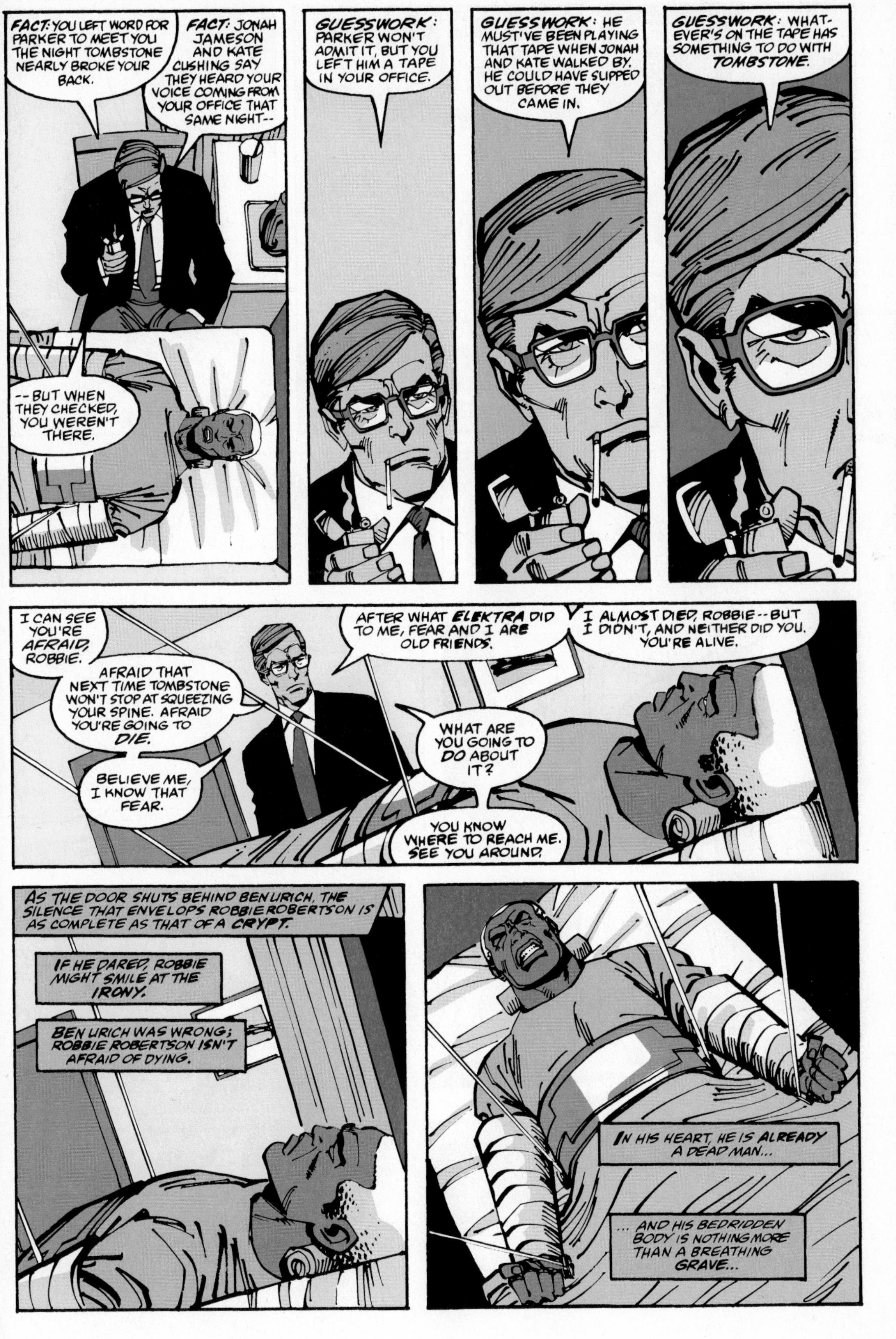
FACT: YOU LEFT WORD FOR PARKER TO MEET YOU THE NIGHT TOMBSTONE NEARLY BROKE YOUR BACK.
FACT: JONAH JAMESON AND KATE CUSHING SAY THEY HEARD YOUR VOICE COMING FROM YOUR OFFICE THAT SAME NIGHT--
--BUT WHEN THEY CHECKED, YOU WEREN'T THERE.
GUESSWORK: PARKER WON'T ADMIT IT, BUT YOU LEFT HIM A TAPE IN YOUR OFFICE.
GUESSWORK: HE MUST'VE BEEN PLAYING THAT TAPE WHEN JONAH AND KATE WALKED BY. HE COULD HAVE SLIPPED OUT BEFORE THEY CAME IN.
GUESSWORK: WHAT-EVER'S ON THE TAPE HAS SOMETHING TO DO WITH TOMBSTONE.
I CAN SEE YOU'RE AFRAID, ROBBIE.
AFRAID THAT NEXT TIME TOMBSTONE WON'T STOP AT SQUEEZING YOUR SPINE. AFRAID YOU'RE GOING TO DIE.
BELIEVE ME, I KNOW THAT FEAR.
AFTER WHAT ELEKTRA DID TO ME, FEAR AND I ARE OLD FRIENDS.
I ALMOST DIED, ROBBIE--BUT I DIDN'T, AND NEITHER DID YOU. YOU'RE ALIVE.
WHAT ARE YOU GOING TO DO ABOUT IT?
YOU KNOW WHERE TO REACH ME. SEE YOU AROUND.
AS THE DOOR SHUTS BEHIND BEN URICH, THE SILENCE THAT ENVELOPS ROBBIE ROBERTSON IS AS COMPLETE AS THAT OF A CRYPT.
IF HE DARED, ROBBIE MIGHT SMILE AT THE IRONY.
BEN URICH WAS WRONG; ROBBIE ROBERTSON ISN'T AFRAID OF DYING.
IN HIS HEART, HE IS ALREADY A DEAD MAN...
...AND HIS BEDRIDDEN BODY IS NOTHING MORE THAN A BREATHING GRAVE...

9:07 A.M.

CREAK

GOLDE

SIZZLE

SIZZLE

CREAK

SIZZZZZS

HOLY

IIIIAAAHH

SIZZZZS

BUDDA-BRAAP!

MY EYES, MAN! MY EYYYESS

WASTE 'IM, YOU STUPID MO-- UNNGH!

TTTATTTARRAT

108

HELP-ME-MAN-YOU GOTTA-HELP ME-MY EYES-MAN-OH-MAN-OH-MAN-YOU GOTTA MY EYES--OH

SHUT UP, DUMMY! SHUT UP, SHUT UP!

GET OFFA ME, GET OFF BEFORE HE--

THUNG

HOW MANY MORE?

GIVE IT TO ME QUICK AND I'LL GET YOU TO A DOCTOR.

TWO-ON-DECK-OH-MAN-I-CAN'T-SEE...

CREAK

GOT IT.

BBBRAAPPAAP

SPLASH

109

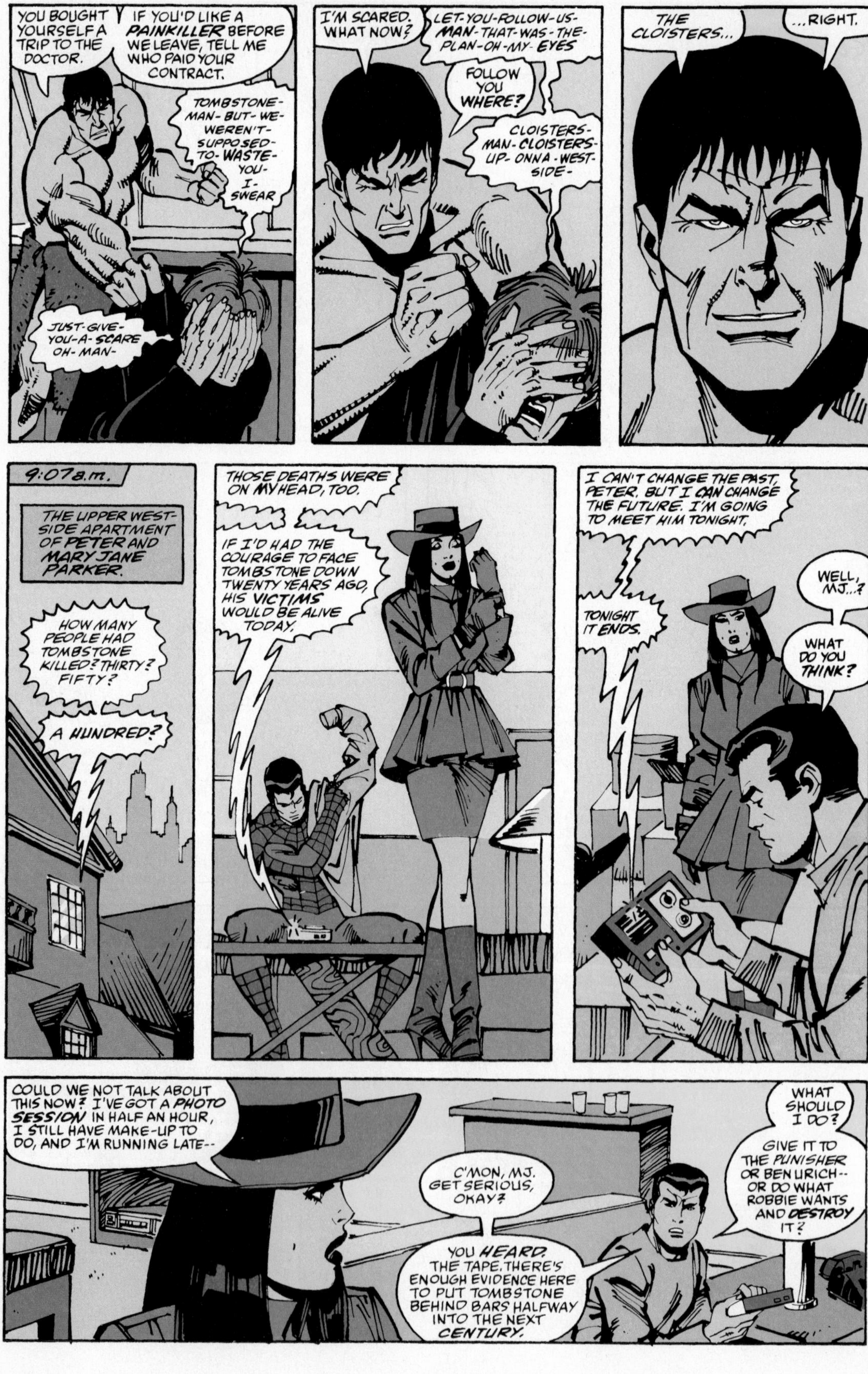

YOU BOUGHT YOURSELF A TRIP TO THE DOCTOR.
IF YOU'D LIKE A PAINKILLER BEFORE WE LEAVE, TELL ME WHO PAID YOUR CONTRACT.
TOMBSTONE-MAN-BUT-WE-WEREN'T-SUPPOSED-TO-WASTE-YOU-I-SWEAR
JUST-GIVE-YOU-A-SCARE OH-MAN-
I'M SCARED. WHAT NOW?
LET-YOU-FOLLOW-US-MAN-THAT-WAS-THE-PLAN-OH-MY-EYES
FOLLOW YOU WHERE?
CLOISTERS-MAN-CLOISTERS-UP-ONNA-WEST-SIDE-
THE CLOISTERS...
...RIGHT.
9:07 a.m.
THE UPPER WEST-SIDE APARTMENT OF PETER AND MARY JANE PARKER.
HOW MANY PEOPLE HAD TOMBSTONE KILLED? THIRTY? FIFTY?
A HUNDRED?
THOSE DEATHS WERE ON MY HEAD, TOO.
IF I'D HAD THE COURAGE TO FACE TOMBSTONE DOWN TWENTY YEARS AGO, HIS VICTIMS WOULD BE ALIVE TODAY.
I CAN'T CHANGE THE PAST, PETER. BUT I CAN CHANGE THE FUTURE. I'M GOING TO MEET HIM TONIGHT.
TONIGHT IT ENDS.
WELL, MJ...?
WHAT DO YOU THINK?
COULD WE NOT TALK ABOUT THIS NOW? I'VE GOT A PHOTO SESSION IN HALF AN HOUR, I STILL HAVE MAKE-UP TO DO, AND I'M RUNNING LATE--
C'MON, MJ. GET SERIOUS, OKAY?
YOU HEARD. THE TAPE. THERE'S ENOUGH EVIDENCE HERE TO PUT TOMBSTONE BEHIND BARS HALFWAY INTO THE NEXT CENTURY.
WHAT SHOULD I DO?
GIVE IT TO THE PUNISHER OR BEN URICH--OR DO WHAT ROBBIE WANTS AND DESTROY IT?

UH-UH, PETER-- THIS IS *YOUR* MORAL DECISION -- NOT MINE.

IF IT WERE UP TO *ME*, I'D SAY BURN THE TAPE AND THROW THE ASHES DOWN THE DEEPEST HOLE YOU CAN FIND.

HUH? *WHY?!*

DON'T YOU CARE THAT THIS GUY TOMB-STONE'S A *KILLER* ON THE LOOSE? AND LOOK WHAT HE DID TO *ROBBIE...*

I HAVEN'T THOUGHT ABOUT *ANYTHING ELSE* SINCE IT HAPPENED, PETER.

I *LOVE* YOU. I DON'T WANT TO SEE YOU HURT.

DO WHAT YOU THINK IS RIGHT, BUT, PLEASE,... DON'T ASK *ME* TO DECIDE. I CAN'T HANDLE IT.

SORRY, KID. I'VE LIVED WITH SPIDER-MAN SO LONG, SOMETIMES I FORGET HOW HARD THIS KIND OF LIFE MUST BE...

I LOVE YOU, TOO.

MMM.

BESIDES, THIS *ISN'T* A DECISION EITHER OF US SHOULD MAKE.

THE TAPE BELONGS TO ROBBIE.

WHAT HE DOES WITH IT IS *HIS* CHOICE, NOT *OURS*.

I'LL LEAVE IT TO HIM.

PETER, I LOVE YOU SO MUCH, THE THOUGHT OF *LOSING* YOU IS MORE THAN I CAN STAND.

THIS LIFE *FRIGHTENS* ME MORE THAN I EVER GUESSED IT WOULD...

" I WANT TO BE STRONG FOR YOU, BUT I DON'T KNOW *HOW.*"

"SHOULD I *TELL* YOU WHAT I FEEL, OR SHOULD I *HIDE* MY SECRET TERRORS BEHIND MY OLD FASHION MODEL MASK?"

"I WISH I HAD SOMEONE TO *TALK* TO, PETER.

"SOMEONE TO SHARE THESE FEELINGS...

"THERE ARE DAYS WHEN I FEEL SO *ALONE.*

TRIER APT 301

PARKER APT 302

CAESAR APT 303

9:27 A.M.

THE *CLOISTERS,* A 12TH CENTURY MONASTERY BROUGHT FROM EUROPE BY THE METROPOLITAN MUSEUM.

MUSEUM HOURS ARE FROM 10:00 A.M. TO 4:45 P.M. DAILY, TUESDAY THROUGH SATURDAY.

THIS IS *MONDAY.*

VERY NEAT. YOU COULDN'T FIND A BETTER SITE FOR AN AMBUSH THAN A WALLED MEDIEVAL *MONASTERY.*

"I'LL GIVE TOMBSTONE THIS MUCH...

...AS A TACTICIAN, HE'S *ALMOST* AS GOOD AS I AM.

--AND SHE WAS STILL *SCREAMIN'* WHEN I WASTED HER.

≥SNIFF≤ WOMEN. NO GUTS.

WHAT'D YOU DO WITH THE BODY? ≥SNIFF≤

DUMPED IT IN CANARSIE AT HER BROTHER'S HOUSE.

PPFTT

NEXT TIME HER FAMILY WILL THINK *TWICE* BEFORE THEY SHORTCHANGE ME AN' MY PEOPLE ON A SHIPMENT.

HEY, DID YA HEAR THAT?

SOUNDED LIKE A--

AH, WOW.

PPFTT

SOONER OR LATER EVERYTHING GOES DOWNHILL.

THERE WAS A TIME WHEN LOSERS LIKE THESE TWO WOULD HAVE BEEN *LAUGHED* OUT OF NEW YORK.

FRANK CASTLE, A.K.A. *THE PUNISHER*, HAS BEEN AWAKE OVER 36 HOURS.

HE'S TIRED.

NOW TOMBSTONE PUTS THEM ON POINT GUARD DUTY.

POOR MANAGEMENT.

THE MAN MUST BE GETTING OVER-CONFIDENT.

TOMBSTONE'S SEDAN.

IT'S RIDING SO LOW, IT MUST HAVE A TON OF ARMOR-PLATING UNDER THAT PAINT JOB.

BETTER USE A FRESH *CLIP*--

TIRED MEN MAKE NEAR-FATAL MISTAKES.

THE PUNISHER JUST MADE *HIS*.

SHADOWS LUNGE FROM TREES AND BUSHES.

THEY SAY NOT A WORD; UNLIKE THE "LOSERS" AT THE FRONT GATE, THESE MEN ARE *PROFESSIONALS*.

IN ONE ADRENALIN-PUMPED INSTANT, CASTLE KNOWS HE WAS SUCKERED INTO A PERFECT *SETUP*...

9:25 a.m.

OKAY... SO I'M AFRAID I DON'T *LIKE* IT.

NOW WHAT DO I DO? SHUT MY EYES AND HOPE THE FEAR GOES AWAY?

YEAH, GOOD *THINKING,* MJ. WE KNOW HOW WELL THAT WORKED BEFORE.

YOU BETTER-- --UH--

OHMIGOSH

YOU KNOW WHO I AM.

NO!

DON'T BOTHER TO LIE-- I SEE IT IN YOUR EYES.

WHERE'S PARKER?

OWWW!

HE'S NOT *HERE*--

REALLY.

LET'S TRY AGAIN.

WHERE'S PARKER?

LET GO OF ME, YOU *CREEP!*

WAS THAT NICE? I ASK A CIVIL QUESTION, AND YOU GET VIOLENT.

LISTEN. ONE WAY OR ANOTHER, YOU'LL TELL ME WHAT I WANT TO KNOW.

HOW MUCH PAIN YOU SUFFER BEFORE YOU DO IS UP TO YOU.

THINK CAREFULLY NOW.

PETER PARKER.

WHERE *IS* HE?

9:31 a.m.

THEY'RE PROFESSIONALS, THESE MEN.

IN AFRICA, THEY FOUGHT ON BOTH SIDES OF SEVERAL CIVIL WARS.

THUD

IN CENTRAL AMERICA, THEY SMUGGLED ARMS.

IN SOUTH AMERICA THEY SMUGGLED DRUGS.

KRAK

CHUNK

IN NEWARK AND CHICAGO THEY SHOT PEOPLE FOR A FEE.

KWHAM

IN ANY OTHER SITUATION, THEY'D BE COLLECTING THEIR CONTRACT MONEY RIGHT ABOUT NOW.

BUT IN THIS SITUATION THE PUNISHER SIMPLY HAS THEM OUTNUMBERED.

KACHAK! CHAK!

THUK!

GO AHEAD...

...TRY ME.

RIGHT.

OKAY, TOMBSTONE.

...I PLAYED YOUR LITTLE GAME OF CAT AND MOUSE...

SNAK

...AND IT'S BEEN A THRILL.

NOW WE PLAY *MY* GAME.

SO GLAD YOU COULD JOIN US, *PUNISHER!*

YOU KNOW ME AS THE *ARRANGER,* OF COURSE.

I WORK FOR MR. FISK... ...THE *KINGPIN.*

MY YOUNG FRIEND HERE IS *ROLAND RAYBURN,* WHOM WE CALL "*PERSUADER.*"

FORGIVE US FOR THOSE MEN OUTSIDE.

THEIR ATTACKS WERE UNPLEASANT, BUT NECESSARY.

PERSUADER IS AT HIS MOST EFFECTIVE WHEN HIS SUBJECT'S ADRENALIN LEVELS AND PULSE-RATE ARE BOTH *ELEVATED.*

AS YOURS ARE *NOW,*

ROLAND IS A MUTANT WITH AN INTRIGUING PSYCHIC ABILITY.

YOU DON'T WANT TO HURT ME, *DO* YOU, PUNISHER?

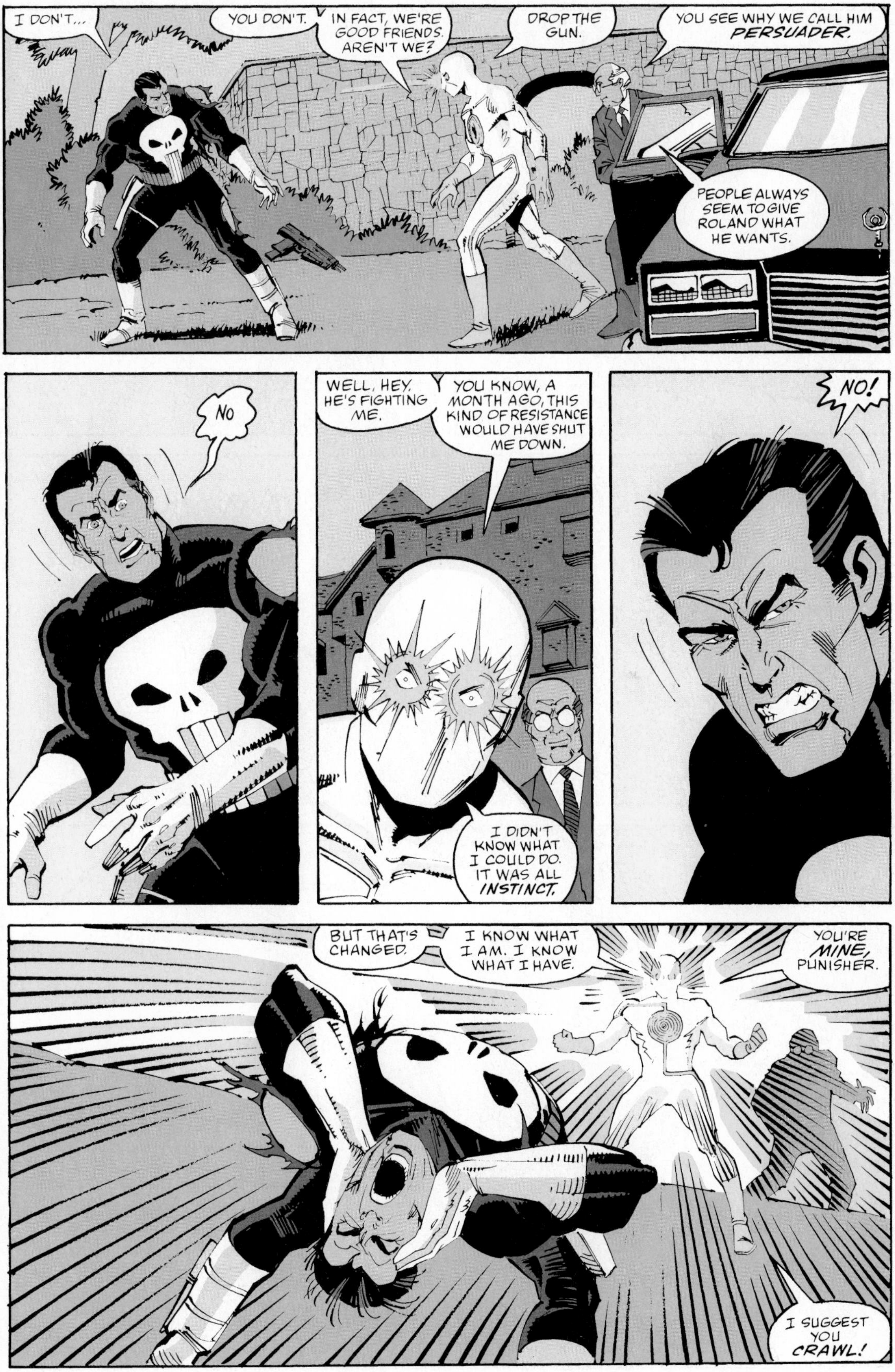
I DON'T...
YOU DON'T.
IN FACT, WE'RE GOOD FRIENDS. AREN'T WE?
DROP THE GUN.
YOU SEE WHY WE CALL HIM PERSUADER.
PEOPLE ALWAYS SEEM TO GIVE ROLAND WHAT HE WANTS.
NO
WELL, HEY. HE'S FIGHTING ME.
YOU KNOW, A MONTH AGO, THIS KIND OF RESISTANCE WOULD HAVE SHUT ME DOWN.
I DIDN'T KNOW WHAT I COULD DO. IT WAS ALL INSTINCT.
NO!
BUT THAT'S CHANGED.
I KNOW WHAT I AM. I KNOW WHAT I HAVE.
YOU'RE MINE, PUNISHER.
I SUGGEST YOU CRAWL!

9:58 a.m.

--IT'S YOUR DECISION, ROBBIE, BUT I THINK YOU'RE MAKING A MISTAKE.

GUYS LIKE TOMBSTONE LIVE ON FEAR. LET HIM SCARE YOU AND HE'LL WIN.

THEN HE WINS, PETER... BECAUSE I'M SCARED.

THAT'S GREAT, JUST GREAT.

SO HE STAYS LOOSE, AND WHAT ABOUT THE NEXT VICTIM HE--

ARE YOU PETER PARKER?

HUH?

YEAH, I'M PARKER.

I THOUGHT SO. ONE OF THE EMERGENCY ROOM NURSES SAID-- YOUR WIFE -- SHE'S BEEN HURT--

MARY JANE!

TO BE CONTINUED...

NEXT ISSUE: "AND ONE WILL FALL"...

120

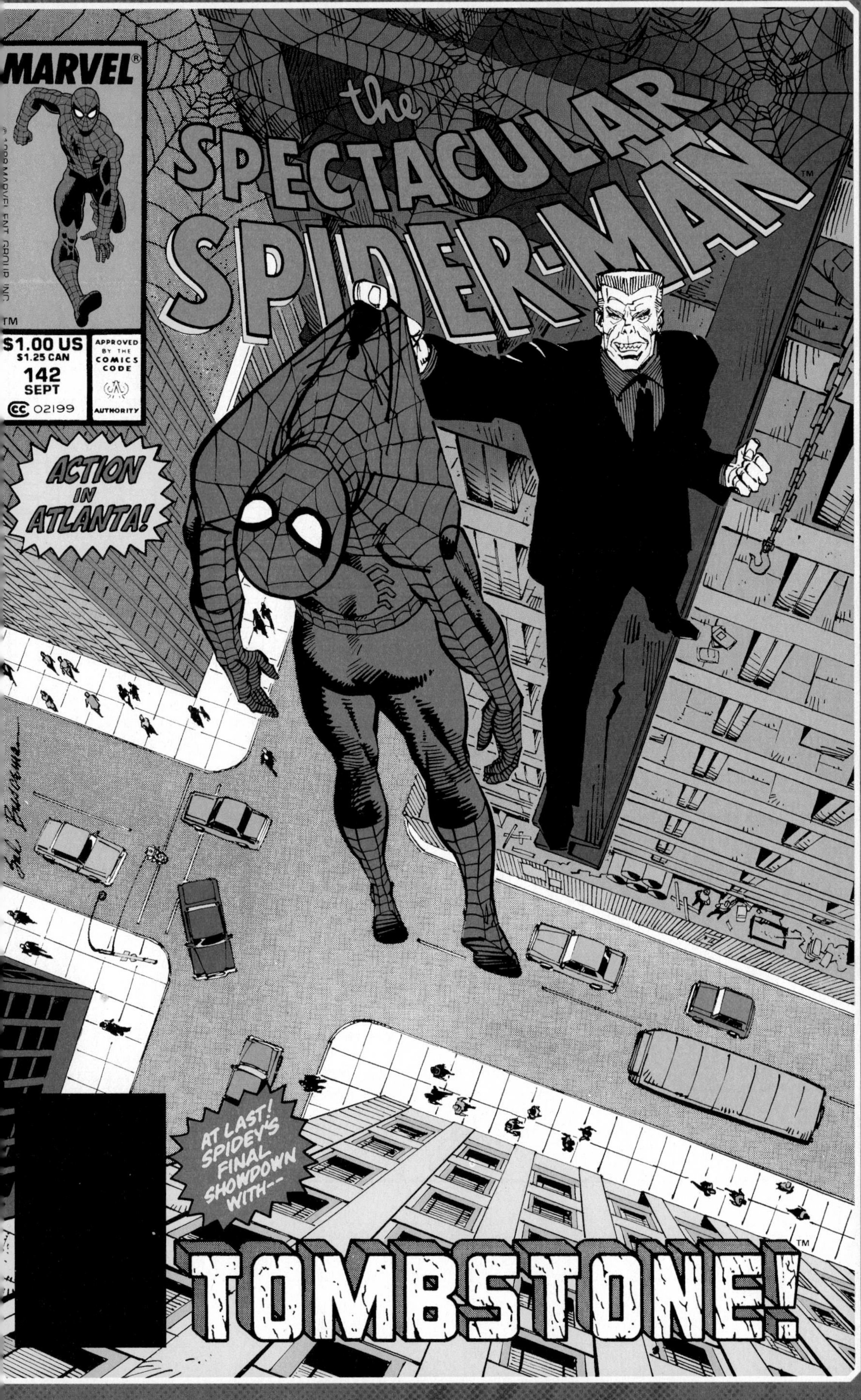
MARVEL
$1.00 US
$1.25 CAN
142
SEPT
02199
APPROVED BY THE COMICS CODE AUTHORITY
the SPECTACULAR SPIDER-MAN
ACTION IN ATLANTA!
AT LAST! SPIDEY'S FINAL SHOWDOWN WITH--
TOMBSTONE!

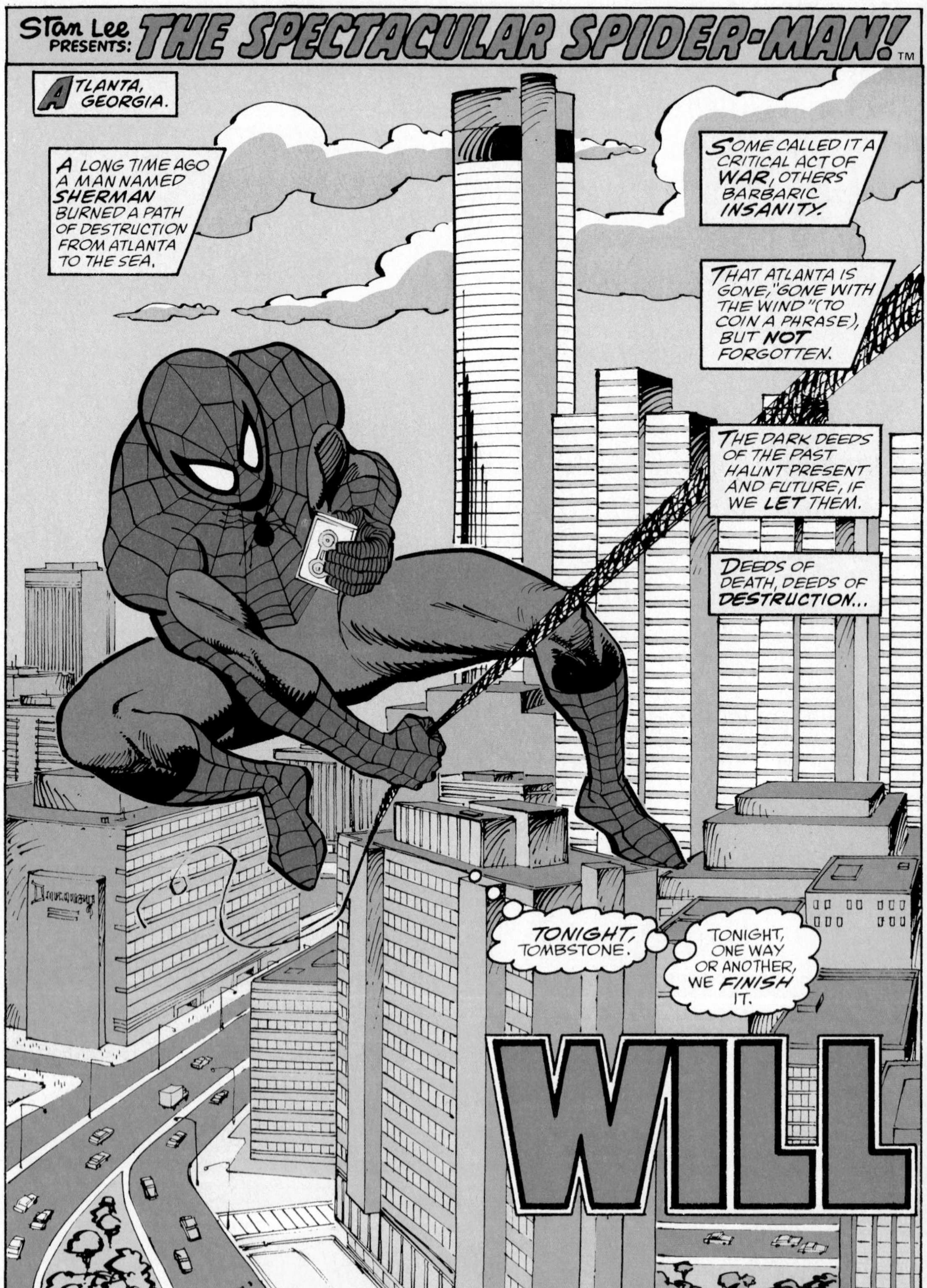
Stan Lee PRESENTS: THE SPECTACULAR SPIDER-MAN! TM
ATLANTA, GEORGIA.
A LONG TIME AGO A MAN NAMED SHERMAN BURNED A PATH OF DESTRUCTION FROM ATLANTA TO THE SEA.
SOME CALLED IT A CRITICAL ACT OF WAR, OTHERS BARBARIC INSANITY.
THAT ATLANTA IS GONE, "GONE WITH THE WIND" (TO COIN A PHRASE), BUT NOT FORGOTTEN.
THE DARK DEEDS OF THE PAST HAUNT PRESENT AND FUTURE, IF WE LET THEM.
DEEDS OF DEATH, DEEDS OF DESTRUCTION...
TONIGHT, TOMBSTONE.
TONIGHT, ONE WAY OR ANOTHER, WE FINISH IT.
WILL

I WAS ANGRY ENOUGH THAT YOU ALMOST SHATTERED ROBBIE ROBERTSON'S *SPINE*--

"--BUT THE MOMENT YOU HURT MY *WIFE*.."

MARY JANE!

"YOU MADE IT *PERSONAL*."

THE NURSE SAID MARY JANE WAS IN *EMERGENCY*-- THAT SHE'D BEEN *INJURED* *--

--BUT WHERE *IS* SHE?

WHERE?!

*SEE LAST ISSUE. --JIM.

MJ?

PETER!

HE SAID YOU WERE NEXT-- I THOUGHT HE'D *KILL* YOU--

"HER **HAIR** SMELLED LIKE STRAWBERRIES AND CREAM.

IT'S ALL RIGHT, I'M ALL RIGHT-- YOU'RE ALL RIGHT, IT'S OVER, DON'T WORRY--

"I LOVE THAT SMELL.

Please BE SEATED *thankyou*

"I LOVE **HER.**

"MORE THAN **LIFE.**"

AFTER YOU LEFT TO SEE **ROBBIE** -- I WAS PUTTING ON MY FACE FOR A MODELING ASSIGNMENT--

YOU DON'T HAVE TO TELL ME NOW.

WHEN I LOOKED UP, HE WAS **THERE** -- AND HE **GRABBED** ME--

TELL HUBBY I WANT THE **ROBERTSON** TAPE, LITTLE GIRL.

DO THAT FOR ME?

NO--

WRONG ANSWER.

OHHH-- YES--

THERE WE GO. THANKS. I APPRECIATE IT.

HE WARNED ME YOU'D BE **NEXT**-- BROUGHT ME HERE--

THEN HE CAN'T BE FAR AWAY--

YOU PARKER?

PHONE CALL.

DON'T TIE IT UP.

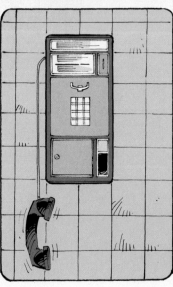

HEY, PETER?

HOW'S THE WIFE?

YOU CREEP.

NOW IS THAT NICE?

WE'RE GOING TO MEET, PETER--

HOSPITAL

--YOU AND ME AND THE ROBERTSON TAPE.

SOMEWHERE OUT OF YOUR TURF, AND JUST BECAUSE I'M A FAIR MAN, SOMEWHERE OUT OF MINE.

OR NEXT TIME, I WON'T TWIST HER ARM.

I'LL TWIST HER LOVELY LITTLE NECK.

WHERE?

I HEAR YOU'RE DOING A BOOK SIGNING.

TOMORROW. MITCHELL BOOKS.

ATLANTA.

PETER, IT WAS HIM, WASN'T IT? WHAT DID HE SAY--?

JUST WHAT YOU'D EXPECT.

MOB HITMEN HAVE AN ELEGANT WAY WITH WORDS.

TOMBSTONE WANTS US TO MEET, AND THAT'S FINE WITH ME...

JONAH JAMESON RAN A FEATURE ARTICLE ABOUT *WEBS*-- MY SPIDER-MAN PHOTO BOOK IN THE SUNDAY *BUGLE*.

TOMBSTONE MUST HAVE READ IT, AND CALLED MY PUBLISHER TO FIND OUT WHERE I'D BE *AUTOGRAPHING* NEXT.

THIS AFTERNOON, WHEN I GOT TO *MITCHELL BOOKS*, THERE WAS A *MESSAGE* WAITING.

FROM TOMBSTONE.

" BRING THE TAPE AND A RECORDER TO *TARA SQUARE*."

" TENTH FLOOR, "

" *SUNDOWN*."

BEFORE I LEFT NEW YORK, I TRIED REACHING *THE PUNISHER*, HE WANTS THE *ROBERTSON TAPE* TOO.

HE'S GOT ALMOST AS MUCH AGAINST TOMBSTONE AS *I* DO.

I FIGURED I'D TIP HIM OFF ABOUT MY MEETING TONIGHT, WITHOUT ANY *DETAILS*...

... SO HE'D BE READY TO MOVE, IN CASE SOMETHING *HAPPENED* TO ME.

BUT HE WASN'T AT HIS TEMPORARY MOBILE HEADQUARTERS IN THE *WEST SIDE MARINA*.

IN FACT, HE WASN'T *ANYWHERE*-- AND I DIDN'T HAVE TIME TO GO LOOKING.

YOU'LL MISS THE *FUN*.

JUST YOUR LUCK, *PUN*...

AAAAHH

NEW YORK.

YOU'RE A SMART MAN, AT LEAST THAT'S WHAT THEY TELL ME.

WHY MAKE THIS HARDER THAN IT HAS TO BE?

SOONER OR LATER I'LL BREAK YOUR WILL, AND YOU'LL DO *EXACTLY* WHAT I SAY. GUARANTEED.

GO...TO... ...BLAZES!

HEART RATE: 190. BLOOD PRESSURE: 280 OVER 140.

KEEP THIS UP, ARRANGER, AND HE'LL HAVE A *STROKE.*

ROLAND, I'M BECOMING QUITE *DISCOURAGED.*

ME, TOO. THIS GUY'S GOT A WILL LIKE ALLOY *STEEL.*

AFTER OUR LITTLE DRUG TREATMENT, YOU *PROMISED* TO USE YOUR MUTANT POWER OF *PERSUASION* ON THE KINGPIN'S BEHALF.

WE'VE GIVEN YOU EVERY MEASURE OF *SUPPORT*--

--EVEN A SPECIALLY-CONSTRUCTED OUTFIT TO ENHANCE AND *FOCUS* YOUR PSYCHIC TALENTS.

AND YET, IN THE LAST *TEN HOURS* YOU HAVEN'T--

SHUT UP. I'M TRYING TO *CONCENTRATE.*

IT'S HAPPENING-- I CAN FEEL IT--!

YEAH--

YEAH!

UNNGH!

YO! *WATCH* IT!

VERY DISCOURAGING. I SHOULD'VE LEFT YOU TRADING STOCKS ON *WALL STREET*, ROLAND.

YOU'VE FAILED MISERAB--

THINK SO?

LOOK AT HIM.

HUH?

ARRANGER, CHECK THIS OUT...

WELL, WELL.

I OWE YOU AN *APOLOGY* PERSUADER.

WELCOME ABOARD, *PUNISHER*.

HOW NICE TO HAVE YOU ON THE *KINGPIN'S* TEAM.

NEW YORK.

MIDTOWN GENERAL HOSPITAL.

I CAN'T DO THIS.

PHYSICAL THERAPY

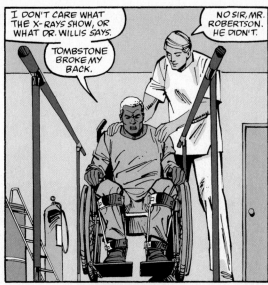

I DON'T CARE WHAT THE X-RAYS SHOW, OR WHAT DR. WILLIS SAYS.

TOMBSTONE BROKE MY BACK.

NO SIR, MR. ROBERTSON. HE DIDN'T.

WHAT HE DID WAS BRUISE AND COMPRESS YOUR SPINAL CORD.

PUT IN LAYMAN'S TERMS, THE NERVES IN YOUR SPINE WERE TRAUMATIZED.

SAW THE SAME THING WHEN I WAS A CORPSMAN IN THE 'NAM.

C'MON, DAD, TAKE A FEW STEPS.

GOT TO KEEP SMILING-- CAN'T LET DAD SEE HOW SCARED I AM.

EVERY TIME SHE VISITS HIM, MOM COMES HOME CRYING.

DAD WAS ALWAYS SO STRONG, SO BRAVE--

-- BUT THESE LAST FEW WEEKS HE'S BEEN A BROKEN OLD MAN.

THAT'S RIGHT, DAD! GO FOR IT!

WHAT HAPPENED TO YOU, DAD? WHY ARE YOU SO AFRAID?

NO...

I CAN'T...

I WARNED YOU, ROBBIE-BOY-- MESS WITH ME AGAIN, I'LL COME AFTER YOUR *FAMILY*.

YOU KEPT YOUR MOUTH SHUT FOR *20 YEARS*.

DAD?

DAD, YOU OKAY?

COULDN'T YOU *KEEP* IT SHUT FOR TWENTY MORE?

AND LET YOU... GO ON KILLING...?

HEY, WHAT'S A FEW *MURDERS* BETWEEN OLD FRIENDS?

WE... WERE... NEVER... FRIENDS...

DAD?

I WAS... AFRAID OF YOU...

...HATED YOU...

YOU SHOULD'VE STAYED IN BED, ROBBIE-BOY.

...HATED *MYSELF*...

...BUT NO MORE...

...NO MORE...

MR. ROBERTSON!

DAD!

ARE YOU ALL RIGHT?

BETTER THAN I'VE BEEN IN WEEKS.

CALL JONAH JAMESON AT THE *DAILY BUGLE*, RANDY.

TELL HIM HIS EDITOR IN CHIEF HAS A *STORY* FOR PAGE ONE.

LANSING, MICHIGAN.

A SUBURBAN HUB COMMUNITY IN THE IDUSTRIAL MIDWEST.

BAXTER HIGH SCHOOL.

THE OTHER TEACHERS LEFT *HOURS* AGO, BUT SHE STAYED ON TO GRADE TESTS FOR HER SOPHOMORE HISTORY CLASS.

SHE LIKES WORKING LATE.

SHE LIKES BEING *USEFUL*.

BEING USEFUL, BELONGING TO A COMMUNITY:

THESE THINGS ARE AN IMPORTANT PART OF HER LIFE.

THEY HELP HER *FORGET* THE PAST.

A FEW YEARS AGO, FORGETTING THE PAST SEEMED LIKE A *FULL-TIME* OCCUPATION.

BUT THOSE *BAD TIMES* ARE OVER NOW.

THESE DAYS, SHE'S *HAPPY*.

131

TOO BAD.

THE BAD TIMES ARE *BACK*.

BZZAMM

EEEE!

IDIOT, YOU ALMOST HIT HER!

THE HIGH EVOLUTIONARY WANTS HER *INTACT*--

--NOT SCATTERED OVER A HIGH SCHOOL *PARKING LOT!*

TIME *SKIPS*.

OLD THOUGHTS AND FEELINGS RETURN.

FEELINGS OF TERROR, CONSTANT *TERROR*.

BMM

AND THOUGHTS OF *PETER*...

PETER CAN HELP HER.

OH, GOOD, WE *LOST* HER.

ACTIVATE THE *GENE TRACER*.

WE FOUND HER ONCE, WE'LL FIND HER AGAIN.

AND NO WAY WE'LL LOSE HER *TWICE*.

PETER WILL SAVE HER.

PETER.

ATLANTA.

GREAT. FORTY MINUTES, AND STILL NO *TOMBSTONE.*

SO WHY DO I FEEL UNEASY?

DID I SCARE HIM OFF?

AFTER ALL, HE EXPECTED PETER PARKER, NOT *SPIDER-MAN.*

NAH. CREEPS LIKE TOMBSTONE DON'T SPOOK. HE'D *LOVE* A CHANCE TO--

THE ELEVATOR! IT'S COMING UP!

CLINK... WARRP

TOMBSTONE MUST BE--

--SPIDER-SENSE TINGLING--

--MOVE!

UH-OH! DROPPED THE TAPE!

CHONK

SWOOSH

DON'T WORRY, I'LL GET IT.

TOMBSTONE!

BELIEVE IT, OR NOT, WEB-SLINGER, YOU'RE A DREAM COME *TRUE.*

HEY--

ATLANTA

133

THANKS FOR COMING, JONAH. YOU, TOO, KATE... AND BEN.

THIS ISN'T EASY. I FEEL AS IF I'VE *BETRAYED* YOU ALL...

NONSENSE. YOU'RE THE BEST BLASTED EDITOR IN THE BUSINESS, AND THE MOST *DECENT* MAN I KNOW.

WHATEVER YOU *THINK* YOU'VE DONE, YOU MUST HAVE HAD A GOOD REASON.

BEST REASON IN THE WORLD, JONAH.

I WAS *AFRAID*.

ATLANTA.

THIS IS GREAT, ALWAYS WANTED SOME FUN WITH A COSTUMED CREEP.

WHEN I CALLED PARKER, I WAS HOPING HE'D CALL YOU.

THWIPP

WE'RE *FALLING!* ARE YOU *CRAZY?!*

FFFT

CRAZY? ME?

YOU'RE THE ONE WEARING THE FUNNY RED-AND-BLUE UNDERWEAR.

THONK

AAAHH!

ANYWAY.

I READ PARKER'S BOOK.

THE WAY HE CAN GET YOUR PHOTO ALL THE TIME--

CAN'T BREATHE. BUT I'VE GOTTA GET UP--

-- I FIGURED YOU HAD TO BE FRIENDS.

BWHOOM

≷UNGH≷

SO I THOUGHT, IF PARKER GETS IN TROUBLE, WHO'S HE GOING TO CALL?

YOU, THAT'S WHO.

THRAK

≷UHHH≷

TWENTY YEARS AGO, I LET TOMBSTONE BULLY ME INTO *SPIKING* AN ARTICLE FOR MY HIGH SCHOOL NEWSPAPER.

WHY? ONE REASON.

I WAS AFRAID.

"A FEW YEARS LATER, IN PHILADELPHIA," ROBBIE CONTINUES, "I WITNESSED A MURDER--TOMBSTONE'S FIRST *MOB HIT.*

"I KEPT *QUIET.*

"I WAS AFRAID.

"FOR YEARS I WATCHED AS TOMBSTONE'S REPUTATION GREW IN OTHER CITIES, WHILE OTHER PEOPLE *DIED*."

CHUNK

"I COULD HAVE STOPPED IT."

"I COULD HAVE COME FORWARD TO *TELL* WHAT I'D SEEN."

KRAK

"BUT I DIDN'T."

"I WAS *AFRAID*."

THAM

THEN THOMPSON CAME TO NEW YORK AND SOMETHING *SNAPPED*. I MADE A TAPE FOR PETER PARKER, TOLD EVERYTHING--

--AND CONFRONTED TOMBSTONE ALONE-- LIKE AN IDIOT-- WITH A *GUN*.

"FOR SOME REASON, HE DIDN'T KILL ME."

"INSTEAD, HE ALMOST BROKE MY BACK, AND THREATENED MY *FAMILY*."

"I TOLD PARKER TO DESTROY THE TAPE.

TOOM

"AND FOR THE LAST FEW WEEKS, I'VE LAIN HERE LIKE A *DEAD* MAN.

" *TOO FRIGHTENED* TO MOVE.

"YESTERDAY MORNING, TOMBSTONE TERRORIZED PETER'S WIFE, *MARY JANE*, LOOKING FOR MY TAPE.

" THAT'S WHEN I FINALLY UNDERSTOOD...

"...THE PRICE OF COWARDICE IS JUST *TOO* HIGH.

" BECAUSE IT'S A PRICE THE *COWARD*, HIMSELF, NEVER HAS TO PAY. "

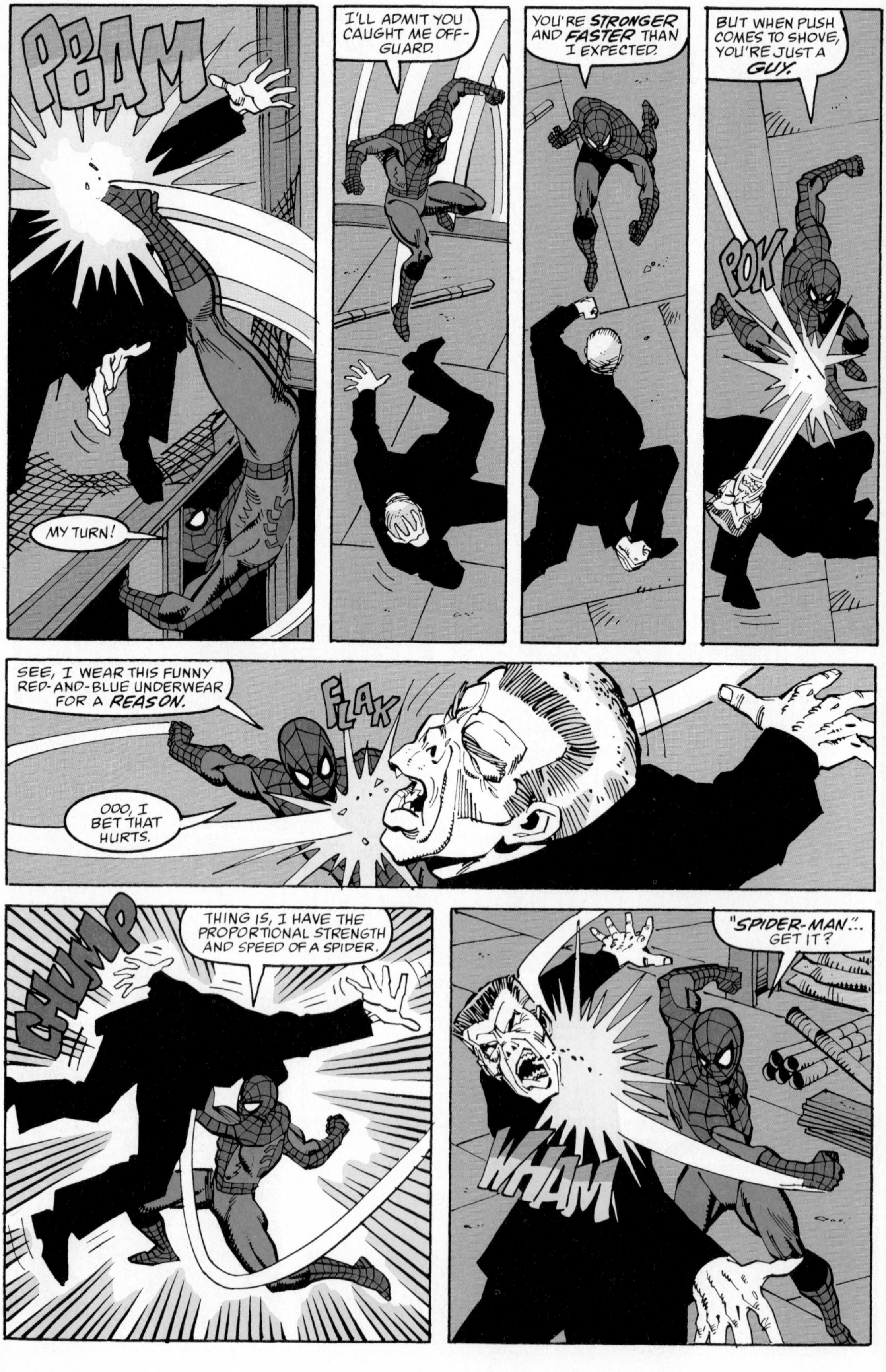
PBAM
MY TURN!
I'LL ADMIT YOU CAUGHT ME OFF-GUARD.
YOU'RE STRONGER AND FASTER THAN I EXPECTED.
BUT WHEN PUSH COMES TO SHOVE, YOU'RE JUST A GUY.
POK
SEE, I WEAR THIS FUNNY RED-AND-BLUE UNDERWEAR FOR A REASON.
FLAK
OOO, I BET THAT HURTS.
CHUMP
THING IS, I HAVE THE PROPORTIONAL STRENGTH AND SPEED OF A SPIDER.
"SPIDER-MAN"... GET IT?
WHAM

AND STRONG AS YOU ARE, FAST AS YOU ARE--

--I'LL *ALWAYS* BE STRONGER AND FASTER!

SEE WHAT I MEAN?

BLONG

I...DON'T... BELIEVE... THIS...

YEAH, WELL, LIFE CAN BE PRETTY UNBELIEVABLE SOMETIMES.

ONE QUESTION BEFORE WE PUT THIS TO BED: WHY DIDN'T YOU *KILL* ROBBIE ROBERTSON WHEN YOU HAD THE CHANCE?

HOW COULD I... KILL HIM?

ROBBIE'S MY FRIEND...

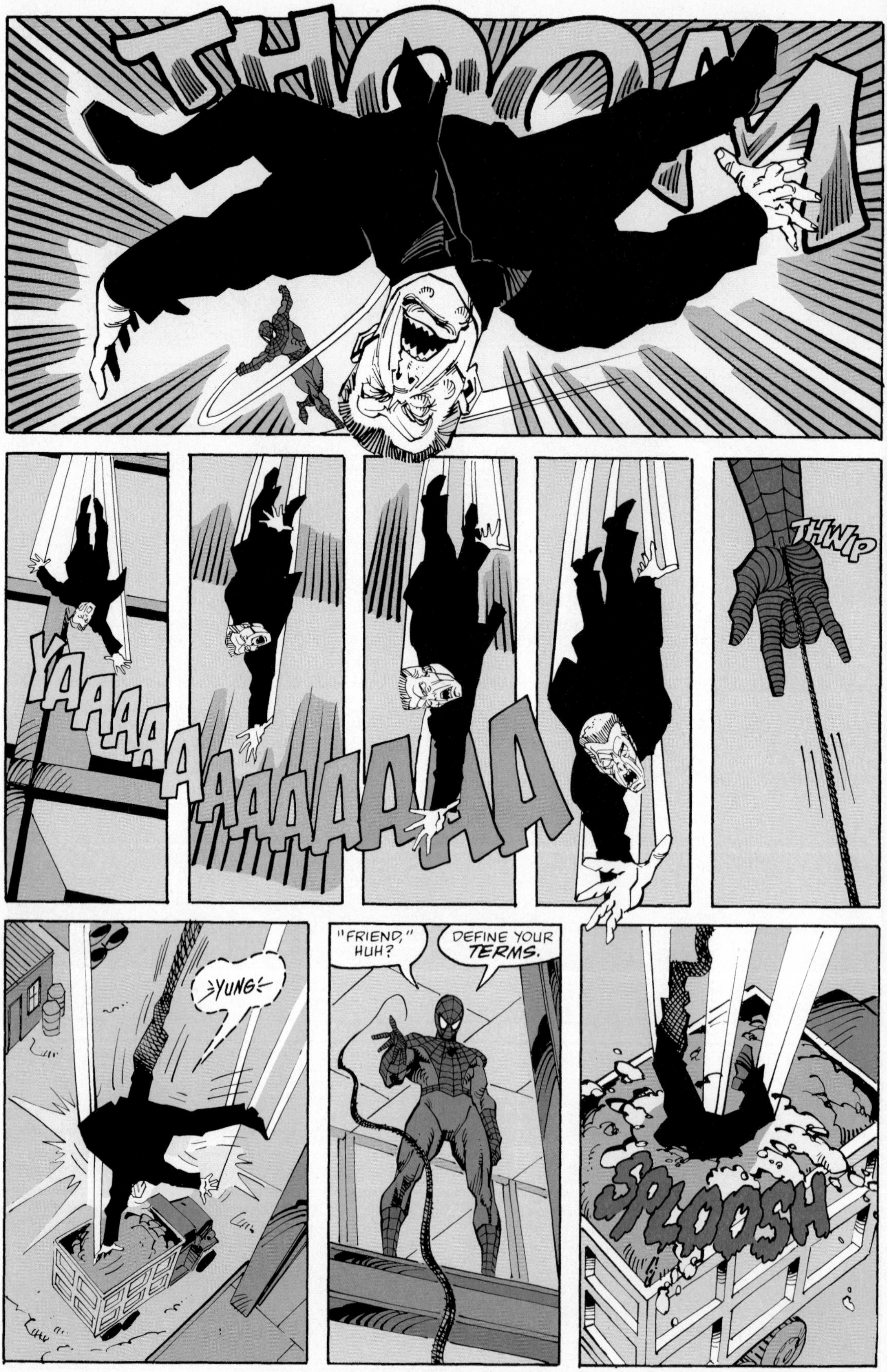
THOOM
YAAAAAAAAAAAAAAAA
THWIP
YUNG
"FRIEND," HUH?
DEFINE YOUR TERMS.
SPLOOSH

THE SICK THING IS, TOMBSTONE PROBABLY **DOES** THINK OF ROBBIE AS A FRIEND.

ROBBIE MIGHT BE THE ONLY "FRIEND" HE EVER HAD.

I DON'T KNOW WHETHER TO LAUGH OR **SCREAM**.

CHEER UP, TOMBS.

A BIG, GOOD-LOOKING GUY LIKE YOU--

--YOU'LL MAKE **LOTS** OF NEW PALS IN **PRISON**.

YEAH, MAYBE. ROBBIE ROBERTSON IS THE ONLY REAL **WITNESS** TO TOMBSTONE'S CRIMES.

IF ROBBIE WON'T TALK, TOMBSTONE GOES **FREE**.

SO WHAT'S IT GOING TO BE, ROBBIE?

IT'S UP TO **YOU**...

...BEFORE YOU ARRIVED, I ASKED MARTHA TO CALL THE **JUSTICE DEPARTMENT**.

I'LL GIVE THEM MY DEPOSITION AGAINST TOMBSTONE.

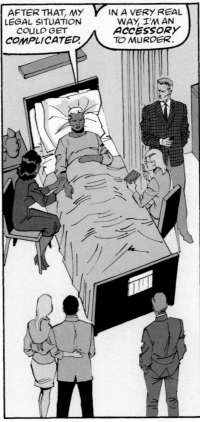

AFTER THAT, MY LEGAL SITUATION COULD GET **COMPLICATED**.

IN A VERY REAL WAY, I'M AN **ACCESSORY** TO MURDER.

NATURALLY, UNDER THE CIRCUMSTANCES, I'LL **RESIGN** AS THE BUGLE'S EDITOR IN CHIEF.

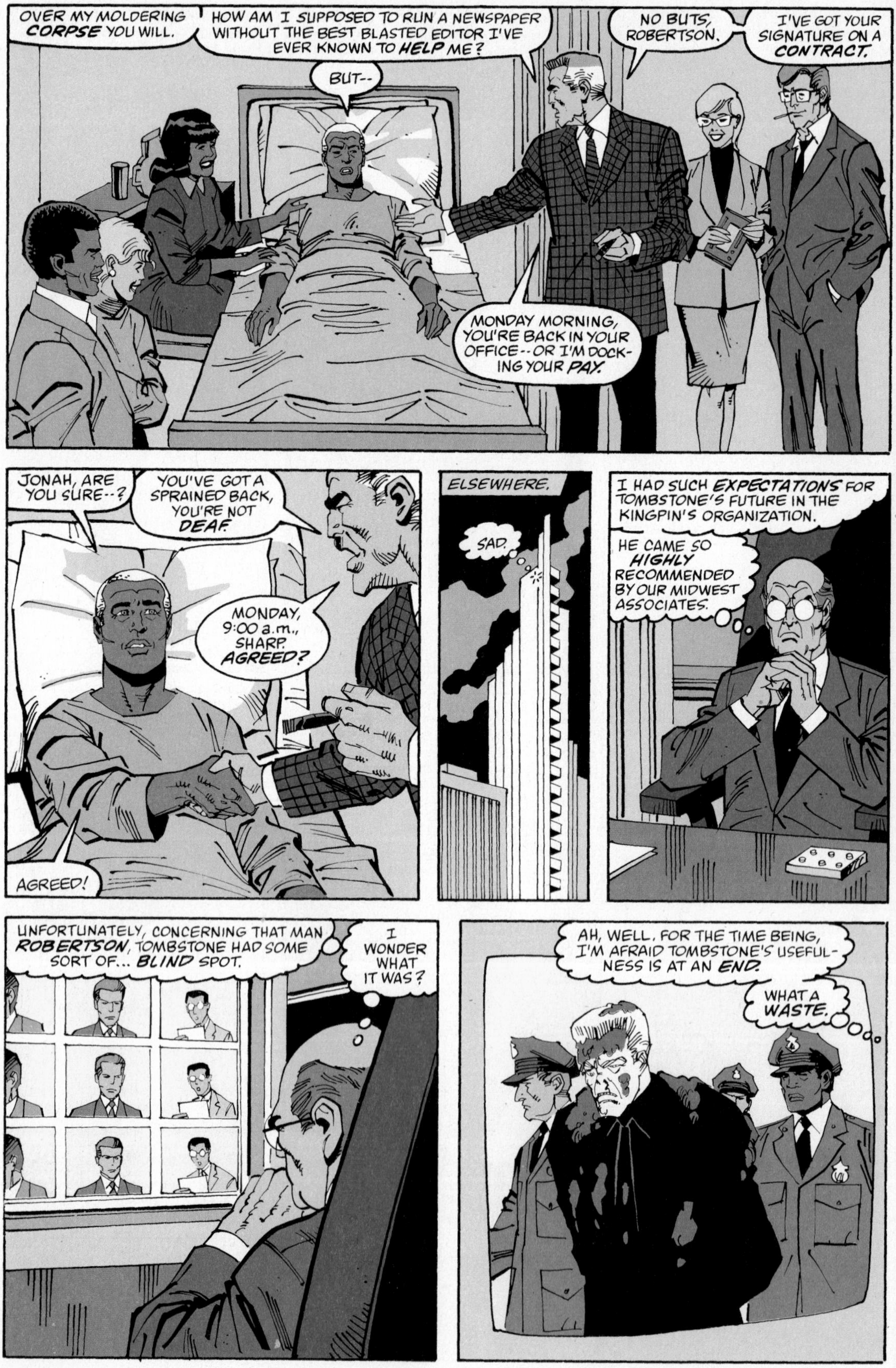

OVER MY MOLDERING CORPSE YOU WILL.
HOW AM I SUPPOSED TO RUN A NEWSPAPER WITHOUT THE BEST BLASTED EDITOR I'VE EVER KNOWN TO HELP ME?
BUT--
NO BUTS, ROBERTSON.
I'VE GOT YOUR SIGNATURE ON A CONTRACT.
MONDAY MORNING, YOU'RE BACK IN YOUR OFFICE--OR I'M DOCKING YOUR PAY.
JONAH, ARE YOU SURE--?
YOU'VE GOT A SPRAINED BACK, YOU'RE NOT DEAF.
MONDAY, 9:00 a.m., SHARP. AGREED?
AGREED!
ELSEWHERE.
SAD.
I HAD SUCH EXPECTATIONS FOR TOMBSTONE'S FUTURE IN THE KINGPIN'S ORGANIZATION.
HE CAME SO HIGHLY RECOMMENDED BY OUR MIDWEST ASSOCIATES.
UNFORTUNATELY, CONCERNING THAT MAN ROBERTSON, TOMBSTONE HAD SOME SORT OF... BLIND SPOT.
I WONDER WHAT IT WAS?
AH, WELL. FOR THE TIME BEING, I'M AFRAID TOMBSTONE'S USEFULNESS IS AT AN END.
WHAT A WASTE.

TOMBSTONE CAME TO NEW YORK AT OUR REQUEST, TO DRAW OUT THE *PUNISHER.*

AT LEAST THAT MUCH OF HIS WORK FOR US WAS *SUCCESSFUL.*

≥SIGH!≤ HOW VERY, VERY *SAD.*

BZZZZT

WELL, NOW. ALL DRESSED AND SHOWERED, FED AND RESTED. COME IN, COME IN.

ARE YOU READY TO ASSUME YOUR NEW *DUTIES?*

AFFIRMATIVE.

JUST POINT ME WHERE YOU WANT ME TO GO.

JUST TELL ME WHO YOU WANT ME TO *KILL.*

*T*O BE CONTINUED...

NEXT ISSUE: DEADLINE IN DALLAS!

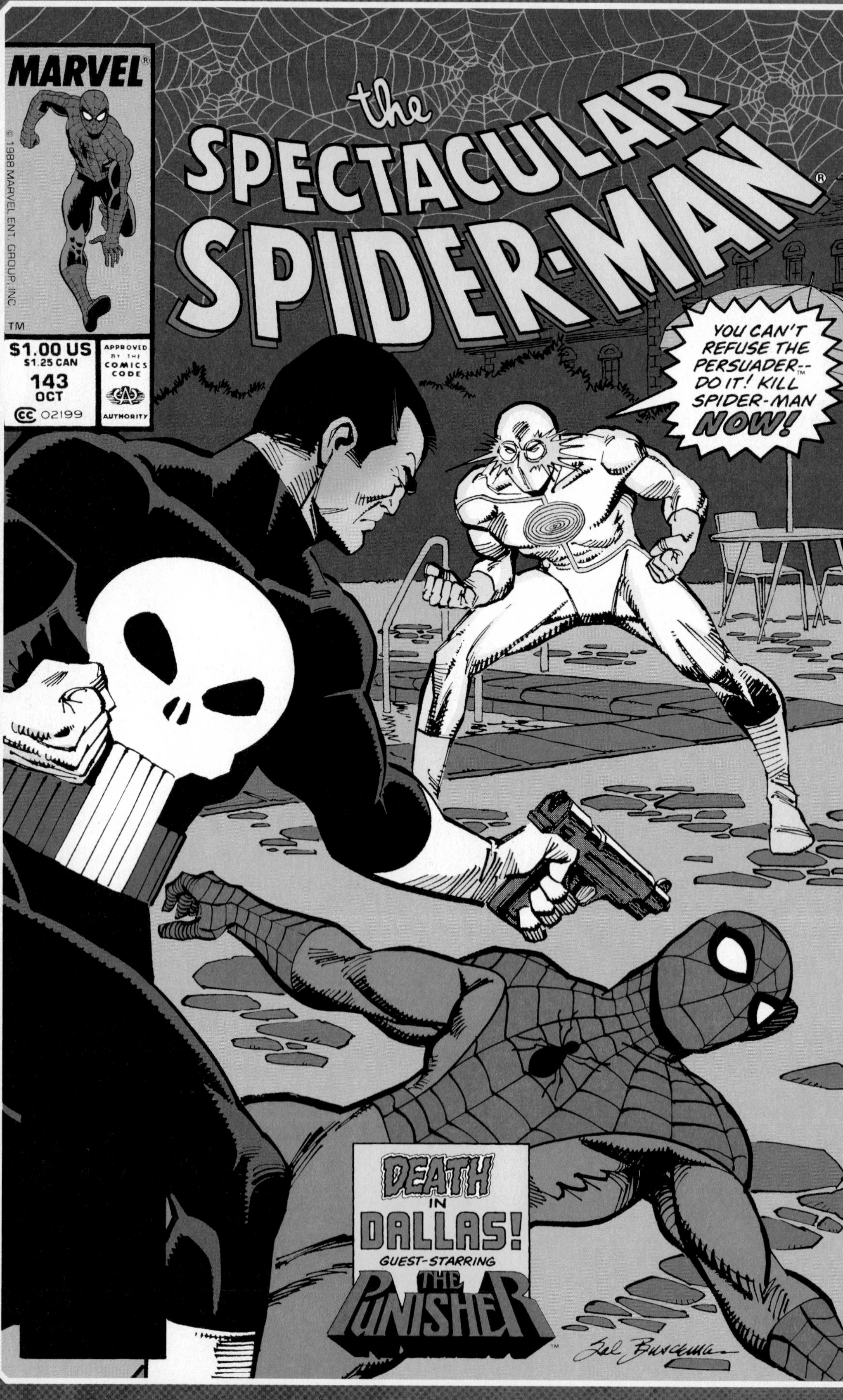
MARVEL
© 1988 MARVEL ENT. GROUP, INC
TM
$1.00 US
$1.25 CAN
143
OCT
CC 02199
APPROVED BY THE COMICS CODE AUTHORITY
the SPECTACULAR SPIDER-MAN
YOU CAN'T REFUSE THE PERSUADER-- DO IT! KILL SPIDER-MAN NOW!
DEATH IN DALLAS!
GUEST-STARRING
THE PUNISHER
Sal Buscema

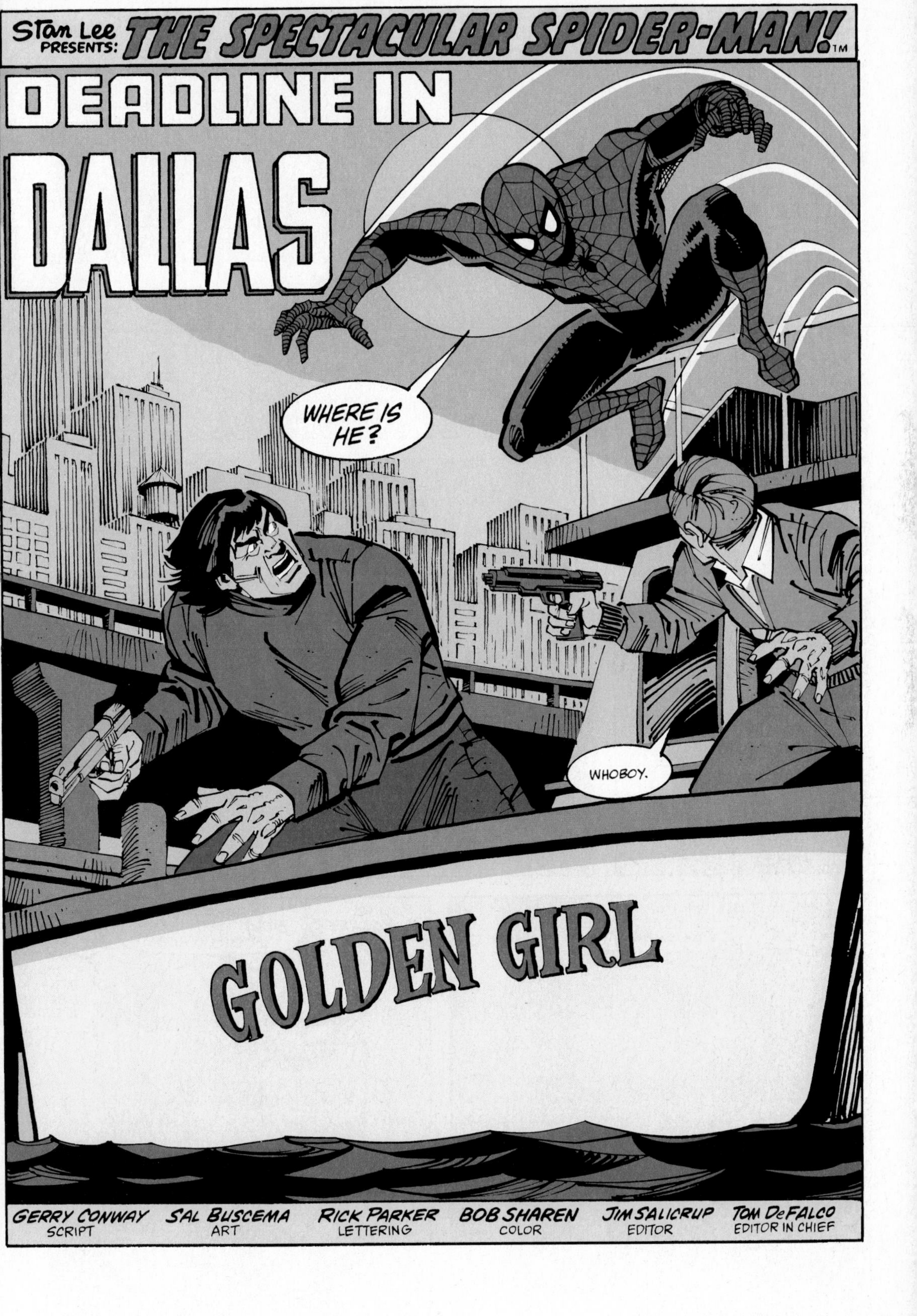
Stan Lee PRESENTS: THE SPECTACULAR SPIDER-MAN! TM
DEADLINE IN DALLAS
WHERE IS HE?
WHOBOY.
GOLDEN GIRL
GERRY CONWAY SCRIPT
SAL BUSCEMA ART
RICK PARKER LETTERING
BOB SHAREN COLOR
JIM SALICRUP EDITOR
TOM DeFALCO EDITOR IN CHIEF

LATER, CHARLIE!

I'M OUTTA HERE!

I'VE CHECKED HIS BOAT OFF AND ON FOR A *WEEK.*

THUMP

AND FOR A WEEK IT'S BEEN AS *EMPTY* AS A POLITICIAN'S PROMISE.

UNTIL *TONIGHT.*

FFFT

TONIGHT I FIND TWO CLOWNS SNEAKING ABOARD WITH GUNS.

SHUK

UNG

SO I ASK MYSELF, WHO *ARE* THESE GUYS?

WHAT DO THEY KNOW ABOUT *THE PUNISHER?*

WHERE IS HE? WHAT *HAPPENED* TO HIM? WHY DID HE *DISAPPEAR?*

ʒNGGʒ

GIMME A BREAK.

ME 'N CHARLIE WERE JUS' LOOKIN' FOR AN EASY RIP... SWEAR.

YOU'RE *BURGLARS?*

DO YOU KNOW WHOSE *BOAT* YOU WERE TRYING TO ROB?

NAWH. JUS' A BOA', UNHG. I THINK I BROKE A TOOF.

PAL, IF THE GUY WHO OWNS THE "GOLDEN GIRL" WERE HERE, YOU WOULD'VE LOST MORE THAN A *TOOTH*.

YOU BOZOS ARE JUST DUMB ENOUGH TO BE *REAL*.

HANG TIGHT TILL THE COPS ARRIVE, OKAY?

BACK TO SQUARE ONE,

WHERE IS HE?

THE PUNISHER DISAPPEARED THE DAY BEFORE I LEFT FOR *ATLANTA*.

AND IT DOESN'T MAKE SENSE. WE WERE WORKING *TOGETHER* TO NAIL *TOMBSTONE*.

"I DON'T KNOW HIM THAT WELL, BUT I CAN'T BELIEVE THE *PUNISHER* WOULD JUST TAKE OFF WITHOUT A WORD."

"SOMETHING HAPPENED, BUT *WHAT?*"

"WHERE IS HE?"

DALLAS/FORT WORTH INTERNATIONAL AIRPORT.

FOURTH BUSIEST AIRPORT IN THE WORLD.

MEL ZIMMERMAN HAS BEEN A SECURITY GUARD AT DALLAS/FT. WORTH FOR *13* YEARS.

FOR MEL, THE JOB LOST ITS RATHER LIMITED *GLAMOUR* LONG AGO.

TO STAY INTERESTED, MEL BECAME A *PEOPLE WATCHER*. HE'S GOOD AT FACES.

THIS ONE TIME, HE'S ALMOST *TOO* GOOD.

WAIT UP. YOU'RE *THE PUNISHER,* I SAW YOU ON AN F.B.I. CIRCULAR MONTHS AGO.

DON'T MAKE A--

HUH? I DON'T *BELIEVE* IT!

YOU DON'T WANT THIS MAN. HE'S NO ONE IMPORTANT.

WHAT DO YOU MEAN, HE'S NO--

OH, YEAH. SILLY ME. HE'S NO ONE IMPORTANT.

WHAT A GREAT LEAD-OFF FOR THE SIX O'CLOCK NEWS-- THE *PUNISHER* IN *DALLAS!* IT MIGHT EVEN GO *NETWORK!*

WONDER WHY THAT GUARD LET HIM GO?

EXIT

WHO CARES? THIS SURE BEATS A *VACATION* IN MAZATLAN...

JUST RELAX AND KEEP WALKING.

WE'RE HERE ON BUSINESS FOR THE *KINGPIN,* REMEMBER?

WHATEVER YOU SAY.

THE DALLAS TIMES HERALD

LOBO BROTHERS FREED IN MISTRIAL

JUST TELL ME WHO YOU WANT ME TO KILL.

NEW YORK, THE KINGPIN'S MIDTOWN HEADQUARTERS.

IT'S ALL **ARRANGED**, MR. FISK.

A FEW WEEKS AGO, WE HIRED THE MIDWESTERN HIT-MAN, *TOMBSTONE*, TO CAPTURE A YOUNG WALL STREET BROKER NAMED *ROLAND RAYMOND.*

RAYMOND IS A **MUTANT** WITH CERTAIN PSYCHIC POWERS OF **PERSUASION.**

BEFORE HE WAS CAPTURED BY SPIDER-MAN IN ATLANTA, TOMBSTONE'S PRESENCE IN NEW YORK LURED *THE PUNISHER* INTO AN AMBUSH. WITH SOME DIFFICILITY, RAYMOND **PERSUADED** THE PUNISHER TO JOIN OUR CAUSE.

THEY'RE NOW IN *DALLAS*, WHERE THE *PUNISHER* WILL ASSASSINATE THE *LOBO BROTHERS*, WHO--

SHUT UP!

YOU HAVE A PATHETIC FASCINATION WITH **DETAIL**, ARRANGER.

I GAVE YOU COMMAND OF OUR SYNDICATE'S DAY-TO-DAY OPERATIONS BECAUSE SUCH MATTERS NO LONGER **INTEREST** ME.

DO WHAT YOU WISH WITH THE LOBO BROTHERS.

MY CONCERNS LIE WITH **DAREDEVIL.**

ENGINEERING HIS EVENTUAL **DESTRUCTION** IS MY ONE SOURCE OF SATISFACTION IN AN OTHER-WISE DISPIRITING EXISTENCE.

INDEED. SOME DAY YOU MIGHT COME TO **REGRET** YOUR PREOCCUPATION WITH THAT MAN, KINGPIN.

IF THE PUNISHER FAILS TO KILL THE LOBO BROTHERS, PERHAPS SOMEDAY **SOON.**

INTERLUDE: A BUS STATION ON THE OUTSKIRTS OF **COLUMBUS,** OHIO.

IT'S TAKEN HER A **WEEK** TO GET THIS FAR.

BY MORNING SHE'LL BE IN **NEW YORK.**

SHE'LL FIND **PETER** IN NEW YORK.

PETER WILL **HELP** HER.

PETER ALWAYS HELPED HER **BEFORE.**

NICE SHOOTING, DAVE.

SURE OUR **TARGET** IS ABOARD THAT BUS?

PROBABILITY 60%, STEVE. CHECK THE **GENE TRACER** YOURSELF IF YOU DON'T BELIEVE ME.

OH, I BELIEVE YOU, ALL RIGHT.

I'M JUST WORRIED WHAT H.E. WILL DO IF **WE** LOSE HER THE WAY THE **LAST** GATHERER TEAM DID.*

*SEE LAST ISSUE. -- JIM.

I GOT A LOOK AT THOSE GUYS BEFORE WE LEFT HQ.

DEVOLUTION ISN'T **PRETTY.**

SO, WHERE **IS** SHE, DAVE?

UH... I DON'T KNOW, STEVE.

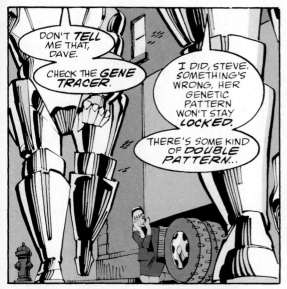

DON'T *TELL* ME THAT, DAVE.

CHECK THE *GENE TRACER.*

I DID, STEVE, SOMETHING'S WRONG. HER GENETIC PATTERN WON'T STAY *LOCKED.*

THERE'S SOME KIND OF *DOUBLE PATTERN...*

GREAT. ALL THIS TECHNOLOGY, AND WE CAN'T LOCATE ONE SCARED *FEMALE.*

NICE KNOWING YOU, DAVE.

F-ZOOM

LAST WEEK AT THE SCHOOL WHERE SHE TAUGHT, TWO OTHER MEN TRIED TO *KIDNAP* HER.

NOW THIS.

SHE DOESN'T KNOW WHAT'S HAPPENING OR WHY, BUT *PETER* WILL HAVE THE ANSWER.

WHEN THEY WERE LOVERS, PETER ALWAYS HAD THE ANSWERS.

END OF INTERLUDE

NEW YORK.

THIS IS NOT GOOD. I NEED A REST.

BETWEEN THE *PUNISHER'S* DISAPPEARANCE--

MIKE's Place

--MY TRIPS AROUND THE COUNTRY PROMOTING "*WEBS*"--

REAR ENTRANCE

--AND MARY JANE'S KIDNAPING BY THAT CREEP, JOHNNY CAESAR, A FEW DAYS AGO *--

--MY LIFE IS SO *COMPLICATED.* I NEED A MAP TO FIND THE BATHROOM WHEN I WAKE UP IN THE MORNING.

* SEE *AMAZING #s 308* & *309.* --JIM.

TO TOP IT OFF, I WAS SUPPOSED TO MEET MARY JANE FOR *DINNER* HERE THIRTY MINUTES AGO.

"SHE'LL PROBABLY *KICK* ME FOR BEING LATE. MJ HATES WAITING IN BARS *ALONE*..."

-- SO WE CLEAR 300 K COMMISSION ON THE *BROKERAGE* FEE ALONE.

NOT A BAD AFTERNOON BUT I'VE HAD BETTER.

BUY YOU A DRINK?

WASTING YOUR TIME, HANDSOME.

MY PORTFOLIO IS ALREADY *FULLY* STOCKED.

RIGHT, TIGER?

RIIIIIGHT.

SORRY I'M LATE. THOSE GUYS BOTHER YOU?

YOU KIDDING? I DIDN'T EVEN WORK UP A SWEAT.

BESIDES, EVEN A MARRIED LADY LIKES TO KNOW MEN STILL FIND HER *ATTRACTIVE.*

HEY, BEN. HOW 'BOUT A *PERRIER* FOR MY MAN, PETEY?

GOTCHA, MS. P.

SO TELL ME, TIGER, WHY THE GLOOM AND DOOM?

TIRED, THAT'S ALL.

COLLEGE STARTS IN A FEW WEEKS AND WITH EVERYTHING THAT'S HAPPENED THIS SUMMER, I HAVEN'T HAD TIME TO *PREPARE.*

THE WAY I FEEL, I COULD SPEND THE NEXT MONTH IN *BED*...

MM. SOUNDS LIKE A PLAN.

LET'S FORGET DINNER, GRAB SUSHI ON THE WAY HOME, SNUGGLE UP, AND--

--IDENTIFIED AS THE NOTORIOUS VIGILANTE KNOWN AS "THE PUNISHER."

DESPITE AN EYEWITNESS IDENTIFICATION BY THIS REPORTER, POLICE REFUSE TO CONFIRM THE PUNISHER'S PRESENCE IN THE DALLAS AREA.

RUMORS CONNECTING THE PUNISHER TO THE NOTORIOUS LOBO BROTHERS CONTINUE TO SPREAD AT THIS HOUR...

DALLAS

PETER, WHAT'S WRONG--?

THAT'S WHAT I'D LIKE TO KNOW, M.J.

I'VE GOT TO CATCH A PLANE TO DALLAS.

WHAT?

WHY--?

THERE'S A MAN I HAVE TO SEE, I'VE A FEELING HE'S IN TROUBLE.

SORRY, HONEY, I'LL CALL YOU FROM THE AIRPORT.

SOOOO...LOOKS LIKE WE'LL BE EATING ALONE, AFTER ALL.

YESSSS... WON'T YOU?

:GNG.:

I'M NOT ANGRY. I'M NOT MAD. PETER WARNED ME THERE WOULD BE NIGHTS LIKE THIS.

I'M FINE.

AND I'M NOT ANGRY.

MUCH.

DALLAS. DUSK.

THE HERDLING REFINERY COMPANY.

GIMME A BREAK, OKAY? I SWEAR I NEVER HURT *NOBODY*, OKAY? LEMME GO, OKAY?

YOU MAKE ME SICK.

YOU ADMIT THIS REFINERY IS A FRONT FOR A SOPHISTICATED *DRUG SMUGGLING* OPERATION?

YEAH, YEAH, I ADMIT IT, OKAY?

THE LOBOS SHIPPED THE STUFF NORTH IN TANKERS, OKAY?

LEMME GO, WHADDA-YASAY, OKAY?

DRUGS KILL CHILDREN, RUIN LIVES, DESTROY WHOLE COMMUNITIES. YOU SAY YOU *KNEW* THIS--

--AND YOU WANT *MERCY*?

IT WAS JUST A *JOB*, OKAY?

NOT OKAY.

THE LOBO BROTHERS NEED TO LEARN A *LESSON*.

YOU'RE IT.

STOP KIDDIN' AROUND, OKAY? *OKAY?*

THIS IS THE *EASY* PART--PERSUADING THE *PUNISHER* TO WRECK AN ILLEGAL DRUG OPERATION.

RELAX, *PERSUADER*, YOU DO GOOD WORK.

THE *ARRANGER* ONLY SENT ME ALONG AS *BACK-UP*... IN CASE OUR BOY GETS *ANTSY*.

OR IN CASE *I* LOSE MY NERVE. BUT I WON'T. I'M BEGINNING TO *ENJOY* THIS KIND OF POWER...

YO, PUNISHER! LET'S BLOW THIS JOINT.

AS SOON AS I--

EH?

TAKATAKA

BRRP

BRRP

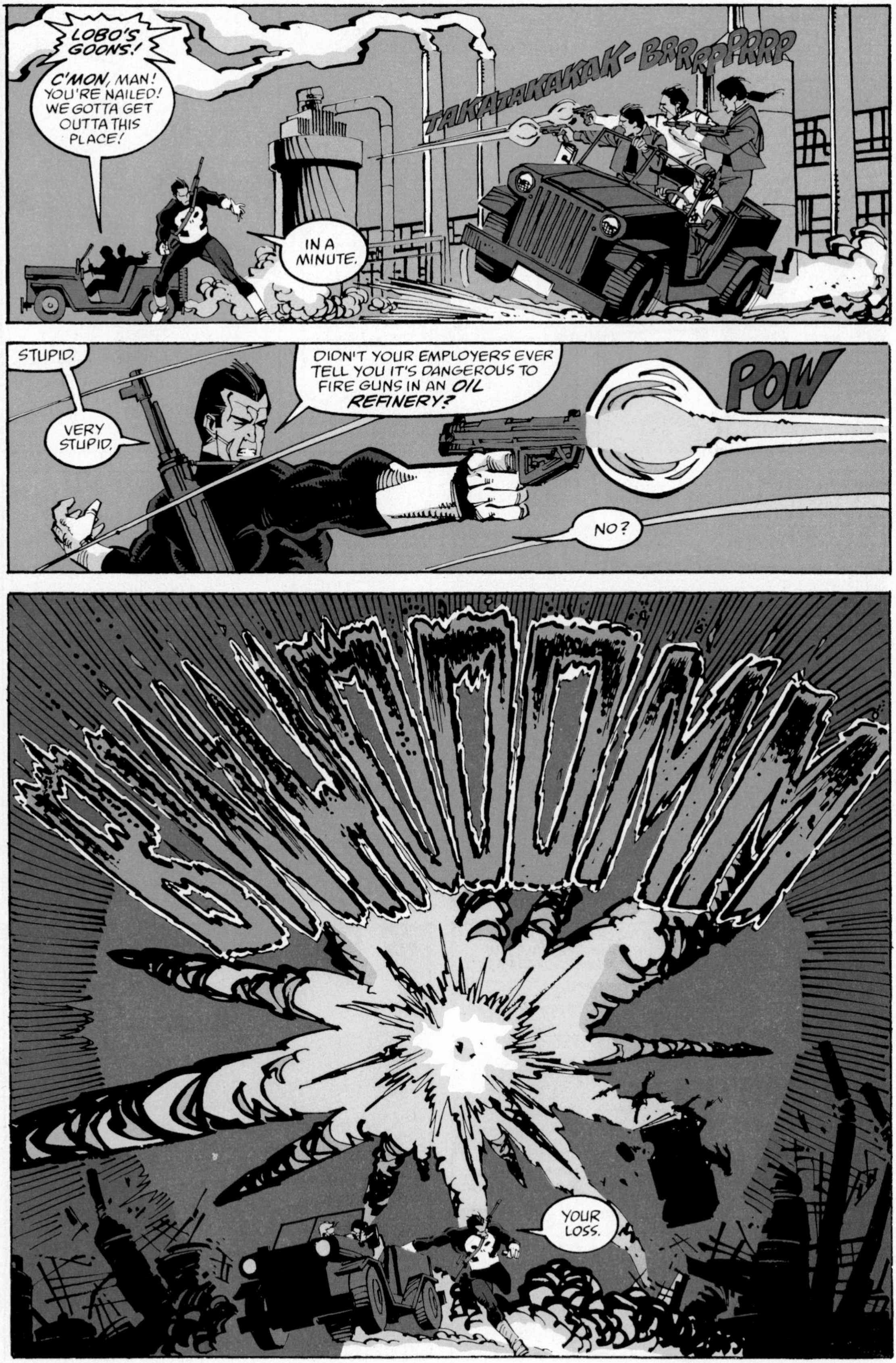

LOBO'S GOONS!
C'MON, MAN! YOU'RE NAILED! WE GOTTA GET OUTTA THIS PLACE!
TAKATAKAKAKAK-BRRRPPRRP
IN A MINUTE.
STUPID.
VERY STUPID.
DIDN'T YOUR EMPLOYERS EVER TELL YOU IT'S DANGEROUS TO FIRE GUNS IN AN OIL REFINERY?
POW
NO?
YOUR LOSS.

ⓒNCE AGAIN, DALLAS/FT. WORTH INTERNATIONAL.

MORNING.

...GINNY IS GOING TO BE *CRUSHED* THAT SHE *MISSED* YOU, MR. PARKER.

CALL ME *PETER.*

IT'S JUST WE DIDN'T *EXPECT* YOU TO *ATTEND* SOMETHING LIKE THIS *CONVENTION,* SINCE IT ISN'T *PART* OF THE REGULARLY-SCHEDULED *PUBLICATION TOUR...*

...AND ON SUCH SHORT *NOTICE.*

GUESS I JUST GOT A HANKERING TO VISIT *DALLAS,* ANDREA.

HOW IS *"WEBS"* SELLING DOWN HERE?

NOT THAT *WELL,* I'M *AFRAID.* IT'S *REALLY* A BOOK WITH MORE *REGIONAL* INTEREST, WOULDN'T YOU *SAY?*

VERY *URBAN* VERY *"NEW YORK."*

DO YOU LIKE TEXAS, MR. PARKER?

WELL... IT'S BIG.

AND IT'S GOING TO BE A LOT HARDER TO FIND THE *PUNISHER* THAN I THOUGHT.

OR MAYBE *NOT.*

YOU KNOW, ANDREA, BACK IN NEW YORK MY SPECIALTY IS *CRIME PHOTOGRAPHY.*

TELL ME ABOUT THE *LOBO BROTHERS.*

OH, *DEAR.*

DALLAS NEWS

PUNISHER AND LOBOS CONNECTED TO OIL REFINERY DISASTER!!

THOSE MEN... THOSE VICIOUS, VICIOUS MEN...

"EDUARDO AND CARLOS LOBO. I DON'T THINK *ANYONE* KNOWS *QUITE* WHERE THEY *CAME* FROM...

"... BUT THE *FIRST* PLACE THEY BECAME *KNOWN* WAS IN *SOUTH TEXAS*, A YEAR AND A *HALF* AGO.

" I REMEMBER *READING* IN THE *NEWSPAPER* -- THERE WAS A *GANG WAR*, SOMETHING TO DO WITH *DRUGS* AND *SMUGGLING*.

" I DON'T KNOW THE *DETAILS* --

"-- BUT A *LOT* OF *PEOPLE* WERE BEING *KILLED*.

" THEN THE *LOBOS* CAME.

"SOMEHOW THEY *STOPPED* THE FIGHTING.

"THE *GANGS* MADE A *PACT*, A KIND OF *PEACE TREATY*.

" *ALL* THE GANGS JOINED *TOGETHER*, CALLING THEMSELVES *'LOS HERMANOS DE LA LUNA'* -- SOMETHING LIKE THAT.

" BUT WHEN IT WAS *OVER*, THE *OTHER* GANG LEADERS WERE *GONE*...

"...AND THE *LOBOS* RULED *SOUTH TEXAS*.

SIX *MONTHS* AGO THEY *MOVED* TO A *MANSION* ON *GRAPEVINE LAKE* OUTSIDE *DALLAS*.

THE POLICE *SAY* THEY'RE *CRIMINALS* BUT THERE'S *NEVER* ANY *PROOF*

UH-HUH. JUST THE SORT OF *UNTOUCHABLE* SCUM THE PUNISHER *THRIVES* ON TAKING DOWN.

SO WHY DO I STILL HAVE A SICK FEELING HE'S IN *SERIOUS* TROUBLE..?

UNFORTUNATELY, FOR THE NEXT FEW HOURS, SIGNING AUTO-GRAPHS AT A LOCAL DALLAS BOOKSTORE, PETER HAS NO CHOICE BUT TO *IGNORE* THAT SICK FEELING...

WOW! NOT ONLY DOES THIS PLACE HAVE A NEAT SUPER HERO *COSTUME CONTEST,* BUT THE GUY WHO TOOK ALL THOSE PI'TURES OF *SPIDER-MAN!*

-- ACTUALLY, FROM A *PHOTOGRAPHER'S* POINT OF VIEW--

--THE NEW OLD COSTUME IS A LOT *EASIER* TO CAPTURE ON FILM THAN THE OLD NEW COSTUME.

I THINK IT STINKS.

G'WAY, KID, YA BOTHER ME.

WHERE DO THEY GET THESE *QUESTIONS?*

ANDREA, I NEED A BREAK. IF I SIGN ONE MORE BOOK, MY *FINGERS* WILL FALL OFF.

OH, OF *COURSE.* WILL AN *HOUR* DO?

TRY *TWO.*

WE'LL MAKE IT AN EARLY *LUNCH.*

I HOPE.

I'M *SO* SORRY-- MR. PARKER WILL BE *BACK* AFTER *ONE.*

THE MORE I THINK ABOUT THE PUNISHER DROPPING OUT OF SIGHT-- THEN SHOWING UP HERE, CONNECTED TO THE *LOBO BROTHERS--*

--THE MORE *CERTAIN* I AM THAT SOME-THING'S WAY OUT OF LINE.

I'VE GOT TO *FIND* HIM.

AND RIGHT NOW, THE ONLY PLACE I CAN THINK TO START LOOKING IS AT THE *LOBOS' MANSION* ON GRAPEVINE LAKE.

YO, DUDE, BLASTIN' THREADS!

RAD!

TOO COOL!

NOT IN *THIS* HEAT, GOLDILOCKS.

TA!

158

THIRTY-EIGHT MINUTES *LATER.*

ON THE OUTSKIRTS OF THE DALLAS COMMUNITY KNOWN AS *GRAPEVINE LAKE...*

THIS IS IT!

MY *SPIDER-SENSE* IS BUZZING LIKE A BROKEN CAR ALARM.

LOOKS LIKE I'VE FOUND THE LOBO BROTHERS' *MANSION--*

--AND JUDGING BY THE CONDITION OF THAT *GATE LOCK--*

--I'M NOT THE *FIRST.*

VOICES COMING FROM THE REAR OF THE HOUSE.

TWO OF THEM ARE LOW, *GUTTURAL--*HISPANIC ACCENTS.

ANOTHER ONE'S ROUGH *STREET-TOUGH--* NEW YORKER.

FOURTH ONE'S SMOOTH, *EDUCATED--* IVY LEAGUE NEW ENGLAND.

AND THE *FIFTH* VOICE...

I'D KNOW THAT STEEL-EDGED QUEENS ACCENT *ANYWHERE.*

FILTH.

TWO-LEGGED VERMIN LIKE YOU KILLED MY WIFE AND CHILDREN. BLOWING UP YOUR DRUG REFINERY WAS DULL DUTY, SHOOTING YOUR GUARDS WAS SIMPLE SELF-DEFENSE-- BUT WASTING YOU IS GOING TO BE A *PLEASURE.*

THEN STOP TALKING AND *DO* IT.

AND TELL YOUR *DUEÑO KINGPIN* WE SPIT ON HIM FOR SENDING OTHERS TO DO THE WORK HE IS TOO AFRAID TO DO *HIMSELF.*

KINGPIN...?

DON'T *LISTEN* TO THEM, PUNISHER.

JUST *SHOOT,* AND LET'S GET OUT OF HERE.

KINGPIN?

SEEMS LIKE EVERY TIME I TURN OVER A ROCK THESE DAYS, *HE* CRAWLS OUT.

THWIPP

SORRY, PUN, BUT MUCH AS THESE CREEPS MAY DESERVE IT--

-- I CAN'T LET YOU KILL ANYONE IN *COLD BLOOD!*

IT'S AGAINST *UNION RULES!*

WHAT..?

SPIDER-MAN! KILL HIM, PUNISHER!

CHECK YOUR "*GOOD-GUY HANDBOOK.*"

PAGE FIFTY-EIGHT, PARAGRAPH 2c.:

UNDER "WASTING SCUM, EXCEPT IN CASES OF SELF-DEFENSE--

--I QUOTE: "DON'T DO IT!"

WATCH YOUR PIECE, PUNISHER! TRYIN' TA KILL SOMEBODY?

KPOW

CARLOS! MI HERMANO, MY BROTHER-- ARE YOU HURT?

¿UHHH!¿

SUCH AS THESE CANNOT HURT US, EDUARDO!

THEY ARE PULGAS--

"--FLEAS ON THE COAT OF THE WOLF!

"LET THEM BITE EACH OTHER, EDUARDO--

"-- WHILE THE WOLVES RUN FREE!"

AND, AS THE LOBOS SLIP AWAY, UNOBSERVED...

BLAST!

ALL I ASK IS ONE CLEAR SHOT, AND THAT WALL-CRAWLER IS A DEAD BUG!

WHY BOTHER?

SPLASH

THE PUNISHER HAS HIM NOW--

"-- AND THE PUNISHER IS COMPLETELY UNDER MY CONTROL!"

"YOU SEE? PUNISHER HAS SPIDER-MAN IN A *CHOKE-HOLD!*"

"SPIDER-MAN CAN'T BRACE HIMSELF, CAN'T FIGHT FREE!"

HE'S GOING *LIMP--* PASSED OUT!

WE *WON!*

GOOD MOVE, MAN!

WAIT'LL THE *ARRANGER* HEARS THIS!

WHAT HE DOES, HE SENDS US HERE TO TOP THE *LOBOS'* FOR PLANNIN' A MOVE INTO KINGPIN TERRITORY UP NORTH--

-- AND WHAT WE DO, WE NAIL A SURPRISE BONUS: *SPIDER-MAN!*

THE LOBOS, YOU IDIOT--

HUH?

THEY'RE *GONE!*

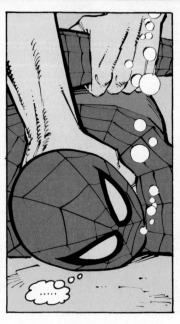

.....

SO MUCH FOR MY GREAT IDEA.

CLEVER ME, I PLAY **DEAD,** FIGURING PUN WILL LOOSEN HIS GRIP ONCE I STOP MOVING

BUT DOES HE?

NOOOOO...

YOU'VE GOT A **SUSPICIOUS MIND,** PUN, OLD PAL.

I GUESS WE DO IT THE **HARD** WAY.

≥EEUNGH!≤

OUF!

YOU'VE BEEN ACTING SO **WEIRD** I DIDN'T WANT TO **HURT** YOU, PUN.

WHUMP

≥HUNGH!≤

BUT THE WAY THINGS ARE **GOING** HERE--

--MAYBE I BETTER KNOCK YOU DOWN **NOW** AND TALK REASON **LATER.**

THE BLOW KNOCKS BOTH THE PUNISHER **AND** THE WEB-SLINGER OFF BALANCE...

TALK AROUND **THIS,** WEB-SPINNER!

BAM

...GIVING THE GUNMAN A CLEAR SHOT...

...UU...

..., AND ONLY HIS SPIDER-SENSE ENABLES SPIDER-MAN TO BARELY DODGE THE BULLET'S FATAL PASSAGE.

--

≈aahaugh≈

ANYBODY GOT AN ASPIRIN?

MY HEAD HURTS LIKE A--

OBOY.

DO IT, PUNISHER. MAKE IT QUICK.

QUIT STALLIN'. TOP 'IM.

WE GOTTA FIND THE LOBOS.

SHUT UP, ANDREW. PUNISHER, YOU KILLED BEFORE -- THOSE MEN AT THE REFINERY, THESE GUARDS, WHAT'S ONE MORE DEATH?

I WANT YOU TO KILL HIM. YOU WANT TO KILL HIM.

SO KILL HIM.

EITHER YOU DO IT OR I DO IT, PAL.

FIVE SECONDS, YOUR CHOICE.

ONE MORE DEATH...

...ONE MORE...

K-POW

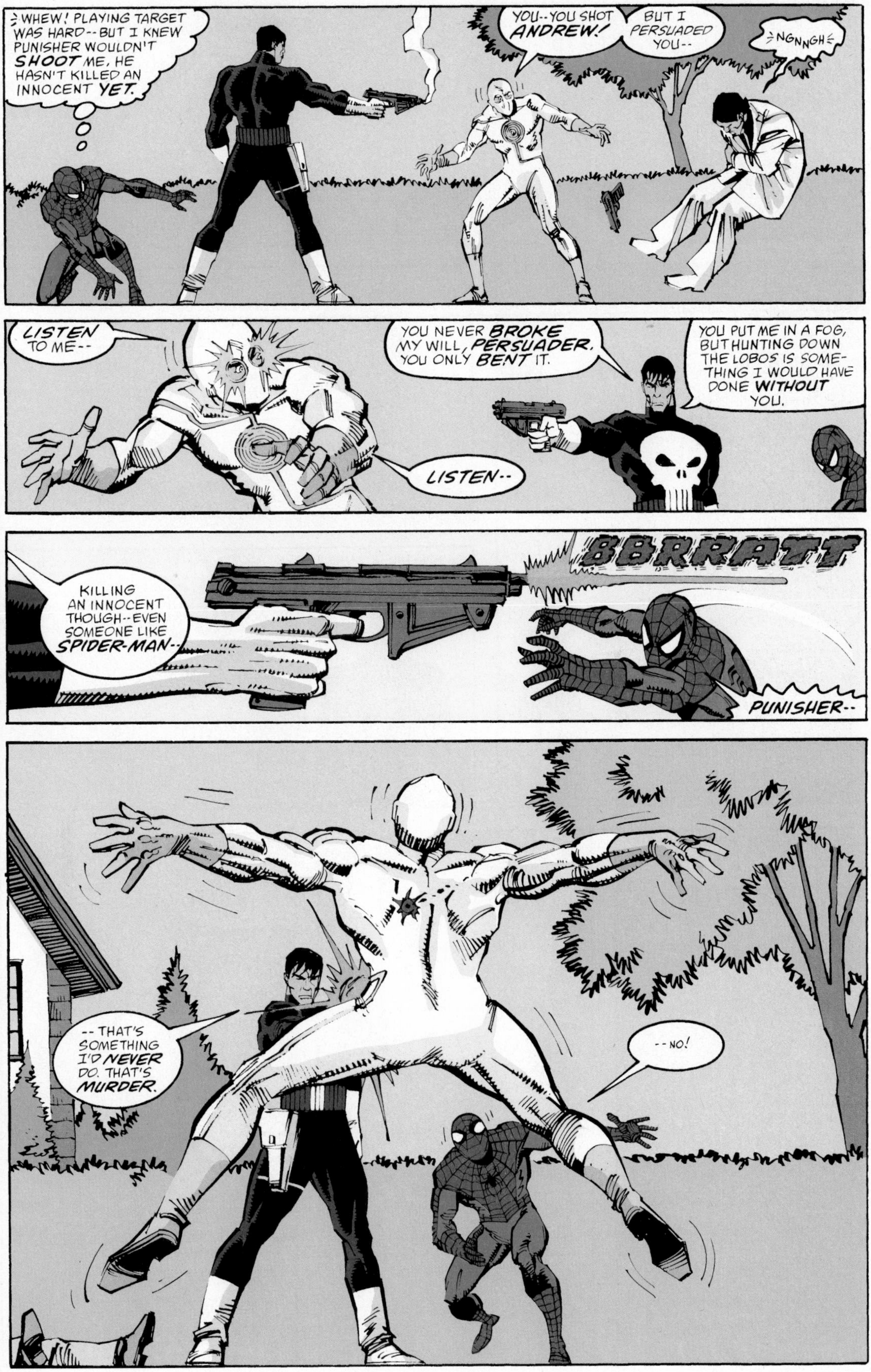
WHEW! PLAYING TARGET WAS HARD--BUT I KNEW PUNISHER WOULDN'T SHOOT ME. HE HASN'T KILLED AN INNOCENT YET.
YOU--YOU SHOT ANDREW!
BUT I PERSUADED YOU--
NGNNGH
LISTEN TO ME--
LISTEN--
YOU NEVER BROKE MY WILL, PERSUADER. YOU ONLY BENT IT.
YOU PUT ME IN A FOG, BUT HUNTING DOWN THE LOBOS IS SOMETHING I WOULD HAVE DONE WITHOUT YOU.
KILLING AN INNOCENT THOUGH--EVEN SOMEONE LIKE SPIDER-MAN--
BBRRATT
PUNISHER--
--THAT'S SOMETHING I'D NEVER DO. THAT'S MURDER.
--NO!

YOU OUGHTTA BE *LEASHED*, YOU KNOW THAT?

THOSE GOONS WORKED FOR THE *KING-PIN.*

WITH THEIR TESTIMONY WE MIGHT HAVE NAILED HIM FOR CONSPIR-ACY TO COMMIT *MURDER!*

INSTEAD, WHAT DO WE HAVE?

TWO MORE *BODIES.*

NO PROOF, NO *NOTHING!*

NOT TO MENTION THE *MINOR* LITTLE DETAIL THAT KILLING *ANYBODY*, UN-LESS IN SELF-DEFENSE, IS AGAINST THE LAW, IMMORAL, AND FLAT-OUT *WRONG!*

YOU LIVE BY *YOUR* MORAL CODE, SPIDER-MAN, I'LL LIVE BY *MINE.*

AS FOR THE *KINGPIN--*

--HIS TIME IS COMING. SOMEDAY SOON,

OH, GREAT.

TRY TO *HELP* A GUY, WHAT DO I GET? TIRED, WET, AND IN *PAIN.*

SO ENOUGH, ALREADY, BOOK TOUR OR NO BOOK TOUR, THIS WEB-SLINGER IS HEADING *HOME.*

GONE.

IT'S *OVER,* CARLOS.

NO, *MI HERMANO,* FOR WHAT HE TRIED TO DO HERE TODAY, THE FAT PIG IN NEW YORK MUST PAY A PRICE.

THE WAR OF *LOS HERMANOS DE LA LUNA* IS NOT OVER, EDUARDO.

IT IS ONLY *BEGINNING...*

NEXT BOOMERANG!

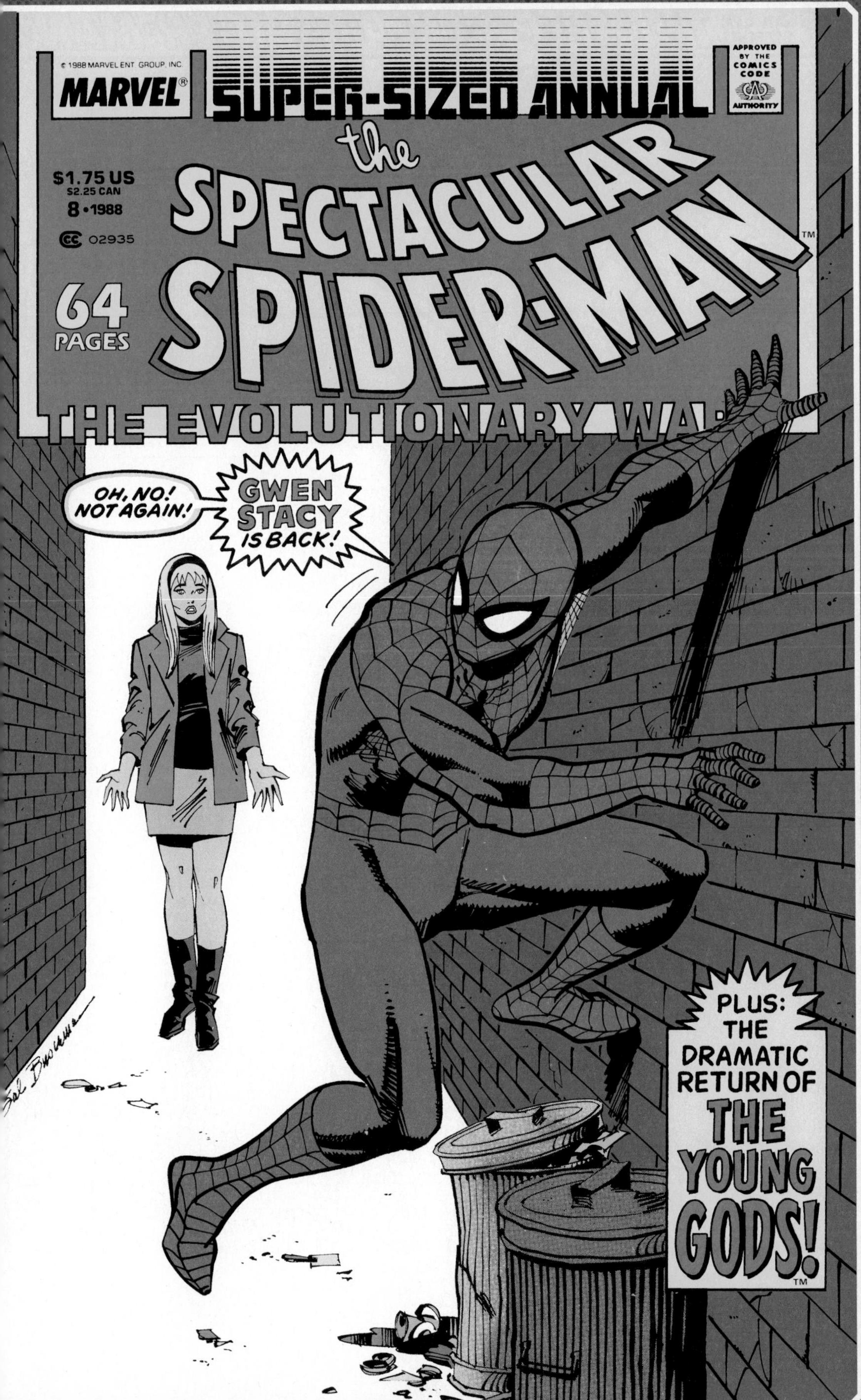

© 1988 MARVEL ENT. GROUP, INC.
MARVEL®
SUPER-SIZED ANNUAL
APPROVED BY THE COMICS CODE AUTHORITY
the SPECTACULAR SPIDER-MAN™
$1.75 US
$2.25 CAN
8 • 1988
02935
64 PAGES
THE EVOLUTIONARY WAR
OH, NO! NOT AGAIN!
GWEN STACY IS BACK!
PLUS: THE DRAMATIC RETURN OF THE YOUNG GODS!™

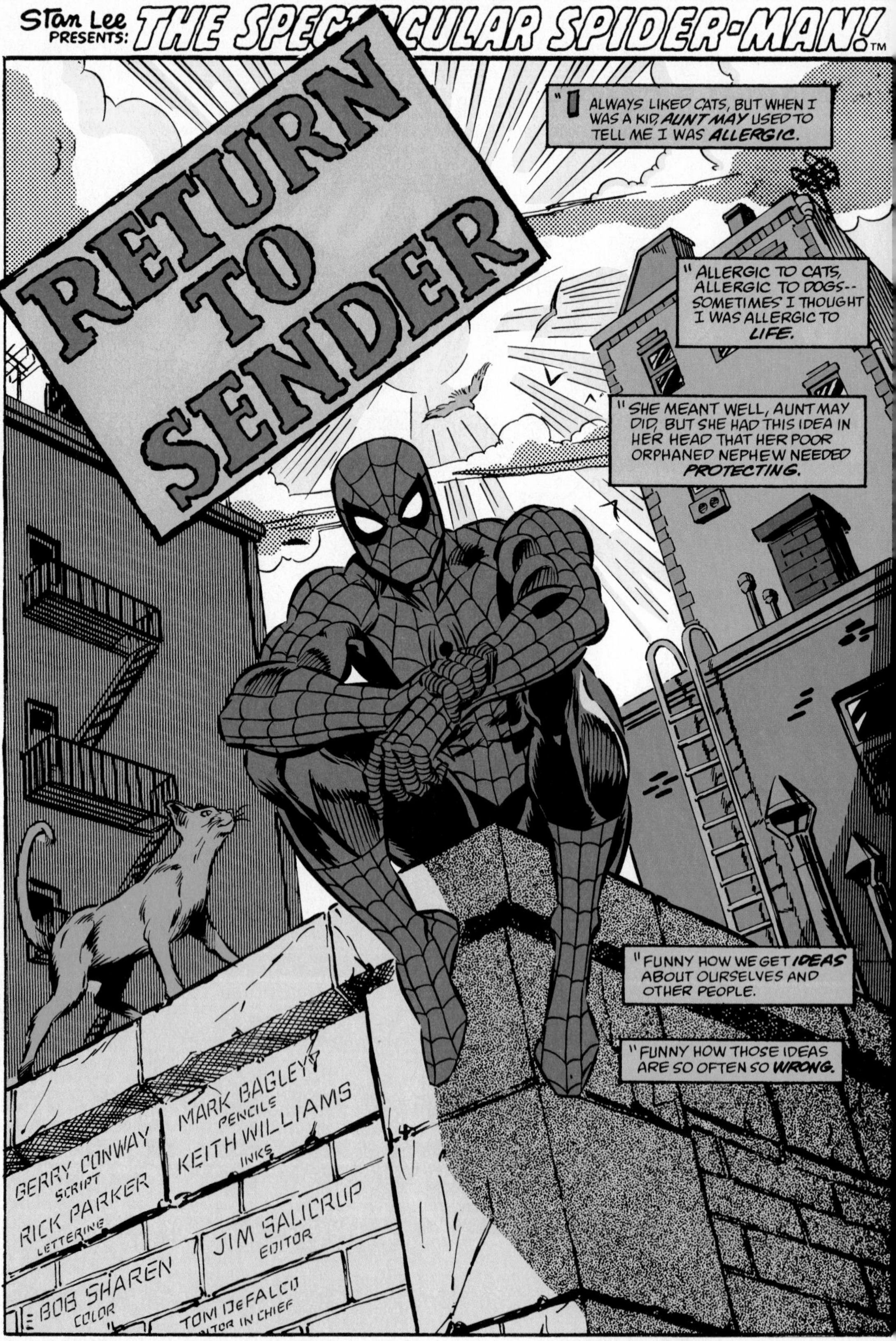
Stan Lee PRESENTS: THE SPECTACULAR SPIDER-MAN! TM
RETURN TO SENDER
"I ALWAYS LIKED CATS, BUT WHEN I WAS A KID, AUNT MAY USED TO TELL ME I WAS ALLERGIC.
"ALLERGIC TO CATS, ALLERGIC TO DOGS-- SOMETIMES I THOUGHT I WAS ALLERGIC TO LIFE.
"SHE MEANT WELL, AUNT MAY DID, BUT SHE HAD THIS IDEA IN HER HEAD THAT HER POOR ORPHANED NEPHEW NEEDED PROTECTING.
"FUNNY HOW WE GET IDEAS ABOUT OURSELVES AND OTHER PEOPLE.
"FUNNY HOW THOSE IDEAS ARE SO OFTEN SO WRONG.
GERRY CONWAY SCRIPT
RICK PARKER LETTERING
MARK BAGLEY PENCILS
KEITH WILLIAMS INKS
JIM SALICRUP EDITOR
BOB SHAREN COLOR
TOM DEFALCO EDITOR IN CHIEF

"TURNS OUT, I WASN'T ALLERGIC AFTER ALL. BIG SURPRISE.

"I WONDER WHAT *MARY JANE* WOULD SAY IF I CAME HOME WITH A CAT.

"I WONDER IF *SHE'S* ALLERGIC.

"WEIRD.

"I'VE KNOWN HER SINCE HIGH SCHOOL, WE'VE BEEN LOVERS FOR YEARS, SHE'S MY WIFE AND BEST FRIEND, BUT I'VE NO IDEA IF SHE EVEN *LIKES* KITTIES.

"SHE ALWAYS CALLED ME *'TIGER.'*

"MAYBE SHE--

"UH-OH.

"MY SPIDER-SENSE IS AN *INSTINCT,* MORE A REFLEX THAN A PROCESS.

"WHEN THE SENSE GOES OFF WITH A WARNING, I'M LIKE A *CAT* ON A *HOT STOVE:*

BZZAM

I JUMP.

"NO THINKING, NO TIME TO REACT. I JUST *MOVE.*

"GOOD THING, TOO.

BZZAM BZZAM

"ALL *THINKING* EVER DID WAS GET ME IN TROUBLE, BUT LIKE MOST FILTHY HABITS, ONCE YOU'VE *GOT* IT, IT'S HARD TO BREAK.

"ODD THING IS, THAT *BLAST* WASN'T AIMED AT *ME.*

"EVEN SO, I'M *ANNOYED.*

"MJ AND I MOVED TO THIS NEIGHBORHOOD 'CAUSE WE WANTED A BIGGER PLACE AND SOME *QUIET.*

"TYPICAL.

"A PERFECTLY FINE FRIDAY NIGHT ON THE UPPER WEST SIDE, AND THESE TWO CLOWNS HAVE TO GO SPOIL IT."

NOT SO CLOSE, YOU MICROCEPHALOID!

SU-SURRY, PRU-PRUFFESSER.

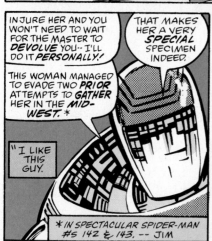

INJURE HER AND YOU WON'T NEED TO WAIT FOR THE MASTER TO DEVOLVE YOU-- I'LL DO IT PERSONALLY!

THIS WOMAN MANAGED TO EVADE TWO PRIOR ATTEMPTS TO GATHER HER IN THE MIDWEST.*

"I LIKE THIS GUY."

THAT MAKES HER A VERY SPECIAL SPECIMEN INDEED.

*IN SPECTACULAR SPIDER-MAN #S 142 & 143. --JIM

"PEOPLE WHO TAKE PRIDE IN THEIR WORK IMPRESS ME.

"BASHING HIM IS GOING TO BE FUN."

YO, BOYS...

...DO YOU FELLAS HAVE A PERMIT FOR STREET-BLASTING?

NO?

GOODNESS, I AM SHOCKED!

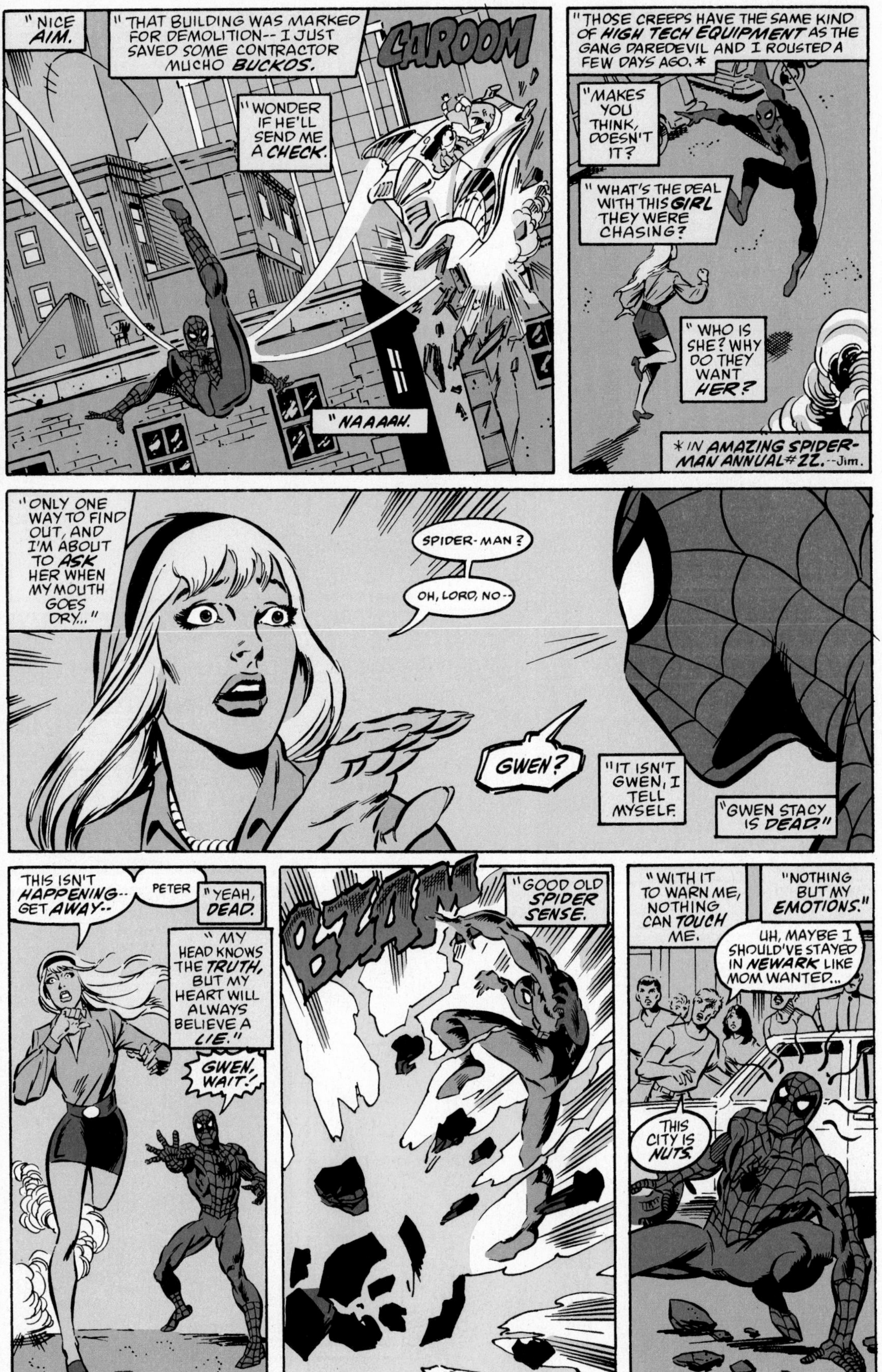

"NICE AIM.
"THAT BUILDING WAS MARKED FOR DEMOLITION-- I JUST SAVED SOME CONTRACTOR MUCHO BUCKOS.
CAROOM
"WONDER IF HE'LL SEND ME A CHECK.
"NAAAAH.
"THOSE CREEPS HAVE THE SAME KIND OF HIGH TECH EQUIPMENT AS THE GANG DAREDEVIL AND I ROUSTED A FEW DAYS AGO.*
"MAKES YOU THINK, DOESN'T IT?
"WHAT'S THE DEAL WITH THIS GIRL THEY WERE CHASING?
"WHO IS SHE? WHY DO THEY WANT HER?
*IN AMAZING SPIDER-MAN ANNUAL #22. --Jim.
"ONLY ONE WAY TO FIND OUT, AND I'M ABOUT TO ASK HER WHEN MY MOUTH GOES DRY..."
SPIDER-MAN?
OH, LORD, NO--
GWEN?
"IT ISN'T GWEN, I TELL MYSELF.
"GWEN STACY IS DEAD."
THIS ISN'T HAPPENING-- GET AWAY--
PETER
"YEAH, DEAD.
"MY HEAD KNOWS THE TRUTH, BUT MY HEART WILL ALWAYS BELIEVE A LIE."
GWEN, WAIT!
BZAM
"GOOD OLD SPIDER SENSE.
"WITH IT TO WARN ME, NOTHING CAN TOUCH ME.
"NOTHING BUT MY EMOTIONS."
UH, MAYBE I SHOULD'VE STAYED IN NEWARK LIKE MOM WANTED...
THIS CITY IS NUTS.

"NO ARGUMENT FROM *ME*, PAL!"

TWICE NOW, THAT WALL-CRAWLER HAS IMPEDED THE MASTER'S OPERATIONS. THAT'S TWO TIMES TOO OFTEN. *DESTROY* HIM!

T-TRYING, PR-PRUFFESSER--

BZAM

BZAM

--BUT HE MOVES TOO *QUICK*--AND WE'RE R-RUNNIN' SO LOW ON *P-POWER*-- I GOTTA--

POOM!

"GONE.

"WHO *WERE* THOSE GUYS?

"WHERE DID THEY *GO*?

"AND WHAT DID THEY WANT WITH *GWEN*?

"I LOOK FOR HER, BUT GWEN'S GONE, TOO.

"NO. *NOT* GWEN.

JIM COLLINS

"I HAVE TO *REMIND* MYSELF:

"GWEN STACY IS DEAD.

SURE.

"MY HEAD KNOWS THE TRUTH, BUT MY *HEART*...

"GET HOME, PAL.

"WE KNOW WHERE SHE'S *HEADED*, DON'T WE?

"AND YOU BETTER BE THERE TO WARN *MARY JANE* BEFORE GWEN ARRIVES..."

INTERLUDE 1

*Somewhere in the depths of the oceans that cover three-quarters of the Earth's surface sails a vast **submarine**, the largest craft of its kind...*

*Since the fall of his stronghold at the South Pole, this has been the mobile **base of operations** of the world's most brilliant geneticist -- the self-appointed architect of humanity's **future**...*

WE DID OUR BEST, **HIGH EVOLUTIONARY.**

IF THE FLIGHT-POD HADN'T BEEN ON THE VERGE OF A TOTAL **POWER LOSS,** WE WOULD HAVE CAPTURED THE GIRL--

-- **AND** DEALT WITH SPIDER-MAN.

I'M DISHEARTENED, QUINT.

WHEN I PROMOTED YOU TO CHIEF **GATHERER,** REPLACING THE DEPARTED, **DR. STACK,** I TOLD YOU THERE REMAINED ONLY **ONE** MISSION FOR YOUR TEAM TO ACCOMPLISH, NOW THAT THE GENETIC BOMB IS ALMOST READY FOR DETONATION.

WHAT IS THAT MISSION, PROFESSOR QUINT?

TO GATHER THE WOMAN WHO CALLS HERSELF **GWEN STACY.** PERHAPS IF YOU TOLD US WHAT MAKES HER SO **SPECIAL--**

SHE IS AN **ANOMALY,** QUINT.

A BEING WHO SHOULD NOT EXIST. A GENETIC FREAK. AN **IMPOSSIBILITY.**

I MUST STUDY HER GENETIC STRUCTURE. I MUST **UNDERSTAND.**

GATHER HER, QUINT. CAN YOU **DO** THAT?

ABSOLUTELY.

PURIFYING THE HUMAN RACE, PREPARING IT FOR ADVANCEMENT TO THE NEXT STAGE OF **EVOLUTION--** THIS IS OUR SACRED OBLIGATION, QUINT.

HUMANITY'S **FUTURE** DEPENDS ON US.

IN THE MEANTIME, ONE TASK REMAINS WHICH ONLY **I** MAY PERFORM.

WE MUST **NOT** FAIL.

THERE EXIST CREATURES WHO WERE ONCE AS HUMAN AS YOU, NOW RAISED TO THE LEVEL OF *GODS*.

ARE THEY HUMANKIND'S *GENETIC FUTURE* QUINT?

I *MUST KNOW*.

I WILL LEARN.

END INTERLUDE

"I *HATE* THIS.

"SNEAKING AROUND BEHIND MJ'S BACK: THAT'S WHAT THIS *FEELS* LIKE...

"I WISH SHE'D BEEN HERE WHEN I GOT HOME.

"MJ.

"NOT GWEN."

UH-HUH.

"I'M SOOO CONFUSED.

"WHY DOES THINKING ABOUT GWEN MAKE ME FEEL *GUILTY*?

"WHAT HAPPENED BETWEEN US *ENDED* LONG AGO ON A BRIDGE, AND I DON'T *THINK* ABOUT IT ANYMORE.

NOT MUCH.

"WHERE *IS* THAT THING?

"I SAW IT WHEN WE WERE PACKING FOR THE MOVE, I'M SURE I PUT IT--

"HERE.

"DO I REALLY WANT TO *LOOK* AT THIS?

YOU BET.

"NOTHING LIKE A GOOD WALLOW IN THE MUDDY PATHWAYS OF *MEMORY* LANE.

"BY THE TIME MARY JANE COMES HOME, MAYBE FIVE MINUTES LATER, I'M ALREADY *REAL* DEPRESSED."

YO, TIGER! LOOK WHAT I GOT:

LOOT!

"I'M *NOT* IGNORING HER."

ONE OF THE PERKS OF HIGH FASHION MODELING: A *DICARMO* ORIGINAL, ALL MINE, 'CAUSE I WAS SUCH A DARLING ON THE SET. LET'S CELEBRATE. MY TREAT.

"I JUST CAN'T THINK OF A THING TO *SAY.*"

DINNER AT SHANIGAN'S, DANCING AT THE *TUNNEL*--

--HELICOPTER CRUISE AT DAWN-- WHAT DO YOU SAY, TI--

--

PETER?

YOU OKAY?

CORNY AS IT SOUNDS, YOU LOOK LIKE A MAN WHO'S SEEN A *GHOST.*

GHOST,

YEAH, THAT'S THE WORD FOR IT, MJ.

SHE'S BACK.

WHO'S BACK, PETER?

BLACK CAT? SILVER SABLE? MADONNA?

OH, NO,...

"*GWEN STACY.*

"THE LOVE OF MY LIFE BEFORE *YOU* WERE THE LOVE OF MY LIFE, MARY JANE.

"I WISH I COULD SAY SHE DOESN'T *MATTER* TO ME ANYMORE.

"I WISH I COULD SAY THE FEELINGS WERE *GONE*...

"I WISH... SHE'D JUST STAY *DEAD,*"

175

INTERLUDE 2

SOMEWHERE NEAR THE CENTRAL EXPLODING CORE OF OUR TEN-BILLION-YEAR-OLD GALAXY, A VAST ALIEN CRAFT DRIFTS ON A TIDE OF NEUTRONS...

...LIKE SOME COSMIC BEHEMOTH DROUSING ON A DEEP OCEAN CURRENT.

LARGER THAN A SMALL STAR, MASSING NO LESS THAN AN ENTIRE PLANETARY SYSTEM, IT IS HOME TO A RACE OF BEINGS KNOWN AS THE CELESTIALS.

WHAT POWERS THESE CELESTIALS POSSESS, WHAT PURPOSES THEY PURSUE, NO HUMAN MIND CAN EASILY IMAGINE.

IN SPITE OF HIMSELF, THE HIGH EVOLUTIONARY IS QUITE... IMPRESSED.

INCREDIBLE.

INCREDIBLE THAT CREATURES AS POWERFUL AS THESE COULD THREATEN THE EARTH--

--AND AFTERWARD, WIPE ALL TRACE OF THEIR EXISTENCE FROM THE MINDS OF ORDINARY MEN.

ORDINARY MEN, BUT NOT THE HIGH EVOLUTIONARY.

I REMEMBER EVERYTHING.

THE CELESTIALS CAME TO *JUDGE* HUMANITY'S GENETIC FITNESS TO SURVIVE.

HUMANITY PASSED THE TEST TO MY CONSIDERABLE *SURPRISE*.

WHEN THEY LEFT EARTH, THE *CELESTIALS* TOOK TWELVE GENETICALLY-ENHANCED HUMANS WITH THEM.

"YOUNG GODS" THEY WERE CALLED--

--WHOSE POWERS REPRESENT THE TWELVE GREAT *ACCOMPLISHMENTS* OF HUMANKIND--

--MEN AND WOMEN CHOSEN FOR TRANSFORMATION BY THE *"GODS"* OF SEVERAL MYTHOLOGICAL PANTHEONS. *

SINCE THEIR ARRIVAL HERE, THE SO-CALLED *YOUNG GODS* HAVE BEEN IN "*TRAINING*"--

--LEARNING THE USE OF THEIR POWERS UNDER THE TUTELAGE OF TWO *ALIEN WARRIORS*.

ALL THIS I LEARNED WHEN I TELEPATHICALLY SCANNED THE CELESTIALS' MOTHERSHIP *MONTHS* AGO.

* SEE OUR *FACT PAGES* FOR MORE DETAILS--JM

AH, THERE THEY ARE.

NOW TO OBSERVE, *UNSEEN* IN MY PSYCHIC PRESENCE.

SLOW DOWN, *MOONSTALKER*.

THIS IS *PRACTICE*, NOT *COMBAT*.

USE BRIGHT SWORD'S GOD-NAME, MOONSTALKER.

HUMAN NAMES FOR *PRIVATE* CONVERSATION ONLY.

YOU ALWAYS SAY I DON'T TAKE TRAINING *SERIOUSLY* ENOUGH, CARTER, AND THEN WHEN I DO--

INUPAIT ESKIMOS UNDERSTAND ALL ABOUT *SECRET* NAMES, KATOS.

THEY'RE FOR *FRIENDS*.

GODS CAN BE FRIENDS, *TOO*, CAN'T WE?

NOT WHEN WE *TRAIN*, LITTLE PUFFIN.

SPIKES!

MINDSINGER!

NO FAIR *CHANGING* YOURSELF WHEN I'M NOT LOOKING!

ALL'S FAIR IN LOVE AND WAR, SPEEDY ONE.

WHAT WAR?

WHY DO WE HAVE TO *TRAIN* ALL THE TIME, ANYWAY? I WANT TO GO *HUNTING!*

177

YOU TRAIN BECAUSE THE CELESTIALS *WISH* IT, MOON-STALKER. THAT'S REASON ENOUGH.

HIGHNOTE, DON'T LET *HARVEST* TANGLE YOU IN THE GRASS *AGAIN*. SING HER A SONG.

SPLICE, WATCH YOUR BACK.

I'M *WATCHING*, JUNIPUR.

KATOS TRAINS HIS PUPILS IN *DEFENSIVE* WARFARE. I'D RATHER MY STUDENTS LEARN AN *AGGRESSIVE OFFENSE*.

UNDERSTAND ME, SPLICE?

YES, JUNIPUR.

THOOM

≈WHEW!≈

IF I RAISED THAT WALL ANY SLOWER, I WOULD HAVE BEEN *CREAMED!*

VARUA, THIS IS WRONG-- LATELY, OUR TRAINING HAS BECOME MORE AND MORE *VIOLENT*.

WE MUST *PROTEST*.

AS OUR SPIRITUAL LEADER, YOU SHOULD--

CALCULUS, SHUT UP...

PARDON?

I SENSE A *PRESENCE*--

SEA WITCH... DON'T--

AYE, AND IT'S *ME* YOU'RE SENSING, VARUA, MY GIRL.

A WEE BIT *TARDY*, I MIGHT ADD.

178

AND MISS THE *FUN* OF SEEIN' MISS HIGH AN' MIGHTY GET DUNKED?

FAITH, BUT EVEN AFTER ALL THIS TIME WE'VE BEEN SPENDING TOGETHER--

--YOU DON'T *KNOW* ME, DO YOU?

SPLOOSH

>COUGH!<

>OOF!<

I HEARD WHAT VARUA SAID, EVERYBODY-- AND I FELT IT, *TOO!*

A PRESENCE IN MY MIND, *WATCHING!*

BUT I KNOW WHAT YOU'RE GOING TO *SAY*... THERE GOES *DAYDREAMER*, "DAYDREAMING" AGAIN!

... SO, JUST TO *PROVE* I'M NOT IMAGINING THINGS...

... I'LL MAKE OUR VISITOR *VISIBLE.*

EXCELLENT, CHILD.

A RATHER *BRUTISH* USE OF MENTAL POWER, BUT WELL DONE IN ITS WAY.

MAY I SAY I FOUND YOUR EXPLOITS HERE *ENTERTAINING*, AS WELL AS *ENLIGHTENING?*

WHO--?

MY NAME IS UNIMPORTANT.

YOUR GENETICS ARE INTRIGUING, I ADMIT, BUT NOW I SEE YOU ARE *IRRELEVANT* TO MY PURPOSES.

I CAME SEEKING GODS, AND FOUND ONLY *CHILDREN* WITH GOD-LIKE POWERS.

FORGIVE THE INTRUSION...

179

CLEARLY, MANKIND'S GENETIC DESTINY LIES ALONG A *DIFFERENT* PATH.

DAYDREAMER, *STOP* HIM! DON'T LET HIM GO!

I'M *TRYING,* BRIGHT SWORD--

--BUT I CAN'T! *I* DEAL IN DREAMS AND VISIONS.

WHOEVER THAT WAS, HIS POWERS WERE *STRONGER* THAN MINE.

ARE YOU ALL RIGHT, KATRINKA? HE DID NOT *HURT* YOU?

OH, I'M *FINE,* GREGOR LOVE. BUT I KEEP TELLING YOU, MY NAME'S *CATHERINE,* NOT--

PLEASE, DAYDREAMER, FOR ONCE, STICK TO THE *SUBJECT.*

DID YOU *SENSE* ANYTHING ELSE--?

BAD *DREAMS,* CALCULUS, *DEADLY* DREAMS.

SURELY YOU *EXAGGERATE.* JUNIPUR HAS TAUGHT YOU AND YOUR TEAM TO SEE ENEMIES *EVERYWHERE*--

I'M AFRAID SHE'S RIGHT THIS TIME, KATOS. I SENSED MUCH THE SAME-- *VIOLENCE,* AND *DEATH...*

GEE, *THANKS,* VARUA, NICE TO KNOW WE SAW THE SAME THING...

...FOR *ONCE.*

NO ARGUING, YOU TWO. DAYDREAMER, SHOW US THE *DREAMS.*

OKAY, JUNIPUR. BUT IF YOU HAVE TROUBLE *SLEEPING* TONIGHT, JUST REMEMBER--

"--YOU *ASKED.*"

A FLASH OF LIGHT, A GLIMPSE OF DARKNESS-- SHIVERING HEAT AND BURNING COLD:

THE IMAGE COMES, IMPRINTING ITSELF IN ALL OF THEIR MINDS IN AN INSTANT.

AND IN AN INSTANT IT IS *GONE.*

THAT BEING PLANS THE EVOLUTIONARY *GENOCIDE* OF HUMAN-KIND.

HORRIBLE. BUT NO CONCERN OF OURS.

ARE YOU *INSANE*..?

KATRINKA!

OOOOHH

THESE DREAMS ARE NOT FOR A *DELICATE* SOUL LIKE YOURS, KATRINKA--

I'M TOUGHER THAN YOU THINK, GREGOR.

"BUT THANKS FOR THE *HAND*, ANYWAY."

KATOS, YOU DON'T SUGGEST WE *IGNORE* THIS?

OUR STUDENTS WERE GRANTED *GODLIKE* POWER.

THEY MUST USE THAT POWER TO *PROTECT* HUMANITY FROM IT-SELF--FROM ITS OWN INHERENT EVIL NATURE.

NO, JUNIPUR.

THIS *EVOLUTIONARY* CRISIS IS A *HUMAN* PROBLEM, TO BE *SOLVED* BY HUMANS.

OUR STUDENTS MUST BE *GUARDIANS*, NOT *PROTECTORS*.

THEY HAVE NO RIGHT TO INTERFERE IN *HUMAN* DESTINY.

WE AGREE.

AND WE *DISAGREE*.

"DON'T INTER-FERE" COST SIX MILLION JEWS THEIR *LIVES* DURING THE *HOLOCAUST*.

AS AN ISRAELI, I WILL NEVER ALLOW SUCH *GENOCIDE* TO HAPPEN AGAIN.

HIGHNOTE, SING US TO *EARTH!*

<¡LO QUE USTED QUIERA, MI AMIGO!>

HIIIIII

MMMMMM, I LOVE IT WHEN RAOUL DOES THAT.

MAKES ME ALL *TINGLY* INSIDE...

NO! STOP! THIS IS--

--WRONG.

VANISHED. HIGH-NOTE HAS *TRANS-PORTED* THEM TO EARTH BY HIS SONG-SPELL.

WHATTA WE *DO*, TEACH?

STOP THEM, CADUCEUS...

HIIIIII

"...BEFORE THEY BRING *DISASTER* TO ALL *HUMANITY*."

END INTERLUDE

I CAN'T BELIEVE THIS IS *HAPPENING*, PETER.

WHEN GWEN WAS ALIVE, I KNEW I NEVER HAD A *CHANCE* WITH YOU.

AFTER ALL, SHE WAS SMART, EDUCATED, A LADY-- AND WHAT WAS *I*?

A CHEAP DATE. EMPHASIS ON *CHEAP*.

DON'T SAY THAT, MJ.

C'MON, TIGER, WE BOTH KNOW IT'S *TRUE*.

IF GWEN STACY WAS A BEAUTY QUEEN, THEN I WAS A PIN-UP GIRL.

STOP IT. YOU'RE JUST *HURTING* YOURSELF.

GWEN IS *DEAD*, MARY JANE.

THAT GIRL IS HER *CLONE*. MY COLLEGE BIOLOGY PROFESSOR CREATED HER SOMEHOW BECAUSE HE WAS *OBSESSED* WITH HER.*

*AS TOLD IN THE SEMI-CLASSIC *AMAZING SPIDER-MAN* #148. --JIM.

PROFESSOR WARREN COULDN'T STAND THE IDEA GWEN WAS *DEAD*--AND IT DROVE HIM *INSANE*, FINALLY *KILLED* HIM.

HE COULDN'T ACCEPT HER DEATH, BUT *I* DID.

GWEN'S JUST A *MEMORY* NOW.

"LIAR."

YOU'RE THE ONE I LOVE, MJ.

ONLY *YOU*...

"LIAR. LIAR. LI--"

BRRNG

"THE DOORKNOB FEELS SLIPPERY."

"MY PALMS ARE WET."

"FUNNY."

"I'VE FACED DOC OCTOPUS, TOMBSTONE, HOBGOBLIN, AND EVEN THE KINGPIN HIMSELF--

"--BUT *NEVER* WITH SWEATY PALMS."

"WHO'D HAVE THOUGHT I'D BE AFRAID OF *HER*?"

PETER!

OH, THANK HEAVEN--!

THESE MEN TRYING TO *KILL* ME--YOU'RE THE ONLY ONE I COULD THINK TO TURN TO--AND THEN YOU'D *MOVED*--CALLED BETTY BRANT--SHE SEEMED SO *STRANGE*, PETER--TOLD ME WHERE TO FIND YOU--

--NEED YOUR HELP--I'M SO *FRIGHT*--

"THE COSTUME,"

NO!

"WHY DIDN'T I TAKE IT OFF?"

"I KNEW SHE'D BE COMING, I KNEW SHE'D BE FRIGHTENED OF SPIDER-MAN."

THE PARKERS

GWEN! COME BACK!

"IS THAT WHY I KEPT IT ON?"

"TO PROTECT MYSELF FROM HER SOMEHOW?"

"SINCE WHEN DO I NEED PROTECTING FROM GWEN STACY?"

MJ, I'VE GOTTA GO AFTER HER.

SHE'S SCARED, IN TROUBLE--AND IT MAY BE TROUBLE BIGGER THAN ALL OF US.

(NOT GWEN. GWEN IS DEAD.)

YOU STILL LOVE HER.

CLONE OR NOT, REAL OR NOT--

YOU LOVE HER,

MJ, THAT'S NOT--

--

TRUE.

LOOK.

I'LL ADMIT I'M CONFUSED.

THIS IS STIRRING UP STUFF I HAVEN'T DEALT WITH IN YEARS.

THEN HELP HER, PETER. HELP HER.

AND WHEN YOU'RE DONE, COME HOME TO ME WITH A CLEAR HEART--

"-- OR DON'T COME HOME AT ALL,"

"FIND HER.

"THERE.

HONK HONK HOOONNK

"SAVE HER--

183

"SAVE HER."

GWEN, WE'VE GOT TO TALK.

GET AWAY FROM ME-- YOU KILLED MY FATHER--

HOONNK

"SHE FEELS SO WARM, SO ALIVE."

"BUT SHE STRUGGLES LIKE A FRIGHTENED CAT."

KILLED YOUR--?

GWEN, CAPT. STACY DIED SAVING A KID FROM A FALLING BUILDING.* I DIDN'T TOUCH HIM.

BUT YOU ALWAYS BLAMED ME FOR THAT, DIDN'T YOU?

"SPIDER-SENSE."

"NOT NOW."

*IN THE CLASSIC AMAZING SPIDER-MAN #90.--J.S.

THE SAME WAY I ALWAYS BLAMED MY-SELF FOR WHAT HAP-PENED TO YO--

YAAA

BRAAM

"STUPID.

"EMOTIONS OVERRODE MY SPIDER-SENSE.

"FORGOT THOSE GUYS WHO WANTED TO GRAB GWEN.

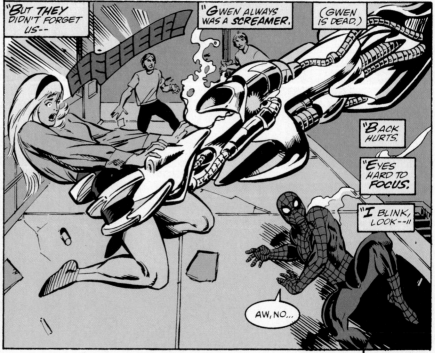

"BUT THEY DIDN'T FORGET US--

"GWEN ALWAYS WAS A SCREAMER.

(GWEN IS DEAD.)

"BACK HURTS.

"EYES HARD TO FOCUS.

"I BLINK, LOOK--"

AW, NO...

184

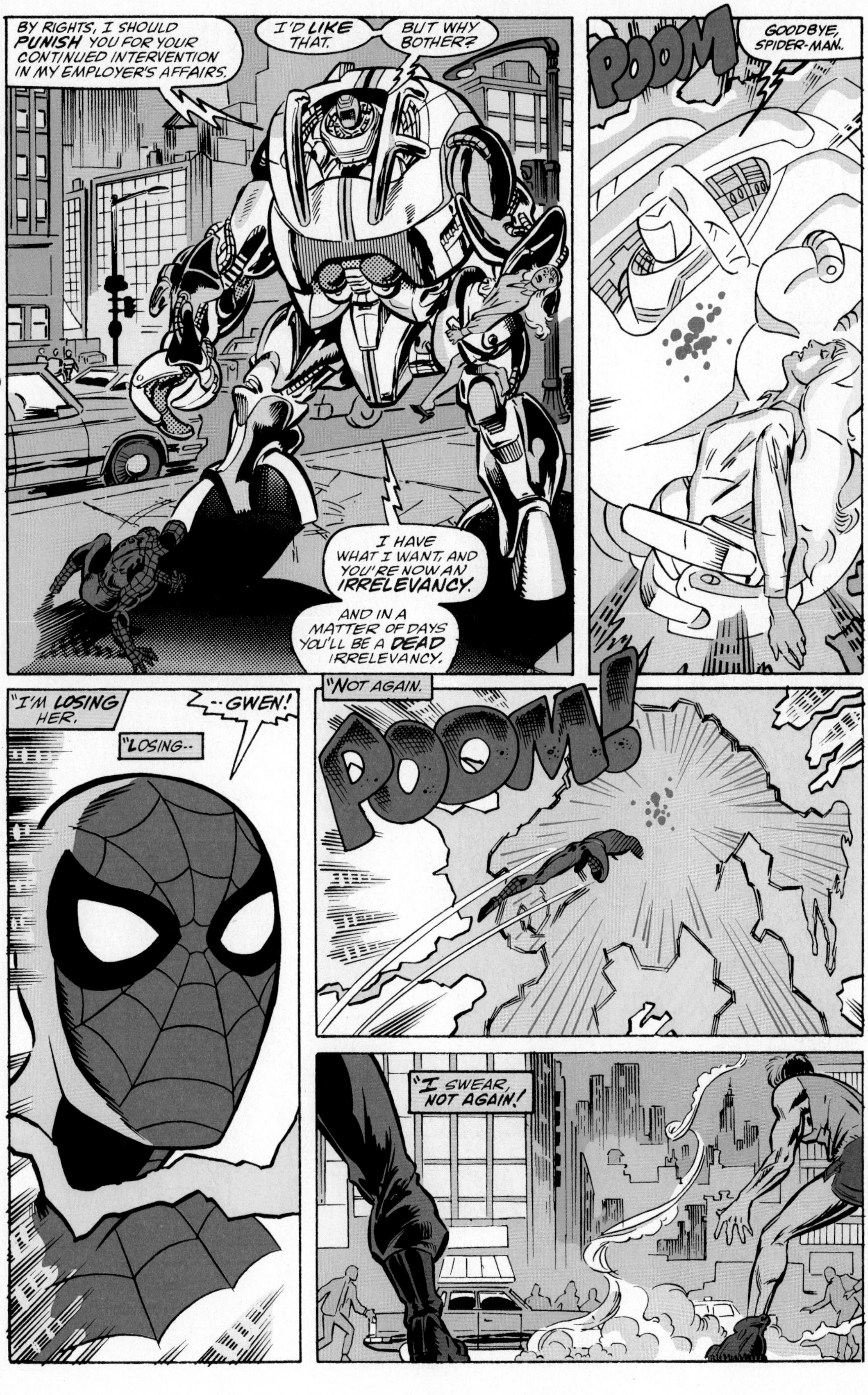
BY RIGHTS, I SHOULD PUNISH YOU FOR YOUR CONTINUED INTERVENTION IN MY EMPLOYER'S AFFAIRS.
I'D LIKE THAT.
BUT WHY BOTHER?
I HAVE WHAT I WANT, AND YOU'RE NOW AN IRRELEVANCY.
AND IN A MATTER OF DAYS YOU'LL BE A DEAD IRRELEVANCY.
POOM
GOODBYE, SPIDER-MAN..
"I'M LOSING HER.
"LOSING--
--GWEN!
"NOT AGAIN.
POOM!
"I SWEAR, NOT AGAIN!

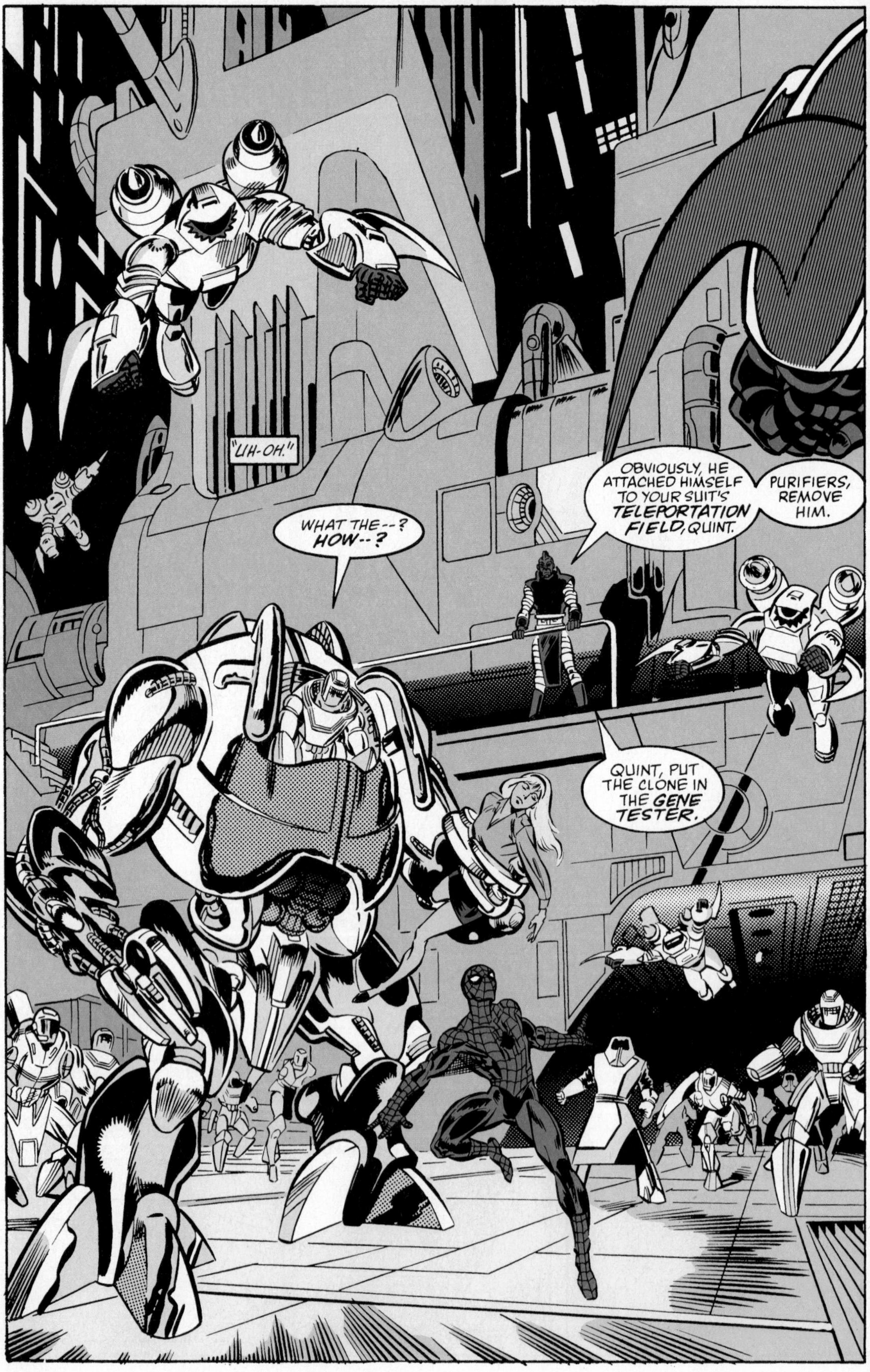
"UH-OH."
WHAT THE--? HOW--?
OBVIOUSLY, HE ATTACHED HIMSELF TO YOUR SUIT'S TELEPORTATION FIELD, QUINT.
PURIFIERS, REMOVE HIM.
QUINT, PUT THE CLONE IN THE GENE TESTER.

WHEW! TALK ABOUT *TENSE*. TALK ABOUT *HOSTILITY*.

BZAM

YOU BOYS NEED A NICE LONG *VACATION*, SOMEWHERE YOU CAN UNWIND, RELAX.

THONK

BLAMM

TIMES SQUARE AT RUSH HOUR, *NEW ORLEANS* DURING MARDI GRAS, *LOS ANGELES* IN AN EARTHQUAKE.

CALL YOUR *TRAVEL* AGENT.

TRUST ME.

"MY HEART'S BEATING FASTER THAN A HEAVY METAL *DRUM* SOLO.

"I CAN'T SEE *GWEN.*"

(YEAH, YEAH, I KNOW, I KNOW.)

"WHERE *IS* SHE?"

"*WHAT* ARE THEY *DOING* TO HER?"

LIGHTEN UP, YOU GUYS.

ZAM

THIS THING'S BEGINNING TO REMIND ME OF AN ACTION-TOY *TV* SHOW.

KZAK

GIANT *ROBOTS*, RAY GUNS, AND *POWER SUITS*--

GIVE ME A *BREAK.*

"NO GOOD.

"TOO MANY OF THEM, TOO FEW OF ME.

ZAK ZAM

"WHAT I NEED IS A *MIRACLE*."

HEY!

HEY--

HIIIII!

"WITH A SOUND LIKE ELLA FITZGERALD BREAKING A WINEGLASS, SEVEN PEOPLE APPEAR OUT OF *NOWHERE.*

"AND RIGHT ON *CUE*, HERE IT COMES.

"UH...

"DID I SAY *PEOPLE*?

"MY MISTAKE."

THOSE ARE THE ONES I *DREAMED* ABOUT!

STOP THEM!

188

MY PLEASURE TO **BEGIN**, KATRINKA. AS **POET**, I RE-MADE LIFE INTO **ART** WITH WORDS. NOW I REMAKE BODY INTO **WEAPON** WITH WORDS.

ROLLER!

AND SO THE GODS **LAUGH**.

BWHOOM

LET THE GODS LAUGH, MIND-SLINGER.

THEY GAVE US OUR POWERS--MADE ME AN **INDESTRUCTIBLE WARRIOR**--

BZAM

THOOM!

--TO SHOW THE **CELESTIALS** HUMANITY WAS WORTHY TO SURVIVE.

THEN THEY **ABANDONED** US. WE OWE THEM **NOTHING**.

SPLICE, YOUR SKILL AS A **CRAFTSWOMAN** WAS LEGENDARY IN 19TH CENTURY AFRICA.

SHOW THESE MEN HOW THE **ZULU** DEITIES GAVE YOU A **GOD-POWER** TO MATCH YOUR **HUMAN** TALENT.

THE FLOOR--IT'S **ALIVE**--

"NOT ALIVE, BUT **CLOSE**.

"THEY SAY A GOOD CRAFTSMAN CAN BREATHE LIFE INTO A CHUNK OF **WOOD** OR A PIECE OF **STONE**.

CRONG!

UH-HUH.

"I LOOK AROUND, AND SPOT THE **BOSS**.

"HE ISN'T WATCHING THE FIGHT, DOESN'T EVEN SEEM **INTERESTED**.

"I LOOK WHERE HE'S LOOKING AND I SEE--"

GWEN!

(IT'S NOT GWEN.)

(IT'S A CLONE, NO MORE REAL THAN A MEMORY.)

"YEAH, BUT MEMORIES ARE REAL.

"AND, CLONE OR NOT, SHE'S REAL, TOO.

YOWW!

"UNFORTUNATELY, SO IS THE GUY IN THE POWER-SUIT WHO GRABS MY ARM.

"THE PAIN'S SO GREAT, I ALMOST BLACK OUT.

"JUST THEN THERE'S ANOTHER FLASH OF LIGHT, A SOUND LIKE A BUBBLE POPPING--

"--AND THINGS REALLY GET COMPLICATED."

VARUA! YOU'VE DECIDED TO JOIN US AFTER ALL!

I'M AFRAID NOT, CARTER.

CALCULUS, TACTICS ARE *YOUR* DEPARTMENT.

GIVE US A *PLAN.*

OPEN YOUR MINDS. SEE THE *PATTERN?*

LOOKS AS EASY AS A THREE-CARD MONTE *SHUFFLE,* BRAIN-GUY.

COMPLIMENTS, CADUCEUS? *ASTOUNDING*

SAVE THE BANTER--

"--LET'S *CHARLESTON.*"

MOONSTALKER, DON'T MAKE ME *HURT* Y--

EH?

YOU CAN'T HURT WHAT YOU CAN'T *TOUCH,* CARTER.

BESIDES--

--THIS TIME, *SHE* ISN'T THE ONE YOU HAVE TO WORRY ABOUT, BRIGHT SWORD--

WHOOM!

--I AM.

HEY, SPLICE-- YOU LOOK *STRESSED.*

GET SOME REST.

DOCTOR'S *ORDERS.*

YOUR PUPILS ARE AS SKILLED AS THEY ARE *MISGUIDED,* KATOS.

WHY DO YOU OPPOSE US SO *FIERCELY?*

BECAUSE HUMANITY MUST BE *FREE,* JUNIPUR.

EVEN IF FREEDOM MEANS *DEATH?*

"ESPECIALLY THEN."

"YEAH, SURE.

"I HEAR THEM TALKING--

"-- BUT RIGHT NOW I'VE GOT PROBLEMS OF MY OWN.

"GWEN HASN'T MOVED FOR THE LAST FIVE MINUTES.

"NEITHER HAS THE BIG BOSS."

"HE JUST STANDS THERE, STARING AT A COMPUTER SCREEN FILLED WITH PATTERNS AND NUMBERS.

"AND THE THING IS, HE DOESN'T LOOK HAPPY.

"EVEN SO, WITH ALL THIS STUFF GOING ON, I CAN'T HELP WONDERING...

"WHY ARE THOSE GUYS FIGHTING EACH OTHER?

"IS THE WHOLE WORLD NUTS, OR IS IT JUST ME?!"

FOLLOW THE *PATTERN,* GENII, DON'T ALLOW BRIGHT SWORD TO REGAIN INITIATIVE.

CADUCEUS, DISENGAGE, YOUR POWERS OF *HEALING* ARE BETTER EMPLOYED DEFENSIVELY.

MOONSTALKER, WATCH YOUR BACK--

YOUR PUPIL CALCULUS IS A FINE *TACTICIAN,* KATOS.

A PITY HE NEVER LEARNED THE *FUTILITY* OF PASSIVE DEFENSE.

STOP HER, JUNIPUR. THIS GOES TOO *FAR.*

--REGROUP WITH HARVEST, AND TOGETHER-- --UH--

GOODNIGHT, CALCULUS.

SWEET DREAMS.

"WHEN I WAS SIX OR SEVEN I HAD THIS RE-CURRING *NIGHTMARE:*

"IT'S RAINING, AND I'M IN THE HOUSE ALONE, AND SUDDENLY THE *LIGHTS* GO OUT.

"WHEN YOU'RE SIX YEARS -OLD, A DARK HOUSE IS SCARY *ENOUGH*...

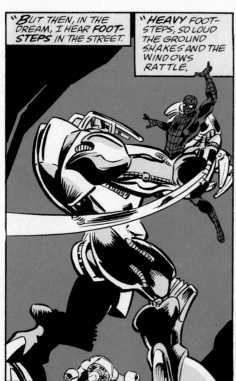

"BUT THEN, IN THE DREAM, I HEAR *FOOTSTEPS* IN THE STREET.

"*HEAVY* FOOTSTEPS, SO LOUD THE GROUND SHAKES AND THE WINDOWS RATTLE,

"I LOOK OUTSIDE AND THERE'S A *GIANT* ON THE LAWN.

"I TRY TO HIDE, BUT THE GIANT SEES ME, AND HE *GRABS* ME...

"...AND HE STARTS TO *SQUEEZE.*"

THE WORLD...

...WHAT HAPPENED TO THE WORLD...

THE WORLD IS A DREAM, CALCULUS, AND YOU JUST WOKE UP.

WHAT DOES YOUR LOGICAL MIND SAY ABOUT *THAT?*

NO...

NOOOOO

OH! CALCULUS, I'M SORRY-- I DIDN'T MEAN TO--

--SOMEBODY, HELP!

NOOOOOOO!

LORDS OF THE NINTH REALM, I WAS AFRAID SOMETHING LIKE THIS MIGHT HAPPEN!

THEY'RE CHILDREN, JUNIPUR-- CHILDREN WITH POWERS BEYOND THEIR CONTROL!

JUNIPUR, SAY HE'LL BE ALL RIGHT!

KATOS?

I DON'T KNOW, JUNIPUR... I DON'T KNOW...

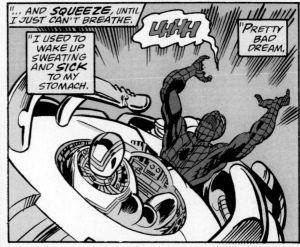

"... AND SQUEEZE, UNTIL I JUST CAN'T BREATHE.

"I USED TO WAKE UP SWEATING AND SICK TO MY STOMACH.

UHHH

"PRETTY BAD DREAM.

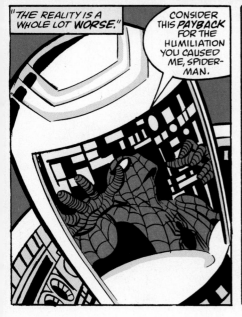

"THE REALITY IS A WHOLE LOT WORSE."

CONSIDER THIS PAYBACK FOR THE HUMILIATION YOU CAUSED ME, SPIDER-MAN.

"I KNOW THIS CREEP.

"HE'S THE CLOWN WHO TAKES PRIDE IN HIS WORK."

HEY, PAL. I'M NO KID, THIS IS NO DREAM--

CHOOM

"-- AND YOU'RE NO *GIANT!*"

"THE CONTROL PANEL CRUMPLES LIKE WET NEWSPAPER."

"WIRES BREAK, CIRCUITS FUSE, THINGS GET *MESSY.*"

SIZZ

YAAAHH!

"AS A NIGHTMARE, THIS GUY'S A *BUST.*"

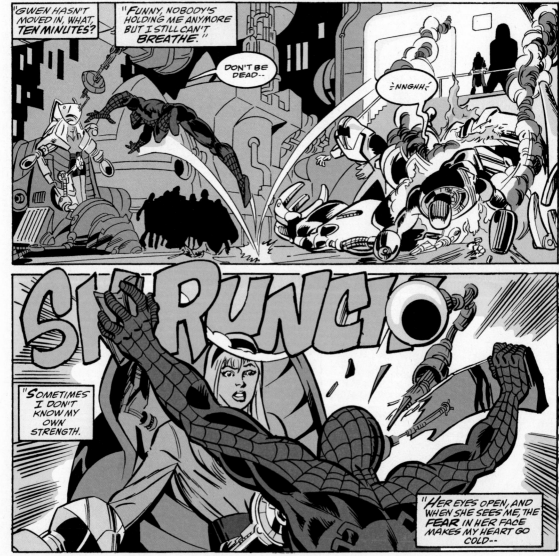

"GWEN HASN'T MOVED IN, WHAT, *TEN MINUTES?*"

"FUNNY, NOBODY'S HOLDING ME ANYMORE BUT I STILL CAN'T *BREATHE.*"

DON'T BE DEAD--

≥NNGHH≤

SK RUNCH

"SOMETIMES I DON'T KNOW MY OWN STRENGTH."

"HER EYES OPEN, AND WHEN SHE SEES ME, THE *FEAR* IN HER FACE MAKES MY HEART GO COLD--"

"-- AND I SAY SOMETHING TRULY *STUPID*:"

DON'T BE AFRAID.

IT'S ME.

PETER.

"THEN SHE'S IN MY ARMS, HER BREATH SHUDDERING ON MY CHEST, AND THE YEARS ARE *GONE*.

"I'VE MISSED YOU.

"THE FEEL OF YOU, THE WARMTH OF YOU.

"THE WAY WE FIT.

"AND JUST LIKE THAT..."

...IT'S OVER.

YOU'RE NOT THE GWEN I KNEW.

AND EVEN IF YOU WERE, EVEN THOUGH I STILL *CARE* FOR YOU...

...I'M IN *LOVE* WITH SOMEONE ELSE.

PETER?

DON'T LEAVE ME...

197

I WON'T.

I'LL GET YOU HOME.

BUT FIRST, NOW THAT THINGS HAVE *SETTLED DOWN* A BIT, I WANT A FEW *ANSWERS*...

HIS MIND'S BUSTED-UP PRETTY BAD.

WHAT'D YOU *DO* DAYDREAMER, USE HIS BRAIN FOR A *PUNCHING BAG?*

I'M S-SORRY...

ANGER HELPS *NOTHING,* CADUCEUS.

CAN YOU *HEAL* HIM?

OR *GOD.*

I'M A *PHYSICAL* HEALER, KATOS.

GOT A BRUISE, A WOUND, A SNIFFLE -- I'M YOUR MAN.

MENTAL STUFF IS MORE *VARUA'S* LINE THAN MINE.

BUT BACK IN CHICAGO, THE SLICKS WORKIN' THE LOOP HAD A *SAYING:*

NOOOOO!

"DON'T TRY, YOU *DIE.*"

GUESS WE WERE RIGHT.

...THE WORLD...

...IT'S BACK. I'M BACK. WHAT HAPPENED?

TELL YOU LATER, CAL OLD PAL. YOU'RE GONNA BE *OKAY.*

JUST DON'T THINK TOO *HARD* THE NEXT FEW DAYS.

198

JUNIPUR, *MI MAESTRA,* WE MADE A *MISTAKE* COMING HERE, I THINK.

PERHAPS, WE SHOULD *NOT* PROTECT HUMANITY, IF IT MEANS WE FIGHT EACH OTHER.

I'M ASHAMED OF YOU, ALL OF YOU.

LEAVE THEN.

WE'LL DISCUSS THIS IN CLASS *TOMORROW.*

UH, EXCUSE ME, "*CLASS*"?

WHO *ARE* YOU PEOPLE?

WE ARE *GODS*--

--OR SOMEDAY *WILL* BE, WHEN WE HAVE LEARNED THE MEANING OF *GODHOOD.*

UNTIL THEN, WE ARE CHILDREN LIKE *YOU.*

HIGHNOTE--

--SING US *HOME.*

HIIIIIIIII

HIIIIIIIIIIIIII

"*EVERY SOUND I EVER HEARD,* EVERY INSTRUMENT, EVERY NOTE--

"--*RAISED PAST THE HIGH END OF HEARING*--

"--*PACKED IN A SINGLE VOICE:*

"*THAT'S THE SONG HIGH-NOTE SINGS.*

"*BEHIND ME GWEN MAKES A CHOKING NOISE.*

"I *KNOW HOW SHE FEELS.*

"*MY TEETH ACHE.*

199

ENOUGH OF THIS, YOU HAVE DISRUPTED MY OPERATIONS AND *DISTRACTED* ME FROM MY MAIN PURPOSE.

WERE I VINDICTIVE, I WOULD *DESTROY* YOU. INSTEAD, YOU MUST LEAVE.

NOT SO FAST, PAL. WHAT DID YOU WANT WITH *GWEN?*

WITH THE WOMAN YOU CALLED GWEN STACY, *NOTHING.*

MY INTEREST WAS WITH THE INDIVIDUAL PURPORTING TO BE HER *CLONE.*

MY GATHERERS LEARNED OF HER EXISTENCE AND ORIGIN FROM THE FILES OF HER "CREATOR," *PROFESSOR MILES WARREN.*

I ASKED MYSELF, HOW COULD A MERE UNIVERSITY BIOLOGY PROFESSOR ACCOMPLISH A TECHNICAL MIRACLE SUCH AS NEARLY INSTANTANEOUS *CLONING?*

MY STUDY OF THIS WOMAN'S GENETIC STRUCTURE, COMPARED TO THAT OF GWEN STACY, SHOWS THAT HE *DID NOT.*

"THIS IS *SURMISE:* WISHING TO RECREATE GWEN STACY, WARREN KIDNAPED *ANOTHER* FEMALE OF SIMILAR AGE AND GENOTYPE,

"HE INFECTED THIS WOMAN WITH A *GENETIC VIRUS* THAT TRANSFORMED HER ON A CELLULAR LEVEL INTO A NEAR DUPLICATE OF THE ORIGINAL.

"BUT THE DUPLICATION, WHILE IMPRESSIVE, WAS NOT *EXACT.*

"THIS WOMAN IS NOT, AND *NEVER WAS,* GWEN STACY'S CLONE."

NO!

WHAT ARE YOU *SAYING?*

THAT I DON'T *EXIST?*

EASY--

IN YOUR HEART, YOU BOTH KNOW THE TRUTH. INDEED, YOU HAVE *ALWAYS* KNOWN.

WHETHER YOU CHOOSE TO ACCEPT OR DENY THE TRUTH IS UP TO *YOU!*

"WE'RE BACK." "I THINK IT SHOULD FEEL LIKE WAKING FROM A DREAM..."

PETER, HE'S WRONG!

HE'S GOT TO BE WRONG--

ISN'T HE?

ISN'T HE?

"...BUT IT DOESN'T.

"IT FEELS TOO REAL.

"WHAT HAPPENS NEXT MAKES ME WONDER..."

IT'S ALL RIGHT.

THE BAD DREAM IS OVER.

TIME TO WAKE UP.

DAYDREAMER, RIGHT?

WHAT DID YOU DO--?

I TOOK AWAY HER ILLUSIONS.

DREAMS AND ILLUSIONS ARE MY SPECIALTY.

I SENSED HER NEED BACK AT THAT FORTRESS, BUT MY FRIENDS WANTED TO GO--

-- AND I WAS UPSET.

I'VE GOT TO GET BACK BEFORE THEY MISS ME. SOMETHING STRANGE IS UP.

KEEP THIS OUR SECRET, OKAY?

"OKAY.

"I WATCH THE OTHER ONE WALK AWAY.

"AND IT HITS ME:

"I DON'T EVEN KNOW HER NAME.

201

"AND I THINK ABOUT THE *TRUTH*."

"DID I KNOW?"

(YES.)

"DID I HOLD ONTO THE *LIE* THAT GWEN WAS "ALIVE" BECAUSE THE PAIN OF LETTING GO WAS JUST TOO *GREAT*?"

(OH, YES.)

GWEN'S GONE, MARY JANE.

SHE'S BEEN GONE A LONG, LONG TIME.

I KNOW. EVEN SO, SHE'S ALWAYS BEEN *BETWEEN* US, PETER. LIKE A GHOST IN YOUR HEART.

DO YOU STILL LOVE HER?

OF COURSE.

BUT I LOVE YOU MORE THAN I *EVER* LOVED HER.

I LOVE HER AND I MISS HER AND SHE'S DEAD.

GWEN WAS MY PAST, M.J. YOU'RE MY FUTURE.

FORGET THE FUTURE. I'D RATHER LIVE RIGHT *NOW*.

ME, TOO. THIS MOMENT IS ALL WE EVER HAVE.

AND IT'S ENOUGH.

MORE THAN ENOUGH...

END

202

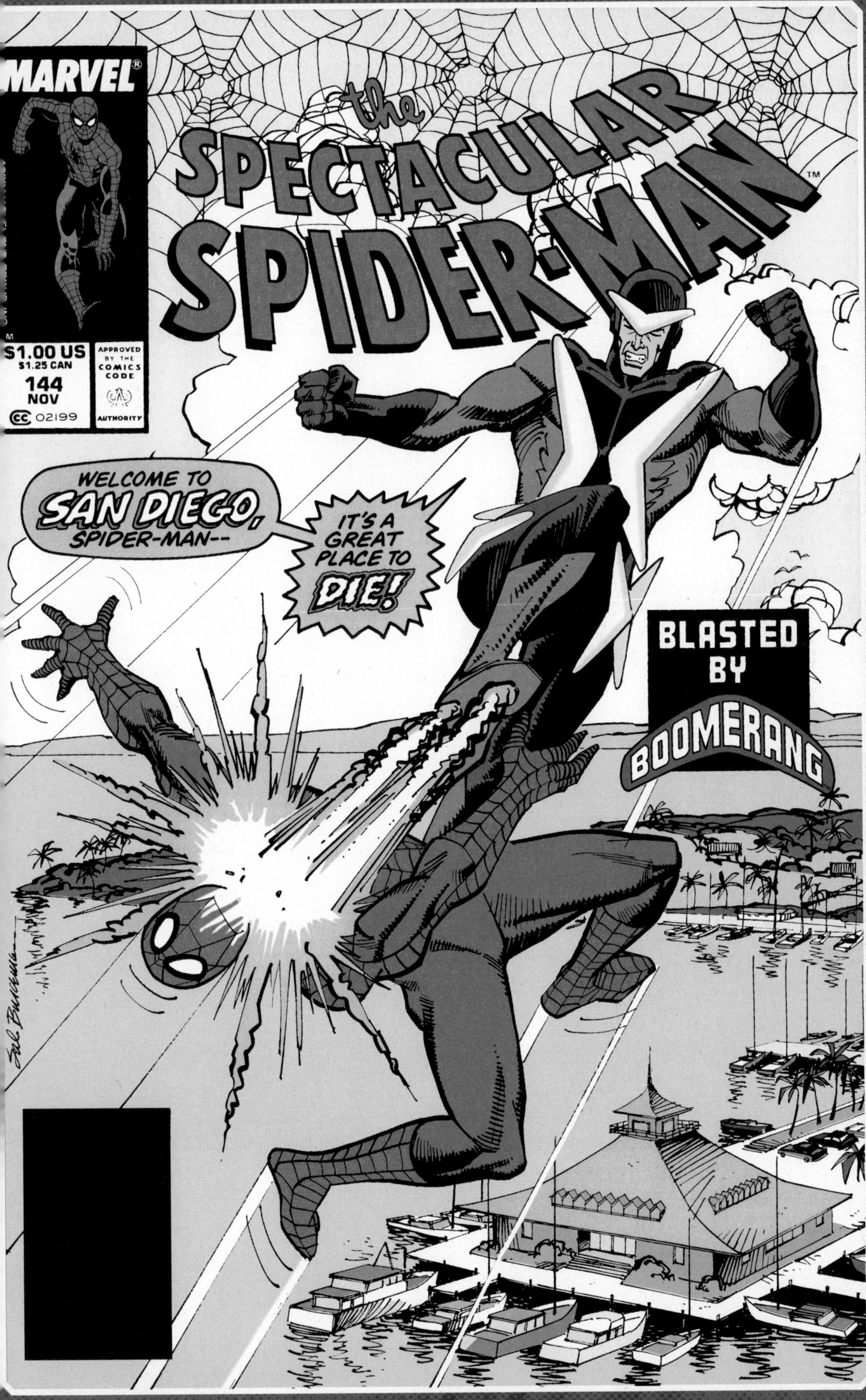
MARVEL®
the SPECTACULAR SPIDER-MAN™
$1.00 US
$1.25 CAN
144
NOV
CC 02199
APPROVED BY THE COMICS CODE AUTHORITY
WELCOME TO SAN DIEGO, SPIDER-MAN--
IT'S A GREAT PLACE TO DIE!
BLASTED BY BOOMERANG

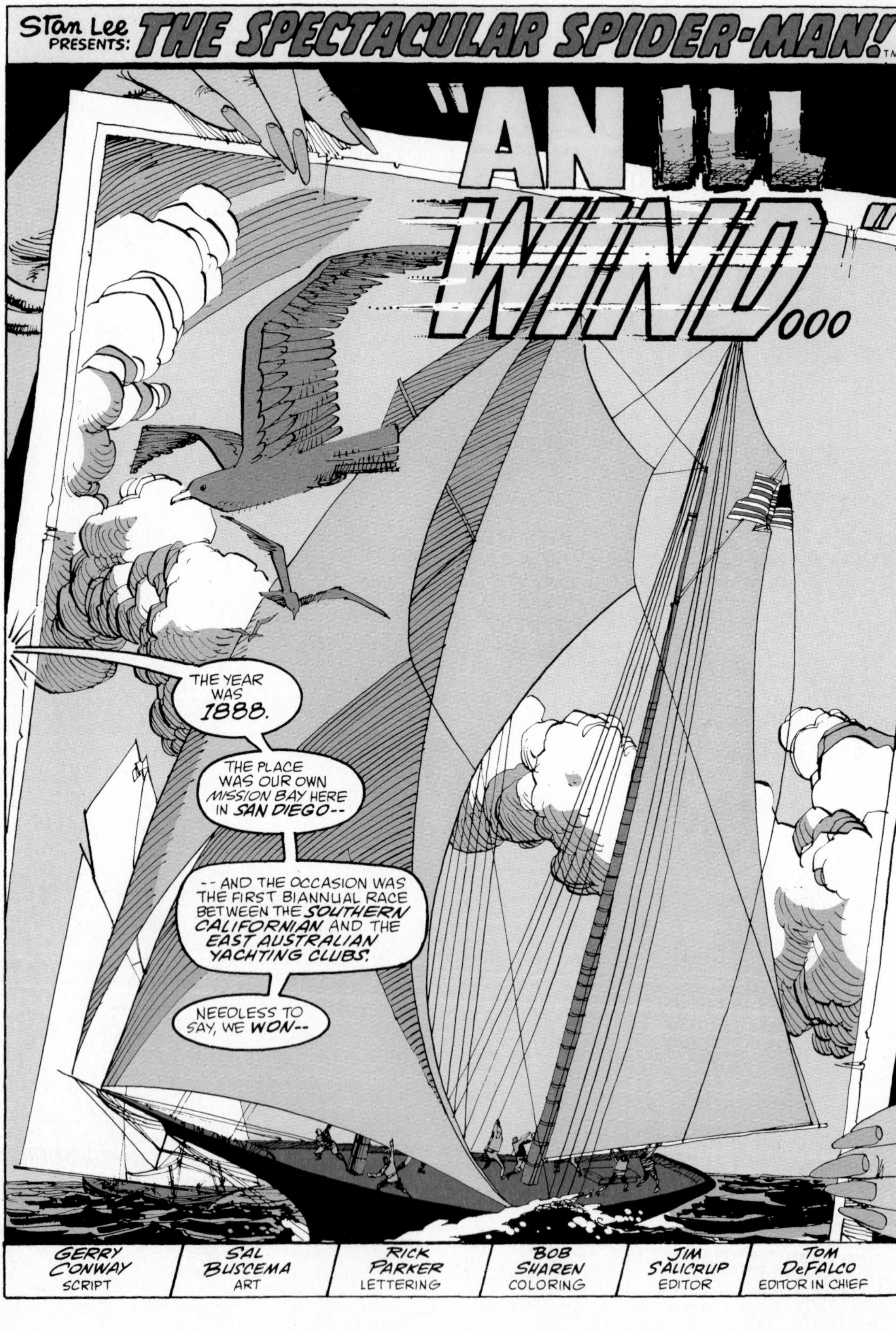
STAN LEE PRESENTS: THE SPECTACULAR SPIDER-MAN!™
"AN ILL WIND"...
THE YEAR WAS 1888.
THE PLACE WAS OUR OWN MISSION BAY HERE IN SAN DIEGO--
-- AND THE OCCASION WAS THE FIRST BIANNUAL RACE BETWEEN THE SOUTHERN CALIFORNIAN AND THE EAST AUSTRALIAN YACHTING CLUBS.
NEEDLESS TO SAY, WE WON--
GERRY CONWAY SCRIPT
SAL BUSCEMA ART
RICK PARKER LETTERING
BOB SHAREN COLORING
JIM SALICRUP EDITOR
TOM DeFALCO EDITOR IN CHIEF

--A FACT OUR AUSSIE COUSINS HAVE *RESENTED* EVER SINCE.

FASCINATING.

FOR THOSE OF YOU WHO TUNED IN LATE, OUR GUEST TODAY ON *"HELLO THERE, SAN DIEGO"* IS LA JOLLA MILLIONAIRE AND YACHTING ENTHUSIAST *LOUIS BAXTER III.*

MR. BAXTER'S YACHT, THE *"GOLDEN CHAMPION,"* WON THE *NORTH AMERICAN CUP* RACE TWO YEARS AGO.

I PREFER TO THINK OF MYSELF AS A YACHTING ENTHUSIAST *FIRST* AND A MILLIONAIRE *SECOND,* RUTH.

THE WEALTH I INHERITED FROM MY FATHER IS *UNIMPORTANT* TO ME--

SAILING IS MY LIFE. I FIND MONEY RATHER *VULGAR.*

--THOUGH OF COURSE WITHOUT IT, THE *"CHAMPION"* MIGHT STILL BE AN IDLE DREAM.

AND WHAT A *TRAGEDY* THAT WOULD BE.

EXPERTS HAVE CALLED THE *"CHAMPION"* THE MOST RADICAL DEVELOPMENT IN SAILING DESIGN SINCE THE INVENTION OF THE JIB.

FIRST TIME ON THE BOOK PROMO CIRCUIT, PARKER?

UH-HUH.

EDUCATIONAL, ISN'T IT?

UM.

TWO DAYS FROM NOW THE *"CHAMPION"* WILL DEFEND THE NORTH AMERICAN CUP AGAINST THE AUSTRALIAN CHALLENGER *"DEFIANT."*

"DEFIANT'S" COLORFUL SKIPPER, MELBOURNE TYCOON *ARTIE CRIPPEN,* HAS SWORN TO RETAKE THE CUP FOR AUSTRALIA "NO MATER WHAT THE COST."

I UNDERSTAND THERE'S SOME *PERSONAL* ANIMOSITY BETWEEN YOU AND CRIPPEN, LOUIS.

I'LL BET. CRIPPEN AND BAXTER MUST HAVE BEEN ON A *TALK SHOW* TOGETHER AND BAXTER NEVER LET CRIPPEN GET A WORD IN.

HEY, PARKER. WHAT'S THE DIFFERENCE BETWEEN BAXTER'S *"CHAMPION"* AND AN EAST EUROPEAN ELECTION?

DON'T DO THIS TO ME, TAMA...

205

...THE EAST EUROPEAN ELECTION IS BETTER-*RIGGED*.

HA!

>AHEM.<

WELL, I SUPPOSE IT'S TIME WE HEARD FROM OUR *OTHER* GUESTS, NEW YORK AUTHORS *PETER PARKER* AND *TAMA JANOWITZ.*

AHA-- AHA-- AHUM

SORRY, RUTH. IT'S BEEN A *LONG* SUMMER.

EVERY TIME I TURN AROUND, IT SEEMS I'M IN A NEW CITY TALKING WITH NEW PEOPLE,

GUESS MY NERVES ARE A LITTLE *SHOT.* I'M NOT A PROFESSIONAL TALK SHOW GUEST.

WHAT I *AM* IS A FREE-LANCE PHOTOGRA-PHER FOR THE *DAILY BUGLE* IN NEW YORK.

SPIDER-MAN IN ACTION
exclusive DAILY BUGLE photographs by PETER PARKER

OVER THE YEARS, I'VE TAKEN HUNDREDS OF ACTION PHOTOS OF A CERTAIN *WALL-CRAWLER*--

-- AND A FEW MONTHS BACK SOME FOLKS GOT THE IDEA TO *COLLECT* THOSE PHOTOS IN A BOOK.

I GUESS THEY KNEW WHAT THEY WERE DOING, BECAUSE, SO FAR, IT'S SELLING LIKE--

KRASH

Y'KNOW, MR. LILY, I REALLY HATE THAT SPIDER-GUY.

LAST TIME WE MET HE LEFT ME TRUSSED LIKE A PIG.

IF MY MATES IN THE *SINISTER SYNDICATE* HADN'T SET ME LOOSE, I'D BE IN *PRISON* NOW. *

AN ALL-TOO-BRIEF RECAP OF AMAZING SPIDER-MAN #281.--JIM.

THE COST OF THAT TELEVISION IS COMING OFF YOUR FEE, MATE.

I HAVE NO *PATIENCE* FOR CHILDISH DISPLAYS OF EMOTION.

RIGHT.

JUST SO WE *UNDERSTAND* EACH OTHER, BOOMERANG.

THIS JOB IS TOO *IMPORTANT* FOR YOU TO SPOIL IT WITH AN ILL-TIMED TEMPER TANTRUM. RIGHT?

RIGHT.

BONZER. LET'S GET TO IT, THEN. I HAD A LONG FLIGHT FROM *MELBOURNE* AND I'M TIRED.

COME HERE.

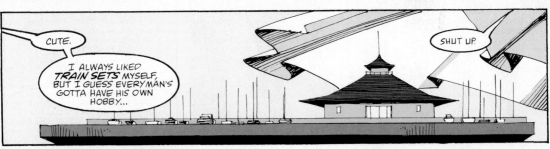

CUTE.

I ALWAYS LIKED *TRAIN SETS* MYSELF, BUT I GUESS EVERYMAN'S GOTTA HAVE HIS OWN HOBBY...

SHUT UP.

YOU'RE LOOKING AT AN EXACT SCALE-MODEL OF THE *SAN LEIBER YACHTING CLUB* MARINA IN MISSION BAY.

THIS SHIP HERE--

DON'T TELL ME.

THE "GOLDEN CHAMPION"-- THAT BLOKE, LOUIS BAXTER'S YACHT.

VERY GOOD, MATE.

THERE'S HOPE FOR YOU YET.

NOW PAY ATTENTION. HERE'S WHAT YOU'RE TO DO, AND I DON'T WANT TO GO THROUGH IT *TWICE...*

IF EVER THERE WAS A CUE FOR A *SCENE TRANSITION*--

-- THAT WAS *IT*.

STUDIO B

WHY DO YOU DO IT, TAMA?

YOU'RE AN IMPORTANT, SERIOUS WRITER-- YOUR BOOK "*SLAVES OF NEW YORK*" IS THE BEST POST-POST MODERN FICTION I'VE EVER READ--YOU'RE FUNNY, AND YOU'RE A *PERSON*, EVEN IF YOU DO DRESS WEIRD.

WITH ALL THAT GOING FOR YOU, WHY RIDE THE BOOK PROMO CIRCUIT?

US SERIOUS WRITERS GOTTA *EAT*, PETE.

AND SPEAKING OF EATING--

MY, MY-- HELLO AGAIN, YOU TWO.

PETER, MY BOY--MAY I CALL YOU PETER, WOULD YOU PREFER "*PETE*"--? PETER, MY BOY, YOU REALLY MUST LEARN TO MAINTAIN YOUR SELF-CONTROL WHEN DEALING WITH THE *MEDIA*.

WELL, IF IT ISN'T *PRINCE DIS- ARMING.*

KBOP

YOU'RE A BRIGHT BOY, PETE, AND YOU HAVE A DELIGHTFUL BOOK, THOUGH I ADMIT THE SUBJECT MATTER ISN'T *QUITE* MY SORT OF THING, BUT YOU MUST LEARN THE SECRET OF SELF-PROMOTION IF YOU WANT TO MAXIMIZE YOUR EXPOSURE.

SELF-ABSORPTION, PETER, THAT'S THE KEY TO SELF-PROMOTION-- TOTAL AND COMPLETE INTEREST IN YOURSELF TO THE EXCLUSION OF ALL OTHER CONCERNS.

BRING EVERY CONVERSATIONAL GAMBIT, EVERY ANECDOTE, EVERY PASSING REMARK BACK TO *YOURSELF* AND YOU'LL DOMINATE EVERY INTERVIEW, I GUARANTEE.

FRIENDLY TIP, PETE MY BOY, FRIENDLY ADVICE.

USE IT IN GOOD HEALTH.

TA.

VROOMM

≷COUGH≷

GEE GOSH, WASN'T THAT HELPFUL?

WHAT DO YOU SAY, PETE, MY BOY... *DINNER?*

SURE, WHY NOT?

AND WHO KNOWS? MAYBE WE'LL LUCK OUT AND RUN INTO BAXTER AGAIN.

I HARDLY KNOW HIM, BUT I'M BEGINNING TO REALLY *HATE* THAT GUY.

--I SWEAR, IF I HAVE TO DO ONE MORE DUMB TALK SHOW, I'M LIABLE TO **STRANGLE** SOMEONE ON CAMERA, MJ.

TOUGH DAY, HUH, TIGER?

NO, I'VE HAD A **WONDERFUL** DAY.

A FIVE-HOUR FLIGHT THAT TOOK TEN HOURS, COUNTING AIRPORT DELAYS--

--A **45** MINUTE TRAFFIC JAM ON THE WAY TO THE BOOKSTORE FOR THE BOOK SIGNING--

--THEN NO BOOKS FOR ME TO SIGN ONCE WE GET TO THE STORE--

--AND THEY WON'T BE HERE TILL TOMORROW--

--THEN AN HOUR OF TORTURE ON "HELLO THERE, SAN DIEGO"--

--AND FINALLY, THE LAST STRAW, WHEN TAMA AND I ARRIVE AT THE HOTEL RESTAURANT FOR DINNER, THE PLACE IS SHUT DOWN FOR **HEALTH CODE VIOLATIONS**--

--AND WE END UP MUNCHING COLD FRIES AND WET BURGERS AT THE DOWNTOWN BUS TERMINAL.

OTHER THAN THAT, THE DAY WAS JUST **PERFECT.**

I LOVE YOU, PETER.

YEAH.

I LOVE YOU, TOO, MJ.

HOW CAN YOU MISS SOMEBODY SO MUCH AFTER ONLY **ONE** DAY?

THAT'S THE **REAL** REASON I FEEL SO TENSE--NOT ALL THIS OTHER STUFF.

I MISS MY WIFE.

I MISS MY HOME.

I MISS....

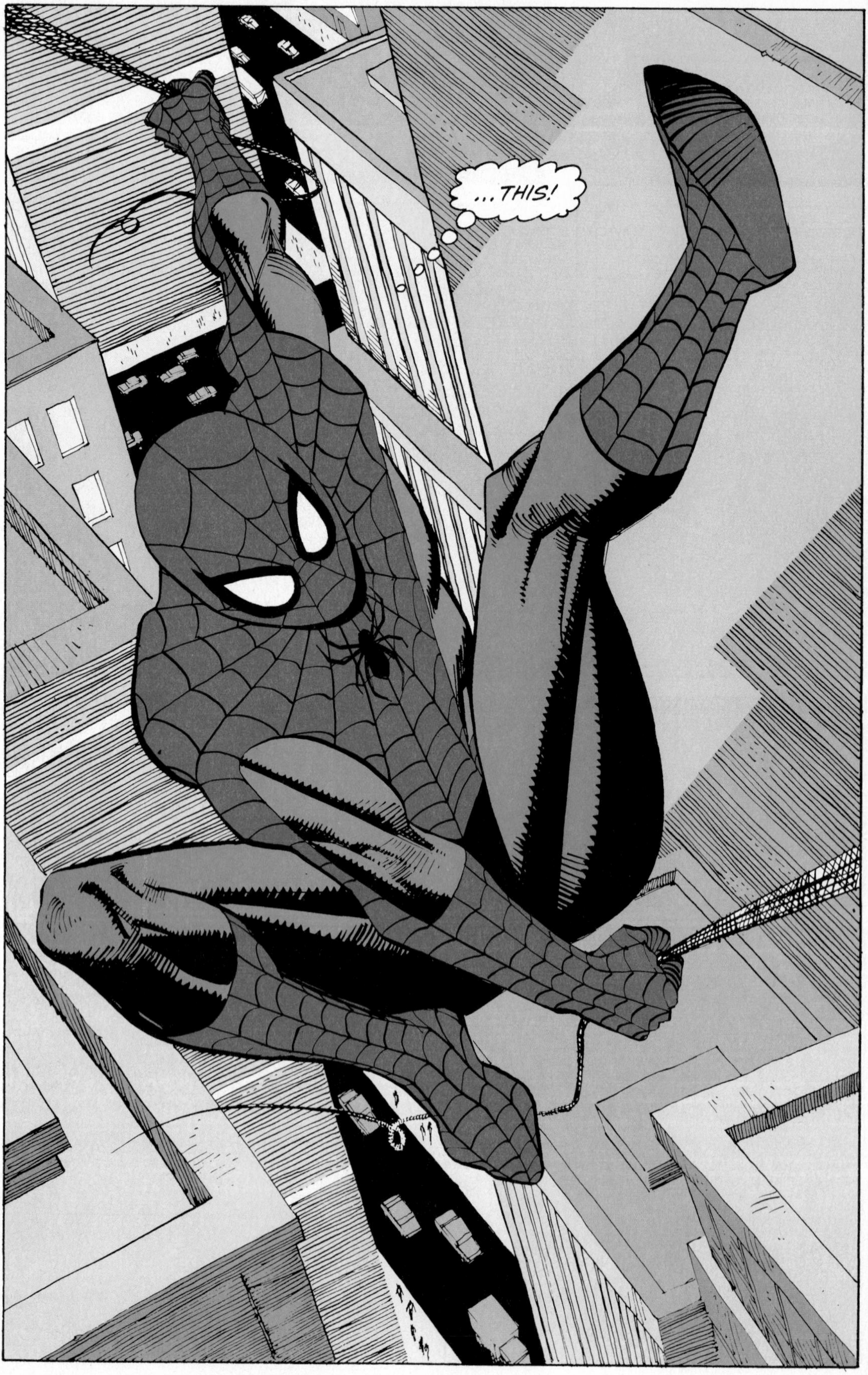
...THIS!

≷WHEW!≷ NOTHING LIKE AN HOUR OF *WEB-SWINGING* TO KNOCK THE KINKS OUT OF YOUR PSYCHE.

YEP, I FEEL *GREAT.*

YEP

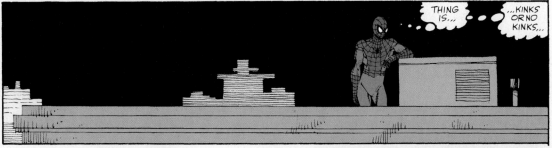

THING IS...

...KINKS OR NO KINKS...

...I'M *STILL* IN SAN DIEGO.

MJ IS *STILL* 3,000 MILES AWAY.

AND I MISS HER...

BWHOOM

IT'S NONE OF YOUR BUSINESS, PARKER.

THIS *ISN'T* YOUR TOWN. THERE ARE POLICE HERE, AND FIREMEN, AND PARAMEDICS, AND HANDLING EMERGENCIES IN SAN DIEGO IS *THEIR* JOB, NOT YOURS.

YOU'RE HERE ON A *BOOK TOUR* THAT'S ALL.

SURE, YOU'RE TENSE, AND YOU MISS YOUR WIFE, AND YOU HAD A LOUSY DAY.

BUT THAT'S NO REASON TO GET INVOLVED, JUST BECAUSE SOMEBODY BLOWS UP A *MARINA.*

RIGHT?

211

RIGHT.

SO FORGET IT . . .

GO BACK TO THE HOTEL, CATCH SOME **Z'S**, MEET TAMA FOR BREAKFAST, WANDER DOWN TO THE BOOKSTORE EARLY--

"-- PAY NO **ATTENTION** TO THOSE SMOKING BOATS--

"-- DON'T **THINK** ABOUT LOUIS BAXTER AND THE 'CHAMPION' AND THE NORTH AMERICAN CUP RACE TWO DAYS FROM NOW-- "

-- AND WHATEVER YOU DO--

-- DON'T **LISTEN** TO THOSE SECURITY GUARDS TALKING DOWN BELOW.

-- FOUND IT ON THE DOCK, RIGHT AFTER THE **EXPLOSION**.

GOT MY KID ONE FOR CHRISTMAS, ONLY HERS WAS **PLASTIC**. NEVER COULD MAKE THE DUMB THING WORK.

WOULDN'T COME BACK NO MATTER HOW HARD WE--

A **BOOMERANG?**

NONE OF YOUR BUSINESS, PARKER.

BUT-- A **BOOMERANG--?**

NONE OF YOUR--

FINE. JUST *FINE.* YOU HAD TO STICK AROUND UNTIL YOUR *SPIDER-SENSE* KICKED IN, DIDN'T YOU?

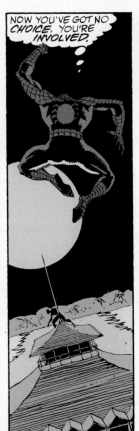

NOW YOU'VE GOT NO *CHOICE,* YOU'RE *INVOLVED.*

TOO BAD, HUH?

SO WHY IS MY *HEART* RACING--

--AND WHY DO I FEEL LIKE *GRIN-NING?*

SPIDER-MAN!

WHAT WAS YOUR *FIRST* CLUE?

JOKE ALL YOU WANT, WEB-SLINGER!

I WAS HOPING YOU'D SHOW UP WHEN I SAW THEY WERE PROMOTING THAT *BOOK* ABOUT YOU.

THIS REALLY *ICES* MY *CAKE.*

ME, TOO, *BOOMERANG.* I MIGHT AS WELL *ADMIT* IT.

I *LOVE* THIS STUFF.

NHAH, *MISSED* ME!

SMART MAN -- YOU GOT IT ALL *FIGURED* OUT.

BY THE WAY, I *DIDN'T MISS.*

DON'T TELL ME WHY YOU'RE HERE, LET ME *GUESS:*

YOU WERE HIRED TO BLOW UP BAXTER'S YACHT-- AM I RIGHT?

OH, *REALLY?*

BNNNNN

IF THAT WASN'T A MISS, I'D LIKE TO SEE WHAT YOU'D CALL A *BULLSEYE.*

SPRAN

ME AND MY MOUTH...

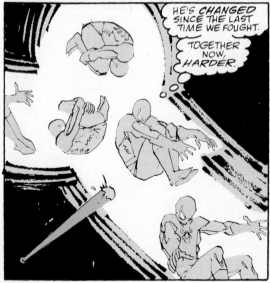

HE'S *CHANGED* SINCE THE LAST TIME WE FOUGHT.

TOGETHER NOW, *HARDER.*

MOST GUYS I FIGHT DON'T *LIKE* ME, BUT BOOMERANG SOUNDS LIKE HE'S CLEAR OVER THE EDGE INTO *HATE.*

THAT MAKES HIM UN- PREDICTABLE, AND UN- PREDICTABLE MAKES HIM *DANGEROUS.*

SO I BETTER BE *CAREFUL...*

JOKING WITH A GUY THAT MAD MIGHT GET ME *KILLED!*

FTOOM

OH, GREAT. THERE HE GOES, OVER THE BAY--NO WAY TO FOLLOW HIM--

FREEZE!

YOU'RE UNDER ARREST--

GIVE ME A BREAK.

WHAT CHARGE?

SUSPECTED ARSON, FOR STARTERS.

SORRY, FELLAS, MUCH AS I RESPECT DUE PROCESS...

...I'M JUST NOT IN THE MOOD.

HEY!

POW

SEE, RON? SEE?

" I TOLD YOU THAT WAS THE REAL SPIDER-MAN, BUT, OH, NO, YOU SAID, 'WHAT WOULD THE REAL SPIDER-MAN BE DOING IN SAN DIEGO? GOTTA BE SOME SHOWOFF IN A COSTUME.'

"SO WHATTAYA SAY NOW, RON? HUH?

"WHATTAYA SAY NOW?"

"OH, SHUT UP."

WELL, GREAT. NOW I'VE GOT THE SAN DIEGO POLICE ON MY CASE. JUST WHAT I NEED.

AT LEAST I MANAGED TO KEEP BOOMIE FROM FINISHING THE JOB HE STARTED. BAXTER'S YACHT IS STILL IN ONE PIECE, AND NOBODY GOT HURT.

THAT'S SOMETHING, RIGHT?

RIGHT.

TOMORROW NIGHT, I'LL FLY HOME, BACK TO N.Y., BACK TO MARY JANE.

LET THE POLICE HANDLE BOOMERANG. LET THEM FIND OUT WHO HIRED HIM.

I DON'T EVEN LIKE BAXTER.

IT'S OVER, FINIS, THE END. ALL DONE.

THIS IS NONE OF MY BUSINESS.

R*I*I*I*I*I*I*I*I*I*GHT.

THE MORNING OF THE FOLLOWING DAY, AT THE OFFICE OF THE *DAILY BUGLE*...

CLAP CLAP CLAP

I DON'T KNOW WHAT TO SAY...

CLAP CLAP CLAP CLAP

...REALLY, I'M *SPEECHLESS.*

ALL YOUR CARDS, ALL YOUR PHONE CALLS OF SUPPORT WHILE I WAS RECUPERATING IN THE *HOSPITAL*... ...NONE OF IT PREPARED ME FOR *THIS.*

SOMETIMES IT TAKES A NEAR TRAGEDY FOR A MAN TO REALIZE WHAT LIFE MEANS TO HIM...HOW MUCH HE *LOVES* THOSE AROUND HIM... AND HOW MUCH THEY LOVE HIM.

WHEN JONAH TOLD ME HE WANTED ME TO START WORKING AGAIN THIS WEEK, I THOUGHT IT WAS TOO *SOON.*

BUT NOW I CAN SEE IT WASN'T SOON *ENOUGH.*

GREAT TO HAVE YOU BACK, ROBBIE.

THE BUGLE HASN'T BEEN THE SAME WITH ITS EDITOR IN CHIEF ON SICK LEAVE.

THANKS, BEN.

≷HRMMPH≷ TIME IS MONEY, ROBERTSON. WE'VE WASTED ENOUGH OF IT ON *SENTIMENT.*

GET TO *WORK.*

YOU'RE NOT FOOLING *ANYONE,* JONAH, YOU BIG SOFTY.

A MAN CAN *TRY,* CAN'T HE?

SORRY TO BREAK UP THE FESTIVITIES, PEOPLE.

ARE YOU *JOSEPH ROBERTSON?*

THAT'S MY NAME.

AND TO THIS OLD NEWSPAPER MAN, YOU GENTLEMEN LOOK LIKE *POLICE.* AM I RIGHT?

FEDERAL MARSHALS, ACTUALLY.

IS THIS ABOUT MY TESTIMONY AGAINST *TOMBSTONE?*

IN A WAY.

ACCORDING TO YOUR SWORN TESTIMONY TO A *FEDERAL GRAND JURY*, YOU WITNESSED TOMBSTONE COMMIT A *MURDER-FOR-HIRE* TWENTY YEARS AGO--YET SAID NOTHING UNTIL NOW.*

THE GRAND JURY JUST *INDICTED* YOU FOR OBSTRUCTION OF JUSTICE AND BEING AN ACCESSORY TO MURDER AFTER THE FACT.

MR. ROBERTSON, YOU'RE *UNDER ARREST*...

* UNLESS YOU MISSED OUR LAST FEW ISSUES, YOU ALREADY KNOW ALL THIS. -- JIM.

SAN DIEGO, CALIFORNIA. THREE TIME ZONES AND SEVERAL HOURS LATER...

BOOKS-R-US

MY BROTHER'S A COP, AND *HE* SAYS SOME COPS SPOTTED SPIDER-MAN AT MISSION BAY LAST NIGHT.

YEAH, RIGHT. WHAT WAS HE DOIN', SWIMMING WITH *SHAMU?*

SPIDEY LIVES IN *NEW YORK*, DUMMY!

≥WHEW!≤ BEING A "CELEBRITY" AS PETER PARKER IS ALMOST *MORE* WORK THAN BEING *SPIDER-MAN!*

AT LEAST WEB-SLINGING DOESN'T GIVE YOU *WRITER'S CRAMP!*

HOW MANY BOOKS DO I HAVE TO SIGN, ED?

UH... THE DISTRIBUTOR FOULED UP OUR *ORDER*, MR. PARKER. WE'VE GOT JUST OVER FIVE HUNDRED...

FIVE HUNDRED! EVEN AT FIVE BOOKS A MINUTE THAT'LL TAKE ME NEARLY--

TWO HOURS, PETE MY BOY. AIN'T THE LITERARY LIFE JUST *GRAND?*

READY FOR A LUNCH BREAK?

LUNCH?

SORRY, TAMA, I ALMOST FORGOT-- I'VE GOT A LUNCH APPOINTMENT AT THE *MARINA CLUB*--

--IN *20* MINUTES!

MAYBE WE CAN CATCH DINNER LATER AT THE BUS TERMINAL. I HEAR THEY HAVE A MEAT BY-PRODUCT HAMBURGER SPECIAL TONIGHT THAT'S ALMOST *EDIBLE.*

ED, I'LL BE BACK IN A COUPLE OF HOURS.

BUT THESE BOOKS-- YOUR *FANS* --

HOLD THE FORT, ED.

IF WORSE COMES TO WORSE, TELL THEM YOU'RE *ME.*

ONE RAPID WEB-SLING ACROSS TOWN *LATER*...

REALLY, I APPRECIATE YOUR CONCERN, PETER LAD-- REALLY, IT'S *TOUCHING*--BUT MY MECHANICS ASSURE ME THE DAMAGE TO *"CHAMPION"* WAS MINIMAL --

-- AND DESPITE RUMORS ABOUT SOME SORT OF *COSTUMED CHARACTER* IN THE MARINA, THE POLICE FOUND NO *CONCRETE* EVIDENCE OF A PLANNED ATTACK --

--SO I REALLY DON'T SEE THE NEED TO MAKE AN UNPLEASANT *FUSS* ABOUT ALL THIS.

YOU MUST TRY THE *BRIOCHE.*

I DIDN'T COME HERE TO DISCUSS *PASTRY,* BAXTER.

I TOLD YOU WHAT *SPIDER-MAN* TOLD *ME.* HE WAS IN TOWN TO HELP PROMOTE *" WEBS "*--

--AND HE SPOTTED *BOOMERANG* MINUTES AFTER YOUR BOAT WAS BOMBED.

BOOMERANG IS A HIRED *KILLER.* YOU SAID YOURSELF IT WAS JUST *LUCK* YOU WEREN'T ABOARD *"CHAMPION"* LAST NIGHT.

SOMEONE WANTS YOU *DEAD?*

OH, PLEASE BE *SERIOUS,* PETER MY BOY.

WHO'D WANT TO KILL A YACHTSMAN-- EVEN ONE ADMITTEDLY AS SUCCESSFUL AND *ENVIED* AS YOUR DEAR NEW FRIEND LOUIS BAXTER?

THE NOTION IS A PATENT *ABSURDITY.*

BAXTER, YOU BLOODY-MAD *DINGO,* I'LL DANCE ON YOUR *GRAVE.*

OF COURSE, THERE'S ALWAYS *ARTIE.*

218

BLOODY RIGHT, THERE'S *ARTIE*-- NO THANKS TO *YOU*.

YOU MUST HAVE SPENT HALF YOUR BLOODY *FORTUNE* TRYING TO KEEP ME OUT OF THIS YEAR'S RACE--

BRIBING OFFICIALS TO CHANGE THE RACING RULES, FORCING ME TO REDESIGN MY SHIP AT THE LAST MINUTE!

SOMEHOW, YOU ALMOST MANAGED TO GET "*DEFIANT*" IMPOUNDED AT U.S. CUSTOMS!

ALL BECAUSE YOU'RE A *CHEAT*, BAXTER-- AND YOU'RE AFRAID I'LL EXPOSE YOU!

CHARMING, AS ALWAYS, HMM, ARTIE?

PETER, MY BOY, MEET ARTIE CRIPPEN, OWNER AND MASTER OF THE GOOD SHIP "*DEFIANT*"-- MY CHIEF OPPONENT IN TOMORROW'S REGATTA.

DON'T MIND ARTIE'S MANNER. ALL AUSTRALIANS ARE *COLORFUL*. ARTIE SIMPLY CARRIES IT FURTHER THAN MOST.

MR. CRIPPEN.

HMM. BOOMERANG IS AUSTRALIAN TOO.

CRIPPEN SURE SEEMS TO *DESPISE* BAXTER-- BUT ENOUGH TO *KILL* HIM?

MAYBE I BETTER--

EH?

TAKE YOUR SUSPICIONS TO THE INTERNATIONAL YACHTING COMMISSION, ARTIE.

I WILL, YOU LOUSY--

SPIDER-SENSE-- TINGLING TO *WARN* ME --

DANGER!

OMIGOSH!

BAXTER--

219

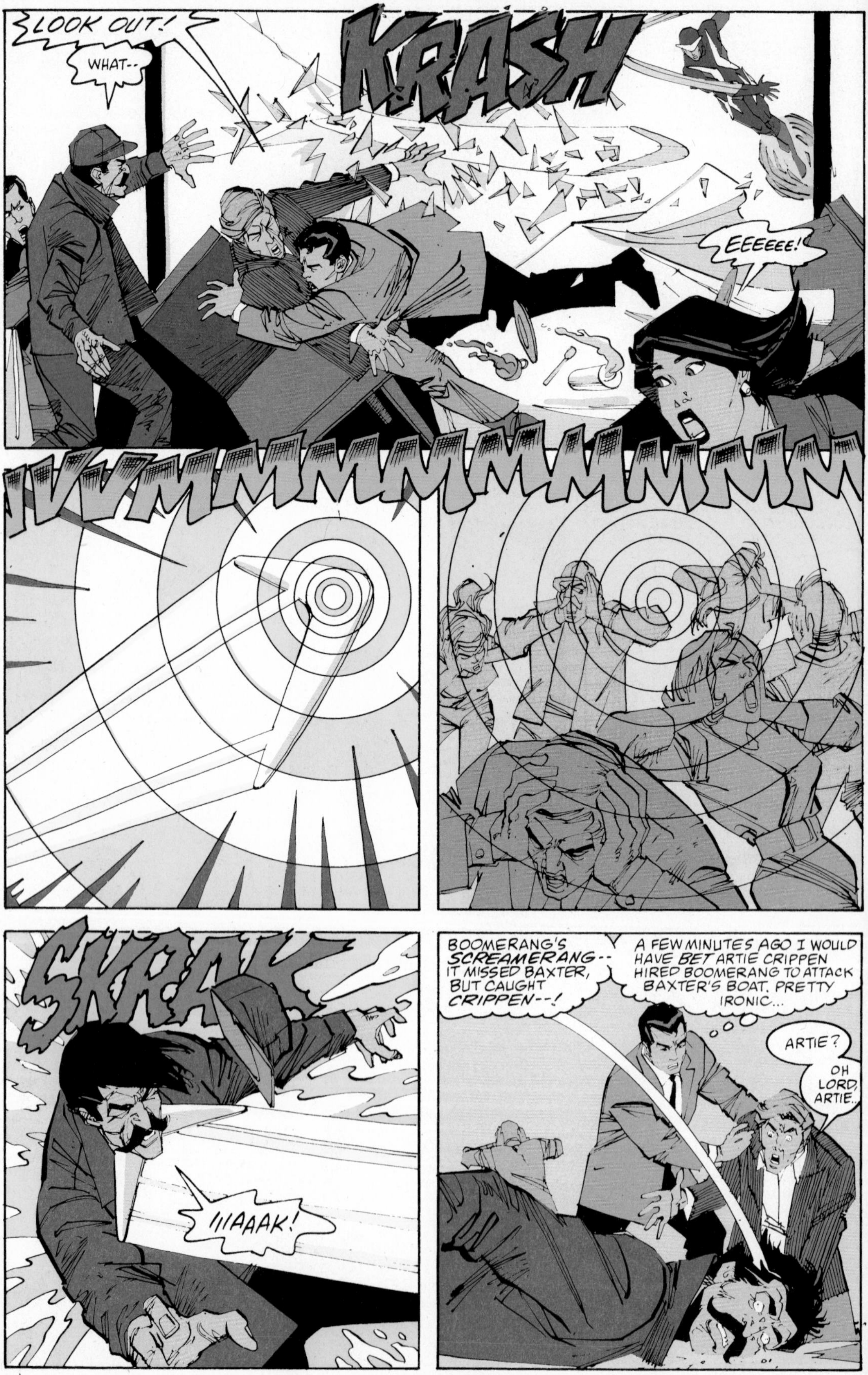
LOOK OUT!
WHAT--
KRASH
EEEEEE!
VMMMMMMMMMMMMM
SKRAK
!!AAAK!
BOOMERANG'S SCREAMERANG-- IT MISSED BAXTER, BUT CAUGHT CRIPPEN--!
A FEW MINUTES AGO I WOULD HAVE BET ARTIE CRIPPEN HIRED BOOMERANG TO ATTACK BAXTER'S BOAT. PRETTY IRONIC...
ARTIE?
OH LORD, ARTIE...

THAT MAN-- IS HE--?

DEAD. THE GUY'S *DEAD!*

AND JUDGING BY THE WAY BAXTER IS TAKING IT, I'D SAY THE "RIVALRY" BETWEEN HIM AND CRIPPEN MUST HAVE BEEN A *PUBLIC RELATIONS* PLOY TO BUILD INTEREST IN THE RACE!

BAXTER'S REALLY *BROKEN UP!*

ARTIE...POOR ARTIE...

DOESN'T MAKE *SENSE.*

IF CRIPPEN AND BAXTER WERE REALLY *FRIENDS--*

--WHO HIRED *BOOMERANG?*

ONE WAY TO FIND OUT--

--*ASK* BOOMERANG WHILE HE'S STILL HANGING AROUND FOR ANOTHER SHOT!

TWO MINUTES LATER, AS *POLICE SIRENS* HOWL IN THE DISTANCE...

AAROOOOO

COPS COMING.

GUESS I DON'T GET A SECOND TRY, AFTER ALL...

SPIDER-MAN!

I WOULDN'T SAY *THAT*, BOOMIE.

YOU'VE GOT A SECOND SHOT AT *ME*.

GOOD.

AH, BUT THERE'S A *DIFFERENCE*:

KRAK

YOU'VE GOT NO PLACE TO CATCH YOUR *WEB-LINE* HERE, SPIDER-MAN.

FALL NOW, AND HOW WILL YOU *SAVE* YOURSELF?

TODAY WON'T BE A *TOTAL* WASH, AT THAT!

LIKE *HEIGHTS*?

GET SERIOUS. YOU'RE TALKING TO A GUY WHO SWINGS OVER *MANHATTAN* FOR CHUCKLES.

BESIDES, HOW MANY ACROPHOBIC HEROES DO *YOU* KNOW, BOOMIE?

HITTING THE WATER FROM *THIS* HEIGHT, UNLESS YOU MAKE A *PERFECT* DIVE--

-- WILL BE LIKE SLAMMING HEAD FIRST INTO A *BRICK WALL* AT **60** M.P.H.!

STOP BEATING AROUND THE BUSH AND 'FESS UP, BOOM.

YOU DON'T *LIKE* ME.

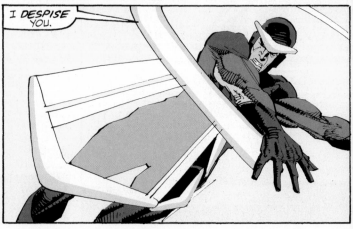

I *DESPISE* YOU.

YEAH, WELL -- YOU'RE NOT ON MY "A" PARTY LIST, EITHER, PAL.

HARD TO *CONNECT* WITH ONE OF THOSE 'RANGS WHEN YOUR TARGET IS SO *CLOSE*, HUH?

MAKE IT EASY ON *BOTH* OF US...

STOP FIGHTING-- *SURRENDER*-- AND TELL ME WHO *HIRED* YOU.

UHHH.

YOU MUST BE *JOKING.*

WHO, ME?

MR. TAKE-ME-SERIOUS? WITH AN OUTFIT LIKE MINE, WOULD I JO--

ZAAANN

ARRRGH!

STUNNED ME WITH HIS *JET-BOOT!*

NOT EVEN MY *SPIDER-SENSE* COULD PROTECT ME FROM THAT ONE!

HAVE TO ANGLE MY FALL--

--MAKE A *PERFECT* DIVE--

--OR SNAP MY *NECK* LIKE A DAY-OLD BREAD-STICK!

DID IT!

SO HOORAY FOR ME. CRIPPEN'S DEAD--BOOMERANG'S FREE--AND I'VE GOT NO MORE IDEA WHO'S *BEHIND* THIS THAN I DID TEN MINUTES AGO!

GREAT JOB.

DAYS LIKE THIS CAN GET EVEN A CHEERFUL GUY LIKE ME DEPRESSED...

223

...YOU FIGURE THE KILLER WAS AIMING FOR YOU, MISSED, AND HIT *CRIPPEN* BY MISTAKE?

OBVIOUSLY.

LAST NIGHT THIS MAN, *BOOMERANG*, ATTEMPTED TO DESTROY MY YACHT. THIS MORNING HE TRIED TO DESTROY ME.

DRAW YOUR OWN CONCLUSIONS.

I SAY SOMEONE HIRED THIS FELLOW TO *SABOTAGE* TO-MORROW'S RACE.

CORONE
CITY OF SA
DIE GO

NEAT GUESS, LOUIE.

WHO AND WHY, THAT'S WHAT I'D LIKE TO KNOW.

BUT *FORGET* IT, PARKER.

REMEMBER, YOU'RE NOT *INVOLVED*.

MR. BAXTER!

SIR, ANY COMMENT ABOUT ARTIE CRIPPEN?

QUITE A FEW *RUMORS* HAVE BEEN FLOATING ABOUT... RUMORS THAT ARTIE AND I WERE *ENEMIES*...

NOTHING COULD BE FURTHER FROM THE TRUTH.

ARTIE CRIPPEN AND I WERE *BROTHERS OF THE SEA*.

HE WAS A *DEAR* FRIEND, AND I SHALL MISS HIM *TERRIBLY*.

AW, RATS. MARY JANE ISN'T GOING TO LIKE IT, BUT I'VE GOT A FEELING I WON'T BE CATCHING TONIGHT'S *RED EYE* FLIGHT TO NEW YORK AFTER ALL...

THAT NIGHT, AS TWILIGHT PURPLES TO NIGHT IN *LA JOLLA...*

ORDINARILY, I HATE SPENDING MONEY.

ONE NEVER SEEMS TO RECEIVE PROPER *VALUE,* IF YOU KNOW WHAT I MEAN.

BUT THIS IS *ONE* CHECK I'M DELIGHTED TO WRITE.

MR. LILY, YOUR PROTEGE HAS FULFILLED *ALL* MY EXPECTATIONS.

THANKS.

YOU DO EXCELLENT WORK, BOOMERANG.

REALLY.

ATTACKING MY YACHT, YOU MADE IT APPEAR *I* WAS THE TARGET. WONDERFUL MISDIRECTION.

THUS, WHEN YOU KILLED CRIPPEN AT THE MARINA TODAY, EVERYONE *ASSUMED* YOU WERE AIMING AT ME.

CINCH.

OVERALL, I'M QUITE SATISFIED.

CRIPPEN IS DEAD, MY *REPUTATION* IS PROTECTED FROM HIS EXPOSURE, THE "*CHAMPION*" IS READY FOR TOMORROW'S RACE--

-- AND ONLY ONE SMALL *COMPLICATION* THREATENS ON THE HORIZON.

NO WORRIES, MR. B.

IF SPIDER-MAN GETS IN THE WAY TO-MORROW--

-- I'LL DO *HIM* FOR *FREE.*

JUST ONCE I WISH YOU WOULD NOT BREAK THE FURNITURE...

TO BE CONTINUED...

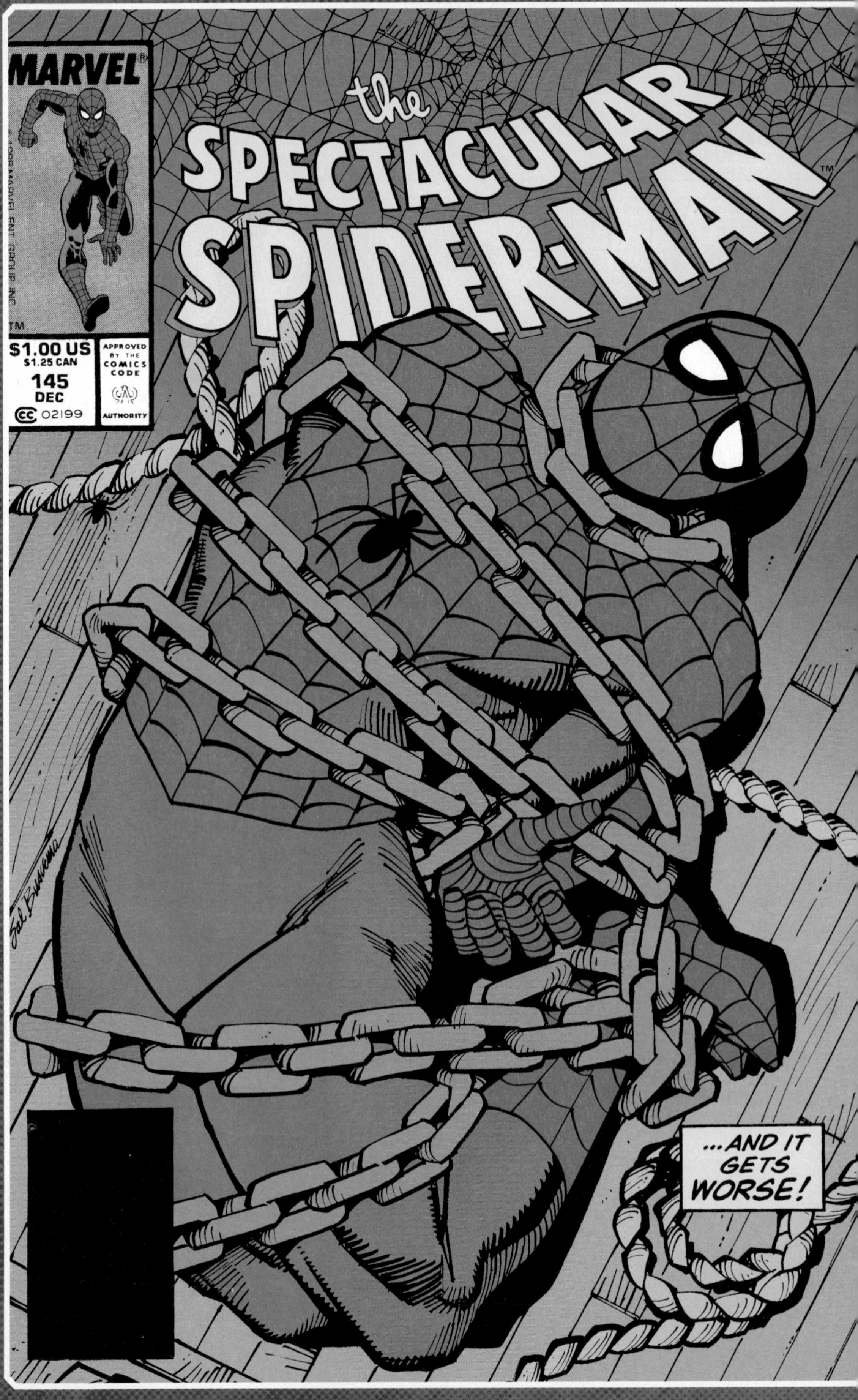
MARVEL
the SPECTACULAR SPIDER-MAN
$1.00 US
$1.25 CAN
145
DEC
02199
APPROVED BY THE COMICS CODE AUTHORITY
...AND IT GETS WORSE!

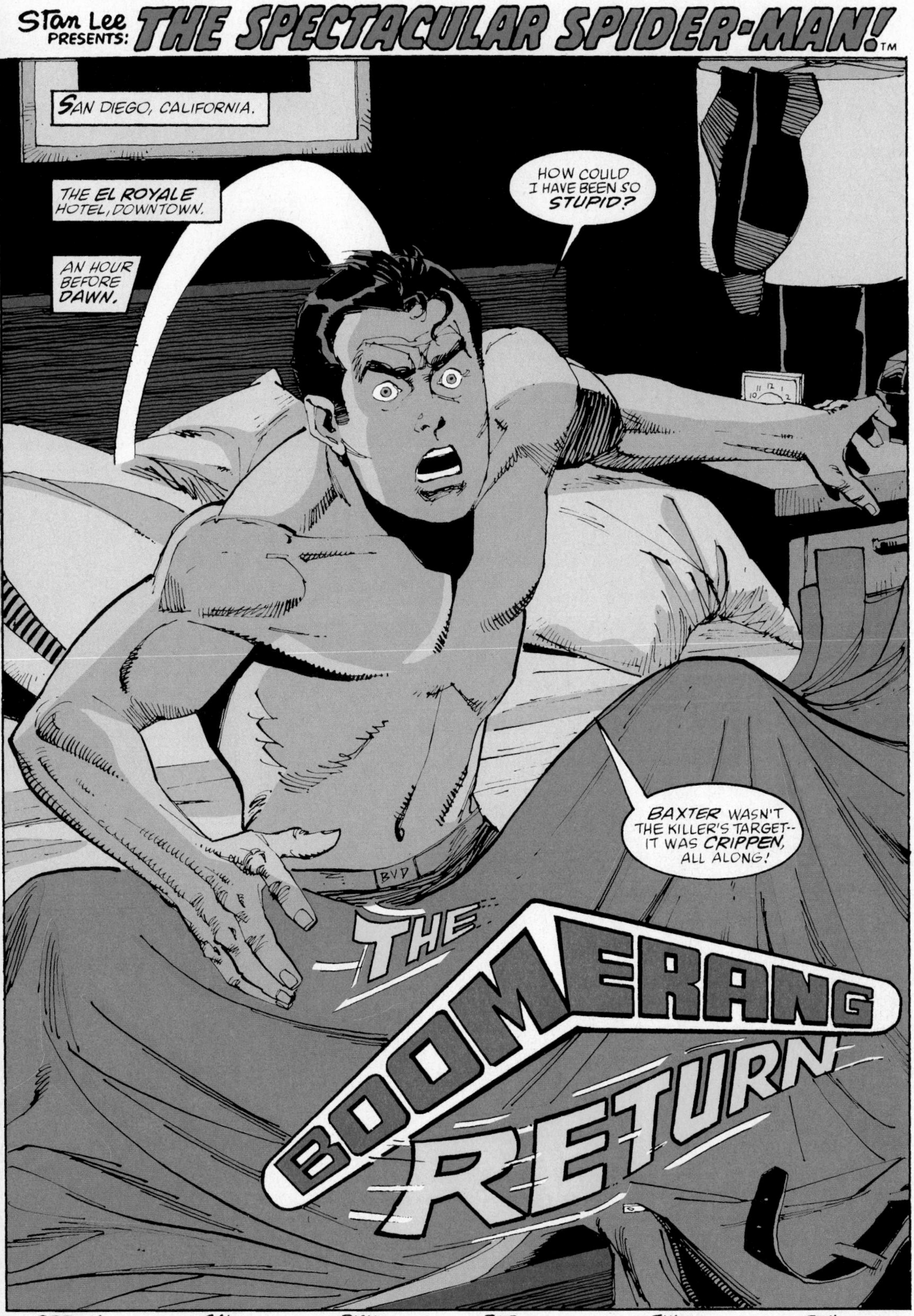
STAN LEE PRESENTS: THE SPECTACULAR SPIDER-MAN!™
SAN DIEGO, CALIFORNIA.
THE EL ROYALE HOTEL, DOWNTOWN.
AN HOUR BEFORE DAWN.
HOW COULD I HAVE BEEN SO STUPID?
BAXTER WASN'T THE KILLER'S TARGET-- IT WAS CRIPPEN, ALL ALONG!
THE BOOMERANG RETURN
GERRY CONWAY SCRIPT
SAL BUSCEMA ART
RICK PARKER LETTERS
BOB SHAREN COLOR
JIM SALICRUP EDITOR
TOM DeFALCO EDITOR IN CHIEF

I COULD *KICK* MYSELF, IT'S ALL SO OBVIOUS! LOUIS BAXTER SET UP ARTIE CRIPPEN'S MURDER--

--AND GAVE HIMSELF THE PERFECT ALIBI BY MAKING IT APPEAR *HE* WAS THE KILLER'S INTENDED VICTIM!

WHAT'S WORSE, HE MADE ME A *WITNESS!*

I NEVER LIKED BAXTER...

"...ESPECIALLY AFTER HE HOGGED ALL THE *ATTENTION* WHEN WE APPEARED TOGETHER ON A LOCAL SAN DIEGO TV TALK SHOW.

"I WAS PROMOTING MY BOOK, '*WEBS*,' AND BAXTER WAS PROMOTING HIMSELF."

BAXTER OWNS THE "GOLDEN CHAMPION"-- A YACHT FAVORED TO WIN TODAY'S *NORTH AMERICA CUP* RACE IN MISSION BAY.

"LAST NIGHT, SOMEONE TRIED TO *BLOW UP* THE 'CHAMPION' WHILE I WAS SWINGING BY THE MARINA.

"I SPOTTED *BOOMERANG* NEARBY-- WE FOUGHT-- AND HE ESCAPED."

AT THE TIME, I THOUGHT SOMEONE HIRED BOOMIE TO *SABOTAGE* BAXTER'S BOAT.

BUT SUPPOSE THE EXPLOSION WAS *FAKED?*

228

"BAXTER'S MAIN RIVAL IN TODAY'S RACE WAS AN AUSTRALIAN NAMED *ARTIE CRIPPEN*.

"YESTERDAY, CRIPPEN WAS *KILLED* -- BY A SCREAM-ERANG AIMED AT BAXTER.

BUT WHAT IF IT ONLY *LOOKED* THAT WAY?

WHAT IF *CRIPPEN* WAS THE TARGET, NOT BAXTER?

EVERYTHING CHANGES.

EVERYTHING.

"THAT'S WHY *BOOMERANG* HUNG AROUND THE MURDER SCENE JUST LONG ENOUGH FOR ME TO CATCH UP WITH HIM.

"HE WANTED A *WITNESS*, AND ONCE HE KNEW I OVERHEARD HIM WISHING FOR A 'SECOND SHOT,' HE BROKE AWAY...

"THE RESULT?"

BAXTER'S ARCH-RIVAL IS DEAD, AND BAXTER IS CLEAR OF *SUSPICION* -- BECAUSE *HE* WAS THE INTENDED TARGET!

ASK ANYONE. ASK PETER PARKER.

ASK *SPIDER-MAN!*

SAN LEIBER YACHT CLUB

BAXTER AND BOOMERANG *USED* ME.

I HATE THAT.

BUT IF I'M GOING TO PROVE BAXTER PLANNED CRIPPEN'S MURDER, I'VE GOT TO HAVE A *MOTIVE*.

AND RIVALRY ALONE DOESN'T QUITE *CUT* IT.

MAYBE THE MOTIVE IS BAXTER'S YACHT, "*GOLDEN CHAMPION.*"

CHAMPION

BEFORE HE DIED, CRIPPEN CALLED BAXTER A *CHEAT.*

SOMETHING ABOUT BAXTER'S BOAT--?

HMMM.

THIS DOESN'T LOOK RIGHT...

HUH?

SPIDER-SENSE...

...BOOMERANG!

230

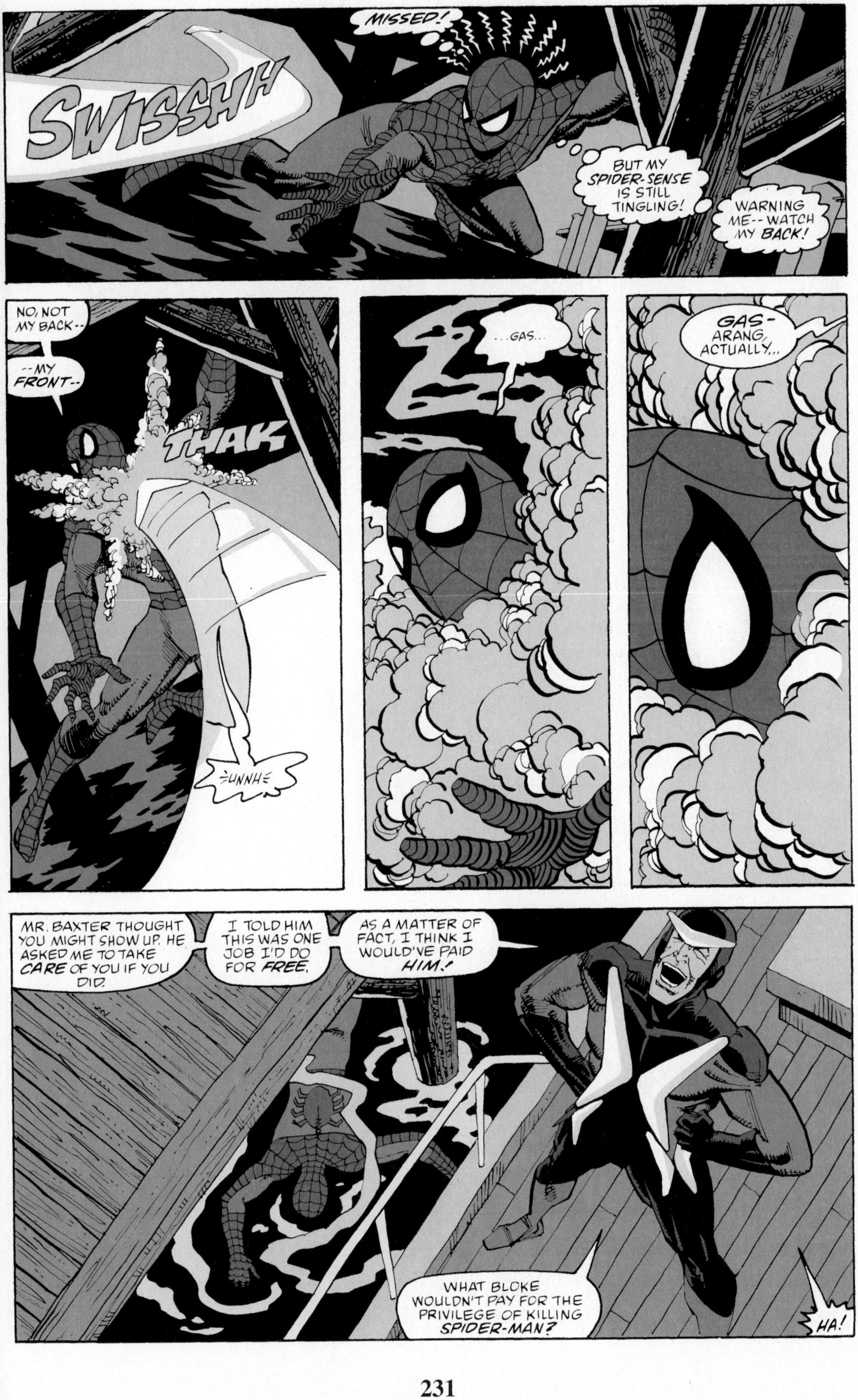
SWISSHH
MISSED!
BUT MY SPIDER-SENSE IS STILL TINGLING!
WARNING ME--WATCH MY BACK!
NO, NOT MY BACK--
--MY FRONT--
THAK
UNNH
...GAS...
GAS-ARANG, ACTUALLY...
MR. BAXTER THOUGHT YOU MIGHT SHOW UP. HE ASKED ME TO TAKE CARE OF YOU IF YOU DID.
I TOLD HIM THIS WAS ONE JOB I'D DO FOR FREE.
AS A MATTER OF FACT, I THINK I WOULD'VE PAID HIM!
WHAT BLOKE WOULDN'T PAY FOR THE PRIVILEGE OF KILLING SPIDER-MAN?
HA!

INTERLUDE 1:

THREE TIME-ZONES AND 3,000 MILES EAST...

...ON THE ISLAND OF MANHATTAN, HEART OF THE MYTHICAL CITY CALLED *NEW YORK*...

TWENTY-THREE YEARS I'VE WORKED THE STREET, URICH.

BENSONHURST, RICHMOND, GRAND CONCOURSE... YOU NAME THE BEAT, I'VE WALKED IT.

CENTRAL PARK ZOO

A COP GETS TO BE MY AGE, DESK JOB STARTS TO LOOK *REAL GOOD.*

ESPECIALLY DAYS I GET A MESSY *MURDER* WITH MY BAGEL FOR BREAKFAST.

THANKS FOR TIPPING THE BUGLE FIRST, FRANK.

I OWE YOU ONE.

YOU OWE ME LOTS MORE'N THAT, BEN, BUT WHO'S COUNTING?

YOU'VE BEEN AROUND. *RECOGNIZE* THE GUY?

TEDDY TONES. ONE OF KINGPIN'S COURIERS.

LOOKS LIKE HE WAS CUT UP PRETTY *GOOD...*

..SO WHERE'S ALL THE *BLOOD?*

CHECK OUT THE CAGE WALL.

SOMEBODY WANTED TO SEND FATSO A *MESSAGE.*

CAN'T WAIT TO HEAR THE *REPLY...*

KINGPIN: WOLVES BITE BACK

INTERLUDE 2:

JUST WEST OF CENTRAL PARK: BEDFORD TOWERS...

I HATE BEING LATE FOR A MODELING ASSIGNMENT.

BUT PETER PROMISED HE'D PHONE BEFORE *BREAKFAST* SAN DIEGO TIME--

--SO I HAD TO WAIT FOR HIS CALL--

-- AND THEN HE *DIDN'T* CALL--

-- AND NOW I'M LATE AND WORRIED *BOTH.*

START YOUR *ENGINE,* RAOUL.

IF WE DON'T MAKE TIME, DOWNTOWN IVES WILL HAVE MY LOVELY RED HEAD FOR A DOORSTO--

¿OOOF!

WHOOP! SORRY!

FINE. JUST *FINE.* THE PERFECT TOPPER TO A TERRIFIC MORNING.

WHY DON'T YOU WATCH WHERE YOU'RE--

HIYA, COUSIN MJ!

COUSIN--?

KRISTY?

KRISTY WATSON, IN THE FLESH! DIDN'T YOU GET MOM'S LETTER? NO, HUH? GOOD OLD FORGETFUL MOM!

I'M HERE TILL EASTER! *GREAT,* HUH?

GREAT...

NOW I GET IT. I'M HAVING A *NIGHTMARE.*

233

INTERLUDE 3:

DOWNTOWN, THE FEDERAL COURT BUILDING...

IT ISN'T *FAIR.*

DAD OFFERED HIMSELF AS A *WITNESS* AGAINST TOMBSTONE-- WITHOUT BARGAINING FOR SPECIAL IMMUNITY--

--AND NOW THEY'RE TURNING HIS OWN WORDS *AGAINST* HIM.

FAIR IS NOT THE *ISSUE,* YOUNG MAN.

MR. ROBERTSON ADMITTED IN DEPOSITION TO KNOWLEDGE OF A *CRIME,* SPECIFICALLY *MURDER,* WHICH KNOWLEDGE HE CONCEALED.

HE FEARED FOR HIS *LIFE,* MS. BERNHAMMER.

AS MR. ROBERTSON'S LEGAL COUNSEL, I'LL CERTAINLY MAKE THAT POINT WHEN THE CASE COMES TO *TRIAL,* MR. JAMESON.

THERE WON'T BE A TRIAL.

BECAUSE OF MY SILENCE, TOMBSTONE SPENT TWENTY YEARS KILLING PEOPLE FOR THE MOB.

RIDICULOUS.

NO, JONAH, I CAN'T ESCAPE *RESPONSIBILITY* AND I DON'T INTEND TO TRY.

MS. BERNHAMMER, AT THE ARRAIGNMENT NEXT WEEK, I WANT YOU TO PLEAD ME *GUILTY.*

ROBBIE, I WON'T ALLOW IT!

I SINCERELY ADVISE--

DAD, *NO...*

PLEASE...

THIS IS *MY* DECISION.

RANDY, LET'S GO HOME.

END OF INTERLUDES.

SAN DIEGO.

'MORNING, MATE.

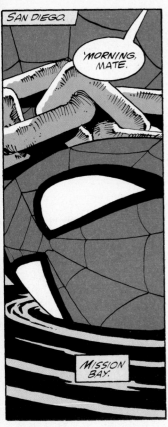

MISSION BAY.

LITTLE TIGHT AROUND THE COLLAR, EH?

WISH I COULD SAY I'M SORRY...

... BUT MY DAD ALWAYS TOLD ME, "NEVER LIE UNLESS IT'S ABSOLUTELY NECESSARY."

I'LL BET YOU'VE GOT IT ALL FIGURED OUT NOW, DON'T YOU?

≤GNNAAGH≥

MY, THAT IS TIGHT, ISN'T IT?

DON'T WORRY, IT WON'T BOTHER YOU LONG.

IF YOU GUESSED BAXTER HIRED ME TO KILL CRIPPEN, YOU'RE RIGHT.

FAKING A BLAST ON HIS YACHT WAS PART OF THE PLAN--

-- AND SO IS WHAT'S GOING TO HAPPEN TO YOLI IN ABOUT FIFTEEN MINUTES.

THIS BOAT IS CARRYING HALF A TON OF PLASTIQUE EXPLOSIVE, SET ON A CONTACT FUSE.

FIFTEEN MINUTES FROM NOW, YOU'LL RAM A BODY ON THE RACE COURSE--

--JUST AFTER THE "CHAMPION" PASSES BY.

SHOULD BE PRETTY IMPRESSIVE.

235

:GYAAH:

YOU'RE *RIGHT*, MATE.

EVERYONE WILL ASSUME IT'S *ANOTHER ATTACK* ON LOUIS BAXTER.

IT'S THE PERFECT FINISH TO HIS *ALIBI* FOR CRIPPEN'S MURDER.

AND THE NICE PART IS, IF YOUR BODY'S EVER FOUND, THEY'LL BLAME *YOU*.

BY THE WAY, REMEMBER *HOG-TIEING* ME THE LAST TIME WE MET?

WELL, AFTER THIS, I FIGURE WE'RE *EVEN*.

HA!

FUNNY GUY.

GLAD HE DOESN'T HOLD A *GRUDGE*.

:GNNYAH:

CHAINS ARE SO TIGHT-- LEVERAGE SO BAD-- I CAN'T MOVE WITHOUT *CHOKING*!

TERRIFIC. IF I MOVE, I CHOKE.

IF I DON'T MOVE, I BLOW UP.

I'D LIKE TO GO HOME NOW, PLEASE.

236

"DEFIANT" IS CLOSING IN ON US, CAPTAIN!

EVEN WITHOUT CRIPPEN AT HER HELM, SHE'S THE FASTEST SAIL SOUTH OF HAWAII!

BUT NOT FASTER THAN "CHAMPION," EH, BOYS?

NO, SIR, CAP'N! NOTHING AFLOAT'S FASTER THAN "CHAMPION!"

THEN LET'S PROVE IT! BRING US INTO THE WIND!

EITHER WE PASS THE TWO-MILE MARKER-BUOY WITH "DEFIANT" TEN MINUTES BEHIND US, OR YOU BOYS START WRITING YOUR RESUMES.

I'VE SPENT A SMALL FORTUNE TO WIN THIS RACE.

AND WHEN LOUIS BAXTER III WINS, HE LIKES TO WIN.

GREAT. SOMETIMES WHEN I FELT REALLY MORBID I USED TO WONDER HOW AND WHERE I'D GET KILLED. IF AND WHEN.

I FIGURED IT'D HAPPEN IN AN ALLEY, OR OFF A ROOFTOP OR IN SOME DINGY WAREHOUSE.

SOMEHOW I NEVER FIGURED THE PACIFIC OCEAN.

JUST GOES TO SHOW.

≥GNNGH≤

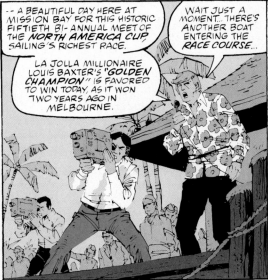

--A BEAUTIFUL DAY HERE AT MISSION BAY FOR THIS HISTORIC FIFTIETH BI-ANNUAL MEET OF THE NORTH AMERICA CUP, SAILING'S RICHEST RACE.

LA JOLLA MILLIONAIRE LOUIS BAXTER'S "GOLDEN CHAMPION" IS FAVORED TO WIN TODAY, AS IT WON TWO YEARS AGO IN MELBOURNE.

WAIT JUST A MOMENT... THERE'S ANOTHER BOAT ENTERING THE RACE COURSE...

"... PROBABLY A YACHTING ENTHUSIAST LOOKING FOR A BETTER VIEW OF THE ACTION. LET'S HOPE HE DOESN'T GET *HURT.*"

≥GNNGH≤

DON'T THINK ABOUT THE *PAIN,* PETER...

≥GNNGH≤

...THINK ABOUT *MARY JANE,* BACK IN NEW YORK.

THINK HOW YOU *LOVE* HER.

VRRMM

≥GNNNGH≤

WHEN YOU LOVE SOMEONE SO MUCH, *ANYTHING* IS POSSIBLE.

ANYTHING!

VRRRM

CHING

OKAY, MY LEG'S FREE. I CAN'T GET UP, I CAN'T GET OUT, I CAN'T SWIM, BUT BOY, I CAN MOVE MY LEG.

THINGS ARE LOOKING UP.

YEAH, *RIGHT.*

320

"THE BUOY IS ONLY A HUNDRED YARDS AWAY-- AND HERE COMES BAXTER'S YACHT.'

"ONE GOOD THING. IF I GET OUT OF THIS, IT'LL BE GREAT PUBLICITY FOR MY *BOOK.*"

MORE *SAIL* -- WE NEED MORE *WIND*, BLAST IT!

SHE'S TAKEN ALL WE HAVE, CAP'N!

"*DEFIANT*" IS CLOSING THE GAP!

IF I WERE A SUPERSTITIOUS MAN, I'D SAY ARTIE CRIPPEN'S *GHOST* MUST BE FILLING HER *SHEETS!*

ALL RIGHT, WE'VE PLAYED ACCORDING TO *THEIR* RULES...

...NOW WE'LL PLAY BY *MINE!*

CLIK

CHAMP

HMMMM

NICE TRICK, MR. BAXTER-- YOUR VERY OWN *CLOUD MACHINE* HIDDEN IN A SECRET HULL PANEL.

SPIDER-MAN NEVER HAD ANY IDEA HOW *CLOSE* HE CAME TO FINDING YOU OUT LAST NIGHT.

ARTIE CRIPPEN FOUND OUT ABOUT YOUR FOG MAKER, DIDN'T HE? THAT'S WHY YOU HAD HIM *KILLED*.

BUT I'LL BET NOT EVEN CRIPPEN GUESSED THE *REAL* SECRET UNDER YOUR HULL...

GNNGH

FORTY FEET TO THE BIG **BOOM**...

...AND SO FAR, ALL I'VE MANAGED TO DO IS FREE A LEG AND TWIST MYSELF AROUND.

IT ISN'T MUCH...

...TO SAVE MY **LIFE!**

CLANG

WHEW

MISSED THE BUOY BY **SIX INCHES** AT THE MOST.

ONLY **TWO** PROBLEMS.

ONE-- I'M HEADING DIRECTLY FOR **BAXTER'S** YACHT.

"AND **TWO**--

"--BY NOW, BOOMERANG MUST HAVE NOTICED I'M **STILL** IN ONE PIECE.

"HE WON'T **LIKE** THAT VERY MUCH."

HE'LL PROBABLY HAVE IDEAS ABOUT **CORRECTING** THE SITUATION.

SUITS ME.

ALL I HAVE TO DO NOW IS HOLD MY BREATH... NOT BLACK OUT... AND **STRETCH.**

AND JUST **HOPE** THIS CHAIN SNAPS BEFORE I DO!

GNNNGH.

≈GAAAHH≈

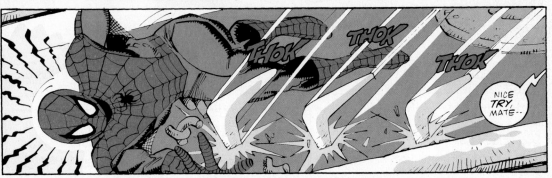

THOK THOK THOK

NICE *TRY*, MATE--

--BUT YOU'RE STILL AS GOOD AS *DEAD!*

WAY OUT HERE IN THE BAY, HOW'RE YOU GOING TO USE *SPIDER-POWERS*, EH?

NO *WALLS* TO CLIMB, NO *STREET LAMPS* TO SWING BY--!

A DINGO IN A BEAR TRAP STANDS A BETTER CHANCE OF SEEING TOMORROW THAN *YOU* DO!

HE'S RIGHT.

OUT OF THE FRYING PAN, INTO THE DEEP BLUE *SEA*...

"I DON'T KNOW IF OUR VIEWERS AT HOME CAN SEE THIS, BUT THERE'S SOMETHING **STRANGE** HAPPENING IN THE BAY.

"THAT **MOTORBOAT** WE SAW BEFORE IS HEADING DIRECTLY ACROSS THE RACE COURSE...

...STRAIGHT INTO A FREAK **FOG BANK** THAT SWALLOWED LOUIS BAXTER'S "**CHAMPION**" LESS THAN A MINUTE AGO! FORTUNATELY, AT THE SPEED THE TWO VESSELS ARE TRAVELING, THE MOTORBOAT SHOULD **MISS** BAXTER'S YACHT BY A LEAST A HUNDRED YARDS!

THIS IS THE PART I LOVE!

CRIPPEN CALLED ME A CHEAT-- BUT IS IT **CHEATING** TO USE YOUR WIT AND SKILL THE WAY I'VE USED MINE?

RULES OF FAIR PLAY ARE FOR MEN WHO HAVEN'T THE **WILL** TO CLAIM EVERY **POSSIBLE** ADVANTAGE!

AND WHAT BETTER ADVANTAGE COULD THERE BE IN A **SAILBOAT** RACE--

--THAN A PAIR OF HIDDEN **TURBO-JETS**?

CHAMPION

SWOOSH

I LOVE THIS COUNTRY. I LOVE THIS SPORT.

WITH ENOUGH WIT, SKILL AND LIQUIDATED CURRENCY, A MAN CAN ACCOMPLISH JUST ABOUT **ANYTHING.**

I'D LIKE TO SAY THIS ISN'T *PERSONAL* BUT IT *IS*.

BACK HOME DOWN UNDER, A MAN'S REPUTATION IS HIS *LIFE*.

HOG-TIED THE WAY I WAS, I'D BE A LAUGHING STOCK IF MY MATES IN MELBOURNE EVER FOUND OUT!

I WON'T TELL IF *YOU* WON'T, BOOMIE-PAL!

SPOOSH!

STILL DON'T *GET* IT, DO YOU?

I KNOW WHAT YOU DID!

I KNOW! AND I'LL NEVER FORGET--

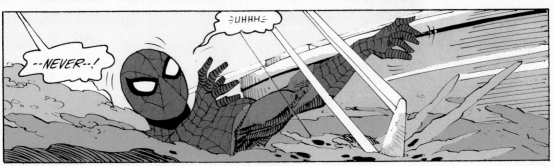

--*NEVER*--!

≥UHHH≥

EH? HE'S GONE *UNDER*--

-- AND HE HASN'T COME UP!

THAT LAST 'RANG MUST HAVE *CLIPPED* HIM!

I DID IT!

I KILLED SPIDER-MAN!

LOOKS LIKE WE'VE STRETCHED THE LEAD BY HALF-A-MILE, CAP'N!

"DEFIANT" CAN'T POSSIBLY CATCH US NOW!

WELL, NOW... I HOPE YOU BOYS LIKE CHAMPAGNE.

I HAVE A CASE OF ROTHSCHILD '58 I'VE BEEN SAVING FOR A SPECIAL OCCASION.

MOTHER LEFT IT TO ME IN HER WILL.

SHE ALWAYS HOPED I'D USE IT AT MY WEDDING.

BUT I'M AFRAID I'M LIKE THE CAPTAINS OF OLD, BOYS.

THE ONLY BRIDE I'LL EVER WANT IS THE SEA.

FOG'S LIFTING.

"LET'S BRING THIS LADY HOME."

SOMETHING'S WRONG.

SPIDER-MAN'S BODY SHOULD'VE FLOATED UP BY NOW!

"MAYBE I BETTER TAKE A CLOSER LOOK..."

244

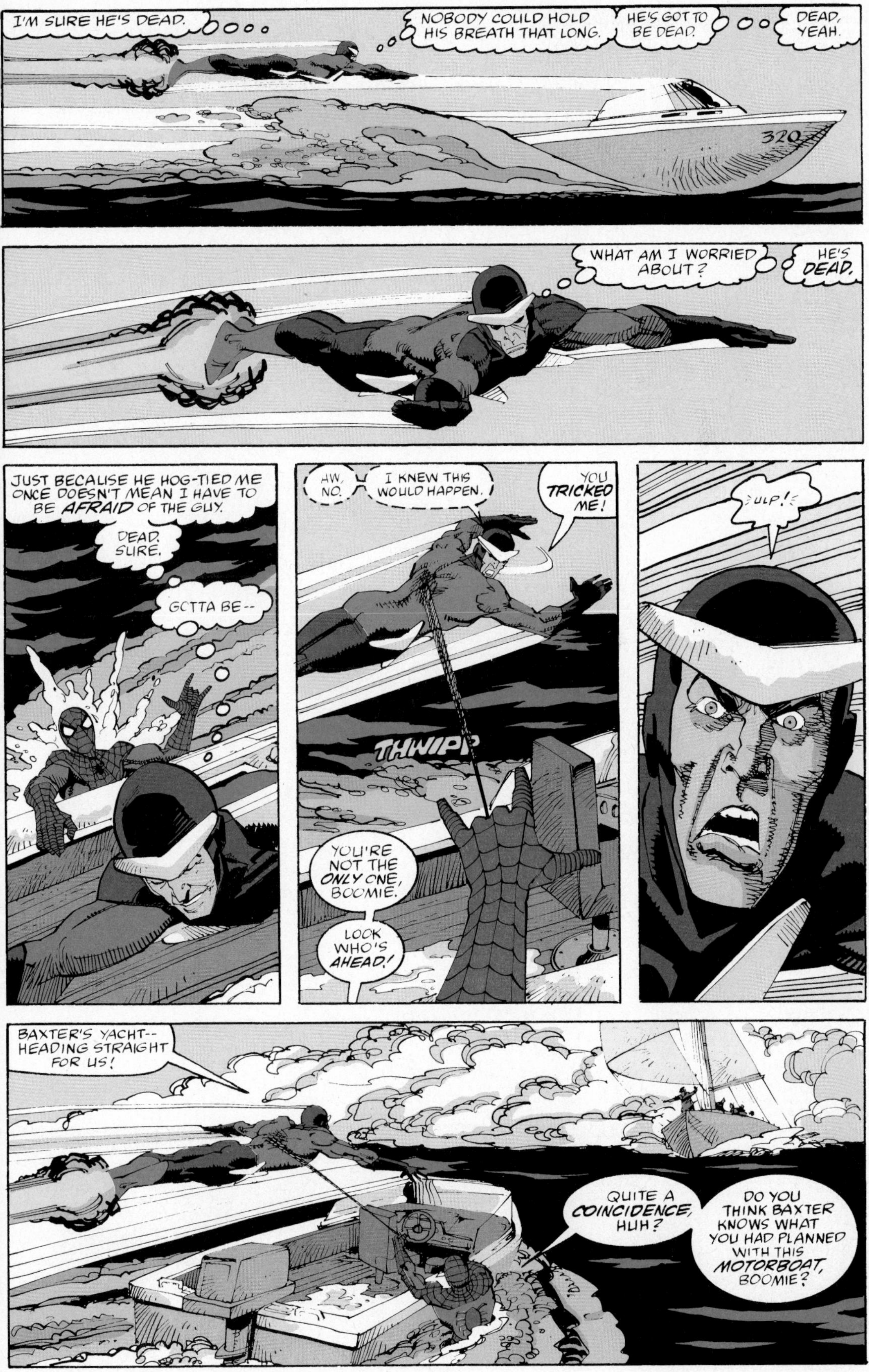
I'M SURE HE'S DEAD.
NOBODY COULD HOLD HIS BREATH THAT LONG.
HE'S GOT TO BE DEAD.
DEAD, YEAH.
320
WHAT AM I WORRIED ABOUT?
HE'S DEAD.
JUST BECAUSE HE HOG-TIED ME ONCE DOESN'T MEAN I HAVE TO BE AFRAID OF THE GUY.
DEAD. SURE.
GOTTA BE--
AW, NO.
I KNEW THIS WOULD HAPPEN.
YOU TRICKED ME!
THWIPP
YOU'RE NOT THE ONLY ONE, BOOMIE.
LOOK WHO'S AHEAD!
ULP!
BAXTER'S YACHT-- HEADING STRAIGHT FOR US!
QUITE A COINCIDENCE, HUH?
DO YOU THINK BAXTER KNOWS WHAT YOU HAD PLANNED WITH THIS MOTORBOAT, BOOMIE?

"GUESS SO.

"I'D SAY IT'S TIME YOU AND I GOT *OUT* OF HERE, WOULDN'T YOU?"

-- MY BOOT-JETS CAN'T *CARRY* US MORE THAN A HUNDRED FEET-- --THEY'RE ALREADY STARTING TO *SPUTTER*--

SHUT UP! I WANT TO *WATCH* THIS.

YEAH, THAT'S WHAT I THOUGHT.

YES--NO--YOU DON'T *UNDER-STAND*--!

WITH YOU HANGING ONTO ME--

"BAXTER NEVER *STRUCK* ME AS THE KIND OF CAPTAIN WHO'D GO DOWN WITH HIS SHIP..."

DO YOU KNOW WHAT YOU *DID*? THIS IS *WORSE* THAN HOG-TYING ME! WHEN WORD GETS OUT I BLEW UP MY OWN CLIENT'S BOAT--

--I'LL BE *THROUGH!*

=UNNNNGGH=

DON'T WORRY ABOUT IT, BOOMIE...

...YOU'RE *ALREADY* THROUGH!

HEY, LOUIE-LOUIE... MIND IF WE *DROP IN*?

SPIDER-MAN... *YOU* DID THIS?

WHEN MY LAWYERS GET FINISHED WITH YOU, YOU'LL OWE ME EVERY DOLLAR YOU MAKE FOR THE NEXT FIFTY--

I'LL GIVE YOU THIS, BAXTER: YOU'VE GOT *NERVE.*

NOBODY EVER THREATENED TO *SUE* ME FOR BUSTING HIS SCAM, BEFORE.

IT FIGURES, ALONG WITH EVERYTHING ELSE, YOU'D BE A *POOR LOSER.*

LOSER?

--THE-- *RACE--*

IT ISN'T *FAIR!* I DESERVED TO WIN! I WAS THE SMARTEST! I HAD THE FASTEST SHIP! I HAD THE MOST *MONEY!*

OH, GIVE IT A REST.

FIRST TIME I SAW YOU, I KNEW YOU WERE MORE *MOUTH* THAN BRAINS.

KNOW WHAT MAKES A *REAL* WINNER, LOUIE?

FACING A CHALLENGE WHEN THE ODDS ARE AGAINST YOU, WHEN YOUR HEAD WANTS TO QUIT, BUT YOUR HEART SAYS DO IT *ANYWAY.*

≷COUGH≷ ≷SPLUT≷ ≷COUGH≷

MOST PEOPLE RUN THAT KIND OF RACE EVERY DAY, BAXTER.

BUT GUYS LIKE YOU AND BOOMERANG NEVER EVEN CROSS THE *STARTING LINE...*

NEXT: INFERNO ™

MARVEL®
the SPECTACULAR SPIDER-MAN®
INFERNO CONTINUES™
$1.00 US
$1.25 CAN
146
JAN
CC 02199
APPROVED BY THE COMICS CODE AUTHORITY
OSBORN CHEMICAL COMPANY
WHAT'S GOING ON? MY FACTORY IS ATTACKING ME!!
NIGHT OF MADNESS!

STAN LEE PRESENTS: THE SPECTACULAR SPIDER-MAN!™

BEDFORD TOWERS, MANHATTAN, DUSK.

WOW!

SOME DAYS ARE SO GOOD, I WANT TO PINCH MYSELF TO SEE IF I'M DREAMING.

I HAD A GREAT TIME IN CLASS AT E.S.U., --

-- MY RELATIONSHIP WITH MARY JANE HAS NEVER BEEN BETTER --

-- AND J. JONAH JAMESON ACTUALLY PAID ME EARLY FOR THE "SPIDER-MAN CAPTURES MYSTERIO" PHOTOS I SOLD HIM.

SO WHY DO I FEEL AS IF AN AXE IS ABOUT TO FALL?

JUST AN INNATE PESSIMIST, THAT'S ME.

GERRY CONWAY | SAL BUSCEMA | RICK PARKER | BOB SHAREN | JIM SALICRUP | TOM DeFALCO
SCRIPT | ART | LETTERS | COLOR | EDITOR | EDITOR IN CHIEF

WHICH IS ONE MORE REASON I LOVE MJ. ME PESSIMIST, SHE *OPTIMIST*.

BETWEEN US, WE MAKE ONE HARD-EYED *REALIST*.

I CAN'T WAIT TO TELL HER ABOUT MY DAY.

I HOPE I'LL HAVE TIME FOR A SHOWER BEFORE SHE AND HER COUSIN *KRISTY* GET HO--

--HOOO!

SKASH

WHAT THE HAIRY HECK IS *THAT*?

-- AND WHY DIDN'T MY SPIDER-SENSE WARN ME IT WAS *COMING*?

LOOKS LIKE A CROSS BETWEEN A *BUZZ-SAW* AND A *MORAY EEL* --

CRUMP

-- ONLY A MORAY EEL WOULD BE A WHOLE LOT *FRIENDLIER!*

THWAP

AFTER SEEING ALL THE WEIRD STUFF HE PULLED YESTERDAY, * I'D ALMOST SWEAR THIS WAS SOMETHING *MYSTERIO* COOKED UP!

* SEE *AMAZING SPIDER-MAN #311.* -- CROSSOVER JIM

251

A KILLER MUTANT FAN-VENT WOULD BE JUST HIS IDEA OF FUN.

CORNY AND CRAZY.

ONLY ONE SMALL, MODERATELY INSIGNIFICANT *PROBLEM*:

RRRRIIP

OL' FISHBOWL-FACE IS IN JAIL.

I TOSSED HIM THERE *MYSELF* LAST NIGHT.

UH... DID I SAY *ONE* PROBLEM? TRY *TWO*:

MYSTERIO IS A SPECIAL-EFFECTS WIZ, NOT AN HONEST-TO-GOLLY *MAGICIAN.*

THERE SHOULD BE ELECTRONICS INSIDE THIS THING -- CIRCUITS, COMPUTERS, *ROBOT* STUFF.

BUT IT'S *EMPTY.*

THERE'S NOTHING IN THIS VENT BUT..

...VENT.

I DON'T BELIEVE IT.

EVEN IN NEW YORK, WEIRD AS IT SOMETIMES IS, FAN-VENTS DON'T JUST COME ALIVE AND *ATTACK* YOU.

USUALLY YOU HAVE TO INSULT THEM FIRST.

NERVOUS HA-HA.

GOOD, NOBODY'S HOME. AT LEAST, WITH KRISTY OUT, I DON'T HAVE TO SNEAK INTO MY OWN APARTMENT. BESIDES, I NEED TIME TO *THINK*.

WHY DIDN'T MY *SPIDER-SENSE* WARN ME I WAS IN DANGER?

THAT WORRIES ME MORE THAN ANY *"MAGIC"* AIR-VENT.

WEIRD THINGS ARE HAPPENING. THE AIR FEELS *ELECTRIC*.

AS IF A STORM WERE ON THE WAY...

" PETER-- TOOK KRISTY SHOPPING FOR DINNER GOODIES. BACK SOON, LOVEYA--*MJ.* "

GUESS I HAVE TIME FOR THAT SHOWER--

MILK

-- BUT SUDDENLY I'M NOT IN THE *MOOD'* ANYMORE.

COLUMBUS AVENUE. 72nd STREET. TWILIGHT.

WHERE DO YOU *PUT* IT ALL, KRISTY?

IF I DON'T WATCH WHAT I EAT, I BLOW UP LIKE A PUFFER FISH--

Loo's MARKET

-- BUT YOU'VE BEEN PACKING-AWAY FOOD SINCE YOU GOT HERE LAST WEEK, AND IF YOU'VE GAINED A POUND, *I* HAVEN'T SEEN IT.

YOU MUST HAVE A METABOLISM LIKE A *BLAST FURNACE.*

CHUM LUMPKY UME GUEMM

WHAT?

> GULP
>
> "JUST LUCKY, I GUESS."
>
> TELL ME MORE ABOUT *MODELING*, MARY JANE.
>
> WHO DO I HAVE TO SEE? HOW DO I BREAK IN? WHERE DO I GET MY PICTURES?
>
> WHOA!

TV REPAIR

Open

NO TRUCKS

TODAY'S SPECIAL

> SORRY... GUESS I GOT CARRIED AWAY.
>
> I'M JUST SO *THRILLED* YOU'RE LETTING ME STAY WITH YOU AND PETER WHILE MY FOLKS TRAVEL IN EUROPE.
>
> OUR PLEASURE.

> I ONLY WISH YOUR MOM HAD GIVEN US SOME *WARNING* BEFORE SHE LEFT.
>
> OH, YEAH... WELL, MOM IS KIND OF A *FLAKE* SOMETIMES.
>
> BUT HOW COULD SHE WARN YOU WHEN SHE DOESN'T EVEN KNOW I'M *GONE?*

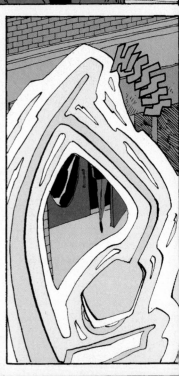

HSSSS

HISSSSS

> JACKSON HEIGHTS, QUEENS.
>
> NIGHTFALL.
>
> WHEW!
>
> MANAGED TO MAKE IT AROUND THE WHOLE *BLOCK* THIS TIME, MARTHA.
>
> THAT'S GOOD, JOE.

BUT DON'T PUSH YOURSELF *TOO* HARD. THE DOCTORS SAID TOMB-STONE CAME CLOSE TO BREAKING YOUR *SPINE*...

"CLOSE" DOESN'T COUNT, MARTHA.

I'VE LEARNED A LOT ABOUT MYSELF, RECOVERING FROM THIS INJURY.

THE HUMAN BODY IS MORE *RESILIENT* THAN WE THINK.

BROKEN BONES HEAL FASTER THAN A BROKEN HEART, JOE.

WHAT DO YOU MEAN--?

I'LL TELL YOU-- I CAN'T BELIEVE YOU'RE NOT GOING TO FIGHT THIS INDICTMENT!

JONAH JAMESON CALLED ME THIS MORNING...

HE SAID HE'S TIRED OF *ARGUING* WITH YOU.

HE DOESN'T UNDERSTAND WHY YOU WANT TO PLEAD *GUILTY* TO THE GOVERNMENT'S CHARGE OF *ACCESSORY TO MURDER* IN THE TOMBSTONE CASE...

..., AND, HONESTLY, JOE, NEITHER DO *I*.

SEEING YOU *QUIT* IS BREAKING MY HEART!

I'M NOT QUITTING, MARTHA, I'M PLEADING GUILTY BECAUSE I *AM* GUILTY.

TWENTY YEARS AGO, I SAW TOMB-STONE KILL A MAN-- AND I KEPT *SILENT*.

IF THAT MAKES ME AN ACCESSORY, I'M GUILTY AS *CHARGED*.

GUILTY OF BEING *HUMAN*, GUILTY OF BEING A YOUNG MAN WITH A *FAMILY* TO FEED AND PROTECT...

YOU DON'T UNDERSTAND.

YOU'RE RIGHT. I DON'T.

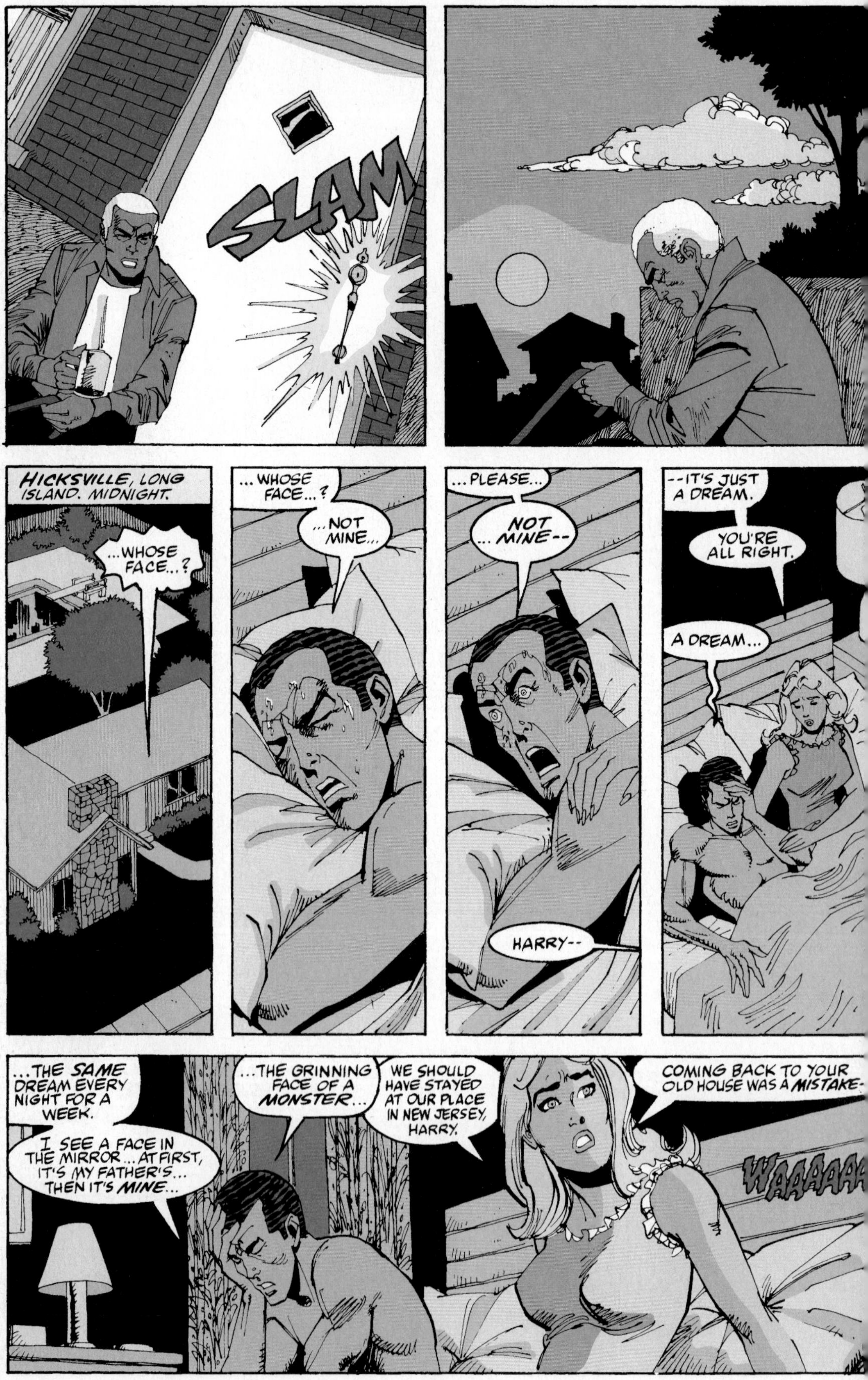
SLAM
HICKSVILLE, LONG ISLAND. MIDNIGHT.
...WHOSE FACE...?
...WHOSE FACE...?
...NOT MINE...
...PLEASE...
NOT ...MINE--
HARRY--
--IT'S JUST A DREAM.
YOU'RE ALL RIGHT.
A DREAM...
...THE SAME DREAM EVERY NIGHT FOR A WEEK.
I SEE A FACE IN THE MIRROR... AT FIRST, IT'S MY FATHER'S... THEN IT'S MINE...
...THE GRINNING FACE OF A MONSTER...
WE SHOULD HAVE STAYED AT OUR PLACE IN NEW JERSEY, HARRY.
COMING BACK TO YOUR OLD HOUSE WAS A MISTAKE-
WAAAAA

AWW, HE MUST HAVE HAD A BAD DREAM TOO.

WELL, YOU'RE GOING TO BE OKAY NOW, NORMIE.

DADDY'S RIGHT HERE.

AND DADDY WON'T LET *ANY* MEAN BOOGIEMEN HURT HIS LITTLE BABY BOY.

I GUESS YOU'RE RIGHT, LIZ. I DON'T KNOW *WHY* IT SEEMED SO IMPORTANT WE MOVE BACK TO THE OLD--

-- OSBORN HOMESTEAD.

SOMETIMES I GET NOTIONS, CRAZY DUMB IDEAS. THIS WAS ONE OF THEM.

WE'LL PACK UP... MOVE BACK TO JERSEY THIS WEEKEND. *OK?*

OK.

THANK HEAVEN.

HARRY DOESN'T REMEMBER THE NIGHTMARES OF HIS PAST-- BUT I DO.

I KNOW WHAT HAPPENED TO HIS FATHER, AND WHAT COULD HAVE HAPPENED TO *HARRY.*

I ALMOST CALLED *PETER PARKER* WHEN HARRY STARTED HAVING THOSE DREAMS AGAIN...

...BUT NOW, I GUESS I'M GLAD I DIDN'T.

IT'S JUST THIS *HOUSE.* THAT'S ALL.

THIS OLD PLACE GIVES ME THE *CREEPS.*

"I FEEL AS IF SOMETHING *EVIL* WERE HIDING HERE...

"...WATCHING...

"...WAITING...

" WAITING FOR MY HARRY TO LOSE HIS *MIND...*"

BEDFORD TOWERS.
MANHATTAN. MORNING.

≈YAWN!≈

I SHOULD HAVE DONE THIS LAST NIGHT.

NOTHING LIKE A HOT-AND-COLD SHOWER TO CLEAR THE--

≈UNGH≈

SOAP IN MY EYE.

MJ! HAND ME A TOWEL, WILLYA?

THANKS, HONEY. I DON'T KNOW WHICH I'D HATE MORE, SOAP IN MY EYES OR RADICAL SPINAL SURGERY.

YOU'RE WELCOME, COUSIN PETER.

OH, HI, KRISTY.

YEAH, SOAP IN MY EYE-- STINGS WAY DOWN IN THAT LITTLE CRACK BETWEEN--

KRISTY?

OHMIGOSH--

DON'T FRET, CUZ.

I'VE GOT THREE OLDER BROTHERS BACK HOME.

'SIDES, I THINK YOU'RE CUTE WHEN YOU'RE WET.

C-C-CUTE?

UHM-HUM.

258

'SPECIALLY THE WAY YOUR **EARS** BLUSH.

YO, COUSIN MJ--MIND IF I MAKE **BREAKFAST**? A GROWING GIRL'S GOTTA EAT.

I'LL BET.

FLIRTING WITH MY MAN GIVE YOU AN **APPETITE**?

FLIRTING? HEY, I DIDN'T--

DON'T KID A KIDDER, KIDDO.

WHEN IT CAME TO TEASING BOYS, MARY JANE WATSON WON THE ALL-CITY FINALS FOUR YEARS RUNNING.

BUT ME NO **BUTS**.

YOU'RE A "GROWING GIRL," ALL RIGHT. JUST DON'T GROW TOO FAST.

AND STAY AWAY FROM MY MAN. **OK?**

OK.

≥SHEESH!≤

BUT I--

≥SHEESH!≤

HAVING KRISTY AROUND THE APARTMENT IS STARTING TO GET REAL **UNCOMFORTABLE.**

BUT WHERE ELSE CAN SHE STAY, WITH HER PARENTS OUT OF--

RRRRRING

PARKER & PARKER, FASHION AND PHOTOS OUR SPECIALTY.

PETER? IT'S HARRY OSBORN.

HARRY! LONG TIME NO SEE!

HOW'RE LIZ AND LITTLE NORMAN? WHEN ARE WE GOING TO GET YOU GUYS OVER FOR DINNER?

PETER--I--LISTEN--I--

CAN YOU COME OUT TO MY CHEMICAL PLANT IN MANHATTAN?

SOMETHING STRANGE IS GOING ON-- I CAN'T EXPLAIN IT-- BUT I NEED TO **TALK**--

I HAVEN'T HEARD HARRY SOUND LIKE THIS SINCE-- **NO.** IT CAN'T BE HAPPENING AGAIN.

HANG TIGHT, PAL. I'LL BE THERE AS SOON AS I CAN.

259

STARLIGHT ROOM, MIDTOWN MANHATTAN.

MORNING.

≥GASP!≤

ARE THEY ALL...

DEAD, YEAH.

GOOD LORD.

THOUGHT YOU WERE TOUGH, URICH.

CRUSTY OLD POLICE-BEAT REPORTER LIKE YOU.

THOUGHT YOU HAD NERVES OF STEEL.

GIVE ME A BREAK, FRANK. THIS PLACE LOOKS LIKE BEIRUT.

WHAT HAPPENED? WHO ARE THESE PEOPLE?

SOME OF 'EM ARE CUT UP PRETTY BAD--HARD TO IDENTIFY...

...BUT NEAR AS WE CAN FIGURE, WE'VE GOT 20 OF YOUR LOCAL MOB LIEU-TENANTS HERE.

I'VE GOT A BAD FEELING YOU'RE GOING TO TELL ME THIS IS CONNECTED TO THAT SLASHER-KILLING AT THE ZOO A FEW NIGHTS AGO...

AMAZING HOW YOU FIGURED THAT OUT, URICH.

TAKE A LOOK.

WAY I SEE IT, THESE BOYS AND GIRLS WERE HAVIN' THEMSELVES A *PRIVATE MEETING*... OR MAYBE A *CELEBRATION* WHO KNOWS...

...AND SOMEBODY CRASHED THEIR PARTY...

KINGPIN-WOLVES KILL

SOMEBODY WITH A REAL NASTY GRIPE AGAINST THE FATBOY.

YOU SAID THIS PLACE LOOKED LIKE BEIRUT, URICH.

I'D SAY YOU'RE RIGHT. WE'RE TALKING WAR ZONE.

OFFICER! OFFICER! WHO'S IN CHARGE HERE?

WELL, WELL. IF IT ISN'T *THE ARRANGER.*

HOW'S YOUR BOSS, BALDY? WHAT'S THE *KINGPIN* THINK ABOUT ALL THIS?

URICH -- YES, I MIGHT HAVE EXPECTED YOU'D BE HERE.

WHERE THERE'S HUMAN DISASTER, CAN THE *DAILY BUGLE'S* TOP "REPORTER" BE FAR AWAY?

I'M SURPRISED THAT PHOTOGRAPHER, *PARKER,* ISN'T WITH YOU TO IMMORTALIZE THE GORY DETAILS.

HEY, I LOVE TO LISTEN TO YOU GUYS TALK, BUT IN CASE YOU HADN'T NOTICED, WE'VE GOT A *SITUATION* HERE.

SOMEBODY'S GUNNING FOR THE *KINGPIN.*

MAKE AN OLD COP'S JOB EASIER- TELL ME *WHO.*

MR. FISK IS A RESPECTABLE *BUSINESSMAN.*

THIS ESTABLISHMENT IS ONE OF HIS *INVESTMENTS.*

I'M ONLY HERE TO PROTECT HIS FISCAL INTERESTS WHILE--

CAN IT!

THE WHOLE TOWN'S READY TO BLOW WIDE OPEN WITH A FULL-SCALE GANG WAR AND YOU'RE GIVING ME NOTHING BUT *HOT GAS!*

TELL YOUR BOSS *FRANK FARROW* ISN'T ABOUT TO SIT BY AND WATCH PEOPLE DIE!

EITHER I GET SOME ANSWERS, AND SOON, OR I'LL HAUL BOTH YOU AND THE KINGPIN DOWNTOWN SO FAST THE FATBOY'S CHINS WON'T STOP JIGGLIN' FOR A *MONTH*.

DO I MAKE MYSELF *CLEAR*?

'LO, JOY? BEN. TAKE THIS DOWN...

HANG A SECOND, BEN. LET ME KEY-UP MY SCREEN.

...OKAY, SHOOT.

TWENTY DEAD... GANGLAND KILLING... STARLIGHT ROOM-- THE *STARLIGHT ROOM*?

WOW, I HAD DINNER THERE, MYSELF, ONLY TWO NIGHTS AGO--

RIGHT, MOB LIEUTENANTS... ALLEGED 'ASSOCIATES' OF WILSON FISK, A.K.A. THE KINGPIN... THIS IS *HOT STUFF*, BEN.

MIND IF I DO SOME RESEARCH ON MY END, SPLIT A *BYLINE*? GREAT. I'LL RUN IT BY KATE AND--

JOY, IF THAT'S *BEN URICH*, JONAH WANTS TO TALK TO HIM.

SURE, GLORY. ANY IDEA WHAT'S UP?

WELL... I'M JUST JONAH'S SECRETARY...

C'MON. *NOBODY* KNOWS THE WAY J.J.J. THINKS BETTER THAN YOU, GLORY.

WELL... SINCE ROBBIE ROBERTSON WENT ON SICK LEAVE, JONAH'S BEEN TAKING A MORE ACTIVE INTEREST IN RUNNING THE *BUGLE*, AND I THINK HE'D LIKE TO--

CUSHING!

WHERE IS SHE?! WHERE'S CUSHING?

BLAST IT ALL! DO I HAVE TO DO *EVERY-THING* AROUND HERE MYSELF?

I USED TO RUN THIS PAPER SINGLE-HANDED, AND BY HEAVEN, I CAN DO IT *AGAIN* IF I HAVE TO-- EH?

JONAH, CALM DOWN, THIS ISN'T A ROAD SHOW VERSION OF "*FRONT PAGE.*"

YOU'RE UPSETTING THE STAFF...

THEY'RE UPSET? *I'M* UPSET! LOOK AT THIS HEADLINE! "*POLTERGEISTS!*"

WHAT ARE WE PUBLISHING, A *NEWS-PAPER* OR A SUPER-MARKET *TRASH SHEET?*

WE'VE HAD ALL KINDS OF WEIRD *SIGHTINGS* ALL AROUND THE CITY, JONAH-- INEXPLICABLE, POSSIBLY *SUPERNATURAL* EVENTS * --

AUTHENTICATED?

* FOR MORE DETAILS, SEE *AMAZING SPIDER-MAN, WEB OF SPIDER-MAN,* AND THE *X-BOOKS* ON SALE NOW! -- TIE-IN JIM

DEFINE YOUR TERMS!

PEOPLE *DISAPPEARING* IN ELEVATORS--INANIMATE OBJECTS GOING *BERSERK*-- RUMORS ABOUT GHOSTS IN THE *EMPIRE STATE BUILDING*--

BUNK!

ANY WINO CAN SEE A GHOST, AND ANY NEWSPAPER CAN RUN A *SCARE HEADLINE!*

BUT THIS IS A *RESPONSIBLE* NEWSPAPER, CUSHING!

AND THIS IS WHAT *I* CALL A RESPONSIBLE HEADLINE!

DAILY BUGLE
POLTERGEISTS?

WHAT YOU PEOPLE WOULD DO WITHOUT ME, I'LL NEVER KNOW.

SOMETIMES THAT MAN CAN BE SO *IRRITATING*...

≥SIGH≤

...ESPECIALLY WHEN HE'S RIGHT.

DON'T LET OLD JJJ GET YOU DOWN, KATE.

I'VE WORKED FOR THE MAN MORE YEARS THAN I CARE TO COUNT, AND BY NOW I KNOW HE'S JUST LIKE AN OLD *DOG* MY UNCLE CAL USED TO KEEP.

HOW'S THAT, GLORY?

THEY BOTH HAVE MORE BARK THAN *TEETH.* SEE YOU AFTER LUNCH.

LET'S SEE. I PROMISED MY NIECE I'D PICK UP A TEDDY BEAR FOR HER AT *F.A.O. SCHWARTZ.*

HARD TO BELIEVE LITTLE YVONNE IS GOING TO BE SEVEN THIS SATURDAY.

WHERE DO ALL THE YEARS *GO?*

ONCE UPON A TIME, I THOUGHT I'D HAVE A DAUGHTER LIKE HER, BUT I NEVER HAD MUCH LUCK WITH--

PERDÓNEME.

OHH!

PLEASE, LET ME.

OH, THAT'S--

--ALL RIGHT.

HE'S GORGEOUS.

NO, IT WAS UNFORGIVABLE.

A MAN MUST ALWAYS TREAT A WOMAN WITH *COURTESY...*

...PARTICULARLY A *BEAUTIFUL* WOMAN.

OH.... WELL.... THANK YOU.

HE'S *GORGEOUS.*

HOW MAY I MAKE AMENDS?

I KNOW.

YOU WILL ALLOW ME TO BUY YOU LUNCH.

PLEASE, IT IS THE LEAST I CAN DO.

I AM A STRANGER TO NEW YORK.

WELL, I...

WHAT RESTAURANTS ARE SUITABLE--

--FOR DINING WITH SUCH A LOVELY AND CHARMING COMPANION?

IS HE TALKING ABOUT HIM OR ME?

I CAN'T TAKE MY *EYES* OFF HIM!

WHO *ARE* YOU?

NEVER MIND. WHEREVER WE GO WILL BE A SPECIAL PLACE--

--BECAUSE *YOU* ARE THERE.

MY NAME IS *EDUARDO LOBO.*

AND I HAVE A FEELING WE WILL BE VERY CLOSE FRIENDS...

"*VERY CLOSE.*"

OSBORN CHEMICAL CORP.

THANKS FOR COMING, PETER.

I DON'T KNOW WHERE TO BEGIN...

TAKE YOUR TIME, HARRY.

YOU SEEM PRETTY *STRESSED.*

I AM-- AND I DON'T KNOW *WHY.*

BUSINESS IS GOOD, LIZ AND NORMAN ARE FINE, EVERY-THING'S *GREAT*---BUT THE LAST WEEK OR SO I'VE HAD *NIGHTMARES* EVERY NIGHT.

THEY STARTED WHEN WE MOVED BACK TO THE OLD HOUSE IN HICKSVILLE.

WHY'D YOU MOVE?

I DON'T HONESTLY KNOW, PETER.

SOMETHING SEEMED TO DRAW ME BACK...

I FEEL AS IF THERE'S *UNFINISHED BUSINESS* I NEED TO COMPLETE...

BUSINESS AS THE *GREEN GOBLIN?*

HARRY DOESN'T *REMEMBER* HIS BRIEF CAREER AS THE *SECOND* GREEN GOBLIN --REPLACING HIS FATHER, THE *ORIGINAL* GOBLIN-- BUT I SURE DO.

"HARRY BECAME THE GOBLIN UNDER THE INFLUENCE OF A *DRUG FLASHBACK...*"

... AND AFTERWARD, HE BLOCKED THE ENTIRE EPISODE FROM HIS CONSCIOUS MEMORY WITH A CASE OF HYSTERICAL *AMNESIA.*

IF THAT AMNESIA IS FINALLY *WEARING OFF...*

HAR, YOU WANT MY ADVICE?

MOVE BACK TO *NEW JERSEY,* RIGHT?

RIGHT.

SELL YOUR DAD'S HOUSE.

TAKE A TRIP.

EASE UP ON YOURSELF AND DON'T--

HUH?

SPIDER-SENSE GOING *NUTS!*

SKREEECH

P-PETER-- WHAT'S HAPPENING?

YOU TELL ME, HAR! YOUR PIPES ARE ATTACKING US!

PETER, DO SOMETHING!

HELP ME!

HANG ON, I'LL GET A FIRE AXE!

METAL PIPES COMING ALIVE--

--LIKE THE FAN VENT ON BEDFORD TOWERS LAST NIGHT!

AND I'VE GOT A SICK FEELING THESE AREN'T ROBOTS, EITHER!

WHAT'S WEIRD IS THE WAY MY SPIDER-SENSE IS ACTING!

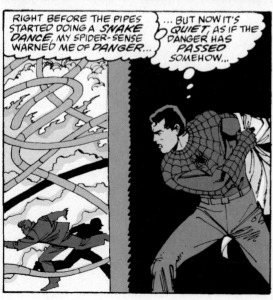

RIGHT BEFORE THE PIPES STARTED DOING A SNAKE DANCE, MY SPIDER-SENSE WARNED ME OF DANGER...

...BUT NOW IT'S QUIET, AS IF THE DANGER HAS PASSED SOMEHOW...

"...BUT THAT'S CRAZY!

"WHAT AM I THINKING?"

THIS WHOLE *SITUATION* IS CRAZY!

PIPES AND FAN VENTS DON'T JUST COME ALIVE!

YEEOWP!

SOMEBODY OR *SOMETHING* IS BEHIND ALL THIS--

SKRAK

SKRUMP

--AND I'M GOING TO FIND OUT WHO OR *WHAT*--

--JUST AS SOON AS I RESCUE POOR OLD *HARRY!*

HE'S UNCONSCIOUS!

MAN, IF HE DIDN'T HAVE NIGHTMARES *BEFORE...*

...HE'LL SURE HAVE THEM *NOW!!*

I WONDER--IT'S A *WILD* IDEA, BUT COULD HARRY'S NIGHTMARE'S BE TIED INTO ALL THE FREAK STUFF THAT'S BEEN HAPPENING THESE LAST FEW DAYS?

SNAKK

HARRY'S NIGHTMARES STARTED A *WEEK* AGO...

...WHEN HE GOT A SUDDEN NOTION TO MOVE BACK TO HIS DAD'S OLD HOUSE IN *HICKSVILLE.*

UHHHHH--

--HA!

SKRIPP

AND IT WAS JUST ABOUT A *WEEK* AGO THAT STRANGE THINGS STARTED HAPPENING AROUND NEW YORK.

FIRE HYDRANTS EXPLODING... ELEVATORS GOING BERSERK... CARS DRIVING OFF ON THEIR OWN...!

I THOUGHT *MYSTERIO* WAS RESPONSIBLE FOR MOST OF IT WITH HIS SPECIAL EFFECTS--

-- BUT WHAT IF HIS PLOT WAS JUST A *COINCIDENCE?*

THWIPP

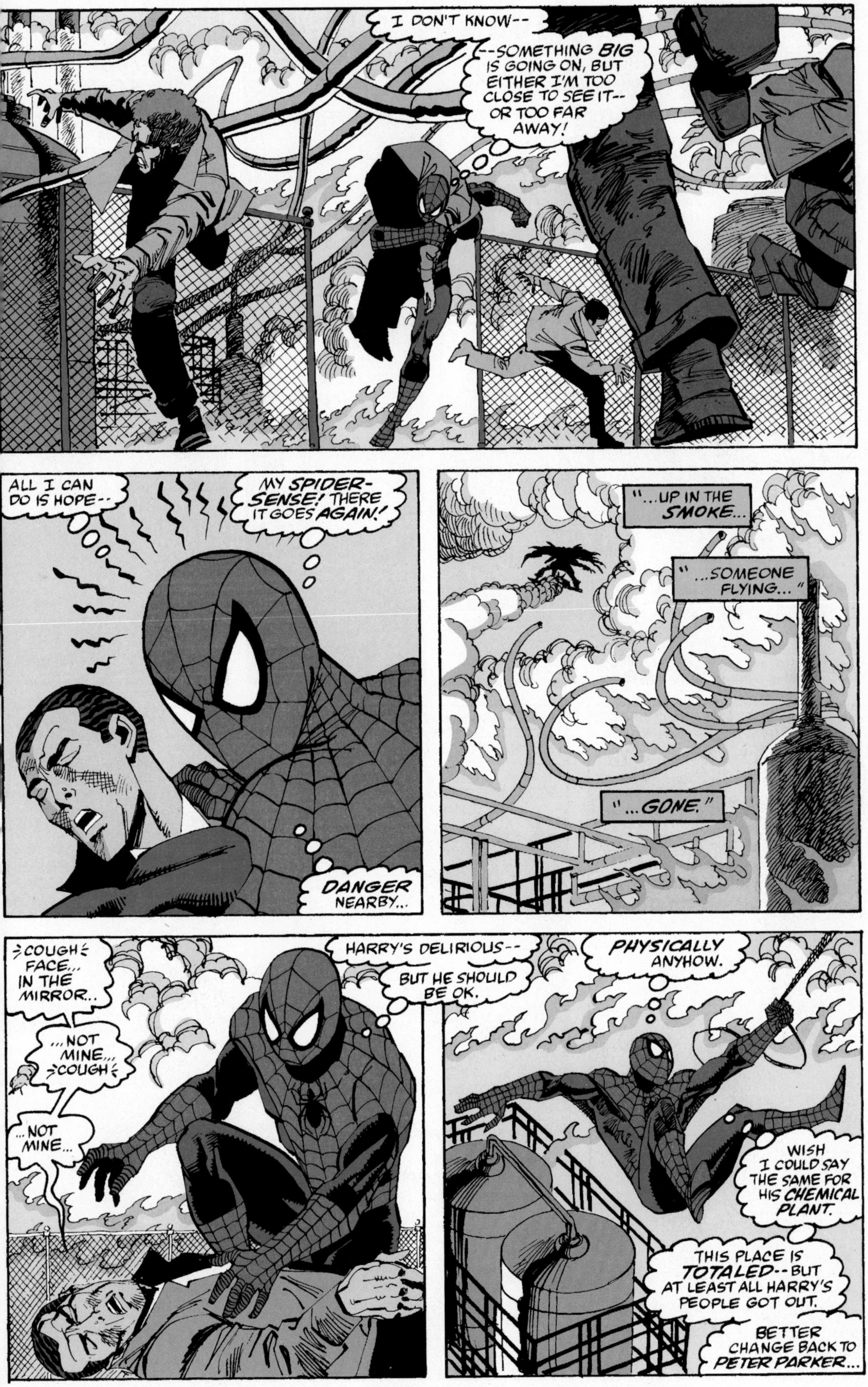
I DON'T KNOW--
--SOMETHING BIG IS GOING ON, BUT EITHER I'M TOO CLOSE TO SEE IT-- OR TOO FAR AWAY!
ALL I CAN DO IS HOPE--
MY SPIDER-SENSE! THERE IT GOES AGAIN!
DANGER NEARBY...
"...UP IN THE SMOKE...
"...SOMEONE FLYING..."
"...GONE."
COUGH FACE... IN THE MIRROR...
...NOT MINE... COUGH
...NOT MINE...
HARRY'S DELIRIOUS--
BUT HE SHOULD BE OK.
PHYSICALLY ANYHOW.
WISH I COULD SAY THE SAME FOR HIS CHEMICAL PLANT.
THIS PLACE IS TOTALED--BUT AT LEAST ALL HARRY'S PEOPLE GOT OUT.
BETTER CHANGE BACK TO PETER PARKER...

"...WHAT HARRY'S GOING TO NEED MOST RIGHT NOW IS A *FRIEND*."

MY DAD USED TO TAKE ME HERE WHEN I WAS A KID, PETER.

OSBORN CHEMICAL CORPORATION

"SOMEDAY ALL THIS WILL BE YOURS, HARRY"-- *CORNY* LINE, HUH? BUT HE SAID THAT, PETER.

HARRY...

HE WAS *PROUD* OF THIS PLANT.

PROUD OF ME, TOO, THOUGH HE NEVER *SHOWED* IT.

AND NOW--

LOOK AT IT.

LOOK AT IT!

HARRY, TRY TO CALM DOWN.

YOU'VE GOT INSURANCE. --YOU'LL REBUILD--

THAT'S NOT THE POINT.

THIS WAS ALL I HAD OF HIM, PETER, AND I'VE LOST IT.

WHATEVER I REBUILD IT'LL NEVER BE THE SAME. *NEVER!*

HARRY ALWAYS *IDOLIZED* HIS FATHER-- EVEN WHEN NORMAN OSBORN TREATED HIM LIKE DIRT.

THAT'S PARTLY WHY HARRY *BECAME* THE GOBLIN WHEN NORMAN DIED.

SUBCON-SCIOUSLY, HE WANTED TO PLEASE HIS OLD MAN.

I'VE GOT A FEELING ABOUT THIS...

... A REAL *BAD* FEELING ABOUT THIS...

...THE FACE...

THE HOUR AFTER MIDNIGHT.

...IN THE MIRROR...

...NOT MINE!

PETER WAS RIGHT.

WE HAVE TO GET OUT OF HERE.

TOMORROW, I'LL TELL LIZ TOMORROW.

TOMORROW'S TOO LATE, HARRY-BOY.

SO WAS TODAY.

YOU'RE MINE, HARRY.

ALWAYS WERE, ALWAYS WILL BE.

DADDY'S LITTLE BOY...

INFERNO RAGES NEXT ISSUE, AND IN WEB OF SPIDER-MAN #47 ON SALE SOON!

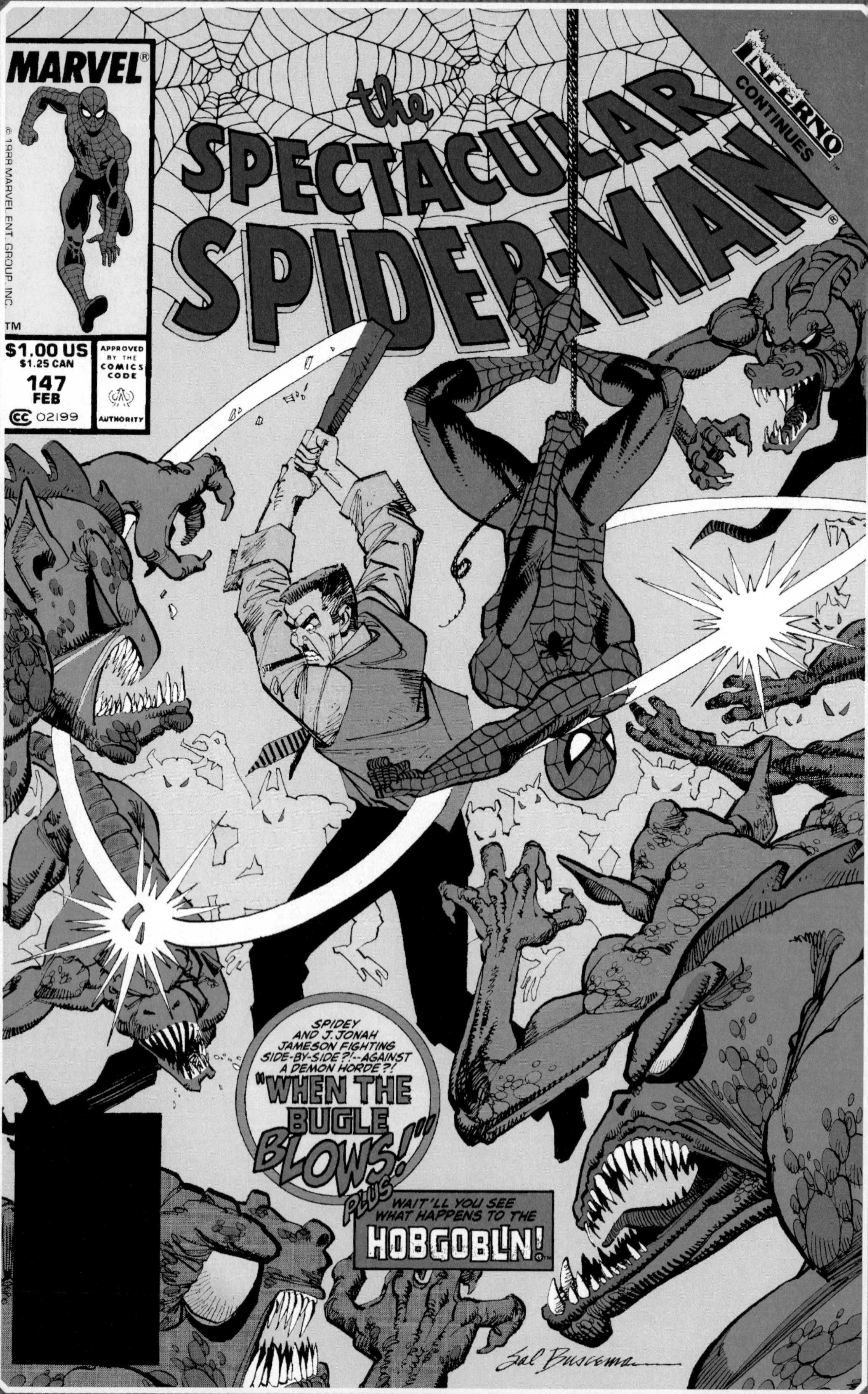

MARVEL®
© 1988 MARVEL ENT. GROUP, INC.
TM
$1.00 US
$1.25 CAN
147
FEB
CC 02199
APPROVED BY THE COMICS CODE AUTHORITY
the SPECTACULAR SPIDER-MAN®
INFERNO CONTINUES™
SPIDEY AND J. JONAH JAMESON FIGHTING SIDE-BY-SIDE?!--AGAINST A DEMON HORDE?!
"WHEN THE BUGLE BLOWS!"
PLUS:
WAIT'LL YOU SEE WHAT HAPPENS TO THE
HOBGOBLIN!
Sal Buscema

Stan Lee PRESENTS: THE SPECTACULAR SPIDER-MAN!™

WHEN THE BUGLE BLOWS

PICTURE OF A RATHER DISAPPOINTED MAN, THE WOULD-BE MASTER VILLAIN KNOWN AS THE HOBGOBLIN!

IT ISN'T FAIR!

I WOULD HAVE WON IF THEY HADN'T TEAMED AGAINST ME!

IT JUST--

--ISN'T--

FAIR!

GERRY CONWAY SCRIPT / SAL BUSCEMA ART / RICK PARKER LETTERS / SHAREN & WILCOX COLOR / JIM SALICRUP EDITOR / TOM DeFALCO EDITOR IN CHIEF

273

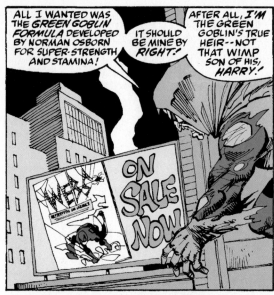

ALL I WANTED WAS THE *GREEN GOBLIN FORMULA* DEVELOPED BY NORMAN OSBORN FOR SUPER-STRENGTH AND STAMINA!

IT SHOULD BE MINE BY *RIGHT!*

AFTER ALL, *I'M* THE GREEN GOBLIN'S *TRUE HEIR*-- NOT THAT WIMP SON OF HIS, *HARRY!*

ALL MY TECHNOLOGY, ALL MY WEAPONS, ALL MY TECHNIQUES ARE *ADAPTED* AND *IMPROVED* FROM THE GOBLIN'S ORIGINAL PLANS!

WHEN THE *FIRST* HOBGOBLIN DIED, I STOLE HIS EQUIPMENT FAIR AND SQUARE!

THE REST OF THE GOBLIN HERITAGE SHOULD BE MINE *TOO!*

AND IT *WOULD* HAVE BEEN, IF HARRY OSBORN AND SPIDER-MAN HADN'T *TRICKED* ME! *

BLAST THEM *BOTH!*

SPAK

* ROUGH RECAP OF *AMAZING #312*, STILL ON SALE. (HINT-HINT.) --JIM

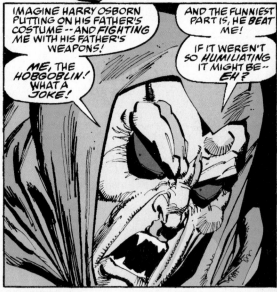

IMAGINE HARRY OSBORN PUTTING ON HIS FATHER'S COSTUME -- AND *FIGHTING* ME WITH HIS FATHER'S WEAPONS!

ME, THE *HOBGOBLIN!* WHAT A *JOKE!*

AND THE FUNNIEST PART IS, HE *BEAT* ME!

IF IT WEREN'T SO *HUMILIATING* IT MIGHT BE-- *EH?*

RROWRR

DEMONS!

IN MY ANGER I'D ALMOST FORGOTTEN THE MADNESS ASSAILING THIS CITY!

TASTY HUMAN! DRESS LIKE DEMON!

BUT YOU DON'T *FOOL* US!

WE EAT YOU UP!

274

YOU PICKED THE WRONG MAN TO ATTACK *THIS DAY*, CREATURES!

WHATEVER YOU *WANT*-- WHATEVER YOU'VE *DONE* TO THE *EMPIRE STATE BUILDING* AND THE REST OF THIS CITY--

--IS NO CONCERN OF MINE AS LONG AS YOU LEAVE *ME* ALONE!

" *DRESS LIKE DEMON*," INDEED! AS IF *I'D* WANT TO BE ONE OF YOU!

ONE OF YOU...

...I WONDER...

AND, AS THE HOB- GOBLIN PONDERS A SUDDEN INSPIRATION--

--ACROSS TOWN, ONE OF HIS ERSTWHILE SPARRING PARTNERS PONDERS A LANDSCAPE GONE LUNATIC:

THIS IS JUST *TOO* WEIRD!

YESTERDAY I THOUGHT *MYSTERIO* WAS BEHIND THE "DEMONS" ATTACKING MANHATTAN--

--NOT TO MENTION THE *FAN VENTS* AND *CHEMICAL PIPES* THAT CAME AFTER ME! *

SO MUCH FOR *THAT* BRIGHT IDEA. THIS KIND OF CRAZINESS IS *WAY* OUT OF MYSTERIO'S LEAGUE.

* LAST ISSUE. --JIM

'SIDES, I TOSSED HIM IN JAIL *MYSELF.*

NO, WHATEVER'S GOING ON IN MANHATTAN IS A LOT MORE *SERIOUS* THAN I THOUGHT.

MAYBE IF I HADN'T BEEN SO WORRIED ABOUT *HARRY* AND THE *HOBGOBLIN*, I MIGHT HAVE PAID MORE *ATTENTION* TO WHAT'S BEEN HAPPENING.

WELL, NO TIME LIKE THE PRESENT TO CORRECT A *MISTAKE.*

I'LL CHECK IN AT THE *DAILY BUGLE* AS PETER PARKER.

JONAH JAMESON WILL KNOW WHAT'S GOING ON, IF ANY- ONE DOES.

THEN I'LL CALL *MARY JANE* AT HAL'S STUDIO, AND SEE HOW SHE'S--

YAAAAAAHH!

SWOOOSH

CALL IT A DEMON WIND.

UNGH!

UNSEEN, UNSUSPECTED EVEN BY *SPIDER-SENSE*, IT PICKS SPIDER-MAN OUT OF THE AIR LIKE A LEAF CAUGHT IN A HURRICANE.

BUT IT ISN'T THE WIND THAT HURTS. OH, NO.

IT'S THE **WALL** THE WIND THROWS HIM AGAINST.

UUUH

THUD

WHAT

HAPPENED

WHAT

"HAPPENED" "CRAZY" IT WAS CRAZY!

THE WIND CAME ALIVE-- ATTACKED ME! AND MY SPIDER-SENSE DIDN'T WARN ME!

BARELY CAUGHT MYSELF ON THIS--

--GARGOYLE!

CHOMP

≥AAAAHH!≤

TA-THUMP

HOW LONG HE LIES UNCON-SCIOUS, HE'LL NEVER KNOW FOR SURE.

LONG ENOUGH.

AND WHEN CONSCIOUSNESS FINALLY RETURNS, THE WORLD IS A CRIMSON BLUR.

THROUGH A HAZE OF PAIN, HE RECOG-NIZES A PLACE NEARBY.

SOMEPLACE FAMILIAR.

SOMEPLACE SAFE.

JOE'S DIN GOOD FOO

DAILY BUGLE BUILDING

FOUNDED 1968 A.D.

278

UPSTAIRS...

OKAY, LET'S CLEAR THIS WRECKAGE.

IF THOSE *DEMONS* COME BACK, I DON'T WANT US STUMBLING OVER BROKEN FURNITURE.

CUSHING, MAKE SOME *BARRICADES* FOR THOSE WINDOWS.

RIGHT, JONAH.

BANNON, CALL THE PRESS ROOM, SEE IF *THEY* WERE ATTACKED TOO.

URICH, DOUSE THAT *FIRE!*

MOVE, PEOPLE.

NEW YORK MAY BE FALLING APART, BUT J. JONAH JAMESON IS AS *ROCK STEADY* AS EVER.

FOR ALL HIS BLUSTER, THAT MAN IS A BORN LEADER.

THANK HEAVEN. WE NEED HIM.

MERCADO, ORGANIZE A FIRST AID TEAM.

IT'LL BE A WHILE BEFORE WE CAN GET OUR INJURED TO A *HOSPITAL.*

GOT IT, JONAH.

CAN'T LET THEM SEE HOW *FRIGHTENED* I AM. WAR, CRIME, CORRUPTION-- THOSE THINGS I CAN *DEAL* WITH.

BUT *THIS--!* IT'S ABSOLUTE *INSANITY!*

EH?

SPIDER-MAN?

HAVEN'T I GOT TROUBLE ENOUGH WITHOUT *YOU* BUTTING IN?

WELL, HIYA, J.J.J.

GOOD

TO SEE YOU TOOOO ½...

MERCADO!

279

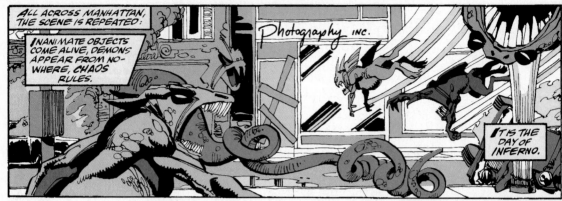

ALL ACROSS MANHATTAN, THE SCENE IS REPEATED:

INANIMATE OBJECTS COME ALIVE, DEMONS APPEAR FROM NO-WHERE, CHAOS RULES.

Photography INC.

IT IS THE DAY OF INFERNO.

AND FOR MARY JANE WATSON-PARKER, CAUGHT IN THE MADNESS WHILE SHOOTING AN EGYPTIAN-MOTIF PHOTO SPREAD, THE DAY HAS GONE FROM BAD TO MUCH, MUCH WORSE...

C'MON, YOU GUYS! BLOCK THAT DOOR!

YOU KNOW WHAT'S OUT THERE!

WHAT'S THE USE? WE DON'T STAND A CHANCE!

YOU CAN'T FIGHT MAGIC! WE'RE ALL DOOMED!

WE'RE GOING TO DIE.

SHUT UP, WEXLER!

NOBODY IS GOING TO--

KRASH

YIII!!

MUNCHIE-MUNCHIE! NICE FAT HUMAN FOR HUNGRY ME!

YUMMY!

HEY, WEXLER--

DUCK!

POOM

WOW. IT BLEW UP. GUESS DEMONS AREN'T AS TOUGH AS THEY *LOOK*...

...LIKE SOME *ADVERTISING AGENCY EXEC-UTIVES* I COULD MENTION.

S-SORRY.

YOU DON'T ADVANCE IN ADVER-TISING BY BEING *COURAGEOUS,* MS. PARKER.

YEAH, BUT IT TAKES *GUTS* TO SUCCEED AS A *MODEL.*

NEXT TO FENDING OFF OVERLY-AMOR-OUS AGENCY REPS, FIGHTING DEMONS IS A *CINCH.*

LET'S *REBUILD* THAT *BARRICADE.*

THEN WHAT? WE HAVE TO GET OUT OF HERE... BUT WHERE CAN WE GO?

I WISH PETER WERE HERE. I HOPE HE'S ALL RIGHT.

HE SAID HE WAS SEEING *HARRY OSBORN* THIS MORNING,* OUT ON LONG ISLAND. I HAVEN'T HEARD FROM HIM SINCE!

* IN *WEB OF SPIDER-MAN* # 47. -- CONTINUITY JIM

PICTURE OF A MAN TRANSFORMED:

YESTERDAY, HARRY OSBORN WAS TORMENTED BY DREAMS AND CON-FOUNDED BY AMNESIA.

TODAY, HE KNOWS HIMSELF... AND HAS MADE PEACE WITH A TROUBLED PAST.

I STILL CAN'T QUITE BELIEVE IT! I BEAT THE *HOBGOBLIN!*

WAIT TILL I GET HOME TO HICKSVILLE AND TELL *LIZ!*

SHE'S PROBABLY WORRIED HALF TO *DEATH* THAT I'VE BECOME THE GREEN GOBLIN AGAIN--

-- THE WAY I DID DURING A DRUG FLASHBACK YEARS AGO.

BUT THIS ISN'T THE *SAME.* I ONLY WORE THE GOBLIN OUTFIT TODAY TO DEFEND MY *FAMILY* FROM THE HOBGOBLIN.

ONCE I GET HOME, I'LL--

HUH?

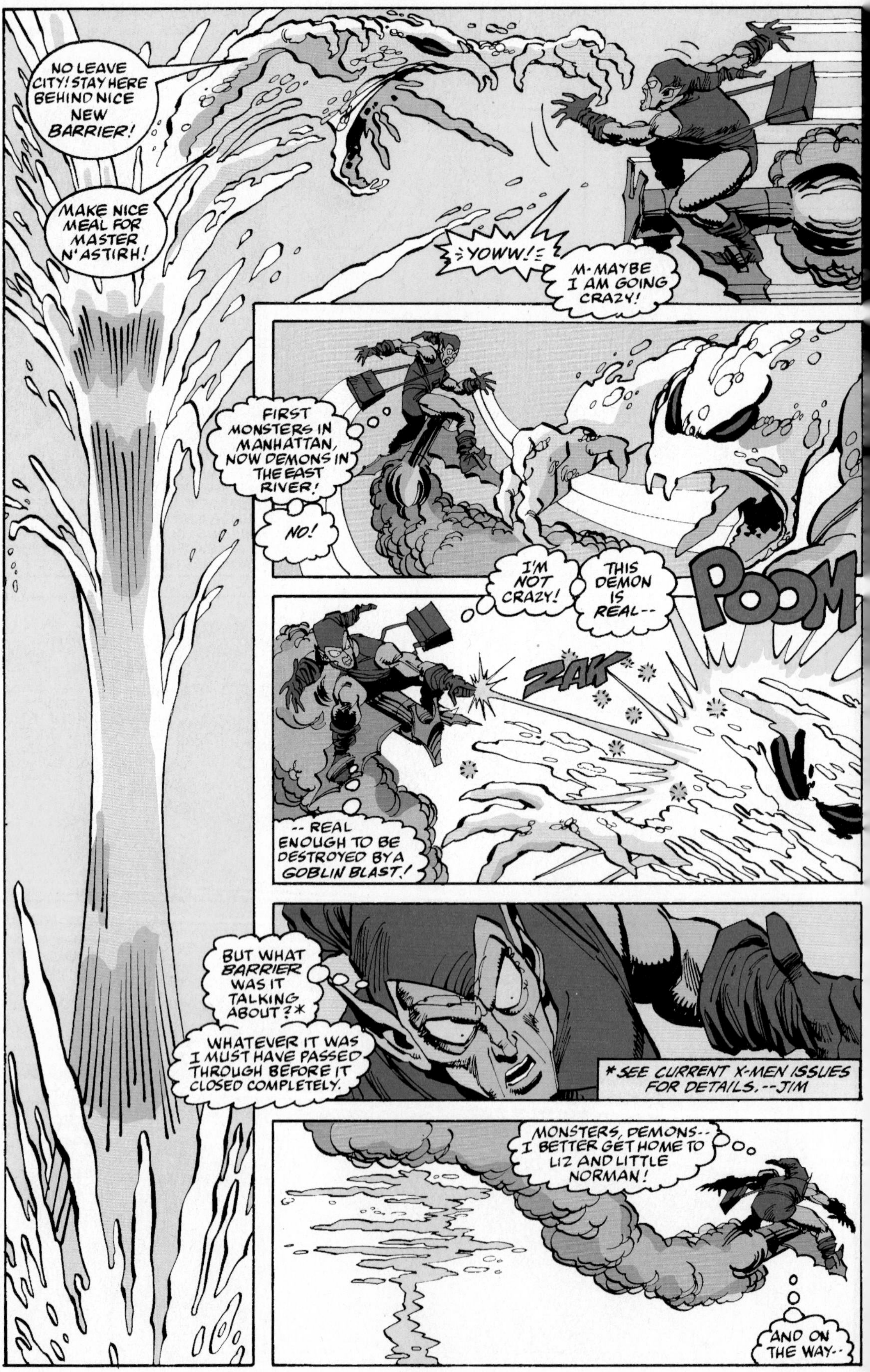
NO LEAVE CITY! STAY HERE BEHIND NICE NEW BARRIER!
MAKE NICE MEAL FOR MASTER N'ASTIRH!
YOWW!
M-MAYBE I AM GOING CRAZY!
FIRST MONSTERS IN MANHATTAN, NOW DEMONS IN THE EAST RIVER!
NO!
I'M NOT CRAZY!
THIS DEMON IS REAL--
POOM
ZAK
-- REAL ENOUGH TO BE DESTROYED BY A GOBLIN BLAST!
BUT WHAT BARRIER WAS IT TALKING ABOUT?*
WHATEVER IT WAS I MUST HAVE PASSED THROUGH BEFORE IT CLOSED COMPLETELY.
*SEE CURRENT X-MEN ISSUES FOR DETAILS. --JIM
MONSTERS, DEMONS-- I BETTER GET HOME TO LIZ AND LITTLE NORMAN!
AND ON THE WAY--

--I'LL STOP BY MAY PARKER'S HOUSE.

IF THERE *IS* SOME KIND OF BARRIER SURROUNDING MANHATTAN, PETER MAY BE WORRIED ABOUT HIS AUNT.

CHECKING ON HER IS THE LEAST I CAN DO FOR AN *OLD FRIEND.*

AND HARRY OSBORN FLIES ON--

--UNAWARE THAT A HANDFUL OF DEMONS HAVE *ALSO* PASSED THROUGH THE CLOSING BARRIER, TO CAPER IN THE STREETS OF QUEENS BELOW.

NOR ARE THEY THE ONLY DANGER FACING THOSE COMMUNITIES CLOSE TO THE INFERNO BARRIER.

IN THE EARLY HOURS BEFORE THE BARRIER'S COMPLETION, *DOZENS OF MADDENED NEW YORKERS* FLED EASTWARD ACROSS THE QUEENSBOROUGH BRIDGE...

MONSTER! KILL YOU!

BRZZZZZ

OUTSIDE HIS HOME, DAILY BUGLE MANAGING EDITOR *JOE ROBERTSON* HAS JUST MET ONE SUCH ESCAPEE.

HE WONDERS IF HE'LL SUR-VIVE TO MEET ANOTHER.

BRZZZZ

MONSTER!

≥UNGH!≤

NEVER THOUGHT I'D BE GRATEFUL FOR THIS CANE!

KRUNK!

JOE! ARE YOU ALL RIGHT? THAT MAN--

HE'S SICK AND FRIGHTENED, MARTHA.

I MAY NOT BE AS *DESPERATE* AS HE IS, BUT IN A WAY I KNOW HOW HE FEELS.

I'M *FRIGHTENED* TOO.

SOMETHING *TERRIBLE* IS HAPPENING IS MANHATTAN. CAN'T YOU *FEEL* IT?

SOMETHING THAT MAKES MY PROBLEM WITH THE *LAW* SEEM UNIMPORTANT.

I TRIED CALLING *JONAH* AT THE *BUGLE*-- BUT OUR LINE'S *DEAD.*

I WAS GOING TO USE A *PUBLIC PHONE* AT THE CORNER MINI-MART WHEN THAT MAN ATTACKED ME.

DAD! MOM! YOU'RE OKAY!

AMANDA AND I GOT *WORRIED* WHEN WE COULDN'T REACH YOU BY PHONE.

EVEN THE *RADIO* ISN'T WORKING...

WE SAW *BUILDINGS* ON FIRE NEAR HERE. AND *RIOTS.*

YOU GUYS BETTER COME HOME WITH *US.*

NO.

SEEING THAT MAN-- HIS *FEAR* HIS *INSANITY*-- I SAW MYSELF.

I'VE BEEN SO AFRAID SINCE *TOMBSTONE* CAME BACK INTO MY LIFE, I HAVEN'T *THOUGHT* STRAIGHT.

ALL I WANTED TO DO IS RUN AWAY.

BUT I'M DONE WITH RUNNING.

IT'S TIME I *FOUGHT BACK*... STARTING HERE. STARTING *NOW.*

MANHATTAN, AT THE HEART OF DARKNESS:

THE ONCE AND FUTURE EMPIRE STATE BUILDING...

...WHERE THE FORCES OF EVIL ARE AS FOCUSED AS THE RAYS OF THE NOONDAY SUN THROUGH A MAGNIFYING GLASS.

FOLLOWING A TRAIL OF DEMONS, THE HOBGOBLIN HAS COME TO THIS PLACE UNSEEN...

...OR SO HE THINKS.

HE IS MISTAKEN.

WELL NOW. WHAT HAVE WE HERE?

RUMBLLE

DINNER!

NO!

TELL YOUR MASTER I WANT TO SEE HIM!

TELL HIM I WANT TO MAKE A DEAL!

THE HUMAN WANTS TO SEE *MASTER N'ASTIRH?*

MASTER WILL *LIKE* THIS. HE WILL BE *AMUSED.*

TELL MASTER.

AFTERWARD, WE *EAT.*

IN SOME SMALL PART OF HIS MIND, HOBGOBLIN REALIZES HE'S GONE INSANE.

HE ALMOST DOESN'T CARE.

ONE *THOUGHT* OBSESSES HIM NOW...

HELLO.

I'M N'ASTIRH.

AMUSE ME.

YOU'RE-- THE *MASTER* OF THESE *MONSTERS?*

OF *COURSE.*

I'M *NOT* LAUGHING YET, BY THE WAY.

YOU CAME HERE FOR A *REASON.*

YOU *WANT* SOMETHING... SOMETHING WE *HUMANS* HAVE TO OFFER...

* SEE THE X-BOOKS FOR ALL THE NASTY DETAILS. --JIM

WHAT I WANT IS NO CONCERN OF YOURS. *

YOU'LL NOTICE I'M STILL *WAITING* TO BE AMUSED. YOU HAVE FIVE SECONDS.

YOU'RE THE *MASTER* OF *DEMONS*-- WHAT ELSE CAN YOU WANT BUT *HUMAN SOULS?*

I'LL TRADE *MY* SOUL FOR *POWER!*

I WANT THE POWER OF A *DEMON!*

DO WE HAVE A *DEAL?*

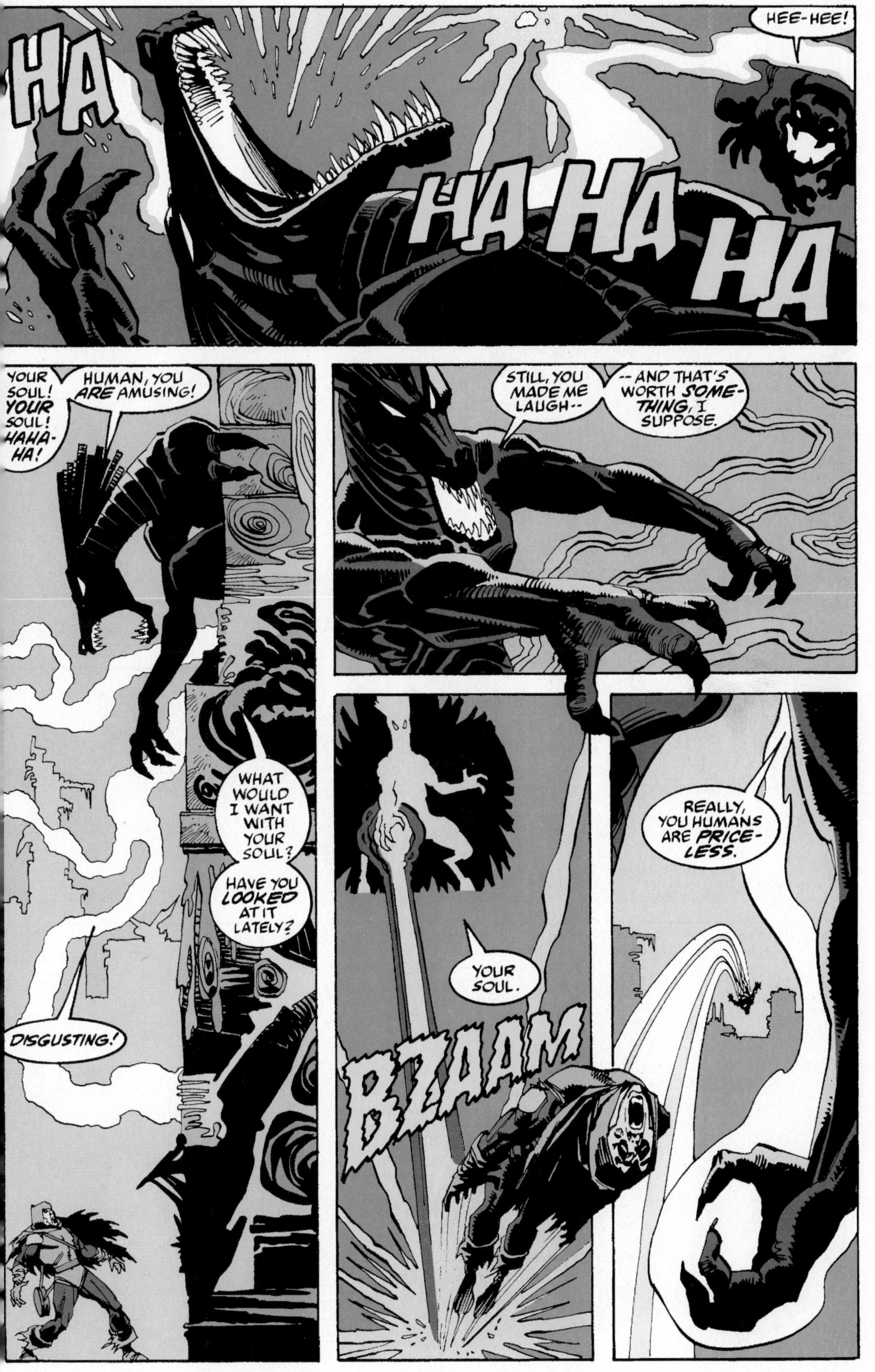
HA
HEE-HEE!
HA HA HA HA
YOUR SOUL! YOUR SOUL! HAHA-HA!
HUMAN, YOU ARE AMUSING!
STILL, YOU MADE ME LAUGH--
-- AND THAT'S WORTH SOME-THING, I SUPPOSE.
WHAT WOULD I WANT WITH YOUR SOUL?
HAVE YOU LOOKED AT IT LATELY?
DISGUSTING!
YOUR SOUL.
BZAAM
REALLY, YOU HUMANS ARE PRICE-LESS.

MIDTOWN.

ONE OF THE JUNIOR COPY EDITORS HEARS IT FIRST, A HIGH-PITCHED *BUZZ* LIKE THE BEATING OF MOSQUITO WINGS.

ONLY LOUDER.

MUCH LOUDER...

KRASH

THEY'RE BACK!

W-WHAT DO WE D-DO?

FIGHT, BLAST IT!

POOM

=AAK=

OO ... ...

KRAK WHAM

FIRST AID

N'ASTIRH LET US PLAY NOW!

WE LIKE TO PLAY WITH HUMANS! HUMANS MAKE *FUNNY NOISES* WHEN THEY'RE SCARED!

MAKE A FUNNY NOISE, HUMAN!

=YAAAAH!=

VERY GOOD!

...

...BEN?

BEN URICH?

MY RIBS ARE IN AGONY...BUT I'VE GOT TO HELP *BEN*...

THWIPP

MAKE FUNNY NOISE *AGAIN*, HUMAN!

THEN I EAT.

YO, *GRUESOME!* OVER HERE!

OW! THAT *HURT!* MY SIDE FEELS LIKE IT'S ON *FIRE!*

EH?

YOU WANT A FUNNY NOISE?

YES!

OKAY.

LISTEN REAL *CLOSELY* NOW!

POOM

≠PFAWH≠

IT BLEW UP! WEIRDER AND WEIRDER!

I'M ONLY TELLING YOU ONCE-- *GET OUT!*

HALF THE CROOKED *POLS* IN THIS CITY HAVE TRIED TO TRASH THE *BUGLE!*

WHOA-BOY, JONAH'S IN TROUBLE!

THEY DIDN'T SUCCEED--

289

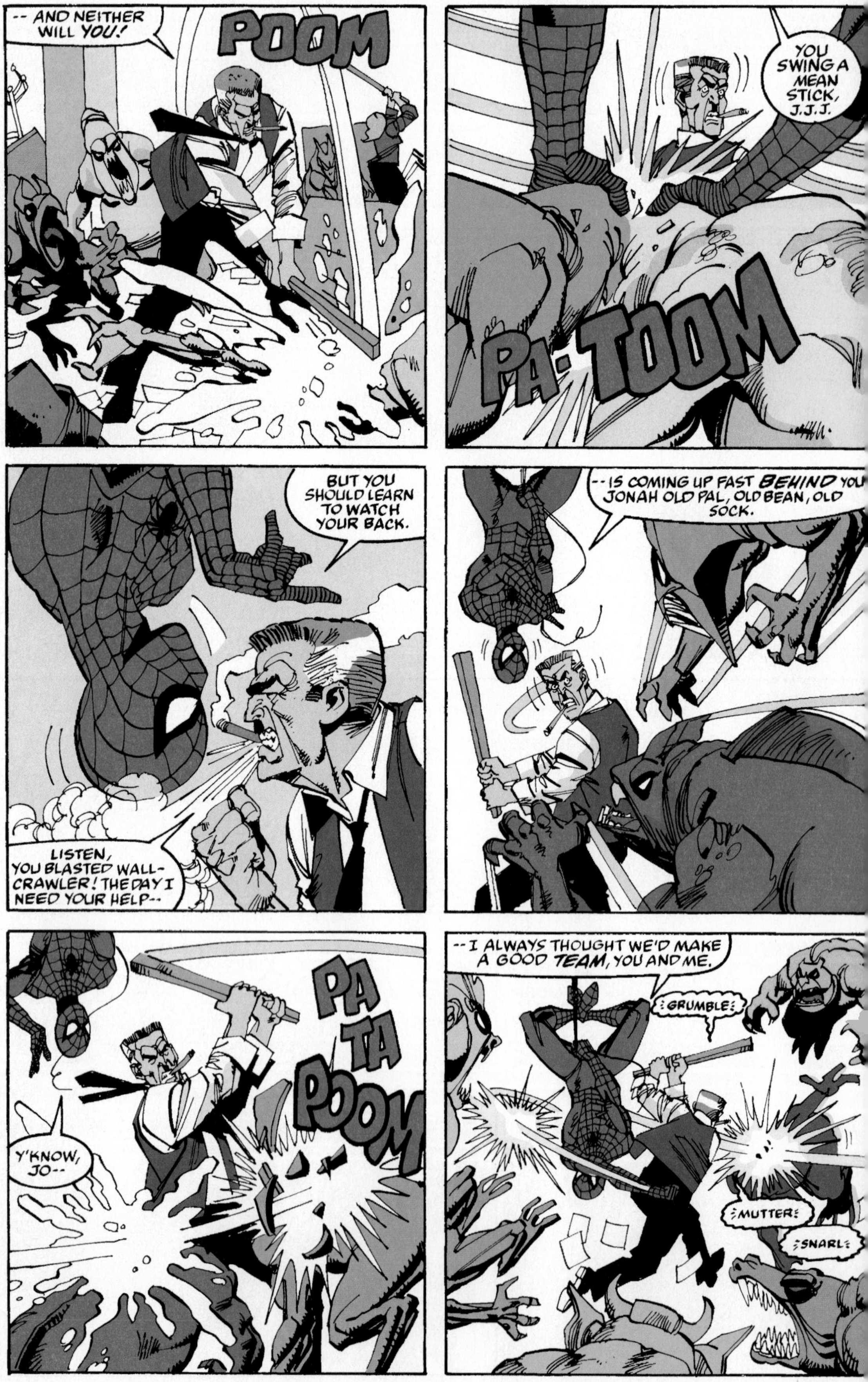
-- AND NEITHER WILL YOU!
POOM
YOU SWING A MEAN STICK, J.J.J.
PA-TOOM
BUT YOU SHOULD LEARN TO WATCH YOUR BACK.
LISTEN, YOU BLASTED WALL-CRAWLER! THE DAY I NEED YOUR HELP--
--IS COMING UP FAST BEHIND YOU, JONAH OLD PAL, OLD BEAN, OLD SOCK.
PA TA POOM
Y'KNOW, JO--
--I ALWAYS THOUGHT WE'D MAKE A GOOD TEAM, YOU AND ME.
GRUMBLE
MUTTER
SNARL

PICTURE OF A CITY BESIEGED (IN MICROCOSM):

THESE ARE MEN AND WOMEN WHOSE LIVES, UNTIL TODAY, HAVE REVOLVED AROUND THE USUAL CRISES OF URBAN LIFE:

STALLED SUBWAY TRAINS.

MISPLACED PAYROLL CHECKS.

POWER BLACK-OUTS.

STOLEN KEYS.

SURLY CAB-DRIVERS.

POOM

BAD PIZZA.

RUDE WAITERS.

TAPOM

INCOMPETENT BANK TELLERS.

AND CHECK-OUT CASHIERS WHOSE PRIMARY LANGUAGE SEEMS TO BE AN OBSCURE SUB-DIALECT OF SERBO-CROATIAN.

PATOOM

THEY'RE NEW YORKERS.

AFTER LIVING IN *THIS* CITY, FIGHTING DEMONS IS A WALK IN THE PARK. *(CENTRAL PARK.)*

LOOKS LIKE WE DROVE THEM OFF... FOR NOW, ANYWAY.

SO WHAT'S THE SCORE, J.J.J.? THINK WE WON?

JONAH?

≶nnnrh≶

≶mrrrh≶

≶ARRRH≶

HA!

SOMEBODY GET A CAMERA! GOT A PAGE ONE PICTURE HERE!

JAMESON IS SO *TENSE*, HE BIT THROUGH HIS *CIGAR!*

HAHA-OW!

THIS CITY IS GOING TO PIECES AND YOU'RE MAKING *JOKES?*

THAT'S ALL I'D *EXPECT* FROM-- EH?

YOUR SIDE'S *BLEED-ING!*

HURTS, TOO.

NOTICE

BUT ONLY WHEN I LAUGH...≶

INFERNO.

FROM HELL'S GATE TO HELL'S KITCHEN, MANHATTAN ISLAND IS CONSUMED BY CHAOS.

ONLY A FEW KNOW WHAT IS HAPPENING, AND ONLY THEY CAN CONFRONT THE EVIL AT ITS SOURCE.*

* OUR LAST X-PLUG. -- XHAUSTED JIM

FOR THE REST OF THOSE TRAPPED ON THIS UNHAPPY ISLE, INFERNO IS A CATASTROPHE WITHOUT RHYME OR REASON.

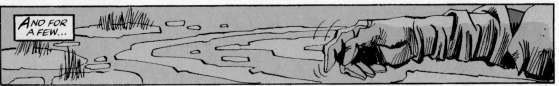

AND FOR A FEW...

...THE CITY'S DISASTER IS OVERSHADOWED BY CALAMITIES OF A MORE PERSONAL NATURE.

MY EYES... ...WHAT DID HE DO TO MY EYES?

I CAN BARELY SEE!

AND THE COLORS--THE LIGHT--THEY'RE ALL WRONG!

WHAT DID HE DO TO MY EYES?

293

YAAAHH!

PICTURE OF A MAN DISMAYED, THE WOULD-BE MASTER VILLAIN KNOWN AS THE HOBGOBLIN:

HE WANTED THE POWER OF A DEMON, AND HE WILL HAVE IT.

BUT ALL POWER COMES WITH A *PRICE*, DEMONIC POWER NO LESS THAN ANY OTHER.

AND AS HE STARES AT HIS REFLECTION IN THE MUDDY WATER OF CENTRAL PARK LAKE, HOBGOBLIN KNOWS, THIS POWER HAS A PRICE HE HAS ONLY *BEGUN* TO PAY...

INFERNO CONTINUES -- IN *WEB OF SPIDER-MAN #48!* AND DON'T MISS NEXT ISSUE'S: "*NIGHT OF THE LIVING NED!*"

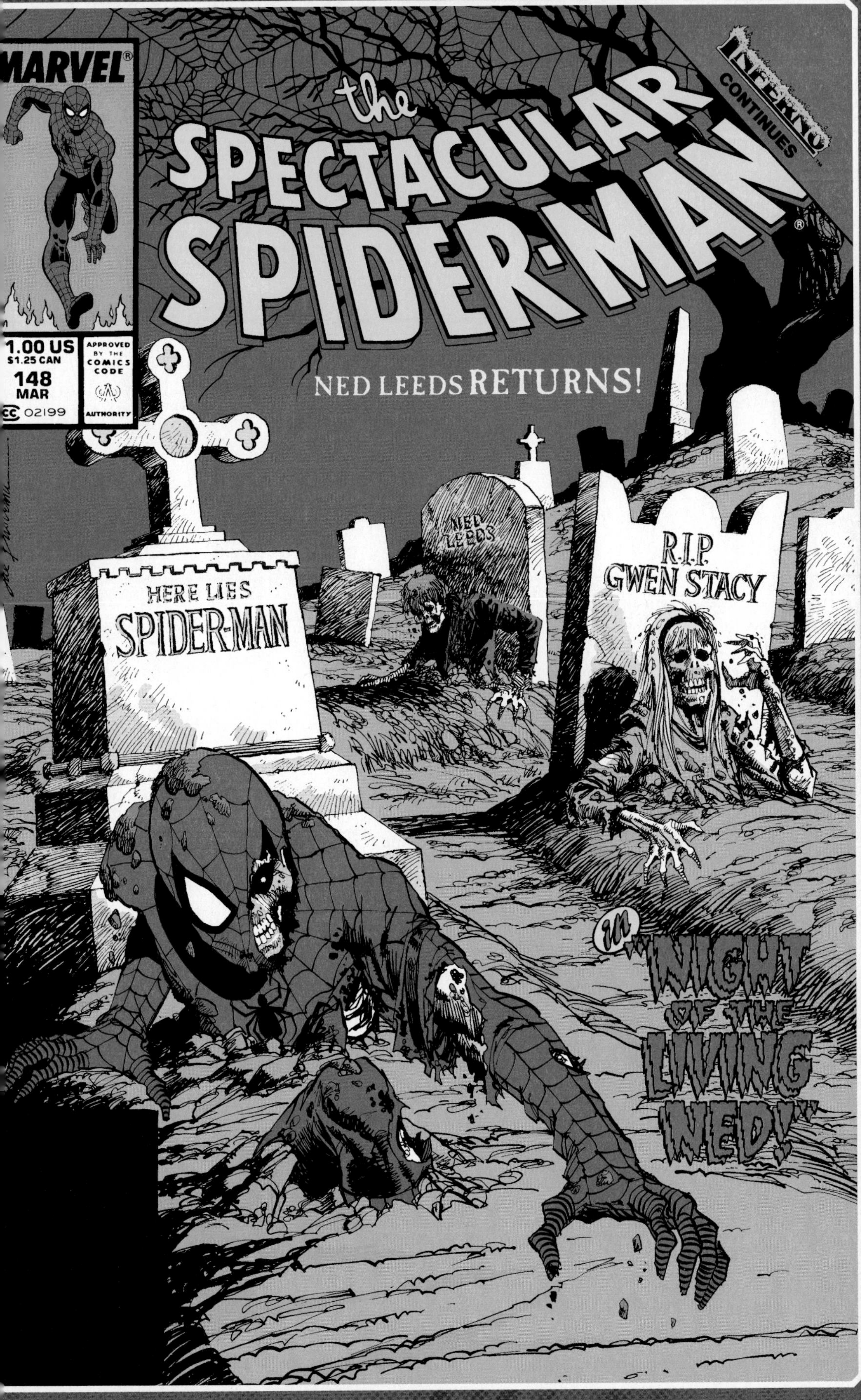

MARVEL
1.00 US
$1.25 CAN
148
MAR
APPROVED BY THE COMICS CODE AUTHORITY
02199
the SPECTACULAR SPIDER-MAN
INFERNO CONTINUES
NED LEEDS RETURNS!
HERE LIES SPIDER-MAN
NED LEEDS
R.I.P. GWEN STACY
in "NIGHT OF THE LIVING NED!"

LIGHTNING BURNS THE NIGHT, RIPPING THROUGH THE CURTAIN OF RAIN LIKE A FORK OF FIRE.

LEEDS NED 1955-1987

THE GRAVE IS JUST HOW SHE REMEMBERS IT FROM THE DAY THEY BURIED HIM HERE.

SHE FEELS A RUMBLE UNDER HER FEET.

LEEDS NED 1955-1985

THE GROUND MOVES.

THE EARTH BREAKS.

IT'S HIM.

I GUESS SOMETIMES LIFE IS LIKE A DRIVE-IN MOVIE.

NIGHT OF THE LIVING NED!

GERRY CONWAY
SCRIPT

SAL BUSCEMA
ART

RICK PARKER
LETTERS

BOB SHAREN
COLOR

JIM SALICRUP
EDITOR

TOM DeFALCO
EDITOR IN CHIEF

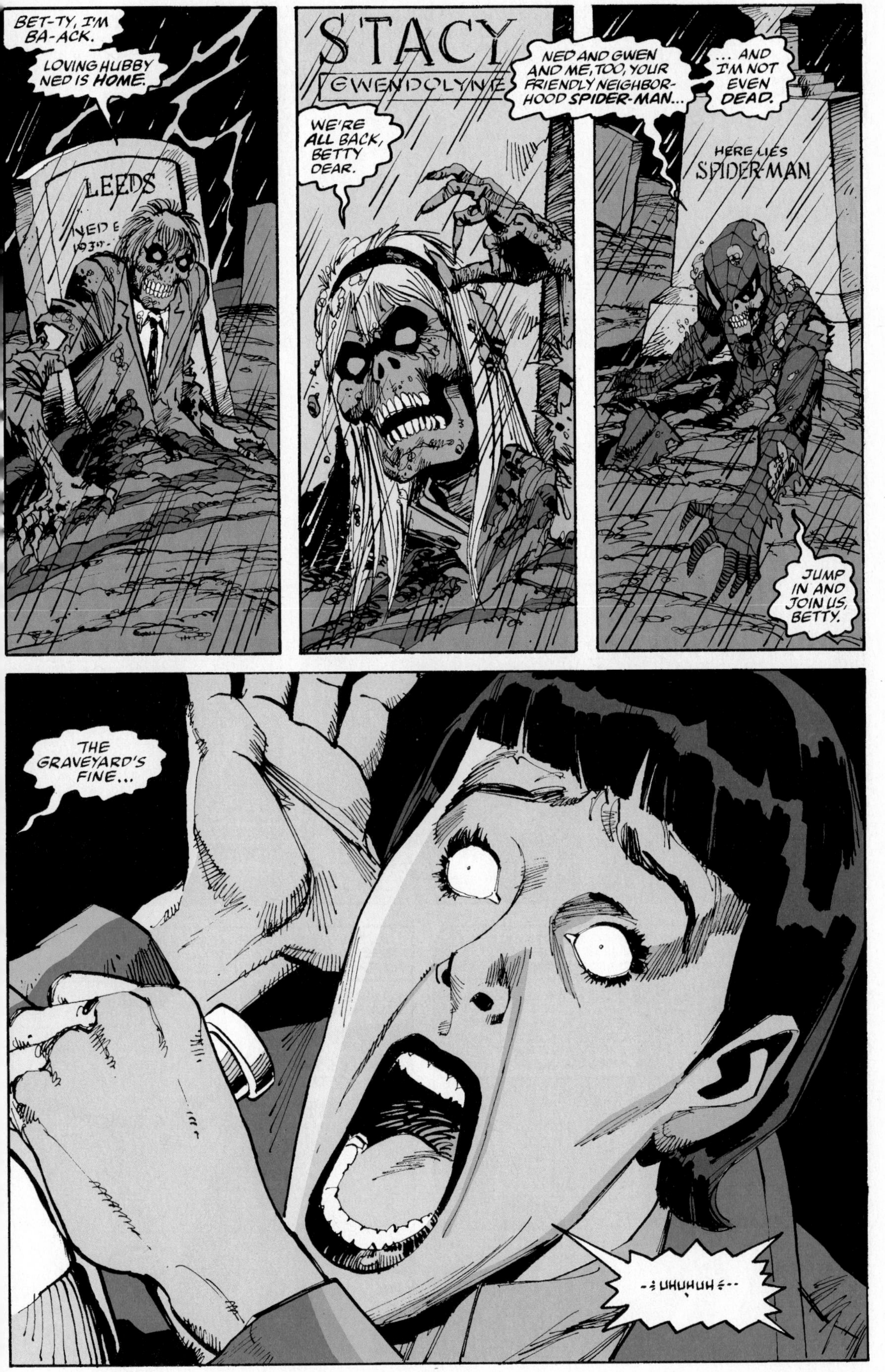
BET-TY, I'M BA-ACK.
LOVING HUBBY NED IS HOME.
LEEDS
STACY
GWENDOLYNE
WE'RE ALL BACK, BETTY DEAR.
NED AND GWEN AND ME, TOO, YOUR FRIENDLY NEIGHBORHOOD SPIDER-MAN...
... AND I'M NOT EVEN DEAD.
HERE LIES SPIDER-MAN
JUMP IN AND JOIN US, BETTY.
THE GRAVEYARD'S FINE...
-UHUHUH--

BETS?

WHAT HAPPENED, WHAT'S *WRONG?*

HE'S BACK, I SAW HIM, NED'S BACK, HE'S DEAD, HE'S ALIVE, HE'S BACK...

I WAS NAILING UP BOARDS ON THE LIVING ROOM DOOR WHEN I HEARD HER MAKE A *CHOKING* SOUND IN THE KITCHEN.

I HEARD A DOG WHIMPER LIKE LIKE THAT, ONCE...

...AFTER A *CAR* RAN OVER ITS RIGHT HIND LEG.

BETTY CLINGS TO ME, AND TELLS ME WHAT SHE SAW: THE LIGHTNING, THE RAIN, NED'S GRAVE...

...AND THE GHOSTS: NED'S GHOST, AND THE OTHERS. HER VOICE IS LOW, AND SHE SHIVERS.

IT WAS A *NIGHTMARE,* BETS. JUST A *DREAM.*

BUT I WAS *AWAKE,* FLASH. AM I GOING *INSANE?*

I WONDER. NED LEEDS WAS BETTY'S HUSBAND; A FEW MONTHS BACK HE WAS KILLED BY TERRORISTS IN BERLIN. HE WAS THE *SECOND* MAN IN BETTY'S LIFE TO BE MURDERED; THE FIRST WAS HER BROTHER, BENNETT, KILLED IN A FIGHT BETWEEN DOC OCTOPUS AND SPIDER-MAN YEARS AGO.

AFTER NED'S DEATH, BETTY HAD A NERVOUS BREAKDOWN, AND WHO COULD BLAME HER.?

FOR A WHILE, SHE FELL UNDER THE INFLUENCE OF A PSEUDO-RELIGIOUS *CULT,* AND I THOUGHT WE'D LOST HER FOR GOOD...

...BUT WITH *SPIDER-MAN'S* HELP, BETTY BROKE FREE. AND SHE'S BEEN WORKING REAL HARD TO PUT HER LIFE BACK TOGETHER EVER SINCE.

YOU'RE NOT CRAZY, BETS.

IT'S THIS CITY...

SOMETHING *WEIRD* IS HAPPENING.

HEAT WAVES, COLD SPELLS, FREAK ACCIDENTS, POWER BLACKOUTS... THE EMPIRE STATE BUILDING IS *GROWING*, PEOPLE ARE *RIOTING* IN THE STREETS... NEW YORK IS *CRACKING UP.* *

YOU SEE *VISIONS* IN THE KITCHEN.

SO *BIG* DEAL.

MID-TOWN HIGH

* SEE CURRENT ISSUES OF-- OH, *NEVER MIND.* IF YOU DON'T KNOW ABOUT *INFERNO* BY NOW, FORGET IT.'---- JADED JIM

A FEW *HALLUCINATIONS* ARE PRETTY MILD STUFF UNDER THE CIRCUMSTANCES, DON'T YOU THINK?

HEY-- WHAT'S WITH THE *HEATER?*

I WAS *COLD,* FLASH. THIS MORNING THE WEATHER WAS SO *HOT,* BUT NOW IT'S *FREEZING.* I FOUND THAT HEATER WITH YOUR CAMPING EQUIPMENT...

AND THAT'S WHERE IT SHOULD *STAY.*

RUNNING A GAS HEATER IN A CLOSED APARTMENT IS *RUSSIAN ROULETTE* WITHOUT A GUN.

I- I'M SORRY. I DON'T KNOW WHAT'S WRONG WITH ME, FLASH... I CAN'T SEEM TO THINK *CLEARLY* ANYMORE.

STRESS, THAT'S ALL.

YOU THINK SO? AFTER NED DIED, MY LIFE BECAME A *BLUR.* NOTHING MADE SENSE. EVERYTHING SEEMED... *UNREAL.*

IT WAS GOOD OF YOU TO LET ME STAY HERE THESE LAST FEW WEEKS.

HEY, WE'VE KNOWN EACH OTHER *FOREVER,* BETS.

SINCE YOU USED TO DATE *PETER PARKER,* WHEN WE WERE KIDS.

A LOT'S CHANGED OVER THE YEARS... YOU, ME AND PETE MOST OF ALL. PETE'S NOT A NERD ANYMORE, I'M NO HIGH SCHOOL FOOTBALL STAR, AND YOU'RE A WIDOW...

...BUT WE ALWAYS STAYED *FRIENDS.*

FRIENDS HANG TOGETHER.

PARTICULARLY *NOW.*

WHAT'S GOING TO HAPPEN TO US, FLASH? I SEE LIGHT EXPLODING OVER THE *EMPIRE STATE BUILDING.*

I HEAR SCREAMS. AND LAUGHTER.

AND THE SOUND OF BABIES CRYING...

I HEAR THEM TOO, BETTY. I DON'T KNOW WHAT IT MEANS.

MAN, I WISH *SPIDER-MAN* WERE HERE. HE'D KNOW WHAT TO DO.

SPIDER-MAN FRIGHTENS ME. BUT YOU *ADMIRE* HIM...

ALWAYS HAVE.

I GUESS EVERY TEEN'S GOTTA HAVE A HERO, AND SPIDER-MAN WAS MINE.

STILL IS.

ALWAYS WILL BE.

NICE.

JUICY.

300

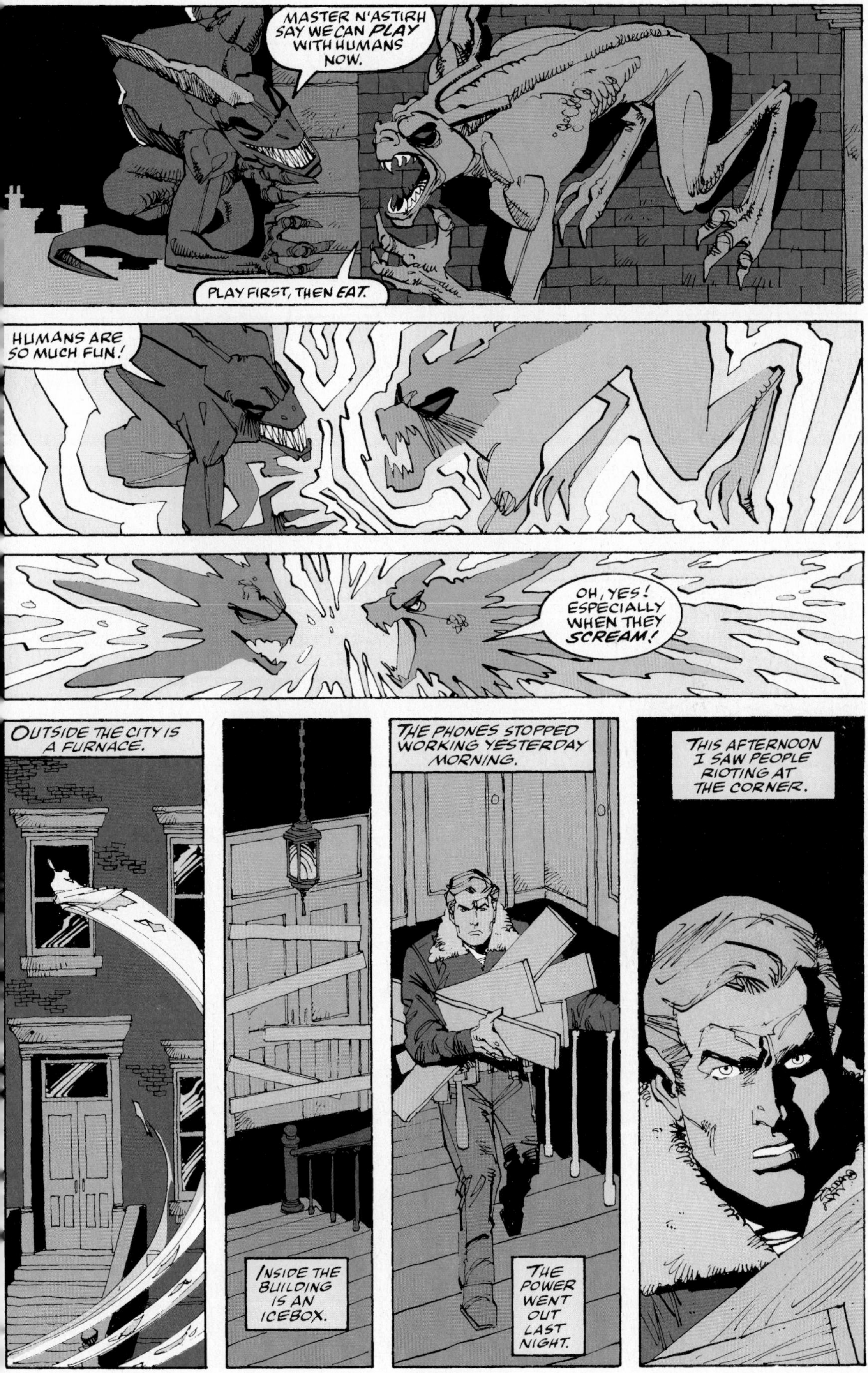
MASTER N'ASTIRH SAY WE CAN PLAY WITH HUMANS NOW.
PLAY FIRST, THEN EAT.
HUMANS ARE SO MUCH FUN!
OH, YES! ESPECIALLY WHEN THEY SCREAM!
OUTSIDE THE CITY IS A FURNACE.
INSIDE THE BUILDING IS AN ICEBOX.
THE PHONES STOPPED WORKING YESTERDAY MORNING.
THE POWER WENT OUT LAST NIGHT.
THIS AFTERNOON I SAW PEOPLE RIOTING AT THE CORNER.

IF I COULD THINK OF SOMEWHERE ELSE TO TAKE BETTY, SOMEWHERE SAFE, WE'D BE GONE IN A MINUTE.

BUT THERE'S NOWHERE TO GO. ALL I CAN DO IS BOARD US IN. AND WAIT.

I HATE FEELING SO HELPLESS. I WANT TO DO SOMETHING. ANYTHING.

WE'RE THE LAST ONES STILL IN THE BUILDING.

EVERYONE ELSE LEFT HOURS AGO.

WHO KNOWS WHERE THEY ARE NOW?

OUT RIOTING, I GUESS.

WHAT'S HAPPENING TO MANHATTAN?

TIMES LIKE THIS, I WISH I'D FINISHED COLLEGE. NOT THAT IT WOULD DO ME MUCH GOOD RIGHT NOW...

...BUT AT LEAST I'D FEEL A WHOLE LOT SMARTER.

FLASH THOMPSON, OVER-AGE JOCK: NO USE TO ANYONE, LEAST OF ALL BETS.

BACK BEFORE WE BECAME FRIENDS, PARKER USED TO TEASE ME FOR NOT BEING AS BRIGHT AS HE IS.

I WONDER IF HE KNEW HOW MUCH THAT HURT?

KNOWING PETE, PROBABLY NOT. HE NEVER --

HI, GUY.

HUH?!

302

SPIDER-MAN!

THIS IS GREAT! I WAS HOPING YOU'D SHOW UP!

NOW WE'LL GET SOME ACTION!

SO WHAT DO WE DO? HOW DO WE GET OUT OF THIS MESS?

WELL, FLASH, THAT'S A REAL GOOD QUESTION.

FORTUNATELY, I'VE GOT A REAL GOOD ANSWER.

YEAH?

WHAT?

WE DON'T.

SKRAK

I DON'T GET IT.

HOW CAN HE BE DOING THIS?

HE'S MY HERO.

MY--

MY NAME IS BETTY LEEDS. ELIZABETH BRANT LEEDS. FLASH CALLS ME *BETS*.

I LIKE FLASH. I TRUST HIM. HE HAS FAITH IN ME.

TAP TAP

(I AM NOT INSANE.)

THERE'S SOMETHING *TAPPING* AT THE WINDOW.

TAP TAP

A BIRD, LOST IN THE NIGHT, DRAWN BY OUR LIGHT. THAT'S ALL.

(I AM NOT INSANE.)

A LITTLE LOST--

--BIRD.

(I AM *NOT* INSANE. I'M NOT.)

(I'M *NOT!*)

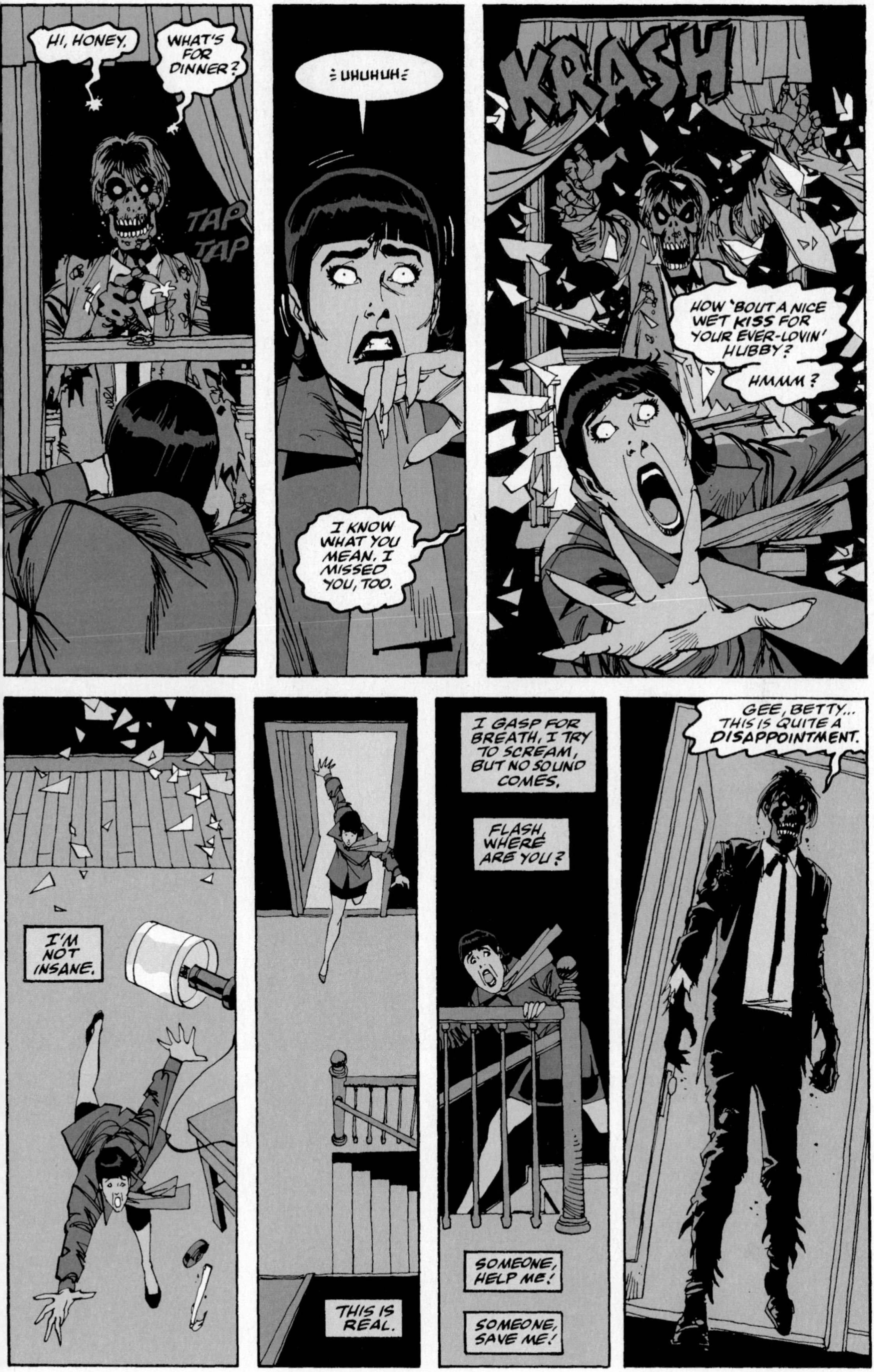
HI, HONEY.
WHAT'S FOR DINNER?
TAP TAP
UHUHUH
I KNOW WHAT YOU MEAN. I MISSED YOU, TOO.
KRASH
HOW 'BOUT A NICE WET KISS FOR YOUR EVER-LOVIN' HUBBY?
HMMM?
I'M NOT INSANE.
THIS IS REAL.
I GASP FOR BREATH, I TRY TO SCREAM, BUT NO SOUND COMES.
FLASH, WHERE ARE YOU?
SOMEONE, HELP ME!
SOMEONE, SAVE ME!
GEE, BETTY... THIS IS QUITE A DISAPPOINTMENT.

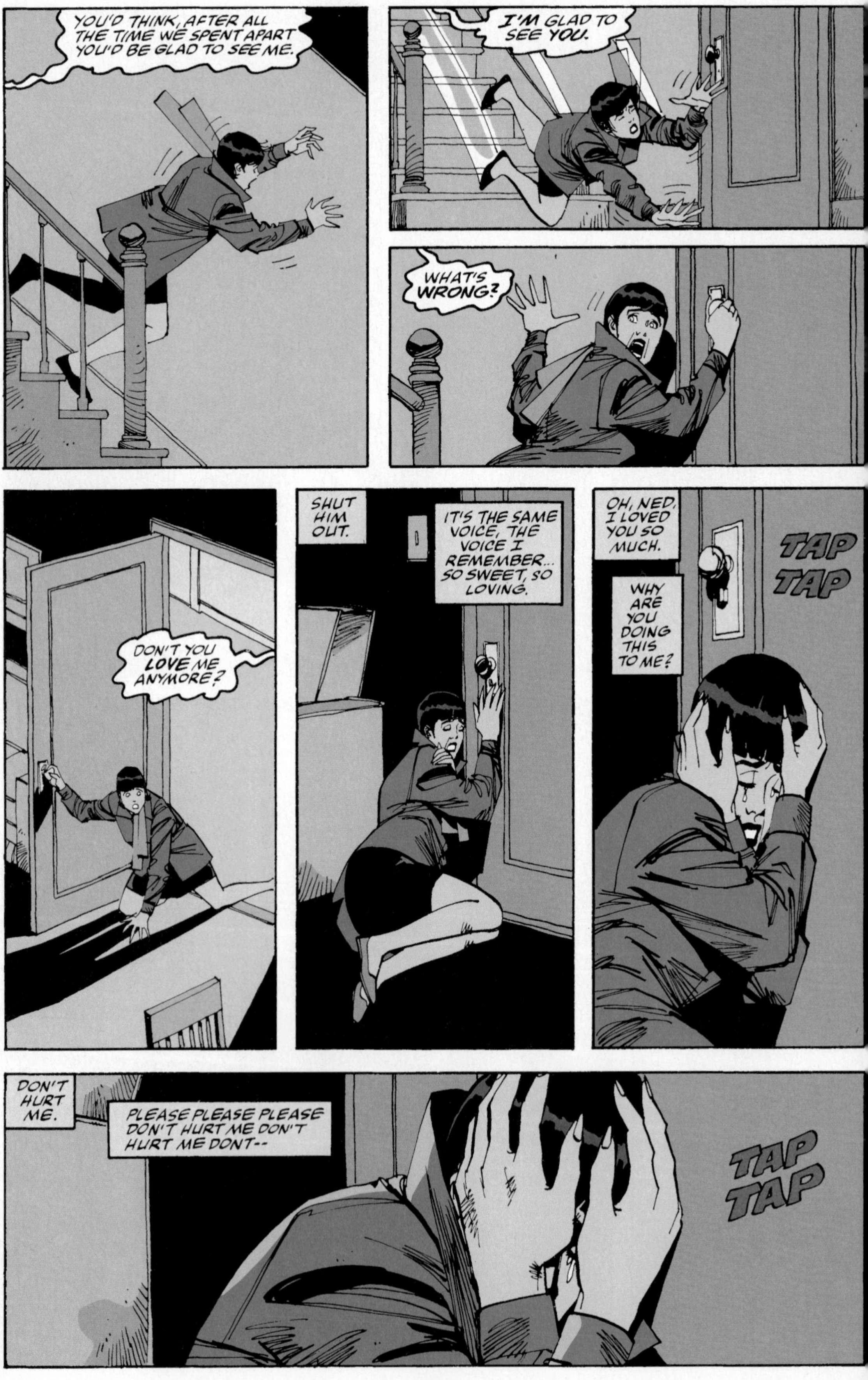
YOU'D THINK, AFTER ALL THE TIME WE SPENT APART YOU'D BE GLAD TO SEE ME.
I'M GLAD TO SEE YOU.
WHAT'S WRONG?
DON'T YOU LOVE ME ANYMORE?
SHUT HIM OUT.
IT'S THE SAME VOICE, THE VOICE I REMEMBER... SO SWEET, SO LOVING.
OH, NED, I LOVED YOU SO MUCH.
WHY ARE YOU DOING THIS TO ME?
TAP TAP
DON'T HURT ME.
PLEASE PLEASE PLEASE DON'T HURT ME DON'T HURT ME DONT--
TAP TAP

--HIT ME AGAIN.

HAD ENOUGH?

IF HE HITS ME AGAIN I'LL PASS OUT.

I CAN'T PASS OUT.

BETTY IS ALONE DOWN-STAIRS.

FOR HER SAKE I'VE GOT TO STAY CONSCIOUS.

YEAH... I'VE HAD ENOUGH.

PHOOEY!

SOME TOUGH GUY YOU TURNED OUT TO BE.

OH, WELL. YOU'RE PROBABLY WON-DERING WHY I WEBBED YOU TO THIS TV ANTENNA.

DON'T TELL ME.

GLAD YOU ASKED.

THAT'S WHY.

KKRAKK

TV ANTENNAE MAKE TERRIFIC LIGHTNING RODS, FLASH!

MOST BUILDINGS HAVE REAL LIGHT-NING RODS ATTACHED TO THEIR ROOFS--

--LIKE THIS ONE.

WITHOUT A ROD TO DEFLECT THE LIGHTNING FROM YOUR ANTENNA, WELL...

I'LL BE ELECTROCUTED!

WHY ARE YOU DOING THIS?

THE TRUTH?

YOU ANNOY ME.

W-WHAT?

YOU HEARD ME.

THIS HERO-WORSHIP ROUTINE OF YOURS MAKES ME WANNA *BARF.*

TOOLS IN MY BELT. NOT MUCH HOPE, BUT I'VE GOTTA TRY.

HOPE HE DOESN'T SEE MY HAND MOVE.

KEEP HIM TALKING...

I THOUGHT WE WERE *PALS...*

PALS? YOU AND ME?

YOU MUST HAVE CAUGHT TOO MANY *TACKLES* DURING YOUR HIGH SCHOOL FOOTBALL CAREER, FLASH OLD CHUM.

EITHER THAT, OR YOU WERE *BORN* DUMB.

THINK ABOUT IT.

I'M A HERO...

...YOU'RE A LOSER.

HEROES DON'T HANG WITH LOSERS.

TALK.

KEEP TALKING.

DON'T LOOK AT MY HAND...

HEROES LIVE AND LOSERS DIE!

TIME TO *DIE,* FLASH, OLD SOCK...

...AND THEN IT'S TIME TO *EAT!*

308

I FEEL AS IF I'VE BEEN FRIGHTENED *FOREVER*. PART OF ME HAS ALWAYS BEEN AFRAID.

I NEED SOMEONE TO TAKE CARE OF ME.

I NEED SOMEONE TO *SAVE* ME.

TAP TAP TAP

BENNETT WAS MY BROTHER; I DEPENDED ON HIM, LEANED ON HIM... *NEEDED* HIM.

TAP TAP TAP

THEN HE DIED, AND I WAS ALONE.

ALL ALONE.

UNTIL *NED* CAME INTO MY LIFE.

TAP TAP TAP

NED WAS SUPPOSED TO SAVE ME...

...THEN *NED* DIED, TOO.

ALL MY MEN DIE.

BETTY.

NED?

YOU DEPEND ON US TOO MUCH. WE'RE ONLY PEOPLE. SOMETIMES WE'RE STRONG, SOMETIMES WE'RE WEAK.

SOMETIMES WE LIVE, SOMETIMES WE DIE.

WE CAN'T *SAVE* YOU, BETTY. YOU HAVE TO SAVE *YOURSELF*.

REMEMBER THE LOVE WE SHARED... AND BE STRONG.

HE'S HERE...

... AND THEN HE'S GONE.

A GHOST? A VISION? A DREAM? A VOICE FROM INSIDE ME?

TAP TAP TAP

I DON'T KNOW...

... AND SUDDENLY, I DON'T CARE.

"NED" WAS RIGHT.

I'VE DEPENDED ON *OTHERS* FOR TOO LONG, AND IT NEARLY DESTROYED MY LIFE.

NO MORE. I FINALLY *GET* IT. I'M ON MY OWN...

309

...AND I'M **SCARED.**

LISTENING TO **THIS GUY,** I FEEL MY **HEART POUNDING.** I'M **AFRAID.**

IT MAKES ME **MAD.**

SPANG!

HAK!

GONNA PULL THE **LIGHTNING DOWN!** GONNA WATCH YOU **BURN!**

ONE **FLASH-FRIED,** COMING UP! HA!

I DON'T LIKE **BEING AFRAID.**

HUH?

WHO ARE YOU?

—WHOOF—

YOU'RE NOT SPIDEY, THAT'S FOR **SURE!**

I NEVER **COULD'VE** RIPPED **HIS** WEB WITH A **SCREW-DRIVER!**

ALL THOSE **THINGS** YOU SAID—ABOUT **HEROES** AND **LOSERS!**

THEY WERE **LIES! ADMIT** IT! **ADMIT IT!**

SPIDER-MAN IS MY **FRIEND!** I'M **NOT** A **LOSER!**

I'M—

—NOT—

OH, **REALLY?**

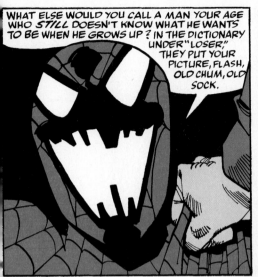

WHAT ELSE WOULD YOU CALL A MAN YOUR AGE WHO *STILL* DOESN'T KNOW WHAT HE WANTS TO BE WHEN HE GROWS UP? IN THE DICTIONARY UNDER "LOSER," THEY PUT YOUR PICTURE, FLASH, OLD CHUM, OLD SOCK.

≥AAAK!≤

DREAMING OF YOUR HIGH SCHOOL *GLORY* DAYS--WHEN EVERYONE *ADMIRED* FLASH THOMPSON, BIG MAN ON CAMPUS.

≥UNNGH≤

THAT FLASH WAS A HERO. LARGER THAN LIFE. A REGULAR *STAR.*

BEHIND YOUR HERO-MASK, YOU'RE A SCARED LITTLE BOY, AFRAID TO BE A MAN!

ISN'T *THAT* WHY YOU ADMIRE SPIDER-MAN?

BECAUSE *HE* WEARS A MASK, TOO?

YOU'VE SEEN THE FACE BEHIND *MY* MASK, FLASH OLD SPOON. I'M THE *REAL THING.*

I'M *EXACTLY* WHAT I SEEM TO BE--A MONSTER OUT OF YOUR BLACKEST NIGHTMARE!

BUT WHAT ARE *YOU,* FLASH? HERO... OR LOSER?

WHO ARE YOU?!!

A FEW MOMENTS AGO, THE TAPPING STOPPED OUTSIDE THE APARTMENT DOWNSTAIRS.

WHEN I LOOKED OUTSIDE, THE HALLWAY WAS EMPTY.

I RAN UP HERE, TO FLASH'S APARTMENT.

I BRACE MYSELF, WONDERING WHAT I'LL FIND INSIDE.

CANDLES, DOZENS OF THEM. THE SMELL OF WAX IS SO THICK IT'S NAUSEATING.

I DIDN'T LIGHT ALL THESE CANDLES. WHO DID?

FLASH?

NO ANSWER.

I'M ALONE.

BUT THAT DOESN'T FRIGHTEN ME AS MUCH AS IT DID BEFORE.

THERE'S A DIFFERENCE. I'M NOT JUST REACTING ANY-MORE.

I'VE GOT A PLAN.

HEY, BABE.

I'VE BEEN WAITING FOR YOU. I LIT A CANDLE TO LIGHT YOUR WAY.

I LIT LOTS OF CANDLES.

YOUR LOVIN' HUBBY HAS BEEN AWFULLY BORED.

STOP PRETENDING, WHATEVER YOU ARE!

I KNOW YOU'RE NOT NED.

DARN.

GAME'S UP.

GUESS THAT MEANS...

...IT'S DINNER TIME!

YOU CAN *RUN* NOW. *HIDE* IF YOU LIKE.

I PROMISE I WON'T LOOK.

NO...

I'M DONE WITH RUNNING AND HIDING.

SCREAM THEN. I LIKE A GOOD SCREAM.

YOU ONLY SCREAM WHEN YOU WANT HELP.

AND I'M THE ONLY HELP I *NEED.*

SNAP

313

BESIDE US, THE ANTENNA TOPPLES, WIRE SNAPPING LIKE A *WHIP.*

GASPING FOR BREATH, I TAKE A CHANCE, *GRAB* THE WIRE AS IT FLAILS BY --

-- AND *PRAY.*

I ALWAYS WANTED TO BE A HERO.

I GUESS SOMETIMES LIFE IS LIKE A DRIVE-IN MOVIE.

SKRASH

FLASH!

HUH?

MY HEART POUNDS AND THERE'S FIRE EVERYWHERE.

THE THING WITH SPIDEY'S FACE SNATCHES AT ME, HISSING--

-- BUT I DODGE, JUST LIKE THE OLD DAYS ON THE MIDTOWN HIGH FOOTBALL FIELD.

I DON'T GET FAR.

SWAK

I NEVER RAN AGAINST A DEFENSE LIKE THIS BEFORE.

GET AWAY FROM HIM, YOU CREEP!

PLOK

HEY!

WATCH IT!

BETTY--?

WHAT DID YOU--

HMMM.

THE GAS HEATER, FLASH!

I BROKE THE VALVE WHEN I TURNED IT ON.

OH, NO!

OH, YEAH!

SAY--

DO YOU HEAR--

HISSSSSS

OH, WELL.

I'D BEEN THINKING ABOUT FINDING A NEW APARTMENT SOON, ANYWAY.

IN THE SMOKE I LOSE SIGHT OF BETS FOR JUST A MOMENT, THEN I FIND HER AGAIN, JUMPING THE STAIRS AHEAD OF ME.

I GRAB HER SHOULDER--

--AND SHE STRUGGLES TO BREAK FREE.

--BUT WHEN SHE SEES MY FACE, HER BODY GOES LIMP--

--AND WE FIND OURSELVES LAUGHING TOGETHER WITH RELIEF.

WOW. "LET GO OF HIM, YOU CREEP!"

REMIND ME NEVER TO GET YOU ANGRY.

RIGHT. I'M DANGEROUS WHEN I'M ANGRY.

OH, FLASH... IS IT OVER? REALLY OVER?

316

ACTUALLY, BETS... I THINK IT IS.

LISTEN... WHAT DO YOU HEAR?

SIRENS IN THE DISTANCE.

...BUT NO MORE *SCREAMS*, NO MORE CRYING BABIES.

THERE ISN'T A DEMON IN SIGHT. ONLY PEOPLE--DAZED AND CONFUSED-- BUT JUST *PEOPLE*.

THE *EMPIRE STATE BUILDING*... IT'S BACK TO NORMAL, TOO!*

* FIND OUT WHY IN *X-FACTOR* #38. (AND THAT'S OUR VERY *LAST* CROSSOVER PLUG!) -- Jim

THEN WE'RE *SAFE?*

I DON'T KNOW ABOUT "SAFE," BUT WE SURVIVED.

WE *DID*, DIDN'T WE? ALL BY OURSELVES...

NO HEROES...NO SAVIORS... JUST US.

YOU AND I. WE DID IT ALONE.

NOT QUITE ALONE.

WE HAD *HELP.*,

...NOT FROM ANY HERO OUT THERE IN THE WORLD,

WE HAD HELP FROM THE ONLY HERO WE EVER *REALLY* NEED...

...THE HERO WE CARRY *INSIDE.*

The End

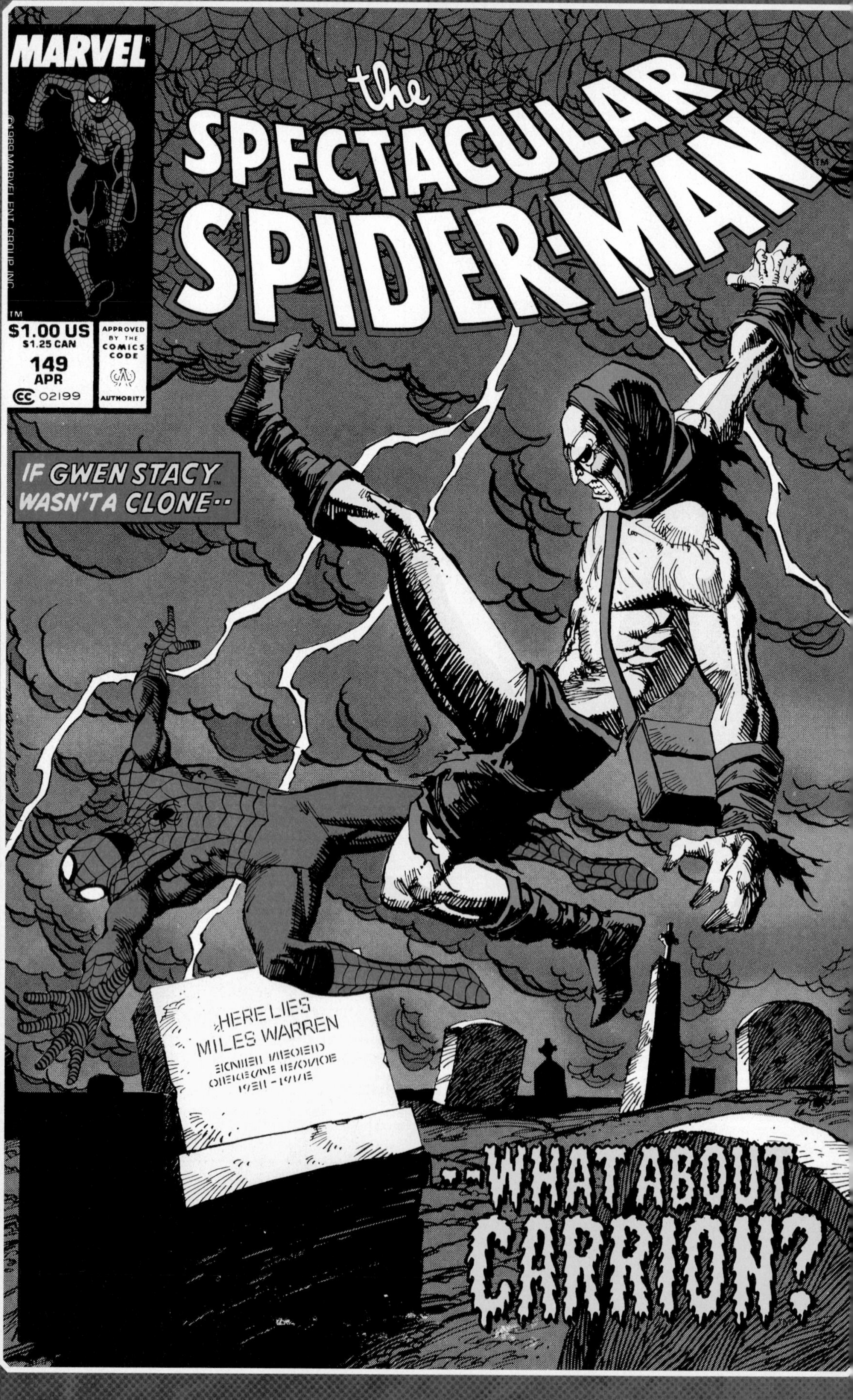
MARVEL
the SPECTACULAR SPIDER-MAN
$1.00 US
$1.25 CAN
149
APR
02199
APPROVED BY THE COMICS CODE AUTHORITY
©1989 MARVEL ENT. GROUP, INC.
IF GWEN STACY WASN'T A CLONE--
HERE LIES
MILES WARREN
--WHAT ABOUT CARRION?

PROLOGUE: MIDTOWN MANHATTAN, 2:45 a.m., HE IS OUTSIDE THE OFFICE TOWER OWNED BY WILSON FISK, A.K.A. "THE KINGPIN OF CRIME."

HE IS FAR FROM HIS HOME...

...AND THE SCENTS OF THIS CITY ARE STRANGE TO HIM.

YET HE HAS NO DIFFICULTY FINDING HIS WAY.

HIS PATH IS WELL LIT BY THE LIGHT OF AN ASHEN MOON,

C'MON, C'MON, WE'RE RUNNIN' LATE.

THIS STUFF'S HEAVY, LOU.

AW... YOU'RE BREAKIN' MY HEART.

I MEAN IT. WHO KNEW CASH COULD WEIGH SO MUCH?

HOW MUCH YOU FIGURE WE GOT HERE? FIVE, MAYBE TEN MILL?

DON'T GET ANY IDEAS.

THAT MONEY BELONGS TO THE KINGPIN. A DAY'S TAKE FROM OPERATIONS AROUND THE CITY.

JUST PUT IT IN THE VAULT, AND KEEP YOUR HANDS--

GRRRRR

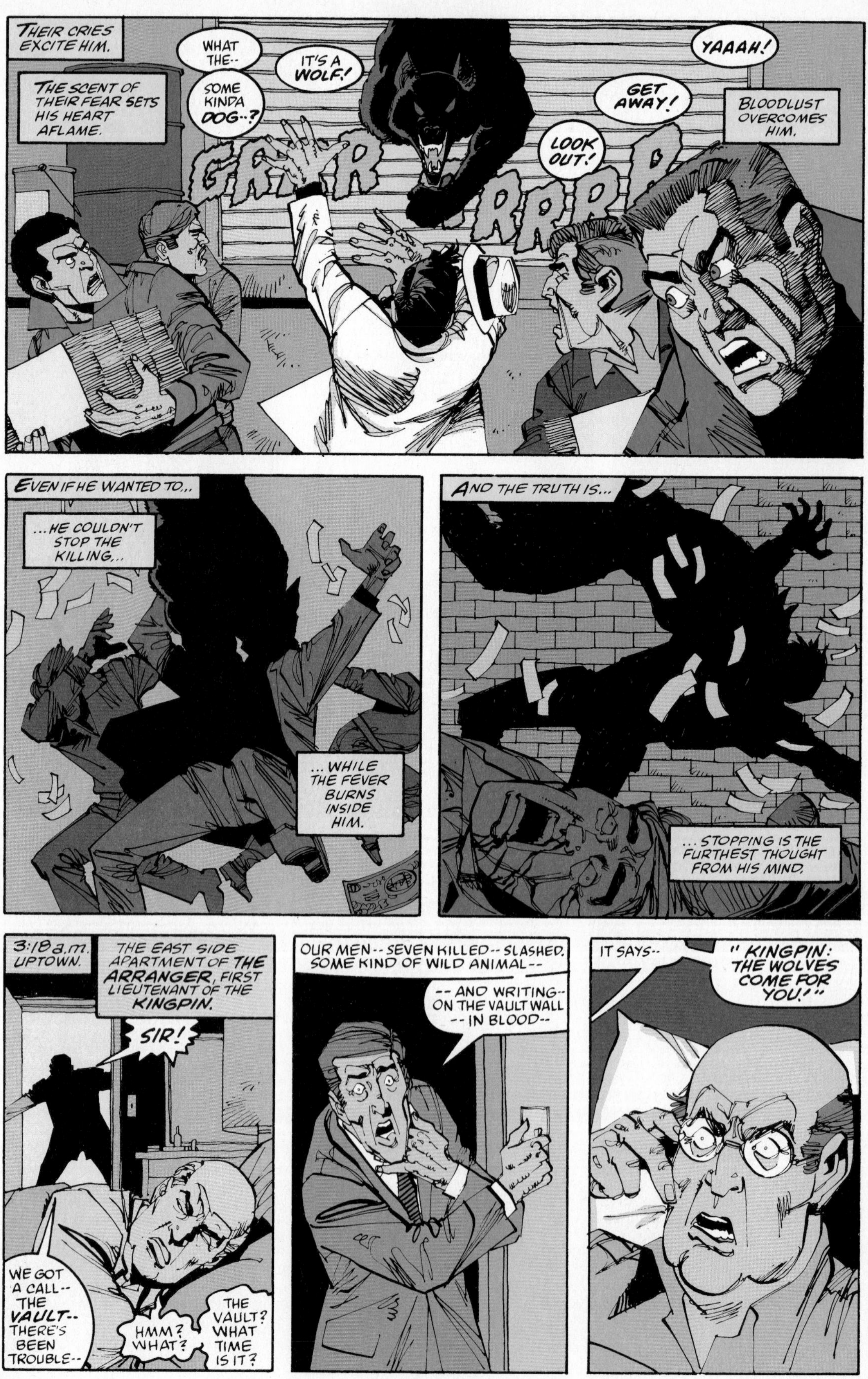
THEIR CRIES EXCITE HIM.
THE SCENT OF THEIR FEAR SETS HIS HEART AFLAME.
WHAT THE--
SOME KINDA DOG..?
IT'S A WOLF!
GRRR RRRR
GET AWAY!
LOOK OUT!
YAAAH!
BLOODLUST OVERCOMES HIM.
EVEN IF HE WANTED TO...
...HE COULDN'T STOP THE KILLING...
...WHILE THE FEVER BURNS INSIDE HIM.
AND THE TRUTH IS...
...STOPPING IS THE FURTHEST THOUGHT FROM HIS MIND.
3:18 a.m. UPTOWN.
THE EAST SIDE APARTMENT OF THE ARRANGER, FIRST LIEUTENANT OF THE KINGPIN.
SIR!
WE GOT A CALL-- THE VAULT-- THERE'S BEEN TROUBLE--
HMM? WHAT?
THE VAULT? WHAT TIME IS IT?
OUR MEN -- SEVEN KILLED -- SLASHED. SOME KIND OF WILD ANIMAL --
-- AND WRITING -- ON THE VAULT WALL -- IN BLOOD--
IT SAYS--
"KINGPIN: THE WOLVES COME FOR YOU!"

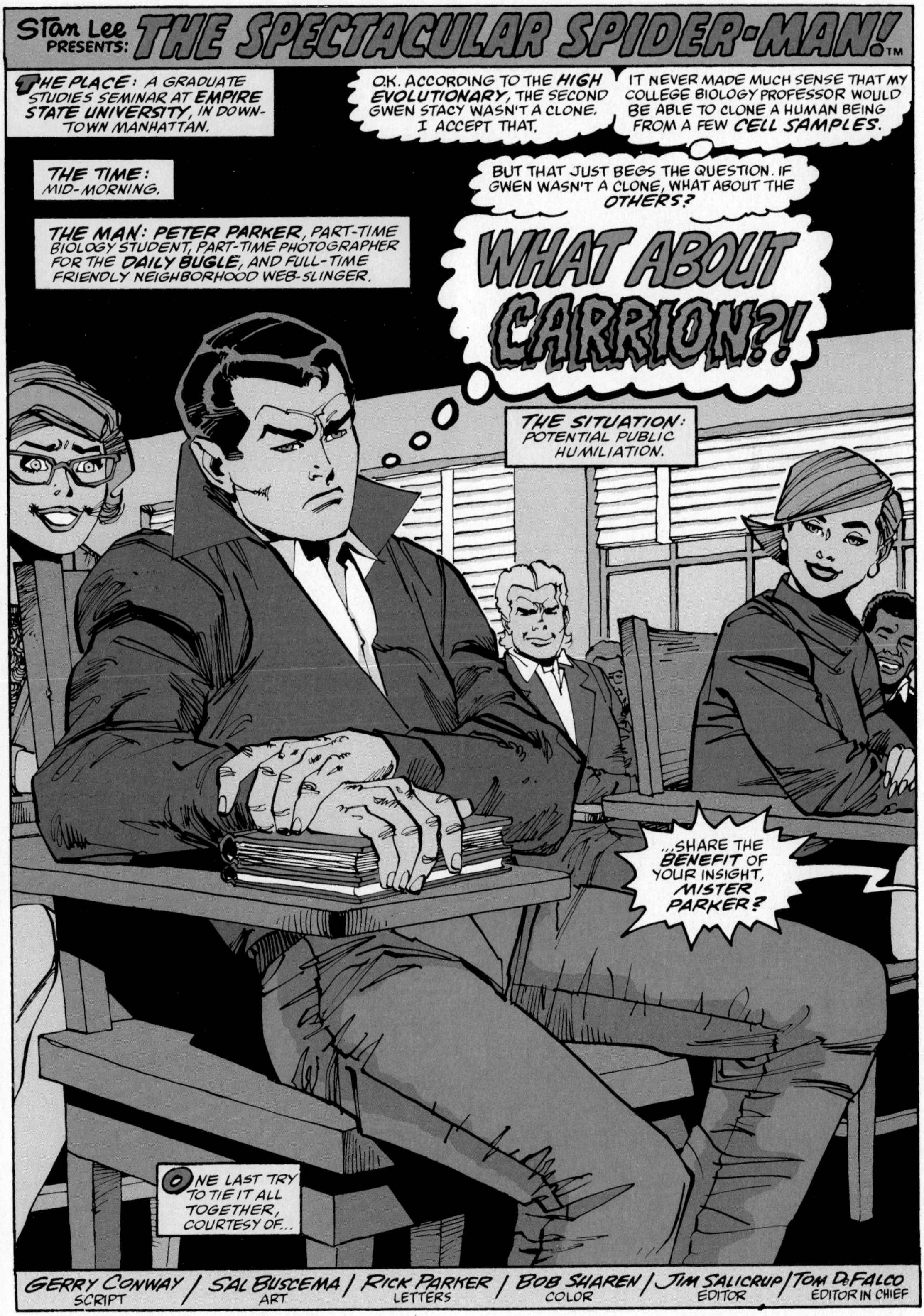
Stan Lee PRESENTS: THE SPECTACULAR SPIDER-MAN! TM
THE PLACE: A GRADUATE STUDIES SEMINAR AT EMPIRE STATE UNIVERSITY, IN DOWNTOWN MANHATTAN.
THE TIME: MID-MORNING.
THE MAN: PETER PARKER, PART-TIME BIOLOGY STUDENT, PART-TIME PHOTOGRAPHER FOR THE DAILY BUGLE, AND FULL-TIME FRIENDLY NEIGHBORHOOD WEB-SLINGER.
O.K. ACCORDING TO THE HIGH EVOLUTIONARY, THE SECOND GWEN STACY WASN'T A CLONE. I ACCEPT THAT.
IT NEVER MADE MUCH SENSE THAT MY COLLEGE BIOLOGY PROFESSOR WOULD BE ABLE TO CLONE A HUMAN BEING FROM A FEW CELL SAMPLES.
BUT THAT JUST BEGS THE QUESTION. IF GWEN WASN'T A CLONE, WHAT ABOUT THE OTHERS?
WHAT ABOUT CARRION?!
THE SITUATION: POTENTIAL PUBLIC HUMILIATION.
...SHARE THE BENEFIT OF YOUR INSIGHT, MISTER PARKER?
ONE LAST TRY TO TIE IT ALL TOGETHER, COURTESY OF...
GERRY CONWAY / SCRIPT
SAL BUSCEMA / ART
RICK PARKER / LETTERS
BOB SHAREN / COLOR
JIM SALICRUP / EDITOR
TOM DeFALCO / EDITOR IN CHIEF

HUH? WHAT? OMIGOSH!

I'M SORRY, SIR-- I WASN'T THINKING-- I MEAN, I *WAS* THINKING, I JUST WASN'T LISTENING-- I MEAN-- I WAS, BUT--

WHAT WAS THE QUESTION?

NEVER-MIND.

I REALIZE YOU'RE A RETURNING STUDENT, MR. PARKER--

--THUS I'M WILLING TO MAKE ALLOWANCES WHILE YOU RE-ADAPT TO ACADEMIA.

BUT THE *NEXT* TIME YOU FALL ASLEEP DURING MY LECTURE...

...I'LL BURN YOUR BUTT.

YOU'RE NOT A CAMPUS SUPER-STAR, ANYMORE, OLD MAN.

MAYBE YOU SPENT TOO MUCH TIME AWAY FROM SCHOOL. YOU'VE LOST YOUR TOUCH.

I'VE BEEN LIVING *LIFE*, McBRIDE.

AND REAL LIFE IS MORE THAN BOOKS.

BUT A GRIND LIKE YOU WOULDN'T KNOW LIFE IF IT BIT HIM IN THE NOSE-- WOULD HE, GIRLS?

SCORE ONE FOR PARKER, MALCOLM.

YEAH...SCORE ONE FOR HIM.

CREEP.

DUMB, PETER...

...MAKING ENEMIES WITH A KID LIKE *MALCOLM McBRIDE*.

HE'S ONLY ANNOYED BECAUSE I ACED HIM OUT OF A SMALL *RESEARCH GRANT* WE BOTH APPLIED FOR LAST MONTH.

McBRIDE RESENTS ME BECAUSE I'M A RETURNING STUDENT.

HE DOESN'T THINK I'M ACADEMICALLY *SERIOUS*...

...AND AFTER THE WAY I ZONED OUT DURING THE SEMINAR, I CAN'T BLAME HIM.

HI, PETER.

HI, ANNE-MARIE... PROFESSOR SWAN.

MIND IF I PURSUE AN *INDEPENDENT STUDY* TODAY?

NOT AT ALL, PETER. GODSPEED.

GOOD THING SWAN AND ANNE-MARIE ARE SO BUSY WITH THE PROFESSOR'S RESEARCH PROJECT.

OTHERWISE HE MIGHT WANT TO KNOW WHAT KIND OF INDEPENDENT STUDY INVOLVES SNEAKING INTO THE LAB BUILDING'S *BASEMENT.*

I THOUGHT ABOUT DOING THIS OFF AND ON FOR WEEKS...

...EVER SINCE I LEARNED THE TRUTH ABOUT GWEN STACY'S "CLONE." *

BUT THERE WERE SO MANY *DISTRACTIONS...*

* SEE SPECTACULAR SPIDER-MAN ANNUAL #*7.* -- JIM

...THE *"WEBS"* PROMOTIONAL TOUR, THE DEMON ATTACK ON NEW YORK, THE HOBGOBLIN'S RETURN...

...SO MANY *DISTRACTIONS,* SO MANY *EXCUSES.*

PROFESSOR WARREN'S LAB.

WHERE GWEN'S "CLONE" WAS BORN-- AND *CARRION* DIED.

WHAT A MESS.

AFTER CARRION'S DEATH, THE POLICE *SEALED* THIS LAB, PENDING AN INVESTIGATION -- WHICH NEVER TOOK PLACE.

I KEPT MEANING TO SEARCH IT, MYSELF, BUT SOMEHOW I NEVER DID.

MAYBE, SUBCONSCIOUSLY, I WAS AFRAID OF WHAT I'D FIND.

SPIDER-SENSE TINGLING... SOMETHING UNDER THIS STONE...

WELL, WELL, WELL.

"THE SECRETS OF LIFE AND DEATH," BY VICTOR VON FRANKENSTEIN?

NO... BUT SOMETHING ALMOST AS GOOD...

...THE PRIVATE RESEARCH JOURNAL OF *PROFESSOR MILES WARREN*...

...a.k.a. *THE JACKAL*...

...a.k.a.--IN ANOTHER INCARNATION-- THE CREATURE CALLED *CARRION.*

MAYBE THIS WILL GIVE ME THE *ANSWER* I'M LOOKING FOR.

YEAH, MAYBE. AND ONCE I *KNOW* THE ANSWER...

...WILL I BE *SORRY* I ASKED THE QUESTION?

CREEP.

I FOLLOWED PARKER OVER HERE TO CHECK OUT HIS RESEARCH PROJECT. HE'S NOT A SERIOUS SCIENTIST.

IF I COULD PROVE HE FUDGED DATA OR FAKED RESULTS, HIS GRANT MIGHT BE RESCINDED.

-- AND THEN THE GRANT MONEY WOULD GO TO *ME.*

BUT I DIDN'T EXPECT THIS.

IT'S DISGRACEFUL.

AN E.S.U. STUDENT SNOOPING ABOUT A SEALED LAB, STEALING BOOKS AND--

AHEM.

WHAT *HAVE* WE HERE?

INTERLUDE:

FEDERAL COURT...

...PHILADELPHIA, PENNSYLVANIA...

FEDERAL COURT BUILDING

...THE TRIAL OF JOSEPH ROBERTSON...

WITNESS FOR THE STATE: LONNIE LINCOLN, a.k.a.. "TOMBSTONE."

MR. LINCOLN, YOU HAVE CONFESSED IN OPEN COURT TO THE MURDER OF ISADORE KIPPER, AN EMPLOYEE OF MR. OSWALD MONTANA...

AM I CORRECT?

...AT THE FEDERAL DOCKYARD IN PHILADELPHIA ON MARCH 14, 1968. *

THAT'S WHAT I SAID.

AND YOU HAVE IDENTIFIED MY CLIENT, JOSEPH ROBERTSON, AS BEING PRESENT AT THE TIME OF THAT MURDER.

* SEEN IN SPECTACULAR SPIDER-MAN #139. --JM

IT IS THE STATE'S CONTENTION THAT MR. ROBERTSON COMMITTED A MISPRISON OF FELONY... WHEN HE FAILED TO IMMEDIATELY NOTIFY THE FEDERAL AUTHORITIES OF WHAT HE WITNESSED.

THE DEFENSE CONTENDS MR. ROBERTSON FEARED BOTH FOR HIS LIFE AND HIS FAMILY'S SAFETY.

ISN'T IT TRUE YOU TRIED TO KILL MR. ROBERTSON WHEN HE FINALLY THREATENED TO EXPOSE YOU EARLIER THIS YEAR?

ME? NEVER.

THIS PHOTO SHOWS JOE ROBERTSON IN A HOSPITAL BED --

-- WHERE YOU PUT HIM.

LADY, I'M A CONFESSED MURDERER.

IF I WANTED ROBBIE DEAD, HE'D BE DEAD.

HONESTLY, I'D NEVER HURT THE GUY.

HE'S MY FRIEND.

OH, ROBBIE...

I'VE COVERED A LOT OF TRIALS SINCE YOU HIRED ME AS A REPORTER FOR THE BUGLE.

IT'S AGONY TO COVER YOURS...

KATE--? JOY MERCADO...

BERNHAMMER JUST FINISHED CROSS-EXAMINING *TOMBSTONE*...

... AND IT LOOKS BAD FOR ROBBIE.

DAILY BUGLE

JUST GIVE ME THE DETAILS.

EDITORIALS ARE *MY* DEPARTMENT, MERCADO.

TOMBSTONE MUST HAVE CUT A PLEA-BARGAIN WITH THE *FEDS* IN EXCHANGE FOR HIS TESTIMONY.

APPARENTLY THEY WANT TO MAKE AN *EXAMPLE* OUT OF ROBBIE.

"*NEWSPAPER EDITOR IN CHIEF SHIELDS CONFESSED MURDERER.*"

AND THE WAY IT'S GOING THEY MIGHT MAKE IT STICK...

JOY'S A CYNIC, LIKE MOST REPORTERS--

-- BUT WHEN SHE MAKES A JUDGMENT, SHE'S USUALLY *ACCURATE*.

OH, ROBBIE...

♪ GOT MY MAN, AND HE LOVES ME... ♪

WHY SO HAPPY, GLORIA?

LOVE'S THE REASON, KATE.

I'M IN *LOVE*.

IMAGINE THAT?

AFTER ALL THESE YEARS AS JAMESON'S SECRETARY, I'M AMAZED YOU'VE GOT A HEART *LEFT*, GLORIA--

-- BUT ALL KIDDING ASIDE, I'M DELIGHTED FOR YOU.

YOU WOULDN'T KNOW HIM. HE'S FROM TEXAS.

WHO'S THE GUY?

HIS NAME IS *EDUARDO LOBO*.

WHAT?!

IT'S LIKE A DREAM...

GLORIA, SIT DOWN. WE *HAVE* TO TALK!

CAN'T. I'M MEETING HIM FOR LUNCH. TA! ♪

GLORIA-- *LISTEN* TO ME--

NO USE! AND HOW CAN I TELL HER THE MAN SHE LOVES IS A KNOWN *CRIMINAL*?

INTERLUDE 2:

Night...

...AT EMPIRE STATE UNIVERSITY...

...IN THE STUDENT DORMS...

STRANGE STUFF, THIS.

BIOCHEMICALLY, IT'S A *VIRUS*...

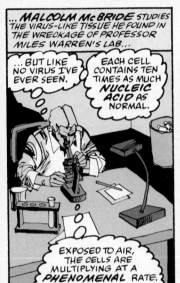

...*MALCOLM McBRIDE* STUDIES THE VIRUS-LIKE TISSUE HE FOUND IN THE WRECKAGE OF PROFESSOR MILES WARREN'S LAB...

...BUT LIKE NO VIRUS I'VE EVER SEEN.

EACH CELL CONTAINS TEN TIMES AS MUCH *NUCLEIC ACID* AS NORMAL.

EXPOSED TO AIR, THE CELLS ARE MULTIPLYING AT A *PHENOMENAL* RATE.

ONLY ONE EXPLANATION: THIS VIRUS WAS CREATED BY RECOMBINANT *DNA* TECHNOLOGY. WHOEVER DESIGNED IT WAS A *GENIUS*.

WHAT A *FIND!*

IF I CAN CLAIM IT AS MY OWN, I'LL BE *RICH*...

SPISH...

OWWW!

MY FACE--

--MY EYES!

MY !!!!

END OF INTERLUDES

MAY PARKER'S BOARDING HOUSE.

FOREST HILLS, QUEENS.

LATE.

HE LIED TO ME!

ALMOST EVERYTHING *THE JACKAL* TOLD ME ABOUT CREATING GWEN'S CLONE WAS A *LIE.*

REALLY.

REMEMBER I TOLD YOU HOW WARREN SAID HE FELT LIKE A *FATHER* TOWARD GWEN?

MM-HMM.

WELL, LISTEN TO THIS, MARY JANE. HIS OWN WORDS...

"September 19th. First day of class, I saw a young woman today... Gwendolyn Stacy. A magnificent creature, so lovely, so alive.

"I'm afraid I fell in love instantly.

"A man my age. How *absurd.*"

"November 4th. Watching Gwendolyn and the other students take blood samples in class today...

"...I almost confessed my feelings.

"I would have appeared quite ridiculous, I'm sure.

"The child hardly knows I'm alive.

"Her only interest is in that boy... Parker.

"I can't stand to see them together.

"I'm really quite obsessed.

"I want to possess her... at any cost."

"May 21st.

"She's dead.

"My love is dead... killed by the Green Goblin...

"...and that costumed vigilante Spider-Man!"

"August 15th. I followed Peter Parker today. I hate him because he knew her love. Love that should have been *MINE!*

"I think... I wanted to kill him.

"At first as I watched him he seemed to *shiver*, as if warned of my presence by some sixth sense."

"Then he shrugged it off..."

"...and did something *incredible*."

"He became *Spider-Man*."

"I thought I despised Parker before, but now I know I barely understood the meaning of the term."

"I must avenge my love."

"I must destroy this man."

"How?"

"How?"

"January 9th."

"Six months of planning, study experimentation..."

"...have brought me to This."

"Today I waylaid a young pupil of mine, Joyce Delany."

"She will be the second subject to undergo cellular-level transformation via the genetic virus I have developed."

"My assistant Anthony Serba, was the first."

"Three days ago, I infected him with a virus derived from Peter Parker's DNA."

"The results were gratifying."

"Every cell of his body invaded and transformed by the virus, Serba almost instantly became 'Peter Parker'..."

"...just as Joyce Delany now becomes 'Gwen Stacy.'"

"Serba remains drugged and unconscious elsewhere in my lab; I'll have use for him later."

"...but this girl, I have use for her now."

"She and Serba will be the instruments of my vengeance."

"And if this plan should fail..."

329

"... I CAN ALWAYS ACTIVATE THE *CARRION* SCENARIO."

THAT'S THE LAST ENTRY.

GOOD.

I'M TIRED.

LET'S HIT THE SACK.

WHY DID HE *LIE* TO ME MARY JANE?

WHAT DIFFERENCE DOES IT MAKE? *WARREN IS DEAD.*

ALL THIS IS *ANCIENT HISTORY.*

"HE MUST HAVE WANTED TO PSYCH ME OUT BEFORE HE SENT ANTHONY SERBA AFTER ME AS THE *SPIDER-MAN CLONE.*"

"HE PROBABLY FIGURED I WOULDN'T FIGHT AS WELL IF I THOUGHT I WAS BATTLING '*MYSELF*'--"

"-- AND HE WAS *RIGHT.*"

"BUT IF SERBA WAS THE SPIDER-MAN CLONE, AND JOYCE DELANY WAS 'GWEN STACY'--

"--WHO WAS *CARRION?*"

PETER, PLEASE LEAVE IT ALONE.

YOU'VE GOT TO PUT THE PAST BEHIND YOU *SOMETIME.*

NOT WHEN THERE ARE STILL SO MANY UNANSWERED QUESTIONS, MJ.

CARRION WAS SUPPOSED TO BE WARREN'S OWN CLONE,

BUT HE DIDN'T APPEAR UNTIL *MONTHS* AFTER THE PROFESSOR'S DEATH.

HOW WAS THAT *POSSIBLE?*

I'VE GOT TO *KNOW.*

WHEN HE'S LIKE THIS, OBSESSED WITH GWEN'S DEATH, I GET SO *FRIGHTENED.*

IT'S AS IF HE'S STUCK IN A *DREAM...*

330

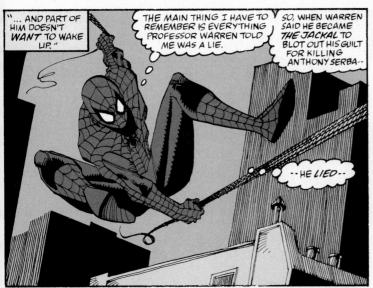

"... AND PART OF HIM DOESN'T *WANT* TO WAKE UP."

THE MAIN THING I HAVE TO REMEMBER IS EVERYTHING PROFESSOR WARREN TOLD ME WAS A LIE.

SO, WHEN WARREN SAID HE BECAME *THE JACKAL* TO BLOT OUT HIS GUILT FOR KILLING ANTHONY *SERBA*--

--HE *LIED*--

--BECAUSE SERBA WASN'T *DEAD.*

EVEN SO, DEEP DOWN, WARREN MUST HAVE FELT *REMORSE* FOR WHAT HE'D DONE TO SERBA AND JOYCE DELANY.

--THAT REMORSE FORCED HIM TO *RESCUE* US--

--AT THE COST OF HIS OWN LIFE. *

AND WHEN HE REALIZED SERBA MIGHT *DIE* DURING OUR BATTLE, IN AN EXPLOSION MEANT FOR *ME*--

*ANOTHER WAY TO LOOK AT EVENTS IN *AMAZING SPIDER-MAN* #149.-- JIM

STILL SO MANY QUESTIONS. MAYBE HERE IN WARREN'S LAB, I'LL FIND--

--SPIDER SENSE--!

HELLO, PARKER.

WHAT GOOD FORTUNE TO FIND YOU HERE, SO SOON AFTER MY *AWAKENING.*

NOW MY REVENGE MAY BE *SWIFT* AS WELL AS *SWEET.*

NO! IT CAN'T BE!

CARRION?

YOU KNOW ME?

HOW ODD.

I'D ASK YOU TO *EXPLAIN*--

331

-- BUT I'D RATHER SEE YOU *DIE!*

EH?

YOU CATCH ME BEFORE I CAN *TOUCH* YOU?

THEN YOU MUST KNOW MY TOUCH MEANS *DEATH!*

AND YOU MUST ALSO KNOW MY BODY *REPELS* ORGANIC MATTER.

YOU CAN'T *HOLD* ME, PARKER.

WHO SAID I WANTED TO HOLD YOU, GRAVEYARD BREATH?

UNNNH

THROOM

FOOL! YOU CAN'T HARM ME. I AM BEYOND DEATH, BEYOND PAIN.

PAIN IS FOR THE *LIVING* --

WHAM

KRASH

--AND I AM *CARRION*, THE UNLIVING CLONE OF *MILES WARREN!*

EEEYOWW!

YOU'RE A GENETIC *VIRUS!*

NO, YOU'RE *NOT.*

SOMEHOW YOU'VE *INFECTED* SOMEONE, TAKEN OVER HIS BODY, HIS LIFE--

JUST LIKE YOU DID BEFORE! BUT *THIS* TIME I'LL--

AAGH!

RED DUST--

--CLINGING TO MY MASK--

--CAN'T BREATHE--

--PASSING--

--OUT--

333

IN THE DREAM HE WAKES IN A **GRAVEYARD**.

STORM LIGHTNING SCORES THE NIGHT.

COLD RAIN FALLS LIKE A HAIL OF NEEDLES.

"IT'S ONLY A DREAM," HE TELLS HIMSELF.

STACY
GWENDOLYNE

"YEAH, RIGHT."

STACY
GEORGE
BORN

STACY
MARTHA
BORN

HELLO AGAIN. I CHANGED MY MIND.

I DECIDED I WANT AN **EXPLANATION** FROM YOU, AFTER ALL.

WELCOME TO THE CLUB.

YOU'RE IN NO POSITION TO MOCK ME, PARKER.

HOW DID YOU LEARN ABOUT THE **REPLICATOR VIRUS**?

I READ PROFESSOR WARREN'S JOURNAL.

AND I'VE MET YOU BEFORE.

IMPOSSIBLE. I ONLY AWOKE A FEW HOURS AGO--UNLESS--

UH-HUH. I MET A DIFFERENT "YOU."

THAT CARRION MUST HAVE BEEN ANOTHER VICTIM OF THE PROFESSOR'S REPLICATOR VIRUS."

WHAT DID WARREN DO, LEAVE SPECIMENS OF THE CARRION-DNA VIRUS HIDDEN AROUND CAMPUS--

--LIKE BIOLOGICAL BOOBY-TRAPS?

I DON'T KNOW. MY MEMORY IS LIMITED.

I KNOW WHAT I-- THAT IS, MILES WARREN.. INTENDED:

I/HE DESIGNED A SPECIAL REPLICA-TOR VIRUS, FROM WARREN'S OWN DNA, ENDOWED WITH UNIQUE POWERS.

I AM THE PRODUCT OF THAT DESIGN, A CREATURE BOTH LIVING AND UNLIVING.

MY PURPOSE IS TO AVENGE THE MURDER OF GWEN STACY.

YOU WERE RESPONSIBLE FOR HER DEATH, PARKER.

THEREFORE CLEARLY, YOU MUST DIE.

UH-UH, MOLD-MOUTH.

I'VE SEEN THIS MOVIE BEFORE.

THWIPP

WHAT--?

THE DEATH DUST--

--YOU MADE ME SPILL IT!

335

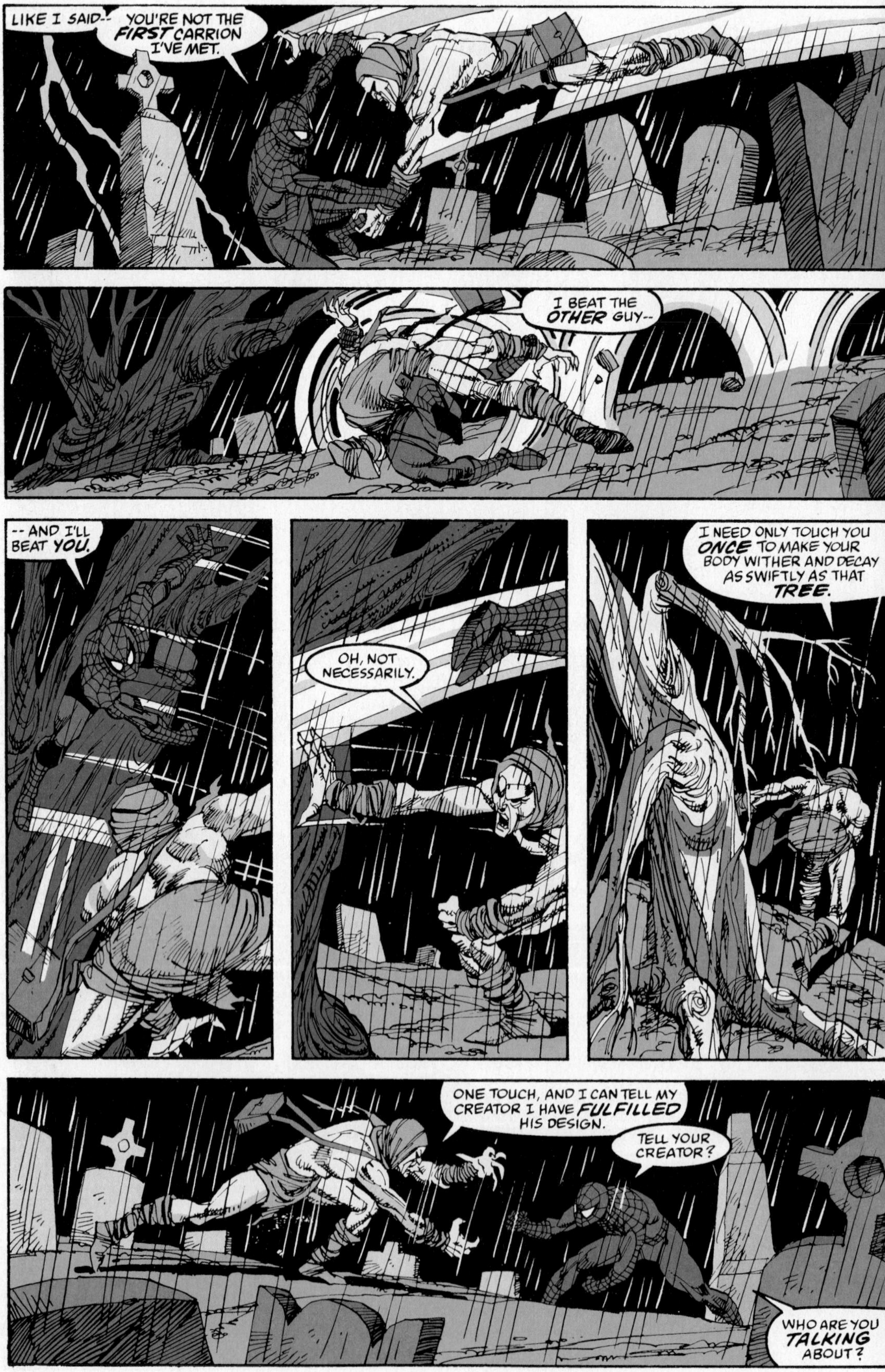
LIKE I SAID-- YOU'RE NOT THE FIRST CARRION I'VE MET.
I BEAT THE OTHER GUY--
-- AND I'LL BEAT YOU.
OH, NOT NECESSARILY.
I NEED ONLY TOUCH YOU ONCE TO MAKE YOUR BODY WITHER AND DECAY AS SWIFTLY AS THAT TREE.
ONE TOUCH, AND I CAN TELL MY CREATOR I HAVE FULFILLED HIS DESIGN.
TELL YOUR CREATOR?
WHO ARE YOU TALKING ABOUT?

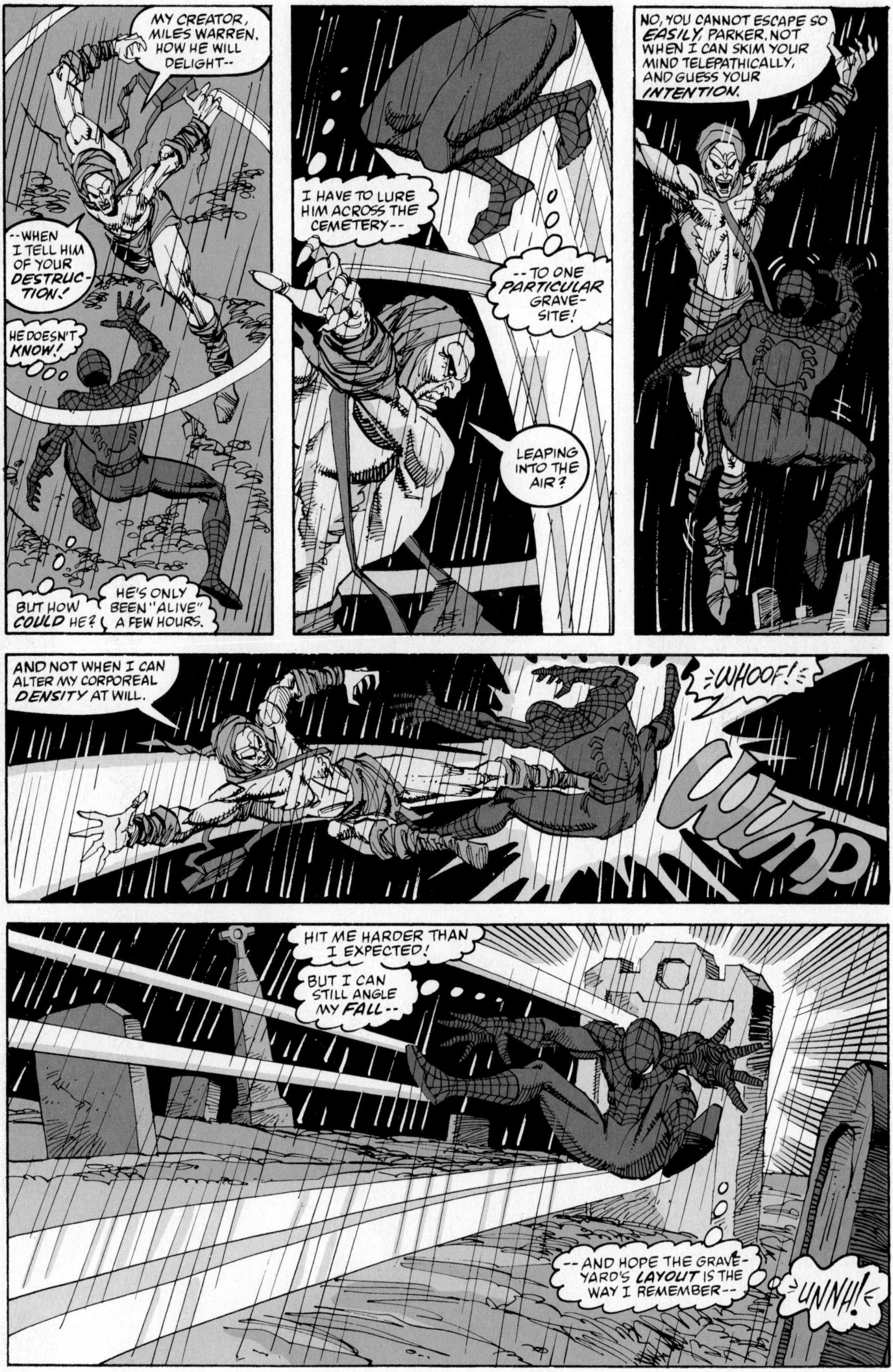
MY CREATOR, MILES WARREN. HOW HE WILL DELIGHT--
--WHEN I TELL HIM OF YOUR DESTRUCTION!
HE DOESN'T KNOW!
BUT HOW COULD HE?
HE'S ONLY BEEN "ALIVE" A FEW HOURS.
I HAVE TO LURE HIM ACROSS THE CEMETERY--
--TO ONE PARTICULAR GRAVE-SITE!
LEAPING INTO THE AIR?
NO, YOU CANNOT ESCAPE SO EASILY, PARKER. NOT WHEN I CAN SKIM YOUR MIND TELEPATHICALLY, AND GUESS YOUR INTENTION.
AND NOT WHEN I CAN ALTER MY CORPOREAL DENSITY AT WILL.
WHOOF!
WUMP
HIT ME HARDER THAN I EXPECTED!
BUT I CAN STILL ANGLE MY FALL--
--AND HOPE THE GRAVEYARD'S LAYOUT IS THE WAY I REMEMBER--
UNNH!

BORN 1972
DIED 1995

SO IT ENDS.

WHY DID YOU WANT TO LEAD ME *HERE*, I WONDER?

YOUR THOUGHTS ARE *DIFFICULT* TO READ. YOU HAVE A STRONG WILL...

...STRONGER THAN I WOULD HAVE *EXPECTED* FROM A BOY YOUR AGE.

IT'S OF NO CONSEQUENCE. THIS IS THE HOUR OF RETRIBUTION.

PREPARE TO DIE, FOR THE MURDER OF --

--MILES WARREN?

HERE LIES
DR. MILES WARREN
BORN 1940
DIED 1909

BTOOM

SURPRISE!

MILES WARREN IS DEAD.

338

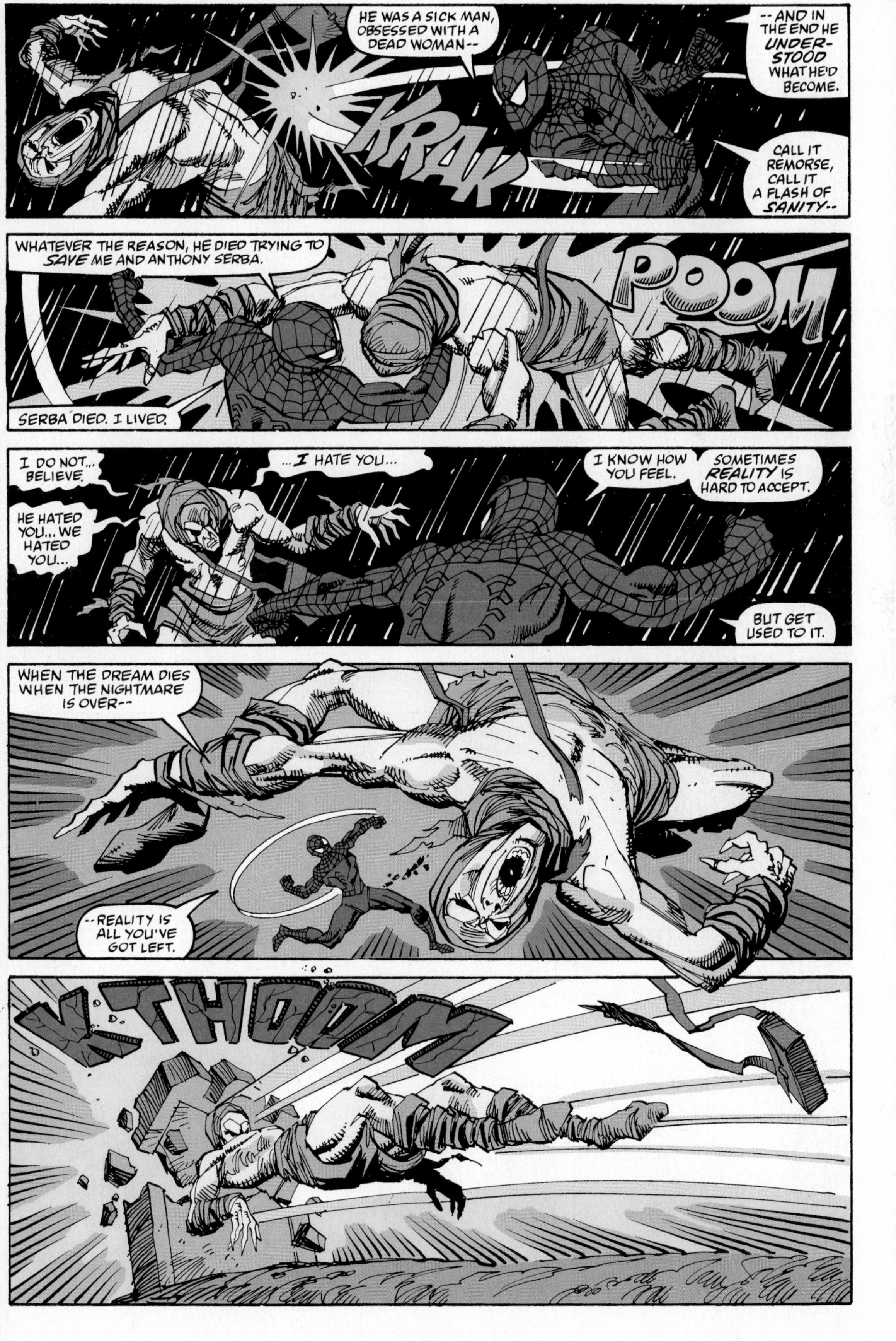
HE WAS A SICK MAN, OBSESSED WITH A DEAD WOMAN--
KRAK
--AND IN THE END HE UNDERSTOOD WHAT HE'D BECOME.
CALL IT REMORSE, CALL IT A FLASH OF SANITY--
WHATEVER THE REASON, HE DIED TRYING TO SAVE ME AND ANTHONY SERBA.
POOM
SERBA DIED. I LIVED.
I DO NOT... BELIEVE.
HE HATED YOU... WE HATED YOU...
...I HATE YOU...
I KNOW HOW YOU FEEL.
SOMETIMES REALITY IS HARD TO ACCEPT.
BUT GET USED TO IT.
WHEN THE DREAM DIES WHEN THE NIGHTMARE IS OVER--
--REALITY IS ALL YOU'VE GOT LEFT.
THOOM

I HAD A HUNCH CARRION MIGHT FREAK OUT WHEN HE DISCOVERED HIS "CREATOR" WAS DEAD.

THAT GAVE ME THE *EDGE* I NEEDED TO BEAT HIM.

BUT I FEEL *STRANGE*-- KNOWING THAT SOMEWHERE INSIDE THE CREATURE CALLED CARRION--

--THERE'S AN INNOCENT MAN.

MAYBE REED RICHARDS CAN FIND A CURE FOR THE *REPLICATOR VIRUS.* I'LL ASK HIS HELP.

IN THE MEANTIME, I'LL DROP CARRION AT *THE VAULT* * AND HOPE HE--

AW, GEE, GWEN.

STACY
GWENDOLYN

* THE GOVERNMENT'S HIGH-SECURITY PRISON FOR SUPER-CRIMINALS. --J.S.

WHAT WAS IT I SAID ABOUT PROFESSOR WARREN?

"HE WAS A SICK MAN, OBSESSED WITH A DEAD WOMAN."

I WONDER WHO ELSE THAT DESCRIPTION MIGHT FIT?

I'VE ALWAYS FELT *RESPONSIBLE* FOR YOUR DEATH, GWEN.

I GUESS THAT'S WHY I FIND IT SO HARD TO LET GO OF YOU.

I STILL HAVE QUESTIONS, BUT NOT EVERY QUESTION NEEDS AN ANSWER.

MARY JANE WAS RIGHT:

I HAVE TO PUT THE PAST BEHIND ME *SOMETIME,*

NOW IS AS GOOD A TIME AS ANY.

AS MUCH AS I ONCE LOVED YOU, GWEN, THIS IS FINALLY...

...*THE END*

340

MARVEL

$1.00 US
$1.25 CAN

150
MAY

APPROVED BY THE COMICS CODE AUTHORITY

CC 02199

the SPECTACULAR SPIDER-MAN

JOE ROBERTSON-- THIS COURT FINDS YOU GUILTY!

ROBBIE'S DAY IN COURT!

PLUS: A WEREWOLF IN MANHATTAN!

WAR BETWEEN THE LOBO BROTHERS AND THE KINGPIN!

...AND WAIT TILL YOU SEE OUR SHOCKING SURPRISE ENDING!

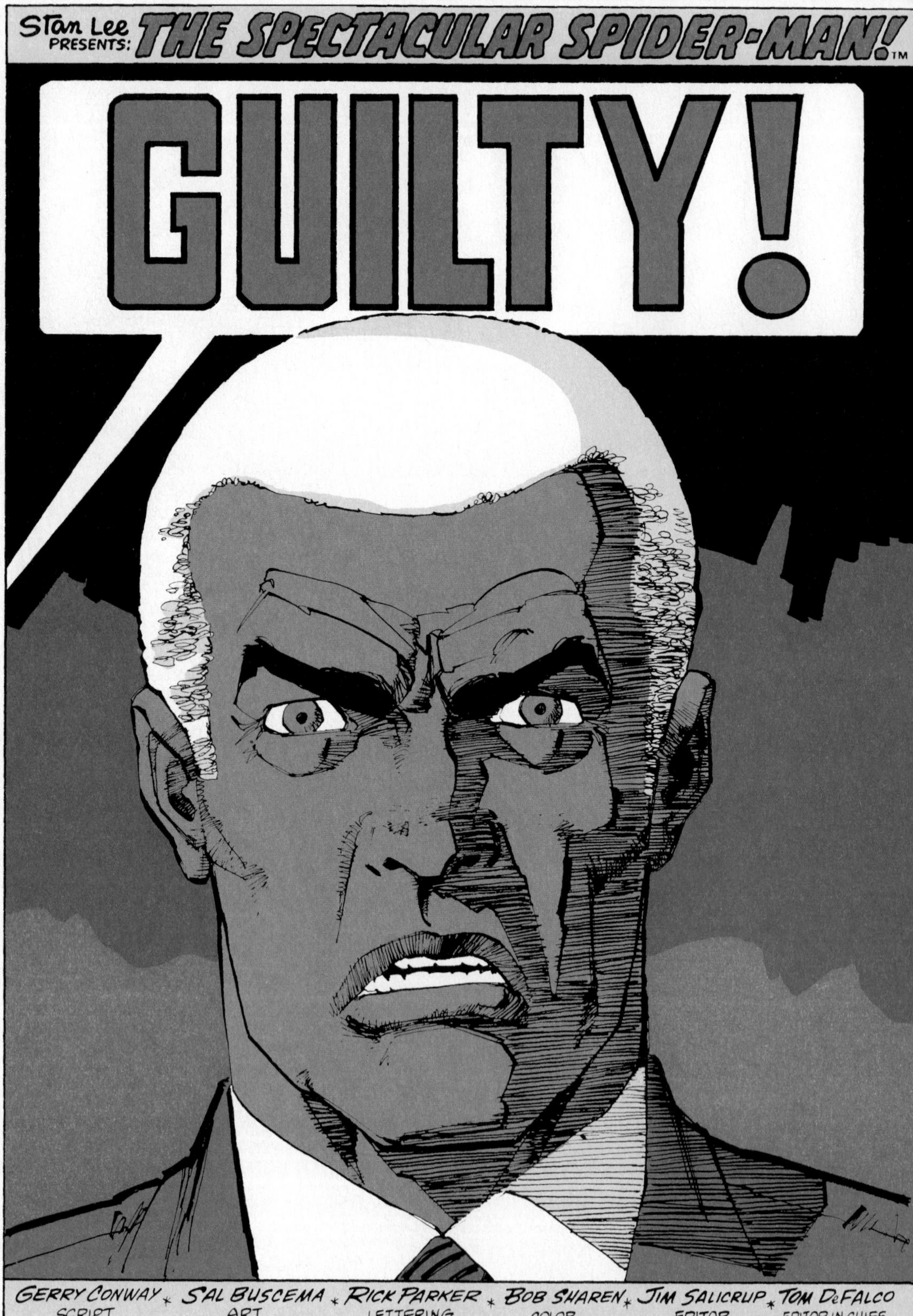
Stan Lee PRESENTS: THE SPECTACULAR SPIDER-MAN!™
GUILTY!
GERRY CONWAY SCRIPT * SAL BUSCEMA ART * RICK PARKER LETTERING * BOB SHAREN COLOR * JIM SALICRUP EDITOR * TOM DeFALCO EDITOR IN CHIEF

A THOUSAND THOUGHTS CROWD ROBBIE ROBERTSON'S MIND, FROM THE RIDICULOUS TO THE *SUBLIME.*

HE REMEMBERS, SUDDENLY, THAT HE HAS TICKETS FOR A KNICKS GAME LATER THIS MONTH.

HE WORRIES WHETHER MARTHA MANAGED TO GET THE STORM WINDOWS UP, WITH A BLIZZARD DUE TO HIT NEW YORK *LATER* THIS EVENING.

AND HE WONDERS, ALMOST DISTANTLY, IF THEY'LL LET HIM KEEP A *NOTEBOOK* IN PRISON.

THE COURT *THANKS* THE JURY FOR ITS PROMPT AND CONSIDERED VERDICT, AND ORDERS THE PANEL DISCHARGED.

IN LIGHT OF THE *SERIOUSNESS* OF THE OFFENSE-- MISPRISION OF A FELONY--

--IN WHICH THE DEFENDANT WILLFULLY *CONCEALED* HIS KNOWLEDGE OF A FEDERAL FELONY FROM THE PROPER AUTHORITIES FOR MORE THAN TWENTY YEARS--

--IT IS THIS COURT'S INTENTION TO CONCLUDE THESE PROCEEDINGS AT THE *EARLIEST* OPPORTUNITY.

COURT WILL RECONVENE FOR *SENTENCING* ON MONDAY AT 9 a.m.

YOUR HONOR--

--IS SUCH HASTE *APPROPRIATE?*

HASTE, MS. BERNHAMMER?

YOUR CLIENT-- A JOURNALIST-- CONCEALED THE IDENTITY OF A *MURDERER* FOR TWO DECADES.

BECAUSE OF HIS INACTION, JUSTICE IN THAT CASE WAS *DELAYED.*

THIS COURT FEELS AN OBLIGATION TO SEE THAT NO *SIMILAR* DELAY OCCURS HERE.

BUT, YOUR HONOR--

COURT IS *ADJOURNED.*

I CAN'T BELIEVE IT! ROBBY HARDLY PUT UP A DEFENSE-- IT'S ALMOST AS IF HE *WANTED* TO BE CONVICTED.

PETER, IT'S *HORRIBLE!* DID YOU SEE MARTHA ROBERTSON'S FACE WHEN THE JURY FOREMAN READ THE VERDICT?

HOW COULD THIS HAPPEN TO A MAN LIKE *ROBBIE*?

WE KNOW *HOW* IT HAPPENED, MARY JANE...

"JOE ROBERTSON WENT TO HIGH SCHOOL WITH A PUNK NAMED *LONNIE LINCOLN*...

"A REGULAR PSYCHOTIC WHO ALMOST *KILLED* HIM WHEN ROBBIE WROTE AN ARTICLE ABOUT LINCOLN'S THUGGERY FOR THE SCHOOL NEWSPAPER...

"YEARS LATER, ROBBIE ACCIDENTALLY WITNESSED LINCOLN STRANGLE A *MOB INFORMANT* ON A FEDERAL DOCKYARD IN PHILADELPHIA.

"BY THEN, LINCOLN HAD BECOME THE HIT MAN KNOWN AS *TOMBSTONE,*

"TERRIFIED FOR HIS LIFE AND HIS FAMILY'S SAFETY, ROBBIE KEPT SILENT ABOUT THE KILLING FOR TWENTY YEARS.

"BUT WHEN TOMBSTONE CAME TO NEW YORK A FEW MONTHS AGO...

"...ROBBIE FINALLY *BROKE* HIS SILENCE...

"...AND THEN CONFRONTED TOMBSTONE MAN TO MAN IN BATTERY PARK.

"I GUESS ROBBIE WANTED TO ABSOLVE HIMSELF OF THE *GUILT* HE FELT BY MAKING A CITIZEN'S ARREST.

"INSTEAD, TOMBSTONE ALMOST *CRUSHED* ROBBIE'S SPINE, AND LEFT HIM FOR *DEAD.*

"ROBBIE DIDN'T DIE, AND HIS BACK WASN'T BROKEN AFTER ALL...

"...BUT MAYBE HIS *SPIRIT* WAS.

"EVEN AFTER I CAUGHT UP TO TOMBSTONE AS *SPIDER-MAN*, AND TURNED HIM OVER TO THE FEDERAL MARSHALS *--

* A RUN-DOWN OF EVENTS IN *SPECTACULAR SPIDER-MAN* #139-142.--JIM

--ROBBIE CONTINUED TO ACT LIKE A GUILTY KID WAITING TO GET HIS WRIST SLAPPED FOR BREAKING THE COOKIE JAR.

AT ONE POINT HE EVEN WANTED TO PLEAD *GUILTY*.

AT LEAST HE CHANGED HIS MIND ABOUT *THAT*--

--BUT WHEN HIS ATTORNEY WANTED TO MOVE FOR DISMISSAL ON A *TECHNICALITY*, THE STATUTE OF LIMITATIONS--

--ROBBIE REFUSED. I CAN'T UNDERSTAND *WHY*.

OH, *JOE*--DARLING, SAY SOMETHING, *DO* SOMETHING...

THEY HAVE TO KNOW YOU'RE A *GOOD* MAN--

MARTHA--?

I-I'M SORRY YOU SAW THIS. RANDY, SON... PLEASE TAKE HER HOME.

NO!

ALL ALONG, YOU'VE TRIED TO FACE THIS *ALONE*...

...AND IT'S DESTROYING YOU, IT'S DESTROYING *US!*

GREAT SHOT, FOLKS. A REGULAR HEARTBREAKER. FRONT PAGE MATERIAL.

HOLD THAT *POSE*.

EH?

JOE, THAT *MAN*--

KATZENBERG, YOU CREEP! WHERE'S YOUR *DECENCY?* YOU WORK FOR THE *DAILY BUGLE* JUST LIKE *DAD*--

--AND YOU'RE TREATING HIM LIKE A *COMMON CRIMINAL!*

345

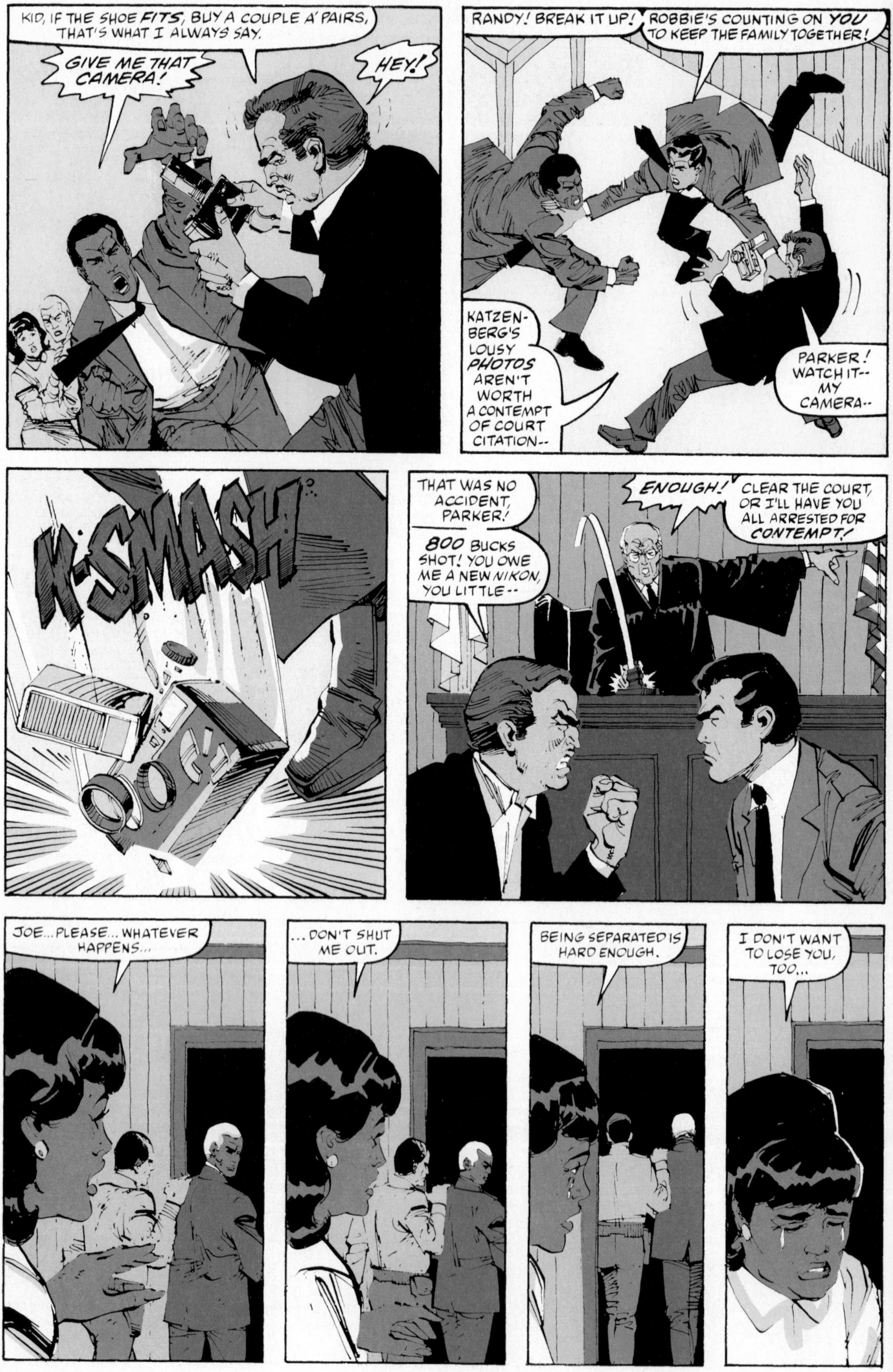
KID, IF THE SHOE FITS, BUY A COUPLE A' PAIRS, THAT'S WHAT I ALWAYS SAY.
GIVE ME THAT CAMERA!
HEY!
RANDY! BREAK IT UP!
ROBBIE'S COUNTING ON YOU TO KEEP THE FAMILY TOGETHER!
KATZENBERG'S LOUSY PHOTOS AREN'T WORTH A CONTEMPT OF COURT CITATION--
PARKER! WATCH IT-- MY CAMERA--
K-SMASH
THAT WAS NO ACCIDENT, PARKER!
800 BUCKS SHOT! YOU OWE ME A NEW NIKON, YOU LITTLE--
ENOUGH!
CLEAR THE COURT, OR I'LL HAVE YOU ALL ARRESTED FOR CONTEMPT!
JOE... PLEASE... WHATEVER HAPPENS...
...DON'T SHUT ME OUT.
BEING SEPARATED IS HARD ENOUGH.
I DON'T WANT TO LOSE YOU, TOO...

MOMENTS LATER, OUTSIDE THE PHILADELPHIA FEDERAL COURTHOUSE...

HEY, PARKER-- WHAT'S YOUR ITCH?

JEALOUS 'CAUSE I GOT THE SHOT AND YOU DIDN'T?

GET SERIOUS.

YOU'RE A PAPARAZZO, KATZENBERG... YOU TAKE EMBARRASSING PHOTOS OF CELEBRITIES FOR SUPERMARKET TABLOIDS.

THE DAILY BUGLE DOESN'T NEED YOUR KIND OF PHOTO-JOURNALISM. RIGHT, JONAH?

WRONG, MY BOY. J. JONAH JAMESON AND THE BUGLE ARE IN THE BUSINESS OF SELLING NEWSPAPERS--

KLINK

--AND NICKIE'S PHOTOS SELL LOTS OF NEWSPAPERS.

PARTICULARLY THOSE PHOTOS THAT CAUGHT SPIDER-MAN RED-HANDED COMMITTING A ROBBERY. *

* SEE WEB OF SPIDER-MAN # 50. -- J.S.

BUT I HAD PHOTOS CLEARING SPIDER-MAN, AND YOU REJECTED THEM!..

YOU BET I DID!

GUILTY OR INNOCENT, THAT WALL-CRAWLER IS A MENACE!

KATZENBERG UNDERSTANDS THAT AND YOU DON'T!

MY SPIDER-SENSE...

...EVERY TIME I'M NEAR JONAH LATELY, IT TINGLES.

COME ON, NICKIE. WE'LL TAKE MY LIMOUSINE BACK TO NEW YORK.

THANKS, JJJ.

CALL ME JONAH.

SORRY ABOUT THAT SCENE IN COURT, PETER. LOOK, WE'RE HAVING SOME PEOPLE OVER TO THE HOUSE IN QUEENS LATER TONIGHT...

WE'D LIKE YOU AND MJ TO BE THERE.

SURE.

YOU GO AHEAD, MJ. I'LL JOIN YOU LATER.

I'VE GOT SOME ERRANDS TO RUN IN THE CITY THIS EVENING...

...AS SPIDER-MAN!

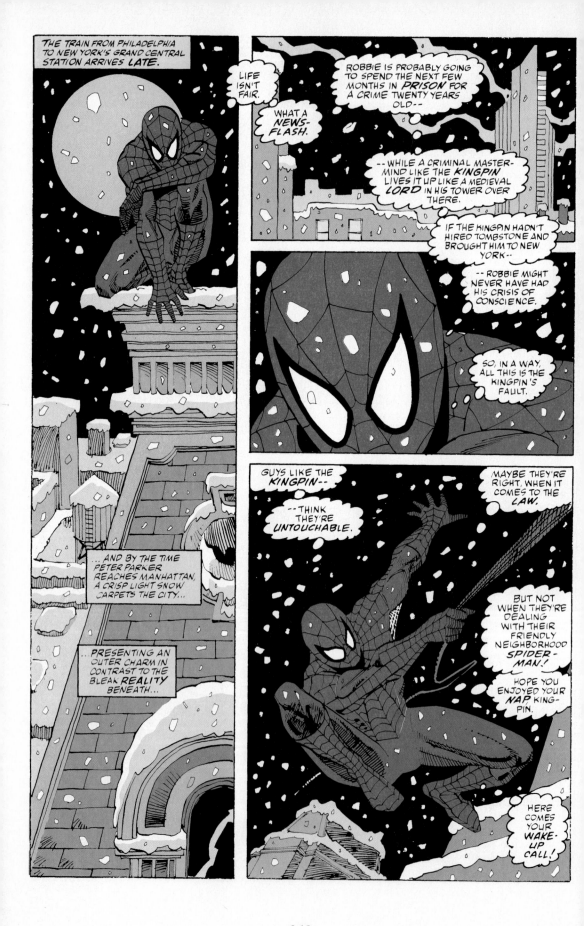

THE TRAIN FROM PHILADELPHIA TO NEW YORK'S GRAND CENTRAL STATION ARRIVES *LATE.*

LIFE ISN'T FAIR.

WHAT A *NEWS-FLASH.*

ROBBIE IS PROBABLY GOING TO SPEND THE NEXT FEW MONTHS IN *PRISON* FOR A CRIME TWENTY YEARS OLD--

--WHILE A CRIMINAL MASTER-MIND LIKE THE *KINGPIN* LIVES IT UP LIKE A MEDIEVAL *LORD* IN HIS TOWER OVER THERE.

IF THE KINGPIN HADN'T HIRED TOMBSTONE AND BROUGHT HIM TO NEW YORK--

--ROBBIE MIGHT NEVER HAVE HAD HIS CRISIS OF CONSCIENCE.

SO, IN A WAY, ALL THIS IS THE KINGPIN'S FAULT.

...AND BY THE TIME *PETER PARKER* REACHES MANHATTAN, A CRISP LIGHT SNOW CARPETS THE CITY...

...PRESENTING AN OUTER CHARM IN CONTRAST TO THE BLEAK *REALITY* BENEATH...

GUYS LIKE THE *KINGPIN*--

--THINK THEY'RE *UNTOUCHABLE.*

MAYBE THEY'RE RIGHT, WHEN IT COMES TO THE *LAW.*

BUT NOT WHEN THEY'RE DEALING WITH THEIR FRIENDLY NEIGHBORHOOD *SPIDER-MAN!*

HOPE YOU ENJOYED YOUR *NAP,* KINGPIN.

HERE COMES YOUR *WAKE-UP CALL!*

348

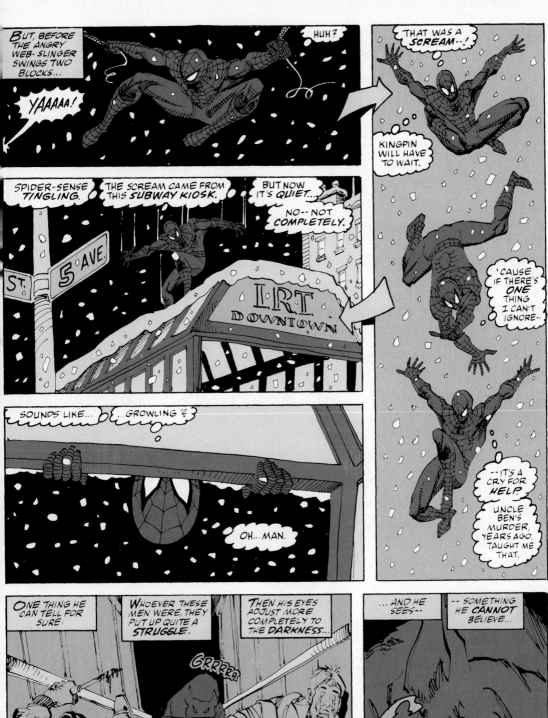

BUT, BEFORE THE ANGRY WEB-SLINGER SWINGS TWO BLOCKS...

YAAAAA!

HUH?

THAT WAS A *SCREAM*--!

KINGPIN WILL HAVE TO WAIT.

'CAUSE IF THERE'S *ONE* THING I CAN'T IGNORE--

--IT'S A CRY FOR *HELP*.

UNCLE BEN'S MURDER, YEARS AGO, TAUGHT ME THAT.

SPIDER-SENSE TINGLING.

THE SCREAM CAME FROM THIS *SUBWAY KIOSK*.

BUT NOW IT'S *QUIET*...

NO-- NOT COMPLETELY.

ST. 5 AVE.

I.R.T. DOWNTOWN

SOUNDS LIKE... ...GROWLING?

OH... MAN.

ONE THING HE CAN TELL FOR SURE:

WHOEVER THESE MEN WERE, THEY PUT UP QUITE A *STRUGGLE*.

THEN HIS EYES ADJUST MORE COMPLETELY TO THE *DARKNESS*...

GRRRR

... AND HE SEES--

-- SOMETHING HE *CANNOT* BELIEVE...

GRRrr...

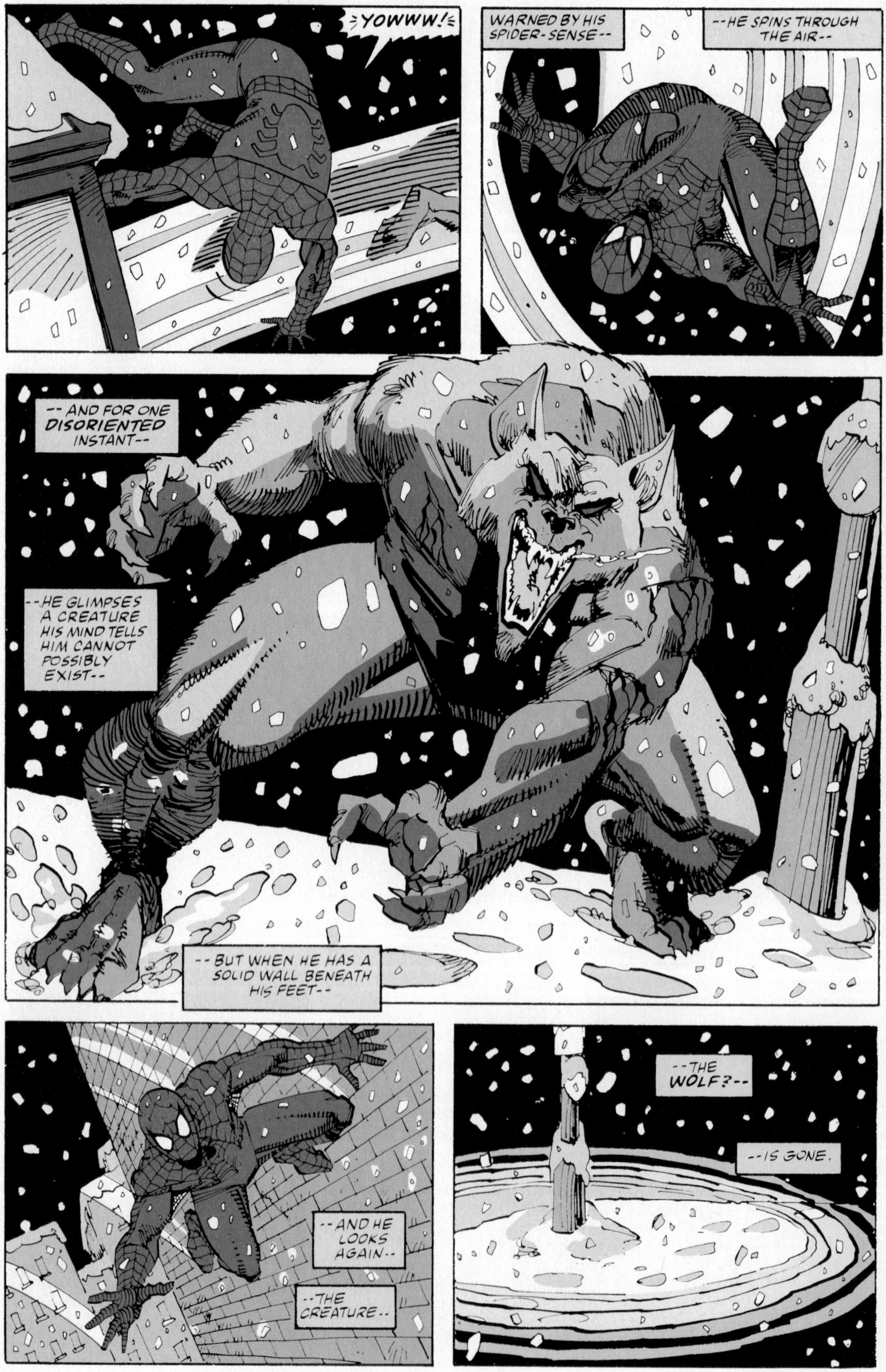
YOWWW!
WARNED BY HIS SPIDER-SENSE--
--HE SPINS THROUGH THE AIR--
--AND FOR ONE DISORIENTED INSTANT--
--HE GLIMPSES A CREATURE HIS MIND TELLS HIM CANNOT POSSIBLY EXIST--
--BUT WHEN HE HAS A SOLID WALL BENEATH HIS FEET--
--AND HE LOOKS AGAIN--
--THE CREATURE--
--THE WOLF?--
--IS GONE.

OH, YEAH, **RIGHT.**

I SAW A WEREWOLF.

SURE I DID.

SOME NUT IN A MONSTER SUIT IS MORE LIKE IT.

BUT THE MEMORY OF **THE INFERNO** IS STILL WITH HIM.

ALONG WITH THE MEMORY OF **CARRION'S** "RETURN FROM THE DEAD" ONLY A FEW WEEKS AGO...

...AND HE'S NOT AS **SURE** AS HE'D LIKE TO BE.

WHAT A MASSACRE.

HEY...

UHHHH.

...THIS GUY IS STILL ALIVE.

HANG TIGHT, BUDDY. I'LL GET YOU TO A HOSPITAL.

TELL THE BOSS.

SET UP... WE WERE SET UP...

WHO'S YOUR BOSS?

...KINGPIN...

HOSPITAL ZONE QUIET

THE KINGPIN, HUH?

DON'T WORRY, PAL. I'LL TELL HIM.

COUNT ON IT.

"*JOY MERCADO,* DAILY BUGLE... TESTING...TESTING...PERSONAL NOTES, CASSETTE TAPE THREE.

"UGH. THIS COFFEE IS *TERRIBLE.*

"BUT AT LEAST IT'S HOT.

"WHERE WAS I?

"FREEZING MY COOKIES IN MY CAR, THAT'S WHERE.

"ANYWAY... I'VE BEEN WORRIED ABOUT *GLORIA GRANT* FOR WEEKS NOW.

"GLORIA IS *JONAH'S* PERSONAL SECRETARY. SHE AND I ARE FRIENDS...

"...BUT SINCE SHE STARTED SEEING THIS NEW MAN OF HERS...

"...SHE'S BEEN ACTING DISTANT AND STRANGE.

"MAYBE I SHOULDN'T BE WATCHING HER APARTMENT THIS WAY...

"...BUT I'M A *REPORTER* BY TRADE...

"...AND SOME HABITS ARE TOO TOUGH TO--*WAIT* A MINUTE.

"WHAT DID I JUST SEE?

THE SNOW'S SO THICK-- WAS THAT A MAN CLIMBING IN GLORIA'S WINDOW?

GLORIA, GIRL--

--WHAT ON EARTH IS HAPPENING TO YOU?

JACKSON HEIGHTS, QUEENS.

THE *ROBERTSON* HOUSE...

THANKS FOR GIVING US A HAND WITH THE REFRESHMENTS, MJ.

MORE PEOPLE SHOWED UP THAN WE EXPECTED.

YOUR FATHER-IN-LAW HAS SO *MANY* FRIENDS, AMANDA.

MORE THAN HE REALIZES.

FRIENDS FROM THE *DAILY BUGLE*...FROM OUR CHURCH, AND THE NEIGHBORHOOD...

I WISH HE HADN'T SHUT THEM OUT, WHEN HE NEEDED THEM THE MOST.

I'M SURPRISED *JONAH* ISN'T HERE, KATE.

HE AND ROBBIE USED TO BE PRETTY *TIGHT.*

JONAH'S BEEN BEHAVING ODDLY FOR *WEEKS,* LANCE...

...EVER SINCE HE HIRED *NICK KATZENBERG.*

TELL ME ABOUT IT.

NICK'S PHOTOS GO FRONT PAGE, MINE GET BURIED--

--AND PARKER HASN'T SOLD A PICTURE TO JONAH IN *WEEKS.*

I WISH ROBBIE WERE BACK.

YEAH...

"...SO DO WE *ALL.*"

LET ME TAKE THOSE SANDWICHES, MARTHA.

NO, DEAR, YOU'VE DONE ENOUGH--

--BESIDES, IT'S BETTER IF I KEEP BUSY.

MY JOE ALWAYS LIKED TO SAY-- OH!

WHOOPS! SORRY, MOM--

I WASN'T LOOKING. IT'S NOT YOUR FAULT.

IT'S NOT ANYONE'S FAULT...

...I JUST CAN'T...

OH, LORD...

WHAT WILL I DO WITHOUT HIM, AMANDA?

I MISS HIM SO MUCH ALREADY...

YOU'D BETTER LIE DOWN.

MARY JANE...?

GO AHEAD. I'LL CLEAN UP HERE.

POOR MARTHA... I ALMOST KNOW HOW SHE FEELS.

PETER LIVES ON THE EDGE, AND SOMETIMES I WORRY THAT I'LL LOSE HIM...

"...AND IF I EVER DID...

"...WHAT WOULD I DO?

"HE'S MY LIFE."

PHILADELPHIA, PENNSYLVANIA.

THE LOOK ON MARTHA'S FACE IN COURT THIS MORNING...

WHAT HAVE I DONE TO HER?

ALL I EVER WANTED TO DO WAS *PROTECT* HER AND THE FAMILY FROM TOMBSTONE'S REPRISALS...

...AND INSTEAD, I DESTROYED US.

SHE SHOULDN'T *SUFFER* FOR MY MISTAKES.

NOBODY BUT ME SHOULD SUFFER FOR WHAT I'VE DONE.

THERE'S ONLY ONE THING I CAN DO TO HELP HER NOW.

I HAVE TO PUSH HER AWAY...

FOR MARTHA'S SAKE, I HAVE TO FACE THIS *ALONE.*

YO, YOU ROBERTSON?

WHO'S ASKING?

NOBODY SPECIAL.

GOT A MESSAGE FOR ROBERTSON FROM THE *MAN.*

THE MAN SAYS, " STAY WELL."

THE MAN SAYS, " I'LL BE LOOKING FOR YOU IN LEWISBURG."

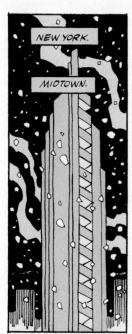

NEW YORK.

MIDTOWN.

THE OFFICES OF **WILSON FISK**...

...A.K.A., **THE KINGPIN OF CRIME**...

KNOCK-KNOCK.

MIND IF I DROP IN?

IT'S **COLD** OUTSIDE.

GET OUT.

WHAT A PERSONALITY.

NO WONDER SOMEONE'S TRYING TO **DESTROY** YOUR MOB.

YOU'RE JUST NO FUN TO BE AROUND ANYMORE.

"DESTROY MY MOB"?

WHAT ARE YOU BLATHERING ABOUT?

YOU REALLY DON'T KNOW, DO YOU?

GREAT. THEN I GET TO BREAK THE **BAD NEWS.**

SOMEBODY IS WASTING YOUR MEN, KINGPIN. IT STARTED **WEEKS** AGO. *

YOU'RE LYING... I WOULD HAVE BEEN TOLD.

*IN **SPECTACULAR SPIDER-MAN** #145, ACTUALLY. -- SPECIFICALLY JIM

356

YEAH, HOW ABOUT THAT? SOMEBODY IN YOUR ORGANIZATION IS KEEPING SECRETS FROM YOU, FAT BOY.

I WONDER WHO. I WONDER **WHY**.

WELL, THAT TURNED OUT BETTER THAN I EXPECTED.

I WENT THERE HOPING TO MAKE THE FAT MAN **NERVOUS**, AND I GUESS I SUCCEEDED.

"HE AND I BOTH KNOW THERE'S ONLY **ONE MAN** WHO CAN KEEP A SECRET FROM THE KINGPIN...

"...AND THAT'S THE **ONE MAN** THE KINGPIN TRUSTS TO RUN HIS MOB DAY TO DAY.

"RIGHT NOW, FISK HAS TO BE WORRYING IF HIS TRUST WAS MISPLACED.

"GOOD.

BZZZ

YES, MR. FISK?

ARRANGER, GET IN HERE.

I WANT A WORD WITH YOU.

"FEEL A LITTLE LESS **SAFE** IN YOUR TOWER, KINGPIN?

"WONDER WHO YOU CAN TRUST?

"AFTER TONIGHT THE ANSWER IS **NO ONE**."

MORNING IN CHELSEA.

GLORIA GRANT HASN'T HAD TO USE AN ALARM CLOCK IN YEARS.

MMMM...

EVERY MORNING, RAIN OR SHINE, SHE WAKES PRECISELY AT 6:45 A.M.

MMMM-MMMM. WHAT A DREAM.

AND RAIN OR SHINE, SHE NEVER FEELS TIRED.

SHE'S ONE OF THOSE DISGUSTING PEOPLE WHO SLEEPS LIKE A LOG...

...AND ALWAYS WAKES ALERT...

...BUT THIS PARTICULAR MORNING--

EDUARDO?

EH? GLORIA?

FORGIVE ME.

I SHOULD NOT BE HERE, MI AMOR. I WILL LEAVE AT ONCE.

--SHE HAS TO WONDER IF SHE'S STILL ASLEEP...

NO... DON'T GO... I JUST DON'T UNDERSTAND...

...WHERE ARE YOUR CLOTHES?

I WOULD EXPLAIN IF I COULD... BUT THERE ARE THINGS ABOUT ME YOU MUST NOT KNOW.

I DON'T KNOW WHY I CAME HERE... OR EVEN HOW.

AT TIMES, I DO THINGS I CANNOT REMEMBER...

YOU'RE HURT.

LET ME HELP YOU...

...I'M BEWILDERED. I'VE NEVER DONE THIS BEFORE.

ALWAYS BEFORE, I'VE BEEN IN *CONTROL*.

IN CONTROL OF WHAT, EDUARDO?

HOW DID YOU GET THESE *WOUNDS*?

MY BROTHER CARLOS AND I AT *WAR* WITH A MAN IN YOUR CITY.

AN EVIL MAN WHO TRIED TO *KILL* US... A MAN WE MUST *DESTROY*.

YOU CAN HELP ME DESTROY HIM, GLORIA.

ME?

EDUARDO, DO YOU KNOW HOW THIS *SOUNDS*?

IT SOUNDS INSANE. BUT LOVE IS INSANE.

GLORIA, QUERIDO, YOU WORK FOR THE *DAILY BUGLE*.

YOU HAVE ACCESS TO *INFORMATION*-- INFORMATION MY BROTHER AND I NEED FOR OUR *WAR*...

WHAT ARE YOU *SAYING*?

HELP ME. GIVE ME THE DAILY BUGLE'S FILE ON WILSON FISK, THE KINGPIN...

...AND SOMEDAY I WILL EXPLAIN *EVERYTHING*.

YOU WANT ME TO--

EDUARDO-- I CAN'T--

IF YOU *LOVE* ME...

...YOU CAN DO *ANYTHING*..

MONDAY MORNING.

HAS THE DEFENDANT ANYTHING TO SAY BEFORE THIS COURT PASSES SENTENCE?

NOTHING, YOUR HONOR.

FEDERAL COURTHOUSE, PHILADELPHIA, PENNSYLVANIA. THE HONORABLE JUDGE R.M. INGERSOLL PRESIDING.

VERY WELL. MR. ROBERTSON, THE COURT HAS CONSIDERED CAREFULLY THE FACTS OF THIS CASE--

--INCLUDING YOUR OUTSTANDING RECORD AS A CITIZEN AND JOURNALIST.

IN FACT, IT IS YOUR RECORD AS A JOURNALIST WHICH MAKES YOUR BEHAVIOR SO DIFFICULT TO COMPREHEND...

...OR CONDONE.

YOUR CRIME, MR. ROBERTSON, WAS MISPRISION OF A FELONY.

YOU CONCEALED KNOWLEDGE OF A CRIME--

--IN DISREGARD OF YOUR DUTY BOTH AS A CITIZEN AND AS A REPORTER.

YOUR ATTORNEY HAS ARGUED "EXTENUATING CIRCUMSTANCES."

THESE CIRCUMSTANCES REDUCE TO ONE UNASSAILABLE FACT: YOU WERE AFRAID.

BUT FEAR IS NO EXCUSE FOR BETRAYING YOUR FELLOW CITIZENS...

...YOUR PROFESSION...

...AND YOURSELF.

360

IN LIGHT OF THIS, I HEREBY ORDER THE PRISONER TO BE REMOVED TO THE FEDERAL PENITENTIARY AT LEWISBURG--

--TO BE DETAINED IN CUSTODY FOR A PERIOD NOT TO EXCEED *THIRTY-SIX MONTHS*.

COURT ADJOURNED.

KLAK

OH, MY LORD... NO... THIS ISN'T HAPPENING...

MOM?

MOM ARE YOU OK?

I COULD TELL FRIDAY THAT THE JUDGE WANTED TO MAKE AN *EXAMPLE* OF ROBBIE...

...BUT THREE YEARS?

THAT'S OUTRAGEOUS!

JOE... THE WAY HE'S *LOOKING* AT ME-- AS IF HE THINKS HE'LL NEVER SEE ME AGAIN!

JOE, OH, JOE... WHATEVER HAPPENS, I LOVE YOU! COME BACK TO ME...

" PLEASE COME BACK TO ME..."

361

LEWISBURG FEDERAL PENITENTIARY.

JOE ROBERTSON REMEMBERS A MORNING WHEN HE WAS SIX YEARS OLD.

THE SKY WAS STILL GREY WHEN HIS FATHER ROUSTED HIM OUT OF BED AND TOLD HIM TO GET DRESSED.

EVEN THOUGH IT WAS EARLY SEPTEMBER, THE FLOORBOARDS IN HIS ROOM WERE COLD...

...AND HIS BREATH FOGGED IN THE EARLY MORNING LIGHT.

BREAKFAST WAS HURRIED, AND JOE WAS SHOCKED TO SEE HIS MOTHER CRYING AS SHE LADLED OATMEAL INTO HIS BOWL.

HE DIDN'T DARE ASK WHAT WAS WRONG.

JOE ONLY KNEW HE MUST HAVE DONE SOMETHING BAD.

AFTER BREAKFAST, HE WENT IN HIS FATHER'S TRUCK, AN OLD FORD PICKUP...

...AND THEY DROVE TO A BUILDING SURROUNDED BY A HIGH IRON FENCE MILES FROM HIS HOME.

JOE'S FATHER LEFT HIM THERE WITH A DRY KISS ON HIS CHEEK...

...AND A PAPER SACK...

...HOLDING A YELLOW No. 2 PENCIL...

...AND A CRISP BALONEY AND LETTUCE SANDWICH.

THERE WERE OTHER KIDS IN THE BUILDING BEHIND THE HIGH IRON FENCE...

...AND THEY LAUGHED TO SEE JOE CRY.

NEVER LET ANYONE KNOW YOU'RE SCARED.

THAT WAS THE FIRST LESSON JOE ROBERTSON LEARNED...

...ON HIS FIRST DAY AT SCHOOL.

NOW ISN'T THIS NICE, ROBBIE-PAL?

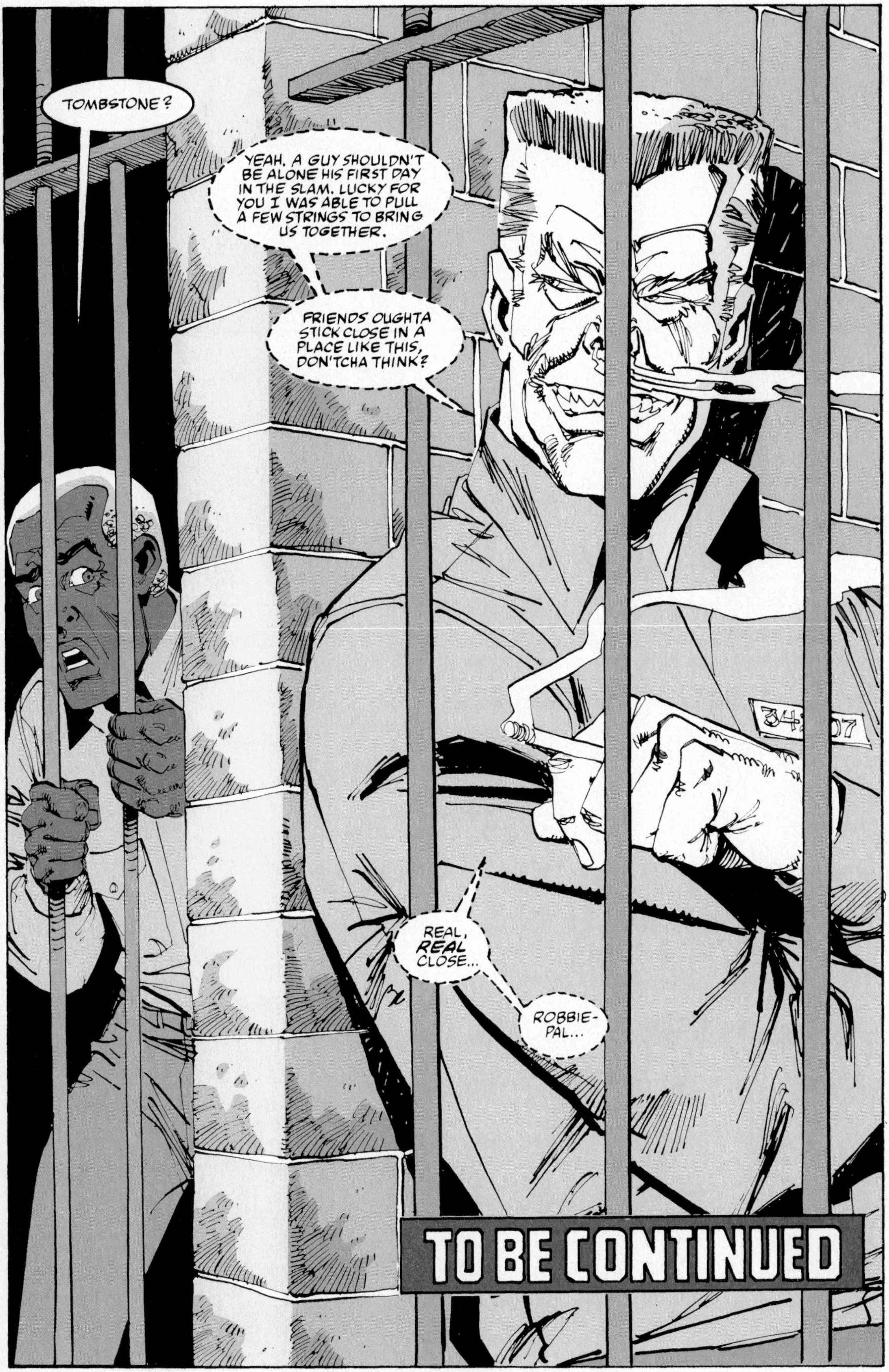
TOMBSTONE?
YEAH. A GUY SHOULDN'T BE ALONE HIS FIRST DAY IN THE SLAM. LUCKY FOR YOU I WAS ABLE TO PULL A FEW STRINGS TO BRING US TOGETHER.
FRIENDS OUGHTA STICK CLOSE IN A PLACE LIKE THIS, DON'TCHA THINK?
REAL, REAL CLOSE...
ROBBIE-PAL...
TO BE CONTINUED

JOE ROBERTSON

TOMBSTONE

TARANTULA

Official Handbook of the Marvel Universe: Update '89 profile art by Sal Buscema, Erik Larsen, Josef Rubinstein & Andy Yanchus

MINDSINGER
(GREGOR BUHKAROV)

BRIGHT SWORD
(CARTER DYAM)

GENII
(JASON KIMBALL)

HARVEST
(CHI LO)

SEA WITCH
(BRIDGET O'HARE)

DAYDREAMER
(CATHERINE MORANIS)

CALCULUS
(JAHAHAREL PATEL)

HIGHNOTE
(RAOUL HERNANDEZ)

CADUCEUS
(MARK CADMON)

MOONSTALKER
(KIANA)

SPLICE
(CHANDRA KU)

VARUA
(MIRA)

Official Handbook of the Marvel Universe: Update '89 profile art by
Tom Sutton, Josef Rubinstein & Andy Yanchus

Spectacular Spider-Man #138,
page 1 art by **Sal Buscema**

Spectacular Spider-Man #141,
page 1 art by **Sal Buscema**

Spectacular Spider-Man #142, pages 1 & 17 art by **Sal Buscema**

Spectacular Spider-Man #142, pages 18 & 19 art by **Sal Buscema**

Spectacular Spider-Man #142,
page 22 art by **Sal Buscema**

Spectacular Spider-Man #146,
cover art by **Sal Buscema**

Marvel Fanfare #41 pinup by
Mike Machlan, John Romita Sr. & Gregory Wright